About the Author

Samuel Willard Crompton is a native of Massachusetts who has visited about thirty of the fifty states. During a break from his literary endeavors he took a thirty-day train trip around the entire perimeter of the country, and he's never been the same since. Some of the highlights were the Four Mile Bridge at Astoria and Cut Bank, Montana. Crompton is the author or editor of many books, including *The Illustrated Atlas of Native American History* and Visible Ink's *The Handy Civil War Answer Book, The Handy Boston Answer Book,* and *The Handy Military History Answer Book.* He is a specialist in the French and Indian Wars and has served as a talking head for the Military Channel on its *First Command* program. Crompton teaches history at Holyoke Community College in Massachusetts, where he has seen his students move from the analog to digital ages. He resides in Hadley, Massachusetts.

Also from Visible Ink Press

The Handy African American History Answer Book
by Jessie Carnie Smith
ISBN: 978-1-57859-452-8

The Handy American History Answer Book
by David L. Hudson Jr.
ISBN: 978-1-57859-471-9

The Handy Anatomy Answer Book, 2nd edition
by Patricia Barnes-Svarney and Thomas E. Svarney
ISBN: 978-1-57859-542-6

The Handy Answer Book for Kids (and Parents), 2nd edition
by Gina Misiroglu
ISBN: 978-1-57859-219-7

The Handy Art History Answer Book
by Madelynn Dickerson
ISBN: 978-1-57859-417-7

The Handy Astronomy Answer Book, 3rd edition
by Charles Liu
ISBN: 978-1-57859-190-9

The Handy Bible Answer Book
by Jennifer Rebecca Prince
ISBN: 978-1-57859-478-8

The Handy Biology Answer Book, 2nd edition
by Patricia Barnes Svarney and Thomas E. Svarney
ISBN: 978-1-57859-490-0

The Handy Boston Answer Book
by Samuel Willard Crompton
ISBN: 978-1-57859-593-8

The Handy California Answer Book
by Kevin S. Hile
ISBN: 978-1-57859-591-4

The Handy Chemistry Answer Book
by Ian C. Stewart and Justin P. Lamont
ISBN: 978-1-57859-374-3

The Handy Civil War Answer Book
by Samuel Willard Crompton
ISBN: 978-1-57859-476-4

The Handy Dinosaur Answer Book, 2nd edition
by Patricia Barnes-Svarney and Thomas E. Svarney
ISBN: 978-1-57859-218-0

The Handy English Grammar Answer Book
by Christine A. Hult, Ph.D.
ISBN: 978-1-57859-520-4

The Handy Geography Answer Book, 3rd edition
by Paul A. Tucci
ISBN: 978-1-57859-215-9

The Handy Geology Answer Book
by Patricia Barnes-Svarney and Thomas E. Svarney
ISBN: 978-1-57859-156-5

The Handy History Answer Book, 3rd edition
by David L. Hudson, Jr.
ISBN: 978-1-57859-372-9

The Handy Hockey Answer Book
by Stan Fischler
ISBN: 978-1-57859-513-6

The Handy Investing Answer Book
by Paul A. Tucci
ISBN: 978-1-57859-486-3

The Handy Islam Answer Book
by John Renard Ph.D.
ISBN: 978-1-57859-510-5

The Handy Law Answer Book
by David L. Hudson Jr.
ISBN: 978-1-57859-217-3

The Handy Math Answer Book, 2nd edition
by Patricia Barnes-Svarney and Thomas E. Svarney
ISBN: 978-1-57859-373-6

The Handy Military History Answer Book
by Samuel Willard Crompton
ISBN: 978-1-57859-509-9

The Handy Mythology Answer Book,
by David A. Leeming, Ph.D.
ISBN: 978-1-57859-475-7

The Handy Nutrition Answer Book
by Patricia Barnes-Svarney and Thomas E. Svarney
ISBN: 978-1-57859-484-9

The Handy Ocean Answer Book
by Patricia Barnes-Svarney and Thomas E. Svarney
ISBN: 978-1-57859-063-6

The Handy Personal Finance Answer Book
by Paul A. Tucci
ISBN: 978-1-57859-322-4

The Handy Philosophy Answer Book
by Naomi Zack
ISBN: 978-1-57859-226-5

The Handy Physics Answer Book, 2nd edition
By Paul W. Zitzewitz, Ph.D.
ISBN: 978-1-57859-305-7

The Handy Politics Answer Book
by Gina Misiroglu
ISBN: 978-1-57859-139-8

The Handy Presidents Answer Book, 2nd edition
by David L. Hudson
ISB N: 978-1-57859-317-0

The Handy Psychology Answer Book, 2nd edition
by Lisa J. Cohen
ISBN: 978-1-57859-508-2

The Handy Religion Answer Book, 2nd edition
by John Renard
ISBN: 978-1-57859-379-8

The Handy Science Answer Book, 4th edition
by The Carnegie Library of Pittsburgh
ISBN: 978-1-57859-321-7

The Handy Supreme Court Answer Book
by David L Hudson, Jr.
ISBN: 978-1-57859-196-1

The Handy Technology Answer Book
by Naomi Bobick and James Balaban
ISBN: 978-1-57859-563-1

The Handy Weather Answer Book, 2nd edition
by Kevin S. Hile
ISBN: 978-1-57859-221-0

Please visit the "HandyAnswers" series website at www.handyanswers.com.

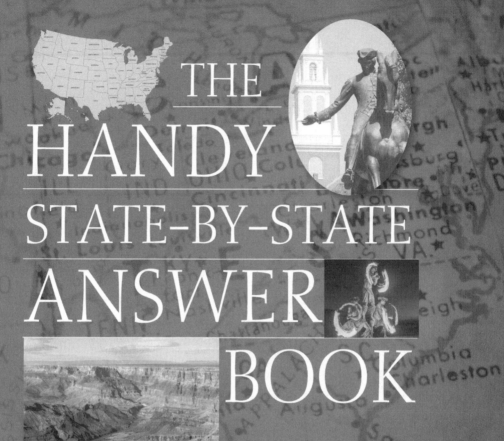

THE
HANDY
STATE-BY-STATE
ANSWER
BOOK

FACES, PLACES, AND FAMOUS
DATES FOR ALL FIFTY STATES

Samuel Willard Crompton

VISIBLE
INK
PRESS

Detroit

THE HANDY STATE–BY–STATE ANSWER BOOK

Visible Ink Press®
43311 Joy Rd., #414
Canton, MI 48187-2075

Visible Ink Press is a registered trademark of Visible Ink Press LLC.

Most Visible Ink Press books are available at special quantity discounts when purchased in bulk by corporations, organizations, or groups. Customized printings, special imprints, messages, and excerpts can be produced to meet your needs. For more information, contact Special Markets Director, Visible Ink Press, www.visibleink.com, or 734-667-3211.

Managing Editor: Kevin S. Hile
Art Director: Mary Claire Krzewinski
Typesetting: Marco DiVita
Proofreaders: Larry Baker and Janet L. Hile
Indexer: Shoshana Hurwitz

Cover images: Image of oil pump, Eric Kounce; all other images, Shutterstock.

10 9 8 7 6 5 4 3 2 1

Library of Congress Cataloging–in–Publication Data

Names: Crompton, Samuel Willard, author.
Title: The handy state–by–state answer book : faces, places, and famous dates for all fifty states / by Samuel Willard Crompton.
Description: Canton, MI : Visible Ink Press, 2016. | Includes index.
Identifiers: LCCN 2016012190 (print) | LCCN 2016012851 (ebook) | ISBN 9781578595655 (pbk. : alk. paper) | ISBN 9781578596041 (uPDF) | ISBN 9781578596058 (ePub) | ISBN 9781578596065 (Kindle)
Subjects: LCSH: U.S. states–Miscellanea. | United States–Miscellanea.
Classification: LCC E180 .C76 2016 (print) | LCC E180 (ebook) | DDC 973–dc23
LC record available at http://lccn.loc.gov/2016012190

Contents

Acknowledgements

Thanks to the staff of various libraries throughout the Pioneer Valley of western Massachusetts, as well as those of several in Marietta, Georgia. Labors of love like this one don't come to fruition without the assistance of all sorts of people, among whom I'd like to single out Elise Bernier-Feeley, John S. Bowman, Richard Shaw, and Sally B. Singingtree.

DEDICATION

This is for my beloved Charlotte, she who came from far away to experience all the diversity America and its states have to offer.

Photo Sources

ABC Television: p. 64.
Acroterion (Wikicommons): p. 199.
Adams, Tim: p. 462.
Akin, Carey: p. 143.
Alabama Department of Archives and History: p. 6.
Anne S. K. Brown Collection, Brown University: pp. 72, 284.
Arnold, Lloyd: p. 124.
Atherton, Jeremy: p. 129.
Basu, Abhinaba: p. 362.
Brady National Photographic Art Gallery: p. 189.
BrokenSphere (Wikicommons): p. 320.
Buttre, Lillian C. American Portrait Gallery: p. 3.
Cadman, Steve: p. 318.
Captain Brenda (Wikicommons): p. 194.
Case, Daniel: p. 313.
Cliff (Flickr and Wikicommons): p. 174.
Cogito ergo imago (Wikicommons, Flikr): p. 504.
Connelly, Chris: p. 83.
Cuerdon, Adam: p. 376.
Daderot (Wikicommons): p. 485.
Dismas (Wikicommons): p. 445.
Doubek, Joshua: p. 340.
Eege Fot vum (Wikicommons): p. 9.
Executive Office of the President of the United States: p. 426.
Federal Emergency Management Agency: p. 359.
ForestWander (Wikicommons): p. 473.
Franklin D. Roosevelt Library: p. 164.
Glasgow, MC: p. 428.
Ha'Eri, Bobak: p. 378.
Harper's Weekly: p. 182.
Hathorn, Billy: p. 304.
Horning, Robert Scott: p. 121.
Hoshua, Y.: p. 138.
Infrogmation of New Orleans: p. 94.
Ingfbruno (Wikicommons): p. 500.
Innerout (Wikicommons): p. 205.
Jeffness (English Wikipedia): 223.
Jglazer75 (Wikicommons): p. 68.
Kevstan (Wikicommons): p. 490.
Klotz, Jerrye & Roy MD: p. 79.
Kronsell, Jan: p. 417.
KRRK (Wikipedia): p. 118.
Library of Congress: pp. 62, 99, 105, 160, 162, 209, 258, 337, 403, 411, 444, 451, 455.
Lien, Hans Olav: p. 467.

Lund, Ken: p. 236.
Messerly, J.: p. 110.
Metro-Goldwyn-Mayer: p. 70.
Moreno, Humberto: p. 457.
MrChocolateShakes: p. 215.
MVASCO (Wikicommons): p. 384.
NASA: pp. 108, 347, 476.
National Archives and Records Administration: pp. 212, 250, 334, 396.
National Maritime Museum, London: p. 191.
Office of Governor Rick Scott: p. 88.
Oregon Historic County Reference Guide: p. 364.
PandamicPhoto.com: p. 172.
Peters, Tony: p. 270.
Prairie Home Companion: p. 226.
Primer, Jonh: p. 240.
Rinehart Indian Photographs, Haskell Indian Nations University: p. 29.
Rodricks, J.: p. 208.
Rolle, Elisa: p. 180.
Sailing Dutchman: p. 244.
Schwen, Daniel: p. 423.
Shutterstock: pp. 14, 15, 22, 24, 32, 42, 47, 54.
Smithsonian Institution: p. 416.
Swampyank (Wikicommons): pp. 49, 296.
Toronto Public Library: p. 141.
UKexpat (Wikicommons): p. 82.
U.S. Army Corpos of Engineers: p. 184.
U.S. Department of Agriculture: p. 102.
U.S. Department of Defense: pp. 58, 148, 330, 390.
U.S. National Oceanic and Atmospheric Administration: p. 353.
U.S. National Park Service: pp. 204, 260, 392, 404, 495.
U.S. Navy: p. 113.
Vadon, Michael: p. 288.
Vasquez, David: p. 278.
Walters Art Museum: p. 264.
Willis, Greg: p. 493.
Wisconsin Historical Society: p. 483.
WPPilot (Wikicommons): p. 316.
Yale University Libraries: p. 435.
Yinan Chen: pp. 218, 232.
Yunker, Chris: p. 98.
Public domain: pp. 37, 40, 74, 92, 132, 133, 149, 152, 169, 202, 221, 230, 254, 268, 274, 286, 297, 302, 308, 325, 329, 343, 345, 356, 366, 373, 381, 421, 433, 440, 453, 466, 478, 486.

Introduction

How much difference can a home state make?

In our hyper-connected world many people believe that states, as well as towns and counties, are less important than in the past. We all live in the fast lanes created by the Internet and mobile devices, they say, and physical boundaries do not count for as much as was previously the case. They are probably correct, just as long as the electricity continues to hum, and the email messages are delivered. Remove those devices and means for even a few days, however, and ninety-nine percent of us become what our parents and grandparents were: thoroughly dependent on local resources and our neighbors.

Family comes first, of course, and is followed by the neighborhood. Towns and counties come next, and are followed by the state, which, in the case of America, is fairly unique. One is hard pressed to think of another nation—large or small—where sovereignty is shared so well between the federal and state levels, and where allegiance or loyalty is so divided. We Americans are long past the idea that a state can defy the federal government. That notion went out with the conclusion of the Civil War. But we have special loyalties to our respective states, loyalties that were formed in the colonial and early national eras. Consider the difference between a Massachusetts person and one from Connecticut.

Both are New Englanders, accustomed to severe winters and the need to keep the house warm. Both are longtime nationalists, meaning that their states supported the Union, rather than the Confederacy, in the Civil War. But the differences can be detected very quickly.

The Massachusetts person—male or female—believes that Boston is the center of the urban universe, and that Tanglewood in the Berkshires represents the highest form of artistic expression; he or she might also vote for Jacobs Pillow, the dance theatre in the same neighborhood. The Massachusetts person believes that the Red Sox are the most important of all sports teams (whether they win or lose), and that Logan International Airport is by far the best way to go.

The Connecticut person, by contrast, believes that Hartford is the finest of state capitals, and that Bradley International Airport is the hub that supports all travel, national and international. He or she acknowledges that Boston is important, but points to Manhattan as the true urban center, the great vortex to which all people are drawn. And while Connecticut does not have a Tanglewood or Jacobs Pillow, its coastal shoreline has so many cultural and recreational spots that no other can compare (certainly not the rocky shoreline of Massachusetts). Did Mark Twain not declare that nothing in the world ever equaled the beauty of a Hartford snowstorm? Did Katharine Hepburn, a favorite daughter, even choose to leave her beloved Connecticut? No, she chose to remain on the Connecticut coast, and to jump into Long Island Sound every day of the year, for purposes of health.

One feels this regional loyalty, which some might even call jingoistic, as he or she approaches a state border. What physical difference separates Arizona from New Mexico? The two are equally composed of sagebrush and endless open spaces. But cross the border from one to the other and a different cultural attitude is almost immediately discovered. The New Mexican tends to be liberal, while the Arizonan tends to be libertarian. The former state is the home of aerospace endeavors and alien possibilities, while the latter is all about natural beauty and personal enjoyment. Perhaps this is why the Four Corners—where Arizona, New Mexico, Colorado, and Nevada come together—is so special; four separate cultures, as well as state entities, touch at that lonely spot.

States, to be sure, are not nations. They do not possess armies, and they cannot compel their residents to go to war. But they do collect taxes, impose regulations, and at times they have served as the boundary stations for ideas and cultural notions. Anyone who doubts this should simply take a canoe ride along the Connecticut River, which separates New Hampshire from Vermont. On the right, or west, bank is a liberal commonwealth, where the majority believe in freedom for the individual from coercion and protection of the group from sickness, disease, and poverty, while on the left, or east, bank is a libertarian state based on the famous motto "Live Free or Die." Likewise, anyone who crosses the border from the Hoosier State of Indiana into the Land of Lincoln, as Illinois is frequently called, immediately knows that the cultural zone has changed. Indiana celebrates its farming past and Civil War heroes, while Illinois rejoices in its urban present and the contributions it has made to the modern nation.

The Civil War put this kind of thinking to an end, and this is why the two great boundaries—one physical and the other chronological—are so vital to understanding the nation as it exists today. Once one passes the chronological boundary of the year 1865, the United States becomes used in the singular meaning: it is one nation. And once one passes the Mississippi River, one enters lands and states where the people seldom, if ever, thought of secession or breaking up the Union. The two things go together, walking hand in hand.

The center point for this new understanding is the Gateway Arch in St. Louis, Missouri. Here, underneath the magnificent structure, one looks back to see the America that grew up in a time of regional loyalties, where it sometimes was questioned whether the nation would endure. And here one looks forward to the endless prairies and plains, to regions where people never questioned that the federal government came first, but wondered, rather, whether they would succeed in planting towns, counties, and states, in light of all the physical hazards.

We know that they succeeded. We know that the United States is one great land, composed of peoples, localities, and states that come together to create a magnificent whole. But it takes a set of foreign eyes—in this case British ones—for us to fully comprehend just how significant our loyalties are.

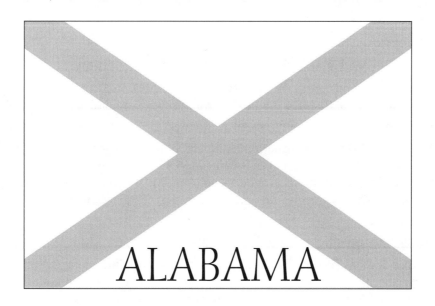

ALABAMA

Nickname: "The Heart of Dixie"
Capital: Montgomery
Statehood: December 14, 1819; 22nd state

AT A GLANCE

Where does the state nickname come from?

Alabama is the heart of Dixie in that the Confederate States of America was established in Montgomery in February 1861. Beyond this, however, the people of Alabama are fonder of their Confederate heritage than almost any other former Confederate state.

What are the major symbols of the Heart of Dixie?

The state motto is "We Dare Maintain Our Rights." This needs little translation, or explication, because Alabama is where the Confederate States of America was founded, in 1861.

The northern flicker (or yellowhammer) is the state bird, and the common camellia is the state flower. The longleaf pine is the state tree.

How large, or small, is Alabama?

The Heart of Dixie is 51,701 square miles (133,905 square kilometers). It is twenty-ninth in size among the states. Its population, as of the year 2010, is 4,779,736, placing it twenty-third in population among the fifty states.

Is Alabama the state that is clearest about its Confederate history?

Just about. The Confederacy was formed in Montgomery, in February 1861, and Alabamians are proud of their role in the Civil War. They are mindful, too, that their state went through some difficult times in the 1960s, during the Civil Rights struggle.

The Heart of Dixie has made some notable strides in recent decades. The state crossed the barrier from a rural to an urban majority as of the census of 1960; Alabama has also moved forward in industrial development. While it remains one of the great strongholds for Dixie sympathy, Alabama has entered the modern world.

Are Alabamians oriented more to the land or the sea?

It's a great question. Though Alabama has only a short coastline, along the Gulf Coast, one part of its culture and economy has always been pointed in that direction. One sees this today with the fishing industry, and tourism as well. But as strong as the pull to the sea is, one finds an equal tug from the land. Alabamians are nothing if not proud of their connection to rural roots.

Alabama's economy, in the early twenty-first century, derives the majority of its revenues from industry. Agricultural products continue to be harvested in large quantities, but they form a small percentage of the state's overall generation of wealth.

How much variety is held within the state of Alabama?

A great deal. The central and southern parts of the state are part of the famous Black Belt, named for the dark-colored soil of the region, which produced more cotton than any other part of the South. But the north is mountainous, with many rivers, and the extreme southern part of Alabama is coastline, about 50 miles (80 kilometers) along the Gulf Coast. Then too, there are many forests in Alabama: about 65 percent of the state has tree cover.

Do Alabamians talk about the weather?

They certainly do. Even though old-timers know precisely what to expect—hot, damp, and humid—they still like to discuss the varieties and oddities that exist. When winter cold does come to Alabama, for instance, it comes as a great shock, and the state can virtually be shut down by an ice storm.

The single greatest threat is posed by tornadoes, however. Alabama is often hit and sometimes ravaged. In recent times the single deadliest outbreak came on April 27, 2011, when an EF4 tornado came through Alabama, hit Tuscaloosa on its eastward pass, and then backtracked to slam sections of Birmingham as it moved west. The maximum recorded wind speed was 190 mph (310 km per hour) and this was enough to cause $2.4 billion in property damage and to claim sixty-four lives (another 1,500 people were injured).

EARLY HISTORY

For how long have humans lived in what we now call the Heart of Dixie?

For thousands of years. In the late 1950s, the National Geographic Society made one of the outstanding archeological discoveries of our time, when its teams excavated Russell Cave in northeast Alabama. Humans have lived in that precise location since at least 6000 B.C.E., the Society declared, and it might well be the single longest inhabited place on the entire continent.

To be sure, we don't know as much as we would like about the early inhabitants of Alabama. We suspect, however, that they lived much as their descendants, the Native Americans of the time of Hernando de Soto and the appearance of the first

Spanish explorer Hernando de Soto explored the southeastern part of North America in 1540, including what is present-day Alabama.

Spaniards. Alabama may have been something of a heaven for the archaic Indians, with plenty of fishing and hunting, and perhaps some farming as well.

Did de Soto and the men of his expedition have anything good—or useful—to say about the Native Americans?

The Spaniards fought battle after battle in Alabama, always prevailing but becoming exhausted in the process. They found the Indians determined adversaries, and they noted the high level of organization that existed in the Native American villages. This was made even plainer by the travels of John Bartram, an eighteenth-century naturalist, who spent much time with the Creek Indians.

SETTLEMENT AND COLONIZATION

When did the first permanent settlements become established?

The French were first on the scene, erecting Fort Dauphin near present-day Mobile in 1702. At about the same time, a handful of Anglo-American merchants, most of them connected with the brisk trade in deerskins, found their way into Alabama, usually sending the trade goods back to South Carolina. There could have been a major confrontation between the English and French in Alabama, but a resurgence of Spanish interest

3

Have the sites of any of the battles and skirmishes been uncovered?

Yes. Major archeological work was done in the 1990s, and we feel fairly confident both about de Soto's route through Alabama and the location of most of the battles. In the process of that work, many people changed their mind about de Soto. Previously he was seen as a great European hero, helping to open the southeast to settlement. Today he is seen as much closer to a vagabond, or even a well-armed thief!

in the region counterbalanced them. As a result, 90 percent of Alabama remained in Native American hands for longer than anyone expected.

Did anyone anticipate the incredible fertility of the soil in south and south-central Alabama?

No one got a hold of this idea in the eighteenth century. Not until the early nineteenth century did the brand new United States show much interest. Indian agent Benjamin Hawkins went among the Creek and Choctaw Indians of the region, trying to interest them in becoming like the white people. He succeeded to such an extent that the Creek and Cherokee became some of the most acculturated of all Native Americans of that time. Hawkins's work did not prevent the Creek War from breaking out, however, and this conflict spelled the ruin of most of what he'd achieved.

Was the Creek War a stand-alone conflict, or part of the wider conflict known as the War of 1812?

Even over the distance of 200 years, it is often difficult to give a precise answer to this question. The British, who had their eye on the Gulf Coast in general and New Orleans in particular, surely incited the Creek to fight the Anglo-Americans; from what we know of that tribe, however, they would not have undertaken any such action if their own leaders did not agree. All we can say for certain is that the Creeks attacked and captured Fort Mims in August 1813, thus igniting the Creek War. Most of the settlers of Fort Mims were massacred in the aftermath of the short siege.

The Creeks did not realize that the militia of the state of Georgia, the state of Tennessee, and the new Mississippi Territory were all determined on revenge. Led by General Andrew Jackson—who later became the seventh president of the United States—the militia smashed the Creek at the Battle of Horseshoe Bend; even Jackson, who was seldom squeamish, admitted that the carnage was simply dreadful. Perhaps 700 Indians died that day, in one of the largest Indian-white conflicts seen east of the Mississippi River. Jackson soon forced a peace treaty on the Creek, taking about seven-eighths of all their land in present-day Alabama.

How soon did the white settlers arrive?

Almost immediately. The end of the War of 1812 opened the door, and the spread of the so-called "Cotton Kingdom" proved a powerful incentive to farmers and merchants alike. Within a decade of Jackson's military victory, much of Alabama was populated by white settlers, and the Creek and Cherokee—at least those who remained—were marginalized in the extreme. Even so, their losses were not complete. One year after becoming president, Andrew Jackson signed the Indian Removal Act, under which virtually all Indians were to be moved west of the Mississippi. Not all of them suffered this fate, but it was not for want of action on the part of the federal government.

The Trail of Tears removed the last of the Cherokee from northern Alabama and southern Tennessee. It is believed that 4,000 Indians died en route to the lands that were promised them.

Was it difficult for Alabama to attain statehood?

No. Alabama came into the Union in 1819, as the twenty-second state. The real struggle for power between Northern and Southern states came one year later, when Missouri applied for admission.

THE CIVIL WAR

Did Alabama become the richest of the Southern states?

No. Louisiana and Mississippi profited even more than the Heart of Dixie. But Alabama was queen of the South in that her culture spread to these other states, and beyond. Even among the desperados that founded the Republic of Texas, many Alabamians were found. And in the years leading to the Civil War, Alabama seemed the most belligerent of the Southern states.

African Americans, meanwhile, were brought to Alabama in great numbers. Many came overland, but others were smuggled through Mobile and the short Alabama coastline even after the U.S. Congress formally outlawed the slave trade in 1808. One can certainly ask whether race slavery in Alabama was any worse than that in other Southern states. The answer, on an anecdotal level, appears to be that it was. There was something about being so truly Southern, and so far removed from the North, that allowed the slaveholders of Alabama to be especially brutal.

I seldom hear much about Alabama's contribution to the Confederate war effort. Why is this?

Perhaps it's because Alabamians are so dead certain that they were the center and heart of the Confederacy that they no longer need to inform outsiders of the fact! South Carolina

The president of the Confederacy, Jefferson Davis, was inaugurated in Montgomery on February 18, 1861.

was the state that started the Civil War, and Virginia is where many of the big battles were fought, but it was a rare battle, or even skirmish, where Alabamians were not involved.

Where does the wonderful expression "Damn the torpedoes" come from?

In August 1864, Union admiral David Farragut led a powerful fleet into Mobile Bay, one of the last ports still open to Confederate shipping. The Confederate forts opened fire, but reports that the waters were mined with torpedoes especially concerned Farragut. His lead ship hit a mine and sank almost immediately, leading many officers to believe the time had come to retire. Farragut thought for only a moment, then issued his famous order, "Damn the torpedoes! Full speed ahead!" Perhaps he was just lucky; then again, fortune often favors the brave. In either case, Farragut's fleet entered the harbor without any further losses. The city of Mobile held out for a few more months, but Farragut's entrance meant that the Confederacy now lacked any substantial communication with nations overseas.

When did Alabamians lay down their arms?

As one might expect, Alabamians were among the last to admit defeat. By the late summer of 1865, however, the Heart of Dixie was as prostrate as the rest of the South. The

Union had won fair and square, and Alabama would clearly be required to change many of its laws, as well as the basic rules of the game (those that had allowed so many African Americans to be enslaved).

How much did white Alabamians suffer under Reconstruction?

Like the other Confederate states, Alabama had to prove its worth and show some repentance just in order to get back in the Union. The state was placed under U.S. military rule, as part of the Third Military District, in 1867, but the occupation lasted only a year. Alabama wrote a new constitution, making plain that African Americans were citizens, but still placed some limits on their right to vote.

Throughout the former Confederate States, the Democratic Party became and remained the one of choice: there was a period where a person could not be elected dogcatcher without demonstrating allegiance to the Democrats. Some of the most extreme cases were seen in Alabama, and by the 1880s, white supremacy had been reinstated. New election laws made it nearly impossible for African Americans to vote, and sharecropping became the order of the day.

MODERN TIMES

What was life in Alabama like at the beginning of the twentieth century?

In some ways the state seemed hardly to have changed at all. Eighty percent of Alabamians lived in towns or villages, and the cities were small, at best. Manufacturing, however, had commenced in Birmingham and elsewhere: Alabama was starting to turn out iron, which became one of the mainstays of its economy.

Was sharecropping entirely a racial system, intended to keep blacks "down"?

That was at least two-thirds of the motivation, but plenty of poor whites suffered under the sharecropping system as well. Under its provisions, tenant farmers got to keep a share of their crop, while handing the rest over to the landlord, who looked a whole lot like the slaveholder had a generation earlier! Making matters worse, many sharecropping landlords required that their tenants purchase all their supplies at the local store, which often turned out to be owned by his brother or cousin. Some make the argument that sharecropping was a necessary evil, a way for the former Confederate states to make it through the dark times at the end of the nineteenth century. Even so, the system benefited a few at the expense of many.

People often ask why African Americans remained in racially oppressive states such as Alabama: the simple answer is that it was very difficult to leave. Starting around 1915, however, many blacks migrated north, to places like Chicago and Detroit, where they found work in the steel and automotive industries. The letters they sent home to relatives encouraged others to join them, and for a time Alabama was on the verge of losing population.

How did Alabama fare in the Great Depression?

The state was hard-hit, but its people were accustomed to economic difficulty. Many of them later claimed they could hardly tell the difference between the 1920s and the 1930s. Like so many other states, Alabama profited from the commencement of World War II: the state sent many young men overseas, and all sorts of industries turned out products for the military during the war. When World War II ended, Alabama looked much the same, but it had, beneath the surface, been fundamentally changed. By 1960, a majority of Alabamians lived in towns of 5,000 or more.

When did Alabama gain a place in the new aerospace industry?

In the 1950s the U.S. Air Force and then the Aeronautical Space Administration looked for a place to develop rockets. They settled on Huntsville, Alabama, which remains the central location for this vital part of the aerospace industry.

Why do so many of the most heartrending stories of the Civil Rights era come from Alabama?

Much of it had to do with identity. White Alabamians were by no means convinced they were wrong to have fought the Civil War; some were so delusional as to insist they had never really lost that conflict! In and around the city of Montgomery—named for one of the white officers under Andrew Jackson at the Battle of Horseshoe Bend—thousands of African Americans traveled by bus each day to the homes of their white employers, where they cooked, cleaned, and washed the dishes (and sometimes participated in raising the white children). It was to this environment that Martin Luther King Jr. and

What persuaded Rosa Parks to make her courageous stand, on December 1, 1955?

Rosa Parks did not intend to be a heroine: she was simply weary of going to the back of the bus whenever white customers came aboard. But on that fateful night, after she had boarded the bus following the end of her work shift, the white section filled up, and she refused to yield her seat to sit in the back of the bus. She was arrested, and something new was born: the Civil Rights movement.

The bus in which Rosa Parks famously stood up for her rights is now preserved at the Henry Ford Museum in Dearborn, Michigan.

other organizers came, and it was decided that Montgomery was a good place to demonstrate the power of nonviolent resistance.

How long did the Montgomery Bus Boycott last?

Over a year. Following the arrest of Rosa Parks, day after day, African Americans chose to walk to work, or even take their chances hitchhiking, rather than ride the buses that were segregated on the basis of race. The white community of Montgomery was certain the bus boycott could not succeed, that the blacks would grow weary of walking all those miles. But the resistance gained strength each month, and in February 1956, the bus companies admitted defeat. From that point on, it was first come, first served when it came to finding seats on the public buses.

This sounds wonderful, a marvelous way to bring about change. But was it the end of the Civil Rights struggle in Alabama?

By no means. Birmingham became the center for white resistance to change, and in 1963, Martin Luther King Jr. led determined African Americans on a protest march through the city. The infamous chief of police, "Bull" O'Connor, had his men unleash attack dogs on the black protestors, but he had, for once, overplayed his hand. National television networks carried the scene on the news, and Americans—white, black, and other—were simply appalled. Almost from that day forward, the segregationist policy was doomed. This doesn't mean that the segregationists gave up trying. Alabama governor George Wallace was one of the strongest opponents of desegregation, even declaring in his inaugural address when he first took office in 1963: "Segregation now, segregation tomorrow, segregation forever." He fought his cause for more than a decade, and when he changed his mind, and declared he had been in error all along, it could not have been more momentous for the people of Alabama.

I've heard of Wallace. Wasn't he also the victim of an assassination attempt?

While running for the Democratic presidential nomination in 1972, Wallace was shot and wounded by Arthur Bremer, a native of Wisconsin, who seems to have been looking for someone to assassinate (he considered killing Richard Nixon, for example). Wallace received much sympathy (from whites and blacks alike) and the failed assassination attempt had a lot to do with his eventual change of heart. In time, Wallace came to believe that he was wrong about segregation, and asked for forgiveness; he even wrote Bremer, declaring his forgiveness for his would-be assassin.

How important was the rock group Lynyrd Skynyrd?

They were a cultural phenomenon. Until the early 1970s, Alabama was known for its folk musicians and country music, but it had not yet produced any rock-and-roll performers who could attract a youthful audience. This changed in a hurry.

In 1974, southern rockers Lynyrd Skynyrd brought out "Sweet Home Alabama," an ode to the state and its culture (not to mention a biting response to fellow rocker Neil Young's songs "Alabama" and "Southern Man," though, ultimately, there was a respect between the two artists. The meaning was clear. Alabama could be vilified in the press, downplayed by the liberal-leaning national media, and perhaps scorned by many Northerners. None of this mattered to real Alabamians: they knew theirs was the best of states. Remarkably, many Northern audiences enjoyed the song, and the group, as much as their Southern counterparts.

These remain some of the best-known words about Alabama ever to be sung:

Big wheels keep on turning
Carry me home to see my kin
Singing songs about the south-land
I miss 'ole 'bamy once again, and I think it's a sin.

What was the turning point for Alabama; the moment at which the state could not go backward?

It's hard to pin it down too precisely, but it was definitely at some point during the 1980s. By 1990, Alabama had taken on a new appearance, that of a cultural anachronism that had shed many of its least-attractive qualities. Alabama did continue to play a major role in Southern politics, however. Where it once had been part of the "Solid South," meaning an area where all the states voted for the Democrats, by 1990, Alabama was part of the solidly Republican South.

Where will the Heart of Dixie be a generation from now?

If recent history is our guide, the likelihood is that Alabama will continue to modernize. Perhaps it will never become a place where Northerners vacation by choice. But Alabama will, most likely, be more hospitable than before, and its climate will doubtless bring many visitors, from other states and other nations.

ALASKA

Nickname: "The Last Frontier"
Capital: Juneau
Statehood: January 3, 1959; 49th state

AT A GLANCE

Where does the state nickname come from?

The Last Frontier clearly applies to the fact that when Alaska came in as a territory, most of the Far West had already been spliced into territories and states. The expression became even more common in the twentieth century, as Alaska became known as the land of hardy folk who crossed the frozen landscape in dog-pulled sleds, and who prospected for oil.

What are the major state symbols?

The state motto is "North to the Future." Officially adopted in 1967, this motto neatly coincides with the Alaskan vision of development and progress.

The willow ptarmigan is the state bird, and the forget-me-not is the state flower. The Sitka spruce is the state tree.

How large, or small, is the Last Frontier?

It is by far the largest of the fifty states, with 590,693 square miles (1,529,888 square kilometers). In all this vast area are only 710,231 people, as of the census of 2010. This means that Alaska is not only the largest of the fifty states, but it has, by far, the fewest number of people per square mile.

What can be said about Alaska that hasn't been said before?

For those who have seen the Last Frontier, no words are necessary; for those who haven't, no number of words can do justice to the raw, unspoiled beauty of Alaska. This is a land that time forgot for centuries, only to rediscover about the time of the American Civil War. This is a landscape that is constantly being reforged, primarily by snow and ice. And this is where the last of the frontier peoples go, to taste something utterly unlike life in the Lower Forty-Eight.

How different is life in Alaska from, say, the Pacific Northwest?

Even though Washington and Oregon are much closer to Alaska than other parts of the nation, even the Pacific Northwest differs considerably from the Last Frontier. While in Washington and Oregon, one can find easy access to metropolitan areas and sophisticated urban living. This is not true in Alaska, where even some of the cities have streets—in some sections—made of mud.

Is there any place in Alaska where the natural scene does not dominate?

There is, perhaps, a tiny section of streets and intersections in each of the few cities, but the minute one departs the city proper, he or she is immediately back in the grip of Mother Nature. And this is the beauty of it: most Alaskans would rather live, and die, at the hand of nature than anything manmade.

Just how big is Alaska?

It is more than twice the size of Texas, which takes some reflection to really absorb. If Alaska were placed smack in the middle of the United States, it would take up one-fifth of the total. And in all this immense, rugged landscape are found fewer than 800,000 human beings. Alaska is extraordinary for the place it fills in the United States, but it is also a citizen of the world. Only Siberia and sections of Australia come even close to it in terms of natural beauty mixed with the feeble, fragile hand of humans.

The Trans-Alaska pipeline taps into Alaska's rich oil fields. Constructed in the 1970s, it runs 800 miles (1,270 kilometers) from Prudhoe Bay in the north to Valdez in the south.

Do Alaskans discuss the weather much? And if so, what do they say?

Alaskans do talk about the weather, but they do it with the attitude of longtime veterans, who expect to handle whatever is thrown at them. When outsiders come to inquire, they are told, with a smile, that Alaska's weather is unpredictable, and that one can move from sweaters to undershirts, and from two layers to four in the blink of an eye.

We all know that Alaska is famous for its long stretches of cold weather. Does it ever experience the opposite?

Yes indeed. The single lowest temperature recorded in Alaska was –82 degrees F (–62 degrees C) at Prospect Creek on January 23, 1971. Given that this took place just as the national conversation about the Trans-Alaska pipeline gathered steam, it caused no end of commentary. Could any pipeline—no matter how well-designed—stand up to weather that brutal? So far, the pipeline has stood the test of time.

The single highest recorded temperature was 100 degrees F (38 degrees C) at Fort Yukon on June 27, 1915. This temperature spike did not cause much conversation at the time. What *has* led to many conversations is the way in which Alaska was spared from the terrible cold that afflicted the Midwest and northern sections of the Lower Forty-Eight in 2014 and 2015. In 2015, *Time* Magazine declared Alaska "ground zero" for discussions of climate change, because the Last Frontier was seeing greater variance than any other, with most of the variance headed in the direction of warmer temperatures.

Is there a recognizable Alaskan culture? And can the Alaskan be told apart from his counterpart in British Columbia or the Yukon?

Alaskan culture is an intriguing mixture of Washington State, Oregon, Russia, and the oldest of the Native American experience. Alaska is the first place to be inhabited by the

Engraving of a gold miner camp in the Klondike in 1898.

hunter-gatherers that came across the Land Bridge about 20,000 years ago, and given the number of glaciers that were in their way, these early Indians may have remained in Alaska for a very long time. The Native Americans that one meets, therefore, are among the oldest of all.

Washington State and Oregon both exerted an outsized influence on Alaska in its early years, because Seattle and Portland were the two major ports of embarkation for those heading to the Gold Rush in the Klondike. Jack London was a Pacific Northwest person, but his writing was deeply informed by the year he spent in Alaska. And finally, although the Russian imperial adventure did not last very long, there are vestiges of Russian culture to be found in Alaska today.

EARLY HISTORY

For how long have humans lived in what we now call the Last Frontier?

For roughly 20,000 years. The Siberian tribespeople who crossed the Bering Land Bridge were, to our knowledge, the first humans ever to come to the Americas, and their descendants can be found all the way from Alaska to Tierra del Fuego. We don't know very much about the lives of these early Native Americans, but we suspect they had short and exciting lives, meaning that the struggle to survive was a mighty endeavor. They may have fought woolly mammoths; almost certainly they wrestled with whales and other sea creatures. The chances are that they did not farm much at all: farming did not become part of the human experience until about 10,000 years ago.

When did people from outside Alaska first hear anything about Alaska?

To our knowledge, this did not happen till the eighteenth century. A few Japanese fishermen may, by chance, have been tossed up on Alaska's shores, but they did not leave any record of their adventures. The Russians, therefore, form our first modern knowledge of the Last Frontier.

During the reign of Czar Peter the Great (an outsized personality if ever there was one), Russia expanded all the way to Kamchatka and the Pacific Ocean. Kamchatka, which is almost as big as Alaska, was a huge project unto itself, but the Russians pressed on eagerly, and in 1741 Vitus Bering caught the first known view of Alaska. He came back the following year and is properly credited as the first outsider to really learn anything about Alaska, even though he died in 1743.

What brought the Russians back, a few decades later?

The pelts of sea otters. These fetched a high price in Moscow and Saint Petersburg, and Russian adventurers were willing to go a very long way to obtain them. The Russians visited the Alaskan coast every year or so for decades, but it was not till the end of the eigh-

> ### Was there ever a genuine chance that
> ### Russia would establish an empire in Alaska?
>
> The chances were remote, but not out of the question. It was during the reign of Czar Alexander I—best known as the czar who fought Napoleon—that Russian influence reached its height, and during the long reign of his younger brother, Czar Nicholas I, that Russian power waned. Russia certainly had the manpower eventually to populate Alaska, but the physical distances were very great.

teenth century that they came back in strength. The Russians established Sitka as their first real town, and the first Orthodox Church was built there. Alexander Baranov, a Russian nobleman, became the leader of the colony.

The Tlingit Indians struck in 1803, wiping out the settlement, but the Russians exacted a terrible vengeance. By now, the Russians had acquired many of the Aleutian Islands. And in 1812, the year war was declared between America and Britain, the Russians went all the way to the coast of California, to establish Fort Ross. This was the maximum extent of the Russian movement, however.

ALASKA IN THE LIFE OF THE NATION

Did the Americans, or their nation, know anything about Alaska at this time?

Only the tiniest bit. Americans were still learning about Oregon and California. But during the 1840s and 1850s, just enough information filtered in that some of the leaders in Washington, D.C., became interested. One of them was William H. Seward.

First governor of New York, then a U.S. senator, and finally the secretary of state, Seward enjoyed a distinguished career. Throughout the 1860s, he was aware that Russia was weary of its imperial experience, but not until 1867 did he learn that Czar Alexander II was ready to sell the "icebox." Negotiations were completed in a remarkably short time, and in April 1867, the U.S. Senate ratified the treaty that brought Alaska to American control for the price of $7.2 million. This was one of the great real estate acquisitions of all human history, but everyone did not see it that way at the time. Some newspapers congratulated Seward for bringing it about, while others labelled the whole endeavor as "Seward's Folly" or "Seward's Icebox."

If the treaty was so controversial, why was it so easily approved by the U.S. Senate?

Seward had previously been a U.S. senator from New York, and he understood the deliberations and predilections of that legislative body. Seward was able to pitch the treaty in such a positive manner—including promoting the vast beauty of Alaska's natural resources—that the vote was overwhelmingly in favor of the purchase.

How might international history have been different, if Seward had *not* purchased Alaska?

The chances are that the Russians would not have found another buyer and that Alaska would have been a burdensome part of their far-flung empire for many decades. But in the twentieth century, *Communist* Russia—or the Soviet Union—would have ended up with possession of Alaska, and that would have made matters quite different. Americans were nervous enough during the Cold War; they would have been much more apprehensive if Russia held Alaska.

How long did it take for Americans to start going, or moving, to Alaska?

Nearly three decades. The first Americans to move to the Last Frontier were interested in getting rich quickly and then moving back to the West Coast in a hurry. Very few people saw much potential in Alaska, which was too cold, too foreign, and just too darned far away. It took the discovery of gold in British Canada to change that perception.

Are you saying that the Alaska Gold Rush was not in Alaska?

That's correct. We Americans tend to be so nationalist-centered that we don't even realize that the great discovery of gold in the Klondike was actually on the Canadian side of the boundary in the Yukon Territory. Quite a few Americans were involved in the early discovery, however, and as the news spread, more Americans than Canadians picked up the axe and pan to move northwest.

The single biggest barrier was formed by Chilkoot Pass. Eight hundred feet high, this mountain pass saw some of the coldest weather in Alaska, and each one of the prospectors coming from the United States had to pass this way. Many newsreels were made, showing would-be miners struggling up the slopes, and film star Charlie Chaplin later made hay with the scene in his film *The Gold Rush*.

How many of these miners became rich?

Very few. Perhaps 80,000 people made it to Alaska and the Yukon between 1897 and 1901: rather few of them remained. Novelist Jack London, who made the trip and lived to tell the tale, came home with only $5 worth of gold dust in his pocket. Of course there were the lucky few who made a pile of money, but even of these, only a few still had their earnings a decade later. Gold rushes are definitely part of the American experience, but they seldom benefit very many of the actual miners.

WORLD WAR II

When did the settlement of Alaska really begin to take off?

Not until World War II. World War I made only a tiny difference to residents of the territory of Alaska. As late as 1940, there were fewer than 60,000 people in the state. Two things conspired to make Alaska better-known to the rest of the nation, however. First came World War II, and then came the bush pilots.

In 1942, as a diversion to distract the Americans from the much more critical Battle of Midway, Japan landed forces that captured two Aleutian Islands: Kiska and Attu. Over the next year, nearly 155,000 American soldiers were brought to bear, to eject a total of fewer than 10,000 Japanese. The first island, Kiska, was a bitter struggle, and less than 1 percent of all the Japanese who fought were taken prisoner. The second island, Attu, was a walkover, because the Japanese had already evacuated. In total, perhaps 200,000 Americans, and consequently their families back home, became more aware of Alaska and what it had to offer.

How and when did the bush pilots go to Alaska?

The flying of aircraft began in the Midwest, but it soon became quite popular in the Pacific Northwest. Until World War II, rather few pilots went north to Alaska, because they had better fields of operation—and larger crowds—in Washington and Oregon. Almost immediately after World War II's conclusion, however, former U.S. Navy pilots began moving to Alaska and earning good money delivering the U.S. mail. This was only the beginning of what became a rage among aviators: to move to Alaska, even if only for a short time. And as a result, parts of the interior previously known only to Native Americans and Inuit suddenly became more open to settlers from the south.

Was statehood a difficult battle for the people of Alaska?

It was, not least because they were so divided on the matter. As late as 1946, a referendum showed only a few thousand more in favor than opposed. And in the U.S. Senate, there were many interests, economic ones especially, that thought it better for Alaska to remain a territory, so that its mineral resources could be developed and used for the good of the nation as a whole. Oddly enough, it was a U.S. congressman from Albany, New York, Leo O'Brien, who pushed the hardest and the longest for statehood; even so, it seemed likely that Hawaii would be admitted as the forty-ninth state and Alaska as the fiftieth.

The logjam was finally broken, and on January 3, 1959, under the administration of President Dwight Eisenhower, Alaska entered the Union. It came in as the forty-ninth state, just over seven months ahead of Hawaii.

What is unique about Juneau, the state capital?

Unlike most state capitals, which tend to be in relatively central locations of a state, Juneau is in the far southeastern part of the state (the largest state at that). Juneau,   **19** named after prospector Joseph Juneau, is the only U.S. capital whose general area borders a foreign country; it is located about forty miles from Canada. But don't try driving there: there are no roads leading into or out of the city, so all goods and citizens/tourists arrive via air or water.

OIL AND ENERGY

Was this when Americans finally became aware of the good reasons for moving to Alaska?

Not quite. Even in the 1960s, it was only the hardiest, and perhaps most adventuresome, Americans who came north from the Lower Forty-Eight. Continuing a long tradition, they tended to remain only a few years, and then return, greatly enriched by the experience. At least they told their family and friends about Alaska, and the Last Frontier became more visible in the eyes of other Americans. But it took the discovery of oil to really put Alaska, once and for all, on the map.

In the late winter of 1968, engineers from ARCO stumbled on one of the greatest oil reserves in the entire world. The waters of Prudhoe Bay, on Alaska's North Slope, contain an estimated 25 billion barrels of oil, meaning that this area has more oil even than Saudi Arabia. The discovery immediately made Alaska much more popular, not only for the oil itself, but also for the revenues, a portion of which, it was promised, would be divided among the residents of the state.

When did the controversy over the Trans-Alaska Pipeline commence?

Almost immediately. Millions of Americans were gung-ho, declaring that the Alaska oil discovery was the greatest find of the twentieth century, and that it would deliver energy independence to them. Millions of others declared that Alaska was one of the last unspoiled places on earth and that it would be a tragedy to risk oil spills in that pristine area. The battle between the oil enthusiasts and the environmentalists would test the tempers of people in Alaska and Washington, D.C.

One of the most poignant issues raised had to do with the caribou, who, for millennia, have migrated across Alaska twice a year. How would the caribou find their way? Would the proposed pipeline doom them as a species? In the end, it was decided to have the pipeline lifted several feet off the ground, placed on stilts, so the caribou could pass underneath. This compromise pleased few people at the time, but it seems to have worked rather well for the caribou.

How long did it take to create that vast pipeline?

Though longer pipelines had been laid, they were all in sunnier, warmer climates. Building the Alaska pipeline meant that thousands of workers came from the Lower Forty-

Eight to work long hours in the cold. They earned good, even excellent, money, and their reports home helped to fuel a continuing trickle of new arrivals in Alaska. One of the big negatives that the oil pipeline workers explained to family and friends, however, was the high cost of living in the Last Frontier. On average, commodities such as peanut butter, bread, eggs, and milk cost about 1.5 times as much as in the Lower Forty-Eight. The pipeline was completed in 1977.

What was the single worst day of Alaska history?

Beyond doubt this was on March 27, 1964, when an extremely powerful earthquake shook the state. The 9.2 mega-quake struck central and southern Alaska with deadly force. Port Valdez suffered a massive underwater landslide; thirty people were killed. In total, the quake and the resulting tsunamis killed 139 people. The property damage was estimated at $311 million.

The shock to the spirits of the people of Alaska was severe.

POPULARITY OF THE STATE

When did Alaska become boom country?

In the 1990s and early 2000s, many Americans left the Lower Forty-Eight in search of more elbow room. They arrived in Alaska to become some of its most productive citizens, involved in fishing, lumber, and the tourist trade. A number of movies were filmed, leading to the general perception that Alaska was one of the best places to be. And while we're on that subject, the television series *Northern Exposure* was surely one of the most positive influences for the state.

Shown on CBS between 1991 and 1998, *Northern Exposure* attempted to show Alaska as a very modern place—one to which an ex-astronaut might retire—and one where all sorts of madcap adventures might be expected. Joel, the village M.D., came all the way from America's East Coast to minister to the people of this little town, only to find they had quite a few things to show him about health and well-being.

How significant was the rise of Sarah Palin?

In the summer of 2008, Republican presidential candidate John S. McCain, of Arizona, surprised almost everyone by picking Alaska governor Sarah Palin as his running mate. The first reports were somewhat shocking: that this middle-aged woman did not speak proper English and that she was a master of the off-the-cuff speech. That perception changed the night she accepted her party's nomination, however. Palin showed herself a master of the cut-and-slash political technique, and she seemed to cultivate sympathy from voters, who did not wish to see her skewered. She performed well in the vice pres-

21

idential debate with Senator Joe Biden of Delaware, but the McCain-Palin ticket lost the general election.

By rights, that should have been it, and Palin would have been lauded by many for her courage and skill, even though these were not enough to prevail. Palin made some poor moves over the next few years, however. She resigned as governor and devoted herself to a series of bus trips, as well as a reality TV show. In 2016, she endorsed Donald Trump, the maverick New York businessman, for the Republican presidential nomination.

Why do discussions of climate change so often bring up discussions of Alaska?

As *Rolling Stone* magazine expressed it, in the autumn of 2015, Alaska had become ground zero for discussions of climate change and its attendant results. The tundra was melting; the Arctic Ocean was becoming more ice-free; and nowhere else in

Sarah Palin was Alaska's governor and a vice presidential candidate on the Republican ticket when Senator John McCain ran in 2008.

the United States were the lives of common people changed so dramatically. President Barack Obama made a special point of visiting Alaska in 2015 to point out his commitment to fighting the battle—which some claimed had become a war—against the negative effects of climate change.

What will Alaska look like a generation from now?

Physically, it will look very much the same, with the soaring mountains, sudden valleys, and calls of the wild that can still rivet a person. Politically and socially, Alaska may well go through some big changes.

ARIZONA

Nickname: "The Grand Canyon State"
Capital: Phoenix
Statehood: February 14, 1912; 48th state

AT A GLANCE

Where does the state nickname come from?

For once, the answer is so plain and clear that it hardly need be stated. Anyone who has ever seen the Grand Canyon, even in photographs, can see why the state would choose to align and identify itself with this superb work of nature.

What are the major state symbols?

"God Enriches" is the state motto. This has been a powerful theme in Arizona history from the time of the earliest Spanish explorers. They came seeking gold, and believed that the Almighty was on their side, that He wanted them to succeed.

The cactus wren is the state bird, and the blossom of the saguaro cactus is the state flower. The palo verde is the state tree.

How large, or small, is the Grand Canyon State?

We would naturally expect the state identified by the Grand Canyon to be large, and Arizona, at 113,990 square miles (295,235 square kilometers) is sixth among the states in geographic size. As of the year 2010, there were 6,392,017 people in Arizona, making it sixteenth among the states in terms of population.

23

One of the most amazing natural wonders of the world, Arizona's Grand Canyon was slowly dug out over millions of years by the Colorado River.

Is there more to Arizona than the Grand Canyon?

Yes indeed. One could easily spend a week at the Grand Canyon and not exhaust what it has to offer. But if the tourist then heads south, he or she will be rewarded by some of the most amazing scenery to be found in the Lower Forty-Eight.

Mesas tower over the scene, while canyons—large and small—crop up all over the place. Enormous sections of land appear, where nothing but cactus grows, and then the scene yields to where the hand of humans has established blooming fields of agriculture. Of course it's all on loan—dependent on the irrigation systems—but that's part of the appeal. The people of Arizona live on the edge, and they know it.

Is there any part of Arizona where the hand of nature is not shown?

Recently some of the suburbs of Phoenix have become so crowded that one can almost feel as if he or she is in the Midwest. All that person has to do, however, is look up, at the mountains in the background, to know that this place is truly different.

Do Arizonans talk about the weather very much?

Not like the rest of us do. They aren't afraid of hurricanes, and tornadoes don't strike their state. The people of Arizona do keep their eyes on the sky, however, because they are always hoping for rain. Most sections of the Grand Canyon State receive only four inches of precipitation per year, so the people have to be on the lookout. They've become expert at trapping and holding water wherever possible.

Can the Arizonan be picked out of a crowd, identified from his fellow Southwesterner?

Definitely. Until the 1990s, Barry Goldwater, the longtime U.S. senator from the Grand Canyon State, personified the Anglo Arizonan. Long, lean, and permanently tanned, Goldwater was a man's man, much liked by his peers, even when they chose to vilify him as an extreme Republican. Goldwater was the "Uncle Sam" stereotype for Arizona.

Born in Phoenix in 1915, Goldwater was an adventurer at heart: like John Wesley Powell, he canoed down the Grand Canyon. Elected to the U.S. Senate in 1952, Goldwater became the exemplar of a new type of American conservative: one who was fairly centrist on social policy, but dead-set on winning the Cold War against the Soviet Union. Well-liked by his colleagues, Goldwater ran for president in 1964. He secured the Republican nomination but was lambasted by attack advertisements that echoed his words, "bomb them back to the Stone Age." Some of his comments were taken out of context, but Goldwater did not complain. He was too proud for that. Though he was swamped by Lyndon B. Johnson in the battle of the cowboy hats (both men were Westerners and proud of the fact), Goldwater remained one of the most popular and well-respected men in Washington, D.C.

Since his death in 1993, Arizona has searched for a similar type of Everyman and it largely has come up short. This isn't really the fault of the Anglo population: it's just that Arizona has become much more interesting, and varied, in its population.

EARLY HISTORY

For how long have humans lived in what we now call the Grand Canyon State?

For thousands of years. We don't know how many people managed to scratch a living out of the Arizonan desert, but there is no doubt that they were there from almost the earliest of times. Not only did they live in Arizona but they developed early forms of irrigation that were in the neighborhood of present-day Phoenix.

When the first Spaniards arrived, they asked the Native Americans who built these systems and they received only shrugs, and the odd answer, "the ancient ones." The Anasazi, as they are known, disappeared by about the thirteenth century of our common era. Whether they are the ancestors of the Native Americans of Arizona today is difficult to say. Many theories have been proposed, including the rather outlandish one that the Anasazi were so highly developed that extraterrestrial beings scooped them up!

25

What did Arizona look like to the first European explorers?

Coronado came north from Mexico City in 1540, looking for silver and gold. He'd hear stories of the Seven Lost Cities of Cibola, and when a Franciscan priest came back from Arizona, saying he'd seen them, Coronado hastened forward. Perhaps the good priest simply saw the bright Arizona sunlight playing off the roofs of the Indian houses. In any case, soon after arriving, Coronado realized he'd been deceived. He and his men pushed on to the north. One of his groups saw, but did not descend to the bottom of the Grand Canyon.

Why didn't Spain do more with the lands Coronado explored?

Imperial Spain was overstretched, and it had plenty of other desert-like areas similar to Arizona (including the Sonoran Desert in northern Mexico). Spain, therefore, did almost nothing about Arizona, and nearly two centuries passed before any more explorers and missionaries went to what is now the Grand Canyon State.

Tucson was established as a military outpost around 1780. That was also the time of Brother Escalante, one of the greatest of all the Spanish explorers. He pioneered new trails across Arizona and was exploring the state at the same time that the Anglo-Americans approved the Declaration of Independence.

What did the brand new U.S. government know about Arizona?

Virtually nothing. Not only was it under Spanish control, but there were no trade routes between the Southwest and the East Coast. Of the different European peoples, only the Spaniards knew much about Arizona, and they weren't telling anyone else.

FROM MEXICAN TO AMERICAN RULE

When did Arizona first become involved with the United States in any way?

The Mexican Revolution of 1811–1821 proved the catalyst. Mexico overthrew Spanish rule and established the new Republic of Mexico. Meanwhile, Anglo-Americans became aware of Arizona because of the Santa Fe Trail, the movement of wagons and goods from Independence, Missouri, to central New Mexico.

The U.S.-Mexican War of 1846–1848 was the second big event that propelled the United States westward. Through the Treaty of Guadalupe-Hidalgo, the United States gained possession of all of New Mexico and Arizona, even though many East Coast Americans did not see these areas as terribly important.

Who were the first white Americans to reach the floor of the Grand Canyon?

This was accomplished by Lieutenant Joseph C. Ives and a party of explorers, dispatched by the federal government in 1857. They came up part of the Colorado River on a steamboat and then marched through areas that had seldom been seen by any whites. On an April morning in 1858, Ives and his party descended to the floor of the Canyon. Though they had no photographic equipment, the journey's artist rendered some impressive sketches. In the journal of the expedition, Ives predicted that his group would be the last whites ever to see this region, because it had nothing of great value and was so separated from the rest of the nation. His might be one of the worst predictions made by any nineteenth-century American explorer!

Why is the story of John Wesley Powell so much better-known than that of Joseph C. Ives?

For one thing, Ives—who was a native of Connecticut—joined the Confederacy during the Civil War: he is therefore not well-remembered. Just as important, however, is that John W. Powell went down the Colorado River on a raft, and that he did much of his work single-handed, without any assistance from the federal government.

Born in upstate New York in 1834, Powell was an academic and a scholar, but as oriented to the outdoors as any true frontiersman. He lost an arm fighting for the Union during the Civil War, and though he suffered recurrent pain throughout his life, this did not deter him from pursuing any of his goals. After leading groups of students on several Western adventures, he set a goal of rafting down the Colorado, and through the Grand Canyon. He accomplished this in 1869, and in the process he came to know the American Southwest better, perhaps, than any white person of his time. Powell was later called upon both by the academic community and the federal government, and his work has stood the test of time.

Did the Civil War play any part in Arizona's development?

Perhaps not for most of the white settlers, but for the Native Americans it was a traumatic time. Christopher "Kit" Carson, one of the most famous of all the Mountain Men, became a brigadier-general in the Union Army; as such, he surrounded and compelled many of the Navajo to surrender. Carson marched them to distant, far-off locations where they could not regroup, and in so doing he virtually condemned many of them to death. Carson does not appear to have been mean-spirited: rather, he was a firm believer in the rule of law, military law in this case.

What did Native Americans of the Southwest think of the white peoples' attempts to "conquer" the Grand Canyon?

Many of the white people seemed arrogant, even foolish, to the Native Americans, but they had great respect for John Wesley Powell. Some of the most poignant of Powell's photographs show him in conversation with leading Indians.

TERRITORIAL DAYS

When did Arizona become a territory, and why was it so difficult for it to attain statehood?

Becoming a U.S. territory was almost demanded by the onset of the American Civil War. The Confederate States laid a vague claim to Arizona and even attempted to establish a government for the area, but they were defeated at the Battle of Glorieta Pass in 1862. President Abraham Lincoln was keen to bring Arizona in as a territory, and this took place in 1863.

What was life like in the Territory of Arizona?

The end of the Civil War and the achievement of statehood by Colorado meant that numerous villains and desperadoes were desperately searching for a new place to live, and the Arizona Territory seemed like the perfect answer. The development of mining camps and towns provided further motivation, and Arizona became known, in the 1870s and 1880s, as the land of stagecoach robberies and bank holdups, as well as numerous battles against the Native Americans. For a time, Arizona was the wildest part of the Wild West.

That did not deter people from moving to the Arizona Territory: the lure of the mineral wealth was far too great. Bisbee, in the southeast corner of Arizona, became one of the first of the big mining successes, and it was followed by Tombstone, about fifteen miles to the north. The nearness of the Mexican border had something to do with the allure: many lawbreakers were pleased to know that they could skip across the boundary with ease and lose themselves for a time in the deserts of northern Mexico.

Was the gunfight at O.K. Corral as violent—and exciting—as they make out?

The event, which took place October 26, 1881, was pretty small so far as Wild West fighting is concerned (only about 30 seconds), but it became famous when a book was published in 1931 and a movie was released in 1946. The shootout involved cowboys Billy Claiborne, brothers Billy and Ike Clanton, and brothers Frank and Tom McLaury on one side and law officials Doc Holliday and brothers Morgan, Virgil, and Wyatt Earp on the other side. Claiborne and Ike Clanton ran from the scene; Holliday and Virgil and Morgan Earp were wounded; Billy Clanton and the McLaurys were killed; and Wyatt Earp was unharmed.

For how long did Geronimo and the Apaches fight the U.S. government?

Some of the soldiers who fought the Apache were Civil War veterans, and they claimed they never encountered a foe as elusive and creative as the Chiricahua Apache. Geronimo was an equal opportunity offender where white people were concerned: he fought the Mexicans just as intensely as the Americans. Time after time, Geronimo escaped after being cornered. But in 1886, he finally surrendered to General Nelson Miles. Geronimo was taken as a prisoner to Florida, where he dictated his autobiography. Years later he was allowed to move to Oklahoma, but he never again saw his beloved Arizona.

How are the Native Americans of Arizona treated today?

Large sections of the state's land are in Indian country, meaning autonomous Indian reservations. This does not mean that living is good on those reservations, however. A long debate has taken place over the values and virtues, as well as the demerits and failures, of the reservation system. It would take a true expert in Indian affairs to give a considered opinion.

An 1898 photograph of Apache chief Geronimo.

How important was copper to the Arizona economy?

Arizonans used to speak of the four big "C's," meaning copper, cattle, cotton, and citrus. Of the four, copper was the number-one income producer between 1880 and 1920.

How and when did Arizona attain statehood?

Arizona endured the single-longest period of any American state in territorial status. It became the Territory of Arizona in 1863 and a state on Valentine's Day of 1912. In-between were a series of initiatives, all of them doomed. East Coast America, which is where the political power lay, was intrinsically distrustful of Arizona and New Mexico, those areas that seemed more Mexican than Anglo. The owners of the copper companies surely could have persuaded the U.S. Congress, but it was in their interest for Arizona to remain a territory.

Theodore Roosevelt was impressed enough to go to Arizona in 1911, to see the opening of the Roosevelt Dam, but it was his handpicked successor, President William Howard Taft, who brought Arizona into the Union on February 14, 1912.

THE EARLY TWENTIETH CENTURY

Did World War I bring any change to the Grand Canyon State?

Not much. Arizona was so far removed from the scene of conflict that its young men were hardly mobilized by the time the war was over. But World War I did have the effect of making Arizona better-known to Americans in other states; when those Arizonans reached the military camps, they informed their fellows of a land so different from the East Coast that it might as well have been on another continent.

Was the Great Depression a shock for many of the people of Arizona?

Again, the events were so far removed that many Arizonans did not take them seriously at first. But when the price of copper took a nose dive, the people of the Grand Canyon State realized that they were in for the fight of their lives, and, for once, they were pleased to have the federal government play a major role.

On October 16, 1936, the lights of the Hoover Dam switched on, and the work was declared complete. The 700-foot-high dam created the 115-mile-long Lake Mead and allowed for the generation and transmission of electricity to Arizona, Nevada, and California (the three states later fought a series of lawsuits to determine who should have the largest share). It was a great moment for the Grand Canyon State and a signature accomplishment of Franklin Roosevelt's New Deal.

Did World War II create any lasting change?

Yes, indeed. The start of the war took Arizona—like the rest of the nation—by surprise, but there was special eagerness to be fully involved in this conflict and for the state to win kudos for its performance. Many thousands of Arizonans served, but perhaps the best-known and most successful of them were the Navajo Code Talkers.

The United States broke the Japanese naval codes by the summer of 1942, and it was deemed vitally important that the Japanese not do the same in reverse. When looking for code transmission and interpreters, the federal government decided that the Navajo Indians, whose language was dramatically different from that of most other Native American tongues, should be used as the primary ones. Navajo Indians served as "code talkers" throughout the war, and to the best of our knowledge none of their transmissions ever were broken by the enemy.

THE SUN BELT

When did the expression "Sun Belt" come into general use?

It was during the 1970s, when the nation as a whole experienced high prices of oil and gasoline. People from around the nation suddenly became aware of the fact that Arizona and New Mexico have more sunlight than almost any other states and that heating costs were significantly lower. Once "Sun Belt" came into use, people also began to speak of "snow birds," meaning people from Northern states who went to Southern states each autumn.

When did Arizona become a destination for retirees?

Many people had already gone to the high desert of Arizona for reasons of health, but it was the post-World War II prosperity that allowed the numbers to increase dramatically.

The 1950s were, perhaps, the key decade, in which East and West Coast Americans became more aware of what the Grand Canyon State had to offer, but the 1970s registered the largest decade of growth of the twentieth century. High costs of heating oil drove many New England residents and Midwesterners to relocate to the Southwest. Though New Mexico was larger, and had more space, Arizona was better served by airports, and it was through these that most of the newcomers came. The majority of those who moved to Arizona reported that their allergies, asthma, or both improved significantly within a short time of their arrival.

When did the Grand Canyon become one of the great tourist destinations for Americans?

The Grand Canyon became a national park in 1915, but the real influx of sightseers began in the 1950s. Numerous *National Geographic* television programs contributed to the Canyon's popularity, but there were also the eyewitness testimonies of literally millions of Americans who informed their friends back home.

In the early twenty-first century, a new distinction arose between those who said they visited the Grand Canyon on its southern rim and those who declared they were among the few who saw it from the northern side. These arguments—and distinctions—were rendered moot when a glass bridge was put across the canyon. From that point forward, visitors were on an equal footing.

MODERN ARIZONA

How on earth did London Bridge ever end up in western Arizona?

Those Americans who love London—and they are many—know that almost twenty bridges span the Thames in the central part of the city. Of these, Tower Bridge, Lambeth Bridge, and London Bridge were the best known, with the last of these three being the oldest. Realizing that London Bridge was slowly breaking down, the City of London decided to remove it, and an American businessman quickly offered to transport it all the way to Lake Havasu City in Arizona. The work was just about as difficult and costly as the moving of the Statue of Liberty from France to New York City, but it was completed in 1971.

What's special about Kitt Peak National Observatory?

This observatory, located 56 miles southwest of Tucson, is the home of the largest solar telescope in the world. Built in 1962, it enables astronomers to view in great detail such features of the sun as sunspots. The 100-foot (30-meter) structure can withstand winds of up to 25 miles (40 km) per hour, moving only 0.0625 inches (0.4 millimeters).

London Bridge was moved from England to Havasu City, Arizona, in 1971, where it has become a popular tourist attraction.

How did Arizona fare toward the end of the twentieth century?

It boomed as never before. Phoenix and Flagstaff were sometimes overcrowded, but the state as a whole had plenty of room for the newcomers. One of the surprising challenges for Arizona was traffic congestion. Unlike East and West Coast cities, Phoenix was built as a long row of suburbs, and very few people were able to walk to work or the mall.

Arizona was also populated by an ever-increasing number of New Age believers, those who believed the world would soon undergo transformative changes. Like their counterparts in New Mexico, these Arizona folks congregated at certain areas, with Sedona being by far the most popular. By 2000, Arizona presented a bifurcated image, with many straight-talking cowboys, numerous high-tech workers, and an increasingly hippie-like subculture.

Did John McCain stand a chance of being the new Barry Goldwater?

Interestingly, rather few political commentators drew the parallel. McCain was not a native of Arizona; he was a U.S. Navy brat who was born in the Panama Canal region. In their straight talk and powerful physical presence, the two were a good deal alike, but, while many respected him for his decades of service in the U.S. Navy (and, especially, the five and a half years he was a prisoner of war during the Vietnam War), McCain never made many friends in the U.S. Senate. He ran for president in 2000 and 2008. In the latter year, he won the Republican nomination but lost the general election to Democrat Barack Obama.

Where will the Grand Canyon State be a generation from now?

The chances are that it will continue to be the leader of the Southwestern states and that its economy will continue to expand. Of course the state faces serious water concerns, but as of this writing, in 2015, Arizona has not suffered the terrible type of drought seen in California.

ARKANSAS

Nickname: "The Natural State"
Capital: Little Rock
Statehood: June 15, 1836; 25th state

AT A GLANCE

Where does the state nickname come from?

While other states have entered the twenty-first century with a bang, embracing computer technology and so forth, the people of Arkansas remain proud of being close to the land.

What are the major state symbols of the Natural State?

"The People Rule" is the state motto. Arkansas is a profoundly conservative state in many ways, but it is a conservatism based on populism. The mockingbird is the state bird, and the apple blossom is the state flower. The shortleaf pine is the state tree.

How large, or small, is Arkansas?

The Natural State has a total of 53,179 square miles (137,733 square kilometers), making it the thirty-second largest of the fifty states. As of the year 2010, there were 2,915,918 people in Arkansas, making it thirty-second among the states in terms of population.

Why does Arkansas have such an old-style feel?

Very likely this is because that's the way the state residents wish things to be. Arkansas is one of the most conservative states of the Union, and its people do not think of *con-*

35

servative in terms of holding back the future but rather in conserving that which is best from the past. They have endured numerous difficulties, including natural disasters and man-made conflicts, and most of them wish to remain what they are: a truly rural people living in a place they call the Natural State.

If the people are so deeply devoted to their landscape, does this mean that it has always worked in their favor?

Far from it. When the first white settlers arrived, around 1810, they found the eastern third of the area an enormous bog, the result of numerous Mississippi River floods. The problem was not truly solved—through drainage and the building of levees—until the late nineteenth century. Tornadoes are a persistent source of concern in Arkansas.

Much like New Englanders who firmly assert they will never become "snowbirds" and flee to southern areas to avoid the cold, the great majority of Arkansans declare they will never leave. The hardships and difficulties that form so integral a part of the state's history are their heritage, and they will always choose to remain in the Natural State.

Do the people of Arkansas discuss the weather very much?

In winter, they tend to congratulate each other for the good fortune of living in a temperate climate. Spring is long and pleasant, and the summer heat is not lacking in charm, but the threat of tornadoes hangs heavy over the region. Many Arkansans have survived or evaded all manner of difficulties, only to be wiped out by the sudden tornado or twister.

Is Arkansas the land of Southern culture flavored by a Midwestern sauce, or the other way around?

People have asked this question for more than a century, and no one has yet formed a convincing answer. Like Missouri, Arkansas is a crossroads state, an area that has seen more travelers and migrants than full-time residents. But if one really has to make a choice, he or she will assert that Arkansas is about 80 percent Southern and 20 percent Midwestern. There's enough of the latter to make the casual visitor *feel* as if he might be in the Midwest, but the former predominates in most communities.

The smallest U.S. national park is located in Arkansas; which one is it?

The popular therapeutic waters of Hot Springs, Arkansas, became a national park on March 4, 1921. At 5,550 acres, it is the smallest national park in the United States. Before then, it was known as Hot Springs Reservation. Native Americans, and then locals, were aware of the hot waters that existed in the region. In 1804, President Thomas Jefferson sent an expedition to the southern part of the area that was part of the previous year's Louisiana Purchase, and soon afterwards, more and more people became aware of what they viewed as the medicinal value of the springs. Tourism followed and Hot Springs became known as the "American Spa."

What chance is there that the people of Arkansas will become more progressive in their thinking and more welcoming of the twenty-first century world?

They are still catching up with twentieth-century developments, and plenty of state residents assert that these are enough. Arkansas has thoroughly modernized its agriculture, and there is more industry than before, but the majority of the state's residents still live in small towns, which have a late nineteenth-century feel.

Does Arkansas have a prominent cultural hero?

If so, he is Sam Walton (1918–1992), the legendary founder of Wal-Mart. Born in

A 1936 photo of Sam Walton, founder of the superstore Wal-Mart.

Oklahoma, Walton lived in Florida, Missouri, and Iowa before settling in Arkansas. He opened the first Wal-Mart Discount City Store in Bentonville in 1962, and the rest—as they say—is history. Friendly, outgoing, and shrewd, Walton built Wal-Mart into the superstore of the twentieth century, to the point where it drove perhaps three-quarters of all its competition out of business. Walton never seemed to need money that much—he was indifferent to wealth and creature comforts—but he left an immense fortune to his family.

EARLY HISTORY

For how long have humans lived in what we now call Arkansas?

For thousands of years. Mound builders lived there perhaps 1,500 years ago, and the tribes that greeted the first European explorers were among their descendants. Prior to the advent of large-scale agriculture, it was difficult to make a living (or even a life) in the region, however, and it was not heavily populated when the Spaniards, and then the French, made their first appearance.

To the best of our knowledge, Hernando de Soto and his much-reduced Spanish force appeared in Arkansas in 1541, having crossed the Mississippi River on rafts. De Soto and company did not remain there for long, but Spain maintained a distant claim to the region for a very long time. The French first appeared in 1673, when Louis Joliet and a few fur traders appeared on the Arkansas River. They, too, did not remain long.

How important was French explorer René-Robert Cavelier de La Salle's claim that all this land belonged to King Louis XIV of France?

To most of us today, the French claim seems rather preposterous, as it was based only on one long canoe trip by La Salle and about twenty companions. But things could have turned out differently. When La Salle stood at the Mississippi's mouth, in 1682, and claimed the entire great river and its many tributaries for France, there was—on the maps at least—a change of political direction. Of course it would have required immense effort for France to settle the region, and, as things turned out, the British and their American subjects never had to fight very hard to gain possession of the soil.

La Salle died in Texas in 1685, but his aide and confidante, Henry de Tonty—who was Italian by birth but in the service of Louis XIV—established Fort Arkansas in 1686, and this was the first permanent European settlement in the region. Tonty was extremely ambitious for the king, and France's claim, and when he died—in 1704—France lost its most ambitious colonizer in the southern part of the Midwest.

What did the Indians think of these various European explorers and colonists?

They were as mystified by the Europeans as the Indians of New England and Virginia were in the early seventeenth century. Why did the white people want the land so much? Didn't they realize that no one owned the land, that it belonged to the Great Spirit? The Indians had the breathing space of nearly a century before the Anglo-Americans showed up, but this respite turned into a nightmare when the Native Americans realized that this group of settlers were different from earlier ones: they intended to stay.

The U.S. Congress first became aware of Arkansas—the name at least—at the time of the Louisiana Purchase in 1803. Even if Louis XIV and France ever had a good claim, it was now gone, thanks to the $15 million the United States paid for the entire area. The advent of the War of 1812 kept the white settlers away a little while longer, but after 1815, Anglo-Americans practically poured across the Mississippi River, looking for ever-greater amounts of land. Tradition has it that Daniel Boone moved to Missouri late in life because he needed more "elbow room"; this was certainly true of those who came to Arkansas.

FROM SETTLEMENT TO STATEHOOD

How rapidly did Arkansas move from territorial status to statehood?

The 1820s and 1830s were a time of great national optimism; a period when it seemed the entire Midwest would be settled in short order. Missouri became a state in 1821; another fifteen years were required before Arkansas entered the Union, in 1836. At the time statehood was achieved, Arkansas had barely more than 50,000 residents, and most of them were in the central and western parts of the state, because of the huge areas of swampland near the west bank of the Mississippi River.

A lifestyle grew up in Arkansas between 1820 and 1860, one based around the tiny village, sometimes with no more than twenty residents. Sawmills were common, as the people of Arkansas began turning their first natural product into a cash cow. Tobacco was grown in some areas, but cotton was not a big success in Arkansas, owing to the temperature difference between the state and those of the Deep South. There was no special reason why slavery should have developed, or flourished, in Arkansas, but there was perhaps a cultural imperative. Most Arkansans were second- or third-generation descendants from men and women of Virginia, Kentucky, and Tennessee, and it seemed natural that slavery would cross the Mississippi River and become part of life in Arkansas.

Was there any chance Arkansas could have stayed out of the Civil War?

President Abraham Lincoln and many Northern leaders earnestly hoped that it would. The mere fact that Arkansas joined the Confederacy (as the eleventh and last state) meant that the Union's task was much tougher. It now involved fighting the Confederates west of the Mississippi, as well as in Virginia and Tennessee. Arkansas fought not especially for the institution of slavery, but from sympathy with its Deep Southern neighbors, and the results were catastrophic. Missouri, it can be argued, suffered even more, but the Natural State saw plenty of fighting, and most of it went against the Confederate cause.

When the Civil War ended, Arkansas was prostrate. It had done wrong, its leaders declared, and it was willing to make restitution, but the Reconstruction imposed by the federal government was too strong, entirely. A new state constitution was written in order to readmit the state, in 1868, and white Arkansans resented its provisions so strongly that they still remembered it a century later when the Civil Rights era commenced.

What was life in Arkansas like near the end of the nineteenth century?

The state had recovered from its economic losses of the Civil War but had not advanced beyond where it was in the year 1860. Lumber, fishing, and occasional mining were the major ways people earned a living, and Arkansans experienced some of the worst conditions of any Southerners during the sharecropping era. Race relations had never been especially good, but they became much worse at the turn of the twentieth century, with an informal segregation taking place: one still sees its echoes in the way blacks are (and are not) represented in certain Arkansas counties. Arkansas also experienced many difficulties enforcing the law (both state and federal). The single most famous case is that of Isaac Parker, often known as the "Hanging Judge."

Is there any truth to the many stories of Hanging Judge Parker?

Born in Ohio, Isaac Charles Parker became a lawyer in Missouri, and in 1875, President Ulysses S. Grant appointed him to the U.S. District Court for the western section of Arkansas. At the time, this included all of what was called Indian Territory, which has since become the state of Oklahoma. Parker was indeed stern on the bench. He spoke out loudly on behalf of the Native Americans, who, he believed, were the victims of encroachment by his fellow whites. Parker is called the "hanging judge" because a total of seventy-nine men were hanged during his twenty-seven years on the bench. While this is certainly a higher number than was true of many of his fellow jurists, most of them did not have as many complications (including the escape of felons into Indian Territory) as Parker faced. Parker died in Fort Smith. His courtroom has been preserved as part of the Fort Smith National Historic Site.

Isaac Parker was known as "Hanging Judge Parker" because of the frequency with which he sentenced men to death.

THE EARLY TWENTIETH CENTURY

When did evangelical Christianity make a powerful appearance in Arkansas?

Arkansas had not previously been known for the religiosity of its people, but most of the state fell within the so-called Bible Belt, and the fundamentalist Christianity that swept the Deep South around 1910 made its way to the Natural State. By 1917—the year the United States entered the First World War—Arkansas was among the most backward of all states of the Union, and perhaps the one where rural communities outnumbered urban ones to the greatest degree.

Who was Hattie Caraway?

Hattie Caraway was married to Thaddeus Caraway, who served as a Democratic senator from Arkansas from 1921 until his death in 1931. As was common back in the day, the governor named Caraway's widow to temporarily fill his seat until a special election could be held. She was elected in the special election in January 1932 to fill out the remaining months of his term, making her the first woman to be elected to the Senate. She surprised people when she announced that she would attempt to remain in office by running on her own in the general election in November. She won that election, as well as in 1938, before losing in the primaries in 1944.

How did Arkansas fare during World War I and World War II?

Both of the world wars presented new opportunities for many Arkansans, especially the young men who went to serve on the battlefronts. They came home with a larger world-view, and quite a few of them advanced the economic cause of the towns to which they returned. At the same time, however, Arkansas witnessed a backlash by some of its most conservative groups, those that declared they did not wish to see any social or cultural change.

The same cannot be said for the Great Depression, however. Arkansas was only in decent economic shape when the Depression commenced, and the 1930s were a fairly desperate time for many people in the Natural State. Arkansas lost perhaps 50,000 people, most of whom moved to California, and there were times when the state was despaired of. This feeling changed quickly with the advent of World War II, however, and by the year 1946, when most of the young men returned, the state had been put on a new footing. Modest discoveries of oil and natural gas advanced the economic front, and Arkansas set its face toward a new future.

Why did the Civil Rights era see its ugliest episode in Little Rock? Why didn't this happen in Richmond, or perhaps Atlanta or Montgomery?

The people of Arkansas were accustomed to living in obscurity, and it did not occur to many of them that the prevention of desegregation would bring national attention. In the late summer of 1957, when it was announced that the public schools of Little Rock would be desegregated (pursuant to the U.S. Supreme Court ruling in *Brown v. Board of Education*), many white folks turned out to make sure this did not happen. Photographs, and even some films, were made that showed white Arkansans spitting on and jeering at a tiny handful of African Americans who wanted nothing more than to attend the local schools.

Given that Arkansas had endured so much—both during and after the Civil War— it seems unfair that its white population should be vilified for their actions during the Civil Rights era, but so it was. Arkansas gained an unenviable record, as the state that resisted the desegregation of white schools.

Who were the Little Rock Nine?

The Little Rock Nine were nine African American students from Little Rock Central High School who bravely attempted to enter the building in September 1957 following the Supreme Court's verdict in *Brown v. Board of Education*, which struck down segregation. Their initial attempts failed when violence ensued and police removed them for their own safety. But they returned later in the month with a U.S. Army 101st Airborne escort, courtesy of President Dwight D. Eisenhower. The school is now a national landmark, a museum is across the street, and a memorial to the Little Rock Nine is on the grounds of the capitol.

Were the people of Arkansas any more racist—any more anti-black—than their counterparts in other Southern states?

No. Arkansas resistance to desegregation grew more out of a desire to honor tradition and prevent change than from an innate dislike of African Americans. Commentators have

41

long observed that the people of Arkansas are more tradition-bound than most of their fellow Americans. The conservative streak runs so deep that a law was passed (in 1895) that specified precisely how the state's name should be pronounced.

When did Arkansas begin to rehabilitate itself in the eyes of the rest of the nation?

A full generation was required for this to happen. Those who watched television in 1957 long remembered the horrible scenes of that year. It required the rise of a local Arkansas politician to prominence to persuade many people that the Natural State had repented of its actions. That person was, of course, William Jefferson Clinton, who became the forty-third president of the United States.

Native son Bill Clinton was one of the most popular U.S. presidents of the twentieth century.

How important is Clinton to the national image of Arkansas?

If any one person can redirect the energy of a state, or reform its image in the mind of the nation as a whole, then that is Bill Clinton. Born in the little town of Hope in 1944, Clinton never knew his father (who died a few weeks earlier). Raised by his mother and stepfather, Clinton showed great intelligence and even greater ambition from an early age. As a teen, he was part of the high school delegation that met President John F. Kennedy in the Rose Garden, and anyone who views the photograph of that event is struck by the sense that the fifteen-year-old Clinton knows he will one day stand in the forty-six-year-old Kennedy's shoes.

After Yale and a Rhodes scholarship, Clinton went into state politics. In 1979, he became the youngest governor Arkansas had ever seen, and in 1981 he became the youngest ex-governor. Dubbing himself the comeback kid, Clinton won election again in 1983, and he remained in the governor's chair until he resigned thirty-nine days after he was elected president in 1992.

We all know that Clinton was one of the most skillful of all twentieth-century politicians. But how was he viewed back home in Arkansas?

With a mixture of pride and despair. Arkansas residents were thrilled to have one of their own in the White House. At the same time, many of them deplored the ethical and some-times personal difficulties that the forty-third president got himself into. Clinton won the general elections of 1992 and 1996, and the country prospered during his White House years, but the Whitewater Scandal and what is sometimes called Lewinskygate (where Clinton got into trouble for his relations with a young White House intern named Monica Lewinsky) brought attention that most Arkansans could do without. Many critics claim that Clinton was a terrific success for himself, but a disaster to the Democratic Party. At any event, Arkansas voters turned to a Republican when choosing their governor in 1996.

What was life in Arkansas like at the turn of the twenty-first century?

More than most states, Arkansas could justly claim that it had not changed. The beloved rivers, streams, hills, and waterfalls were all intact. The people of Arkansas continued to spend much of their time outdoors, and they took longer than most to adapt to the computer and Internet revolutions. At the same time, there were those who argued that Arkansas had changed more than most other states, which seems to suggest that the state had—as of about the year 1950—been very far behind.

Will people continue to move to Arkansas? Or will it be one of the enclaves where most people claim to be fourth- and fifth-generation state residents?

It's unlikely that Arkansas will witness any major immigration. The state is committed to its rural past, and one does not imagine subdivisions and suburbs cropping up any time soon. The chances are that Arkansas will remain one of the most homogeneous places—in terms of lack of new immigration—in the Union.

Nickname: "The Golden State"
Capital: Sacramento
Statehood: September 9, 1850; 31st state

AT A GLANCE

Where does the state nickname come from?

Some people say it is for the golden-like hills of the area, but more people believe it is from the gold fields that brought so many prospectors in 1849–1850. It's no exaggeration to say that the Gold Rush led to the establishment of the state itself.

What are the major state symbols for the Golden State?

"I Have Found It" is the California state motto, an obvious reference to the finding of gold in 1848. The California valley quail is the state bird, and the golden poppy is the state flower. The redwood, which many foreigners take to be *the* symbol, is the state tree.

How large, or small, is the Golden State?

California is third among the fifty states in size, with 158,608 square miles (410,793 square kilometers). As of the year 2010, there were 37,245,956 people in the Golden State, making it by far the most populous. To put it another way, there are more people in California than in all of Canada.

Is there one special spot from which the best of California can be seen?

The Golden State abounds in beauty, both from the hand of nature and the work of humans. Even so, if one had to choose just one specific place, it would very likely be either a view of the Golden Gate Bridge or the view *from* that magnificent bridge.

45

The bridge, which opened in 1937, is best seen by walking, rather than driving the car across. Even the most casual observer will be impressed by the width of the bridge, its exceptional sturdiness, and the way it "moves" or "gives" with the flow of the water below. The engineers designed the Golden Gate Bridge this way, and their decisions have been rewarded with exceptional stability. It is one of the wonders of the Western world, so well designed that it can withstand the pressures of time, tide, and, likely, earthquakes. There was only one occasion in its history when the bridge was in danger, and that was when too many people stood on it at one time: during the fiftieth anniversary celebration in 1987!

Can anyone really do justice to the natural beauty of California?

Many people have tried. Numerous travel books, National Park Service brochures, and so forth testify to the natural beauty of the Golden State. But California is one of the places one really has to see in order to fully appreciate it.

Redwood trees—some more than a thousand years old; endless vistas of the Pacific Ocean—sometimes with sudden drop-offs that the tourist must take care to avoid; Yosemite National Park; Simi Valley; all these and more form the heart of what is truly one of the most beautiful states in the Union and one of the most exciting places on the entire planet. Of course all this natural wonder has its share of hazards.

Is it true that there are trees so big and wide that you can drive your car through them?

Yes, three such trees exist. Giant redwood trees in Klamath, Myers Flat, and Leggett have openings wide enough to drive your car through them. The most famous drive-through tree was the Wawona sequoia tree in Yosemite National Park. But a heavy snowfall in 1969 resulted in the giant tree falling down.

Do Californians discuss the weather very much?

Not in the way that the rest of us do. Normal weather in California is so splendid that no one has to say very much about it: bright, sunny, with a chance of a cloudless day. But when disaster strikes, and it often comes as a result of the weather, Californians can speak of nothing else. They have experienced mudslides, hurricanes, tornadoes, and forest fires that would send most of us running far away. They know their state is vulnerable to tsunamis, though it's been awhile since California was hit. The Golden State is vulnerable to drought, too. In January 2015, for instance, California entered the fourth year of a record-breaking drought. Governor Jerry Brown declared a state of emergency in terms of water usage. And, to top off everything else, Californians live with the distinct knowledge that a massive earthquake will come someday. The question, of course, is when?

What are some of the highs and lows, so far as temperature is concerned?

California sees mostly balmy weather, with more sunlit days than other states, but when the weather does turn, it can be ominous. The coldest temperature ever recorded in

A testimony to engineering and human determination, San Francisco's Golden Gate Bridge has a total length of 1.7 miles (2.7 kilometers) and services over a hundred thousand cars and trucks a day.

California came on January 20, 1937, when –45 degrees F (–43 degrees C) was seen at Boca. That record low came in a decade of some sensationally low temperatures, but many of them were in the Midwestern states, and this one came as quite a shock to Californians. As for extreme heat, California has seen plenty, over time, but the single most sensational—indeed the single highest temperature recorded anywhere in the United States, was at Greenland Ranch in Death Valley, on July 10, 1913. The mercury recorded 134 degrees F (57 degrees C).

How different are Californians from their East Coast counterparts?

The differences are striking. Californians—male or female—tend to be more athletic and to spend a greater period of time out-of-doors. They are just as interested in material success as people living on the East Coast, but that success is pursued in a more happy-go-lucky way.

Can Californians be identified, picked out of a group?

Yes. Whether they are Anglo, Hispanic, or Asian, and whether they have lived in the Golden State for two years or all their life, the typical Californian is much sunnier and optimistic than the rest of us. Some of this comes from the weather, which is delightful so much of the time; another part derives from the fact that California is constantly being resettled, meaning that it receives new immigrant groups. The boundless optimism they bring is part of the reason for California's success.

Who are some of the best-loved of California sons and daughters?

It makes for a very long list. John A. Sutter, whose fort was very close to where gold was found, in 1848, is perhaps the earliest of them all. But as the nineteenth century gave way to the twentieth, California had a veritable slew of heroes and heroines: perhaps the aspect that unites them is that they were multidimensional, not people of tunnel vision. In the 1960s, Governor Edmund "Pat" Brown was the hero of many Anglo Californians; at about the same time, Cesar Chavez became the idol of many California Hispanics. California beach culture has been celebrated by many popular rock groups, most successfully the Beach Boys. Since the computer revolution, Bill Gates and Steve Jobs have run neck-and-neck as heroes for young Californians.

EARLY HISTORY

For how long have humans lived in what we now call the Golden State?

For thousands of years. We don't know when the first Native Americans came to California, or what they did for a living, but we know that their descendants were there in great numbers when the first European explorers arrived.

When Spaniards first made their way up the California coast, in the sixteenth century, they found at least 100 different tribes living in what is now the Golden State. These various Indian peoples had lifestyles that can—even now—be envied. An abundance of fish and shellfish existed along the coast and major rivers, while deer, elk, and bear populated the hinterland. Given that the Native peoples were so expert at hunting and fishing, they had little need to farm, and most of the evidence suggests they did not do so. The early Native Americans of California lived in something close to paradise.

Why didn't the Spaniards move in and soak up more of what California had to offer?

There is an image—and not entirely a mistaken one—of a gold-crazed Spaniard, lurching through the American Southwest, seeking valuable minerals but unaware of the treasure that actually lies right beneath his feet: the fine land. This is half-true of the Spaniards that came to California. Ever eager to get rich quick, they moved on, looking for the Lost Cities of Cibola, and endless gods. They missed out almost entirely.

The few Spaniards who devoted any attention or time to California tended to be men of the cloth: Franciscan and Dominican friars and priests who wished to convert the Native Americans to Roman Catholicism. Their efforts have been criticized many times, and not without reason, but we will never know how many Native American lives these priests and monks saved, just by keeping them out of the clutches of the Spanish military. Father Junípero Serra is one of the favored sons of California: he established more missions on the southern California coast than any other person.

TRAPPERS AND TRAVELERS

Given how far California is from the East Coast, how and when did East Coast Americans become aware of what lay on the other side of the continent?

This happened through two means. First came the fur trappers, rather desperate fellows who crossed the Rocky Mountains and then the Sierra Nevada to enter California from the east. And during the 1830s, a handful of American ships paid call at Mexican ports along the California coast. The fur trappers did not tend to leave diaries or journals, but some of the American sailors did. One of the most famous of these was *Two Years Before the Mast*, by Richard Henry Dana Jr.

How did Mexican-held California fall into the hands of the United States?

When he came into the White House in 1845, President James K. Polk was determined that the United States should acquire all of California and all of the Oregon Country (which was bigger than the present-day state of Oregon). Polk provoked the Republic of Mexico into starting the conflict that we call the Mexican War. In what seemed like no time, the Americans conquered most of Arizona and New Mexico, and all of California. For a short time, perhaps as little as four weeks, it seemed as though California would become its own nation. Americans who had crossed from the Sierra Nevada in the preceding decade overthrew the Mexican authorities and established what they called the Bear Flag Republic. It is honored today, on the California state flag. But the arrival of units of the U.S. Navy quickly persuaded the Bear Flaggers to back down, and California came under the rule of the Stars and Stripes.

Was gold discovered in one place or spread out through the state?

In January 1848, James W. Marshall of the United States and Johann Augustus Sutter of Switzerland found nuggets of gold along the banks of the American River in what is now Sacramento, the state capital. They hurried the metal to San Francisco, where it was assayed, and they soon received the news that this was the real deal: gold. However, news also reached Samuel Brannan, one of the editors of San Francisco's first newspapers, the *California Star*, and he spread it like wildfire. "Gold!" he shouted. And with that the Gold Rush commenced.

This stone landmark indicates the exact spot where the original Sutter's Mill was located.

How did San Francisco rise so quickly, to become one of the great American cities?

In 1845, when the U.S. Navy took over, the area was called Yerba Buena, meaning "place of the good herb," and it was inhabited by only about 800 Mexicans. Three years later, when the Gold Rush began, San Francisco had perhaps 10,000 people. The Gold Rush provided nearly all the newcomers, who included many sailors from transport ships. Arriving at San Francisco, the crews of these ships decided the gold fields should not be left only to the travelers, and they abandoned their ships, in a desperate attempt to be among those who got rich. A few years later, San Francisco had 100,000 residents. Almost no other American city has ever risen with such speed.

CALIFORNIA IN THE LIFE OF THE NATION

How quickly did California go from being a conquered province of Mexico to becoming the thirty-first state?

This happened with great speed. James K. Polk had left the White House, and it was during the administration of Zachary Taylor that the question of California was debated. Many Southern sympathizers were determined to bring California in as a slave state, but the residents decided otherwise. The question of statehood was then submitted to the U.S. Congress, where it threatened to upset the balance of power between pro-slavery states and those that forbade slavery. It required all the efforts of U.S. senator Henry Clay of Kentucky to bring about the Compromise of 1850, which brought California in as a free state, while providing a new Fugitive Slave Law to the Southern states.

Did California play any role in the American Civil War?

Militarily, the Golden State provided only one or two battalions. But in terms of mineral wealth, and thereby the funding of the Union war effort, California was quite important.

What happened to the Pony Express?

Beginning in 1859, dispatch riders carried the mail all the way from St. Joseph, Missouri, to Sacramento. The image of the daring express rider, galloping across the Great Plains, rising up into the Rocky Mountains, and then arriving in California, is one of the most brilliant and wonderful from the mid-nineteenth century. Just two and a half years later, however, the Pony Express was rendered obsolete by the connection of the transcontinental telegraph, and the ponies, and their riders, faded into the background.

President Lincoln was determined that California not fall into Confederate hands, and he found the brand new transcontinental telegraph, completed in the autumn of 1861, very useful in keeping Californians on his side.

What are some of the great fortunes that were made in nineteenth-century California?

Levi Strauss, who produced the first known blue jeans, was surely one of the most successful businessmen. As is often the case, the people who made the most money from the mineral rush were the merchants who produced the boots, clothing, tents, and so forth. Quite a few other fortunes were established in the late nineteenth century, though, and the people who possessed this money came to live in a section of San Francisco called Nob Hill.

What was life in California like toward the end of the nineteenth century?

It was close to paradise, but it was for white Americans only. The Native Americans virtually disappeared in the two decades that followed statehood. Many were clearly forced off their lands; others were perhaps "encouraged" to depart. What we can say for certain is that the Indians were no longer a significant presence by 1900. And in 1916 came the sad story that Ishi, the last of the Yahi tribe, had died.

How good was life for the Anglo-Americans in California? It was wonderful. There was plenty of hard work, but the rich agricultural land of central California was bountiful. Rather few people who moved from the East Coast ever chose to go back. California was on its way to becoming an integral part of the American Dream.

Was there ever a time when California's prospects dimmed, or when the golden dream of California was about to go away?

No. Regardless of how much difficulty was involved, or how many hazards might come forth, the people of California seemed pleased with their choice and were determined to get on with business. Even the great San Francisco Earthquake of 1906 did not deter people from moving to the Golden State. The great philosopher William James was in San Francisco at the time of the quake, and he marveled at how the natural disaster brought about the best in people, making them more alive and more willing to perform heroic deeds. Much the same can be said of other natural disasters, which came later.

MODERN CALIFORNIA– THE WORLD WARS

How did California fare during World War I and World War II?

World War I did not change life in California very much, because the scene of action was in Europe and it involved primarily the use of the Atlantic Fleet. World War II, however, was an enormous shot in the arm to the Golden State. The naval base at San Diego was the scene of departure for hundreds of thousands of young servicemen, many of whom later decided to resettle in the Golden State. San Francisco Bay was the location for hundreds of naval vessels, which swept the coast for mines, in order to deter the Japanese navy. The factories of California turned out tremendous work orders throughout the war. But there was one great shame involved, and Californians have never gotten over it entirely.

Soon after the beginning of World War II, President Franklin D. Roosevelt ordered the internment of the great majority of Japanese Americans, many of whom lived in California. Some of them were recent arrivals, whose loyalty could be questioned, but many of them were second- and third-generation Japanese Americans, who thought of themselves as Americans. Over 110,000 were rounded up and sent to camps far from the coast. Many years later, Congress officially apologized and provided restitution to the descendants of those who were interred.

What was life in California like during the 1950s?

This, according to most anecdotal reports, was the best of times. California had plenty of workers to fill the tasks, but the state was not overcrowded. California had a clear majority culture, composed of Anglo-Americans who did not believe minorities would ever become a potent political force. And the truly amazing system of public higher education was substantially in place by the year 1955.

Long before any other state, California determined that higher education should be accessible and affordable. Tuition at the community colleges was sometimes as low as $5 for a three-credit course! At the same time, California had become perhaps the most important state in terms of the defense industry. The combination of high brainpower and abundant labor meant that the Golden State was the choice for many new industries and mercantile concerns. And at the same time, California's fields actually turned out more products than ever. This was, for many people who experienced it, the best of times.

YOUTH REBELLION

What happened during the 1960s?

Just about everything. Youth rebellion; the heavy use of drugs; and the dropout—sometimes only for short times—of many young people from the system. California was as well-positioned as any state to handle the tumult of the Sixties: neither its leaders nor the common person expected just how tumultuous the decade would be.

The incredible success of California's public system of higher education opened the door to many of the problems of the Sixties. Young people, many of whom did not need to work while in college, served as mouthpieces for the disapproval of an entire generation. The Free Speech movement began at the University of California at Berkeley, and an entire generation of young people seemed ready to drop out of the traditional American approach to life.

What was the height of the youth protest movement?

The year 1967 was dubbed the "Summer of Love" as millions of young people contemplated going to California, even if only to spend a short time in San Francisco. This was the height of the youth movement, the protests against the Vietnam War, and the glamorization of the use of drugs. California never had a Woodstock-like experience like New York; instead it had the Haight-Ashbury era in the late 1960s. Named for a section of San Francisco, Haight-Ashbury stood for all that was countercultural in California and as an example to the rest of the nation. Numerous drugs were taken by the young people in this low-rent district, and free love was practiced as well. Haight-Ashbury—both the name and the experience—was loathed by many traditionalist Californians, but it was, temporarily, embraced by many people under the age of thirty.

How important was rock music to San Francisco during this tumultuous time?

Very important. Many up-and-coming bands got their start and first fame during the psychedelic era of the late sixties. The Jefferson Airplane, the Grateful Dead, Janis Joplin and Big Brother and the Holding Company, Sly and the Family Stone, and Creedence Clearwater Revival were some of the more prominent Bay Area bands whose music related to the youth of that time.

Who was the quintessential politician from California: Richard Nixon or Ronald Reagan?

Nixon was a native Californian while Reagan was a transplant from the Midwest, but Californians are much fonder of the latter. Rising to become governor of California, Reagan went on to win two presidential elections and serve in the White House from 1981 to 1989. But even he was not quite as perfectly Californian—in the mercurial sense of the word—as Jerry Brown. Son of the very popular Pat Brown, who was governor in the 1960s, Jerry Brown rose to serve as governor from 1975 to 1983. A dropout from a Jesuit seminary, Brown was an effective governor. Following his two-term stint as the state's chief executive, he unsuccessfully ran for U.S. Senate; he then dropped out of politics, only to return in 1998 when he was elected mayor of Oakland, a position he held from 1999 to 2007. He then served as the state's attorney general from 2007 to 2011, and then became the state's governor again in 2011. Brown also ran unsuccessfully for president in 1976, 1980, and 1992. At the time of this writing, he is still chief executive of the Golden State.

Was there ever a time when it seemed that California was "going to the dogs"?

Many middle-class Californians felt this way in the early 1970s. They built a coalition based on anti-immigration and anti-public service themes. At the time, it seemed unlikely they would ever prevail, given California's long history of progressive politics.

Many critics of California's liberal politics and easygoing social mores pointed to the "no-fault" divorce law that was enacted by California in July 1970. The Golden State was the first in the nation to allow divorce in cases of incurable insanity and irreconcilable differences.

When did the backlash against California liberalism commence?

It arrived with a thud in the spring of 1978, when California voters approved Proposition 13. The first of its kind, this ballot initiative prevented property taxes from rising more than 2.5 percent in any given year, meaning it would take a total of forty years for them to double. From 1978 on, California was more split than ever before, between its middle-aged property owners and its youth, who wanted a freer, more open culture.

MODERN CULTURE AND EVENTS

How and when did the computer industry become so large a presence in California?

Like other aspects of late-twentieth-century life, the computer grew out of a combination of high-tech talent, mixed with an abundance of leisure time. In the heyday of California prosperity, it was relatively easy for people like Steve Jobs and Steve Wozniak to tinker in their garage and to come up with something like the first Apple computer. One of the extraordinary aspects, though, was the amount of venture capital that could be raised in California, allowing the computer to burst from the gates so rapidly.

What was the second biggest disaster in California history?

The first was, of course, the Great San Francisco Quake of 1906, and the fire that came hours later. The second was the Bay Area Quake, which struck at 5:04 p.m. Pacific Time on October 17, 1989, just as fans

The "other half" of Apple Computers, Steve Wozniak was key in making the computer company one of the most successful and innovative in the world.

I know the expression "Silicon Valley," but I don't know what it means.

Silicon is the substance of which computer chips are made, and Silicon Valley is the name for the area in central California where the computer industry built its biggest high-rises and established its biggest corporations.

of two Bay Area teams—the San Francisco Giants and the Oakland A's—were settling into their seats at San Francisco's Candlestick Park for Game 3 of the World Series.

The Bay Area Quake did not kill nearly as many people as that of 1906, but it was "seen" by television viewers around the nation, and the reporting went on for weeks; some of the most terrifying images were of the Bay Bridge, a part of which collapsed, between Oakland and San Francisco. Fires raged in parts of San Francisco for days after the actual event.

Didn't anyone ever say "enough," declaring that the Bay Area is too dangerous?

Some naysayers emerged in the aftermath of the 1989 quake, but their voices were low compared to the demands of those who wanted everything rebuilt. And the Bay Area recovered very quickly.

What was life in California like at the turn of the twenty-first century?

It was not the best of times. California, as so often in the past, led the nation in the deregulation of its electrical power industry, and the state went through a number of brownouts in 2000 and 2001. There were all the usual concerns as well, with forest fires and floods. But the great majority of Californians remained upbeat and optimistic, and when the state came close to the financial rocks, the people exercised a ballot initiative to recall their governor.

Democrat Gray Davis was recalled and Independent Arnold Schwarzenegger came in as the new governor of the Golden State. Schwarzenegger claimed he would rid California of crony politics and cut back on the immense state budget, but the legislature had the upper hand in most of their mutual dealings.

How many of the Golden State's many problems had been solved by the year 2010?

Rather few. The state struggled with water shortages, runaway spending, and a culture that was split between the former Anglo-Saxon majority and various minority groups. Yet the California spirit remained much the same: darn the difficulties, move straight ahead. 55

POPULAR CULTURE

Can one really discuss the Golden State without describing the Beach Boys?

They were only one of a number of popular rock groups, but they stood out, through the purity of their melodies. Hitting the scene a little earlier than the Beatles, the Beach Boys, who formed in the Los Angeles-area city of Hawthorne, were greatly loved. Even though later revelations about their personal lives—that of Brian Wilson especially—tended to be depressing, millions of fans, around the world, only think of positives when a Beach Boys song comes on the air.

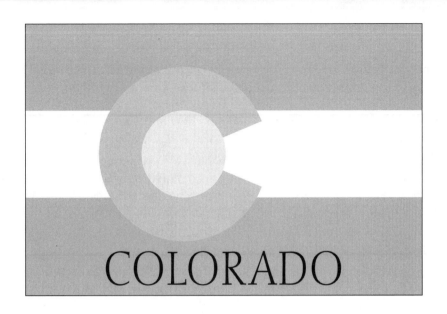

COLORADO

Nickname: "The Centennial State"
Capital: Denver
Statehood: August 1, 1876; 38th state

AT A GLANCE

Where did Colorado gain its nickname?

Colorado entered the Union in 1876, the year America celebrated its centennial as a nation. That was enough to trigger the nickname, which has remained ever since.

What are the major symbols of the Centennial State?

"Nothing without Providence" is the state motto. Those who know the people of Colorado declare that nothing can be accomplished without help from above, but that most of the work has been accomplished through the willpower of the residents. The lark bunting is the state bird, and the Rocky Mountain columbine is the state flower. The Colorado blue spruce is the state tree.

How large, or small, is Colorado?

At 104,094 square miles (269,605 square kilometers), Colorado is eighth largest of the fifty states. As of the year 2010, the state had 5,029,196 residents, making it twenty-second in size of population.

What makes Colorado so special, from a visual point of view?

The mountains! The Centennial State is where the western edge of the Great Plains meets the foothills of the Rocky Mountains, and the westernmost part of the state sees those mountains soar, in some cases to over 14,000 feet in altitude. There's plenty to love about Colorado, even without the mountains, but they form the top of the wedding cake.

How different is Colorado from its neighbors, New Mexico and Utah?

The Centennial State has much more water than its neighbors, water that comes from the spring runoff from those incredible mountains. To be sure, this has its problems. Colorado is infamous for the flash floods that can trap the unwary. In general, though, the abundance of water means that Colorado does not face the pressing concerns of its neighbors, and it receives quite a few immigrants from other states.

Do Coloradans talk about the weather very much?

They certainly do, and it isn't the type of casual conversation seen in many other states. To Coloradans, the weather is about half the story of the day. The state is known for incredible blizzards that sweep from the Rockies, for flash floods that seem to come out of nowhere, and for blinding sunshine and heat. It all makes for a marvelous combination, but it's not for the faint of heart!

We know that Colorado is famous for its swings from extreme cold to severe heat. Can you give a poignant example?

Colorado is of course well-known for the cold that sweeps down from the Rocky Mountains. Residents of high altitude locations begin to get ready for winter in early October. The single coldest temperature ever recorded in Colorado was –61 degrees F (–52 degrees C), at Moffat on February 1, 1985. The wind chill factor is a constant in Colorado weather history. But the Centennial State also sees its share of severe heat. The highest recorded temperature was 114 degree F (46 degrees C) at Las Animas on July 1, 1933.

Who are some of the best-known and loved of Colorado sons and daughters?

Colorado has yet to produce a statesman on the national level: some argue that the Centennial State is too liberal for its own good in this regard. Colorado heroes, therefore, tend to be athletes and musicians. The Denver Broncos are one of the most beloved of all American sports teams, and quarterback John Elway—at his peak—was one of the most beloved of all Colorado athletes.

Broncos quarterback John Elway played for the Denver team from 1983 to 1998; he is currently executive vice president of football operations for the team.

Can the Colorado person be picked out in a crowd?

No longer. As recently as 1960, the Colorado male was unmistakable. He went nowhere without wearing a hat, and his clothing reflected the rugged life he led. His wife was the stereotypical Western woman in the best sense of the term, meaning that her skill and enthusiasm were demonstrated in almost everything she put her hand to. All this changed between about 1960 and 1990. Today, Coloradans are just as likely to wear dreadlocks and sandals, and to discuss the delights of marijuana, which was legalized in 2012.

Of course there are some holdouts, areas where the traditional Colorado has been preserved. But as Colorado continues to move in a leftist direction (politically speaking), the state is ever more divided, culturally speaking.

EARLY HISTORY

For how long have humans lived in what we call the Centennial State?

For thousands of years. When the first Paleo-Americans arrived, they may well have thought the area resembled the Alaska they had traveled through, albeit somewhat warmer. The combination of plains and mountains made the area especially appealing, although, until the appearance of the horse, just 300 years ago, the state was difficult to traverse.

When the first people of European descent arrived, they found several Indian tribes in Colorado: the Cheyenne, Ute, Shoshone, and others. These Indians did not find the first white people threatening or intimidating; rather, the Indians thought them a rather pitiful group, who would not make it in the rugged terrain. Only later, when huge numbers of settlers arrived by wagon, did the Native Americans realize the mistake they had made.

Who were the first explorers and settlers?

The Spaniards came first, during the time of Coronado's expedition (1540–1541), but they did not remain. There was nothing visible to be gained in Colorado, and imperial Spain already possessed lots of open areas with magnificent sunshine, including the Sonoran Desert of Mexico. Though they did nothing with the land, the Spaniards were jealous of it, however, and when they learned that an American explorer was in the area, they moved to chase him out. This was Lieutenant Zebulon M. Pike, for whom Pike's Peak is named.

Pike explored eastern Colorado and he sighted—but did not have time to ascend—the peak that is named for him. Escorted out of the area by Spanish authorities, he returned to the East Coast where his written report suggested there was little to be gained by settling Colorado. This belief was echoed by Major Stephen H. Long, who led an exploratory party in 1820–1821. Long labelled much of the western Great Plains the "Great American Desert," and this tended to discourage settlement for some time.

MINERS AND SETTLERS

How did the miners find their way to Colorado?

The California Gold Rush brought thousands of skillful and experienced prospectors and miners to the Golden State, and when the Rush ended, they naturally looked for other places to go to. Some moved to the interior, and were joined by handfuls of East Coast miners, who settled on Colorado as their best bet.

William Greeneberry Russell, a Georgia native who had done well in California, discovered the first Colorado gold in the spring of 1858, in what is now the Denver suburb of Englewood. Russell was followed by dozens of others, but these early prospectors were soon overwhelmed by tens of thousands who came to Colorado in 1859 and 1860. Known either as the Colorado Gold Rush or Pike's Peak Gold Rush, this was one of the truly momentous events in the history of the West. Wagons departed Independence, Missouri, with "Pike's Peak or Bust!" painted on their sides.

Wasn't there any skepticism, any sense that it might all be a hoax?

When it comes to gold, silver, or oil, Americans are the least skeptical people in the world. Throughout our history, it has been enough to learn that a commodity exists, in order to persuade thousands of people to drop everything and go in search of it. What made the Colorado Gold Rush so special was the visual component. There were few photographs, but many watercolor illustrators went west, and painted the eager emigrants, pushing for Pike's Peak.

Did Colorado play any part in the American Civil War?

A very small one. The territory was formed just as the war began, in order to ward off any possible Confederate infiltration, but there was little need for concern. Cotton was what made slavery viable in the American South; the discovery of silver and gold was something quite different, leading to a different type of economy. The Confederate leaders realized this, and though they made some attempt to penetrate Arizona and New Mexico, they did not expend any energy on Colorado.

NATIVE AMERICANS VERSUS WHITES

How did the Native Americans of Colorado respond to the white encroachment?

Many of them knew it was hopeless to resist, and there was—at that point—still enough empty land to the west for them to move to. But the Southern Cheyenne took the brunt of the settlers' incursion, and they paid the heaviest price.

Chief Black Kettle and a large group of Southern Cheyenne were viciously attacked by a Denver militia on November 24, 1864; this became known as the Sand Creek Massacre. Black Kettle survived, after being shot and wounded at least four times, but his trust, and that of his people, was permanently forfeited. It's true that there had been Indian raids in the months leading up to the Sand Creek Massacre; it's equally true that the militia was out for blood and that Colorado has never entirely erased the shame of that event.

How did Colorado attain statehood so rapidly?

The sheer number of emigrants—those who came looking for Pike's Peak—made it possible, but the pressure of the Civil War contributed too. President Abraham Lincoln brought in Colorado as a territory, and President Andrew Johnson made it the thirty-eighth star on the flag, in 1876. That was the Centennial Year, when America celebrated its hundredth birthday, and Colorado quickly gained the nickname of "Centennial State."

Colorado boomed in the two decades following statehood. Miners, farmers, and technically skilled people flocked to the Centennial State, which promised more wide-open spaces and opportunity than almost any other. Denver rose quickly, to become the queen city of the state, but Boulder was not far behind. Even in those early days, there was great optimism that the Rocky Mountains would be conquered—or harnessed—and used for the spread of American civilization.

COLORADO IN THE EYES OF THE NATION

What was the high point for Colorado, so far as it was understood on the East Coast?

On a summer day in 1893, Katharine Lee Bates (1859–1929) went up Pike's Peak on a wagon. She was one of a number of East Coast teachers who had gone to Colorado to teach for a short time. On reaching the summit, Bates was overcome by the beauty that lay in a 360-degree angle. She hastily wrote down the words that first appeared in print in 1895.

O beautiful for spacious skies,
For amber waves of grain
For purple mountain majesties,
Above the fruited plain!

Anyone who has seen Colorado's mountains, and gazed back at the fruited plain that leads to them, tends to agree with the message of this song: there is something very special about the Centennial State. "America the Beautiful" became well-known during the Great Depression years; it remains one of the best-loved of all songs of the American people.

Were there any bleak times, when the bright promise appeared to fade?

Only in certain areas. There are former mining towns that one can visit today, which are sometimes populated by less than a few dozen people. They suffered in the downturn of gold and silver prices at the end of the nineteenth century. But, almost regardless of what boom faded, there seemed to be another to take its place. Miners turned into electricians, stringing wires across the state, first for the telegraph and then the telephone company. Sod busters moved into Denver, becoming some of the state's first urbanites. But the unbridled optimism did run into snags, and something much worse in the Cripple Creek Massacre of 1913.

It seems as if Colorado generally enjoys good times, but that when something goes wrong, it really goes wrong. Is this accurate?

The lyrics to the patriotic song "America the Beautiful" were penned by Katharine Lee Bates; William Arms Fisher put it to music.

From the Sand Creek Massacre to Cripple Creek and then to Columbine, Colorado has a history of sudden "explosions" of violence. Most of the time Coloradans seem as peaceful and happy as any other group in the nation, but the state has seen some rather horrific events.

In the spring of 1914, the Cripple Creek coal region was struck first by a workers' strike, and then an attack on the striking workers in Ludlow by the National Guard. Dozens of people were killed and more than one hundred injured, in one of the worst outbreaks of internal violence in the history of the nation. Public blame fastened on John D. Rockefeller Jr., who ran those mining camps from a distance. All of Colorado felt the stain of the Ludlow Massacre, however.

How did the Centennial State fare during the First World War?

As one historian expresses it, Colorado was ahead well before the rest of the nation. Not until April 1917, did Congress declare war; by that time, Colorado was fully mobilized. The reason is not far to seek: the Centennial State wished to demonstrate its loyalty to the nation and to erase the shame associated with the Ludlow Massacre. Coloradans were at the forefront of the American military effort in 1917–1918. Then the bottom fell out.

The end of World War I spelled disaster both for Colorado's agriculture, in the eastern third of the state, and its mining industry, in the center and western sections. As a result, Colorado entered the Great Depression almost a decade ahead of the rest of the nation and languished there a very long time. State population figures tell part, but not all, of the story. The Centennial State went from a population of 539,700 in 1900 to 939,629, boasting one of the most aggressive growth stories in the nation. Between 1920 and 1940, however, Colorado grew only from 939,629 to 1,123,296.

How bad was the Great Depression in Colorado?

No one has ever been able to determine just how many young men "rode the rails" during the Great Depression, traveling as hobos, but it's a good bet that many of them were from the Far West, and that Colorado contributed more than its share. Many homes were abandoned, and towns that formerly thrived staggered throughout the Great Depression. It took the advent of World War II to bring Colorado back, and even then the results were not fully evident till the mid-1950s.

The building of new homes was a big business in Colorado in the two decades that followed World War II, and the state rapidly moved toward being an urban-suburban mix, with true rural dwellers becoming the minority. The state's economic and political fortunes improved significantly when the brand new U.S. Air Force Academy was established in Colorado Springs in 1954. The first graduating class was in 1959.

What is the city of Loveland best known for?

Each year more than a hundred thousand valentine cards are sent to Loveland so that they can be resent and postmarked *from* Loveland. Workers hand-stamp a unique Valentine's Day stamp and verse and send them off from the so-called Sweetheart City.

What's the story behind Denver getting the 1976 Olympics—and then not getting them?

In 1970, the International Olympics Committee awarded the 1976 Winter Games to Denver. Many rejoiced, many did not. Within a couple years, Colorado assemblyman (and fu-

---

I've seen photos of the outside of the Air Force Academy, and I can't quite make out what those shining metal strips are. Can you inform me?

Built between 1959 and 1961, the Air Force Academy Cadet Chapel is one of the most unusual places for worship to be found in the United States. Futuristic, built of granite shipped from Missouri, the chapel has seventeen distinctive spires that look more like spikes than rounded chapels or cathedral ceilings.

ture governor) Richard Lamm led a group opposed to hosting the Olympics, citing the high expense to the region (public funding would be required). The question of "to host or not to host" went to a vote in November 1972, with citizens deciding 60% to 40% against Denver being the host city. The games wound up in Innsbruck, Austria, instead.

How important was John Denver to the self-concept of the people of Colorado?

Born in Roswell, New Mexico, in 1943, John Denver (whose birth name was Henry John Deutschendorf Jr.) was a talented acoustic guitar player. At a time

Although he wasn't born in the state, the late pop and country-Western singer John Denver loved the state and will forever be associated with it for penning songs such as "Rocky Mountain High."

when many country music singers were against what the nation stood for—against the Vietnam War especially—John Denver sang of the virtues and wonders of rural life. He scored in a big way with "Take Me Home, Country Roads," in 1971, but even bigger with "Rocky Mountain High," which came out in 1973. Denver popularized the image of Colorado, in much the same way Katharine Lee Bate's had done for Pike's Peak.

> But the Colorado rocky mountain high,
> I've seen it raining fire in the sky
> The shadow from the starlight is softer than a lullaby
> Rocky Mountain high.

Where, meanwhile, had Colorado gone in a political sense?

The Great Depression spelled the end to Colorado's Progressive tradition (in the political sense of the word) and led to almost a half-century of Republican Party dominance. This faded in the mid-1970s, however, as Colorado began moving in a left-of-center, but also libertarian, direction. The largest cities of Colorado, too, showed definite signs of liberalism during the 1980s and 1990s. Boulder became known as one of the leading cities in the entire nation for massage therapists, New Age healers, promoters of macrobiotic diets, and so forth.

RECENT TRAGEDIES

What happened at Columbine High School in 1999?

It was one of those magical sunlit mornings in Colorado, as the nation was preparing to celebrate Earth Day, when two high school students used machine guns to kill almost fifteen of their classmates. There had been high school shootings before, but none had been so brutally casual, or had shown how devastating modern weapons could be in that environment.

The state of Colorado virtually shut down for several days. Even when material life went back to normal, the feel of life in Colorado was not the same. Why did this happen to us, people asked? How could this have happened in a comfortable suburban community? Those questions have never really been answered, and the nation as a whole has seen several other tragedies, including another mass shooting in Colorado in 2012.

What are the details surrounding the mass shooting in 2012?

A man threw tear gas grenades into an Aurora, Colorado, theater filled with approximately 400 moviegoers who had gathered to watch *The Dark Knight Rises*. Amidst the chaos of the smoke, the man started randomly shooting. When the terror had ended, twelve people lost their lives and seventy more were injured. The shooter was apprehended in the parking lot shortly thereafter.

When did Colorado make such a sharp turn to the left?

Somewhere between 2004 and 2012. As recently as 2004, Colorado was still about evenly split between white-collar conservative communities and communities of aging hippies. No one has yet defined it precisely, but a major change happened during the ballot initiative of 2012, especially the one that allowed the legal use of marijuana. Colorado voters approved this initiative, and the Centennial State, which has often touted its squeaky clean image, suddenly was the first state in the nation to allow the smoking of pot.

Where will Colorado and its people be a generation from now?

The chances are they will continue to be a people that look to the outdoors. Even the most suburban of Colorado communities has a focus on the great outdoors that will not disappear. The Centennial State has plenty of issues to deal with, not the least being its air quality, but the chances are that its people—who will continue to diversify, as Hispanics become a larger share of the population—will continue to demonstrate the "Rocky Mountain High" that John Denver so beautifully expressed in 1973.

CONNECTICUT

Nicknames: "The Nutmeg State"; "Constitution State"
Capital: Hartford
Statehood: January 9, 1788; 5th state

AT A GLANCE

Which of the two nicknames is more commonly used?

Constitution State is the more common of the two, and it reflects the fact that Connecticut's approval of the U.S. Constitution put that document "over the top," meaning that it became the law of the land.

What are the major state symbols?

"He Who Transplanted Still Sustains" is the state motto. The origin of the expression is biblical, but the modern-day meaning stems from Puritan times, when men and women of Old England came across the ocean, determined to establish a godly commonwealth. The robin is the state bird, and the mountain laurel is the state flower. The white oak is the state tree.

How large, or small, is Connecticut?

The Constitution State is comprised of 5,004 square miles (12,690 square kilometers), making it forty-eighth among the fifty states in physical size. As of the year 2010, there were 3,574,097 residents, making Connecticut twenty-ninth among the states in terms of population.

How has Connecticut, which is the nation's richest state per capita, managed to keep so low a profile over the decades, indeed centuries?

Most Connecticut residents prefer not to discuss the matter, but when pressed they will admit that the relative anonymity confers many benefits. Even in a time when all budgets—federal and state—are pressed to the max, few federal facilities in Connecticut are closed. Then too, the state, for a long time, was able to go without a state income tax. This doesn't mean that everything in Connecticut is cozy, but the Nutmeg State has, throughout its history, been able to make the most of what it has.

Where does Connecticut's wealth come from?

As one drives past abandoned factory buildings and warehouses, primarily in southwestern Connecticut, he or she is tempted to believe that the good times have passed. Connecticut has a flair for reinventing itself, however, and the wealth that once came from the production of firearms shifted to the insurance industry, which remains the number-one employer in the Nutmeg State. There's a lot of old wealth in Connecticut, too, which helps to keep real estate property values high.

Completed in 1878, the Connecticut State House in Hartford is an iconic piece of beautiful architecture that represents the best qualities of the state.

Is there any one, iconic scene that goes a long way to expressing the best of Connecticut?

For the tourist, the answer almost certainly lies in the vicinity of the Connecticut State House, in downtown Hartford. The golden dome is one of the most beautiful in the nation. Less than two miles away is the Mark Twain House, beloved home of America's single most famous humorist. Only after taking a tour does the average tourist learn that Mark Twain had to give up this treasured place, after financial reverses, and that he was—in many respects—never the same again.

Does anyone go to Connecticut for the scenery?

Well, Connecticut is not Vermont or New Hampshire, whose ski resorts draw people from hundreds and even thousands of miles. The Nutmeg State, rather, draws people in for an afternoon or weekend of pleasant automobiling, and the chances are good they will come again. Connecticut has a number of public beaches that draw tourists. Its single biggest success along the coast is involved with Mystic Seaport, one of the great outdoor museums of the United States.

Speaking of Mystic Seaport, what were the Connecticut mariners known for?

Connecticut has a long maritime tradition, with men shipping out for whaling trips that sometimes exceeded three years. Beyond this, however, Connecticut also provided many of the vessels that participated in the triangular trade of the Atlantic, which included the shipment of slaves from West Africa.

Is the weather—or climate—a topic of conversation in Connecticut?

Back when the village general store was commonplace, the people of Connecticut used to exchange weather anecdotes, much in the style of a Norman Rockwell painting. But the Nutmeg State has become more harried in recent years, and the corner store has quite likely been replaced by a shopping mall or plaza. When the locals do talk about the weather, they admit that Connecticut is rather fortunate: neither the extremes of winter nor the blasting heat of summer affects the rural towns very much. Unlike their neighbors in Massachusetts, the people of Connecticut do not, on average, suffer very much during the winter, even if it is long.

What are the highest and lowest temperatures ever seen in Connecticut?

In 1995, Connecticut experienced one of the hottest summers in recent U.S. history. Connecticut recorded its single highest temperature on July 15, 1995, when the mercury reached 104 degrees F (41 degrees C) at Danbury. Connecticut's coldest recorded temperature was –32 degrees F (–36 degrees C) at Falls Village on February 16, 1943.

Is there a way to tell the Connecticut person apart from his New York State counterpart?

Definitely. All one has to do is stroll across the border from western Connecticut to eastern New York in order to see the cultural transition.

Connecticut tends to be filled with small towns, usually placed about six miles apart. The towns are self-supporting, in that the local services are contracted with people who are known quantities, and Connecticut people wouldn't have it any other way. Once one crosses into New York State, a relative blizzard of corporations and big-time service contractors tend to dominate the scene. Of course it is the height of irony that Connecticut, which prides itself so much on regional management, is also the center of the insurance industry: many of the big names in insurance have their corporate headquarters in Hartford.

For how long has Connecticut been—in some respects—a cultural expansion of greater New York City?

One felt it as early as the 1920s, and quite a few Connecticut writers lamented the change. The Puritan and Yankee ethos seemed to disappear, as the people and state were swallowed up by the incredible commercial power of greater Manhattan. Over time, however, many Connecticut residents realized how lucky they were to benefit from New York City's wealth, and an increasing number of business executives took the train in each morning.

Is Connecticut the land of Mark Twain? Or of Katharine Hepburn?

In either case, the state wouldn't be doing badly. Mark Twain was not a Connecticut native. Born in Missouri, he came to Hartford in his thirties and fell completely in love with the place. This man, who saw so much of the world in his long life, declared there was nothing so beautiful as his Hartford home in the immediate aftermath of a major snowstorm. But Twain fell on hard times, had to sell his beloved home, and was—for the rest of his life—a wanderer.

One of the classiest Hollywood actresses from the Golden Age of film, Katharine Hepburn was a Connecticut native.

Katharine Hepburn's story was quite different. Born and raised in Connecticut, she, too, got to see much of the world, as perhaps the most famous of all twentieth-century actresses, but she always returned home. Late in life she gave an interview to *60 Minutes* in which she declared that she jumped into Long Island Sound first thing, every single day of the year, in order to wake up her body and spirit.

EARLY HISTORY

For how long have humans lived in what we often call the Constitution State?

For nearly 10,000 years. Little physical evidence of these early inhabitants remains, but we believe they were often nomadic peoples, who wandered well into Vermont during the summer, and returned to southern Connecticut to ride out the winter.

When the first white settlers appeared, in the seventeenth century, they found a number of tribes in Connecticut, with the Pequot predominating along the coast and the Mohegan or Mahican the most numerous in the north. In neither case were the Indians especially dangerous, but the Puritan mindset was that anyone who was not of the fold was suspect at best.

How was Connecticut populated by white settlers?

This happened rather quickly. In the mid-1630s, one group of Puritans walked overland from Boston, forming one of the first landward migrations in American history. At about the same time, a few shiploads full of settlers arrived from Old England and began populating the coast. The two groups met about a decade later, and the colony of Connecticut soon received its charter from King Charles II.

I've heard of the Pequot. Are they still around today?

The Pequot took a terrible beating in the so-called Pequot War in 1636–1637. Between them, Boston, Plymouth, and Hartford sent white militia forces that smashed the Pequot; in the climactic battle, at present-day Mystic, 700 Indians, including women and children, perished when the militia set their fort afire. But the Pequot are indeed around today. In 1988, they were allowed to establish the Mashantucket Pequot casino, in Ledyard, Connecticut, and the tribe has been rather prosperous ever since.

Speaking of Ledyard, I seem to recollect that name as well. Who was he?

John Ledyard wanted to be the first person to walk completely around the globe (minus the ocean sections of course). He set out in 1787, took a ship for Europe, and walked all the way to western Siberia before being detained by the Czarist police. He was returned to Western Europe, with a warning not to make the attempt again.

FROM COLONY TO STATE

Is there anything to the story of the Charter Oak?

There is. In October 1687, Sir Edmund Andros, governor of Massachusetts, arrived in Hartford to demand the surrender of the charter that had been granted two decades earlier. The scroll was brought forth and laid on the table in front of Sir Edmund, but just as he reached out to take it, someone blew out the candles. When the room was relit, the charter was gone.

Tradition has it that Joseph Wadsworth, a member of the family for whom the famous Hartford art museum is named, spirited away the charter and hid it in a local oak tree. Precisely which oak tree long remained in doubt, but when a massive oak came down in a thunderstorm in 1858, locals claimed that this was the very one.

How did Connecticut fare during the late colonial period?

Connecticut had one of the best and most effective of all the colonial economies. This was because it had a mixture of farming, shipping, and light industry. Big fortunes were the exception rather than the rule, but there was a trickle-down effect, and when the American Revolution commenced, Connecticut was, quite likely, the most prosperous of all the colonies, just as it is the richest state per capita today.

Did Connecticut play a role in the French and Indian Wars?

Connecticut was sheltered by the fact that Massachusetts lay to its north and New York to the west. The Nutmeg State was not seriously endangered in any of the colonial conflicts. Connecticut supplied many soldiers to the colonial efforts, however, and a good deal of the gunpowder that was used came from Connecticut.

Was there any chance Connecticut would not join the patriot cause during the American Revolution?

Virtually none. Connecticut never suffered much under British rule, but the colony's people had developed a well-founded identity decades prior to the Revolution. Their economy was based on a combination of farming and merchant trading, and the people of Connecticut were eager for independence from Great Britain.

Did Connecticut provide any outstanding military leaders during the Revolutionary War?

Only one, and he is not the type we like to speak about. Benedict Arnold was born in Norwich, Connecticut, and was a druggist prior to the war. Once the war began, he proved an outstanding military leader, perhaps the most gifted one on either side during the eight-year conflict. Arnold be-

Before he was known for betraying his country to the English, Connecticut-born Benedict Arnold was a hero during the Revolutionary War.

trayed his country for gold, however (20,000 pounds to be precise), and he ended up in England, despised both by the people he'd forsaken and by those he went over to.

Connecticut did provide a number of important civic leaders, however, among whom Governor Jonathan Trumbull was perhaps the most significant. George Washington took Trumbull's advice so many times that he later quipped, "Let us consult Brother Jonathan" whenever he faced an important decision. Then too, Roger Sherman of Connecticut was the only person to sign all three of the key documents in the founding of the nation: the Declaration of Independence, the Articles of Confederation, and the U.S. Constitution.

CONNECTICUT IN THE LIFE OF THE NATION

How did Connecticut fare in the decades that followed the establishment of the nation?

There was some resentment on the part of Connecticut that the state was not allowed to expand to the west. It was unfair, many declared, that New York had gotten in the way, preventing Connecticut from any further expansion. The only exception to this was the so-called Ohio Preserve, a section of Ohio meant for settlers from Connecticut. But this did not last, and the people of Connecticut had to adjust to the fact that they were constricted within the same 5,000 square miles that their descendants possess today.

Connecticut more than made up for this, however, by going in for industrial development. Most people know that Eli Whitney was a Massachusetts Yankee who went south and helped the South by making the world's first cotton gin. Less known is that Whitney soon returned to the North, and that he established one of the first real factories in the Northeast, turning out muskets for the U.S. government. Whitney did not invent the concept of interchangeable parts, but he was the first gun maker to adopt the principle.

Guns … pistols … tobacco…. Sometimes it sounds as if Connecticut was all about material development, and nothing else.

Don't tell that to the descendants of the Connecticut missionaries who went overseas (there were thousands of them). And don't mention it when you're in New Haven, home to Yale University. The people of Connecticut are justly proud of their connection to higher education.

Yale was founded in 1701, as an alternative to Harvard, which many of the old-line Puritan ministers believed had become too liberal and "soft." The long rivalry between Yale and Harvard is celebrated in many ways, most especially by the football game each November.

Was there ever a concern that Connecticut would lose most of its population to the new states, those being formed in the Midwest?

This was a nightmare scenario that haunted the dreams of many Connecticut leaders. The single worst of all the times came in 1816 and 1817. After 1816—which is known as the Year without a Summer—thousands of Connecticut residents packed up and moved, primarily to Ohio. The Connecticut economy was in serious peril, but it—and the state—were rescued by, of all things, the Erie Canal. Completion of the canal, in 1825, allowed goods to move more rapidly across New York State, allowing Connecticut merchants to sell their wares further inland. Connecticut was already known for the expertise of its clockmakers and watchmakers; other mechanical specialists began to fill niches, allowing Connecticut to weather a very difficult time.

CIVIL WAR PROSPERITY

How important was Connecticut to the Union effort during the American Civil War?

Could the Union have won the war without the assistance of Connecticut? Perhaps, but the war would have taken much longer. Connecticut provided most of the pistols, many of the rifles, and a majority of the uniforms for the Union between 1861 and 1865. It's true, however, that the Nutmeg State does not celebrate its Civil War connection in the way it does its memory of the Revolutionary War.

When did Connecticut become the land of "old money"?

Sometime in the 1870s and 1880s. Connecticut had already done quite well, with a majority of its farmers and industrialists making it, but the advent of the insurance industry brought about a great boom to the Connecticut economy. It was at this time, too, that some of the first suburbs of the nation were laid out. Hartford required a concentric ring of towns to supply its labor force, but the even greater demand came from the southwest, from New York City.

Connecticut has a love-hate relationship with New York City. Culturally, the

Connecticut has become a mecca for insurance companies in the United States (the Phoenix Mutual Life Building in Hartford is pictured here).

Connecticut people are quite distinct, and in their private moments they may even consider themselves superior to their New York counterparts. In terms of economic influence, however, Connecticut is the tail that perennially follows the dog: Manhattan sets the style and Connecticut complies. Starting in the 1890s, large numbers of Connecticut businessmen began making the trek to Manhattan, and their great-great-grandchildren are doing the same today.

Longer commutes—and bigger traffic jams—than those in southern Connecticut are often seen elsewhere. Why do the people of the Nutmeg State make so big a deal about going to Manhattan?

First, it irritates them that they have to go out of state to make a living. Second, the towns and suburbs of southern Connecticut are so numerous that it seems one is making a cross-country trip. Third, and perhaps most important is that the trip *home*, in the late afternoon, is so much more difficult. That's when it really becomes unbearable, at least for some.

Connecticut businesspeople have been trying to find a way around the problem for nearly a century, and they haven't come even close. In order for Connecticut to retain its rural feel, it has to send a lot of its people to greater Manhattan every day.

How did Connecticut fare in World War I and World War II?

The Nutmeg State did not prosper as a result of either of the world wars. The insurance industry did make a major move upward in the aftermath of World War II, however, and it was during the 1950s that the popular image of Connecticut was one based on wealth (the many films of Katharine Hepburn made hay with this scenario). It was the formation of the Groton submarine base after World War II that really helped Connecticut, however.

During the 1950s, too, Connecticut was perceived as the land of leisure *par excellence*. This image was displayed in numerous magazines and periodicals, most of which showcased a man of leisure standing in front of his rural mansion, almost always with an oak tree in the foreground. The image appeared to declare that Connecticut was the best of all possible places.

Did Connecticut escape the 1960s?

It seemed to. There were plenty of campus protests at Yale and elsewhere, but the rural communities were little-affected. Life in the Nutmeg State seemed to go pretty much as usual. What did change was the average age of state residents. Many young people left Connecticut in their twenties and did not return, and the average age of people in many rural communities rose considerably.

What was the single worst day in Connecticut history?

Until quite recently the answer was always the same: September 21–22, 1938. The Hurricane of '38 slammed Connecticut, with houses and barns destroyed, and terrible flooding, especially along the Connecticut River. But in December 2012 came the shootings in Newtown, and they have claimed the dubious distinction of Connecticut's worst disaster ever since.

On December 14, 2012, twenty-year-old Adam Lanza entered Sandy Hook Elementary School and shot and killed twenty children and six adult staffers. The numbers were horrific enough, but that the tragedy happened at Christmas time made it resonate ever more powerfully. A national conversation about the merits and demerits of high-powered guns ensued, with Connecticut suddenly receiving more attention than is usually the case.

What will Connecticut look like a generation from now?

The chances are that it will still be one of the wealthiest states in the Union, but that much of the really "old wealth" will have migrated to other states. Connecticut will continue to be a leader in higher education.

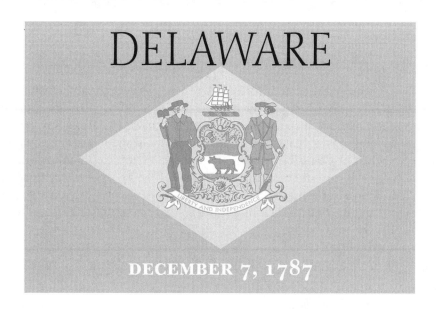

DELAWARE

DECEMBER 7, 1787

Nickname: "The First State"
Capital: Dover
Statehood: December 7, 1787; 1st state

AT A GLANCE

Where does the state nickname come from?

First State refers to the fact that Delaware was the first state to give official approval to the U.S. Constitution.

What are the major symbols for the First State?

"Liberty and Independence" is the state motto. Adopted in 1847, the motto harkens to Delaware's difficult position as the southernmost of the northern states, and the northernmost of the southern ones. The blue hen chicken is the state bird, the American holly is the state tree, and the peach blossom is the state flower.

How large, or small, is the First State?

Comprising only 2,023 square miles (5,240 square kilometers), Delaware is forty-ninth among the states in geographic size. Only Rhode Island is smaller. As of the year 2010, there were 897,934 state residents, making Delaware forty-fifth among the states in terms of population. Few people realize that these 897,000 people are more than live in all of Alaska, the nation's largest state.

How did so small a state become so important to the national economy?

Perhaps this is because the people of Delaware realized, early on, that they would never make it, or prosper, if they competed with bigger states on ordinary terms, which, in the early nineteenth century, meant farming. Though Delaware had, and still possesses, quite a few farms, the First State gave itself to commercial and industrial development early on. The DuPont Company, known once as a major supplier of gunpowder, is in Delaware: today it turns out chemicals for all sorts of industries. Early railroad development, too, thrived in Delaware. In more recent times, however, it is Delaware's willingness to embrace major corporations—banks and credit institutions especially—that have proved the key to success.

When I think of Delaware I get confused. Is it primarily sea coast, or primarily inland?

Delaware has only twenty-eight miles that lie on the Atlantic Ocean, but it has Delaware Bay and much of the Delaware River. It is rare to be more than twenty miles from water, wherever one stands in Delaware. Within that twenty-mile range, however, there is some pretty decent diversity, including rolling hills and flat farmland. About the only thing Delaware really lacks is any sort of large hills or mountains, though this can be seen as an advantage: the lack of natural obstacles makes it more possible for commerce to succeed in Delaware.

Is there any variety in Delaware's weather?

Quite a bit. Winters tend to be short and rather mild, albeit with plenty of rain, and summers are long and known for their humidity, which can be stifling at times. Spring and autumn are both rather short, but in a pleasant way. About the only major threat that the people of Delaware experience is that of hurricanes, and the state has mostly been spared the worst of these. The coastal area is vulnerable, but many hurricanes make a turn out to sea just before they are ready to smack the First State.

Delaware temperatures are usually moderate, thanks to the state's coastal orientation. There have been the occasional severe temperatures, however. The mercury rose to 110 degrees F (43 degrees C) at Millsboro on July 21, 1930, and it sank to –17 degrees F (–27 degrees C) at the same place on January 17, 1893.

Does Delaware have a recognizable culture?

Yes, but it is of a very mild variety. Though they are proud of their state, the people of Delaware are neither flag-wavers nor great enthusiasts. They know that Delaware survives—and thrives—by virtue of its proximity to the great urban corridor that runs from Boston in the north to Washington, D.C., in the south. Delawareans, therefore, tend not to say very much about themselves or their state: They allow visitors to come and see for themselves. In terms of politics, the First State is about equally divided between the two major parties.

EARLY HISTORY

What was life like for the Indians of present-day Delaware?

Not much of their material culture survives, but we conjecture that they led one of the easier physical existences of the many different Native American groups. Fish and shell-fish were abundant, as were deer and bear, leading to what may have been one of the most varied and plentiful diets seen along the East Coast.

Who were the first Europeans to arrive, and what Native American groups did they encounter?

Virginians, led by Captain John Smith, were the first white Europeans to spend any time in Delaware, and they were not deeply impressed. Compared to Virginia and Maryland, Delaware seemed like too much work for too small a reward. Tobacco ensured the survival of Virginia and Maryland, but Delaware, by contrast, lacked any one powerful crop that would call to new settler groups. It fell, therefore, to colonists from Sweden to put down the first roots.

The first Swedish settlers arrived in 1631. They established a tiny settlement they called Zwaanendael at present-day Lewes, on the coast. The settlers were wiped out by a series of attacks by the Leni-Lenape (or Delaware) tribe the following year, however. The Swedes returned in 1636, however, and they soon established Fort Christina, in pre-

sent-day Wilmington. Named for Queen Christina, who later won infamy by abdicating her throne, Fort Christina was intended as the center for a major Swedish colony in North America.

How did first the Dutch, and then the English, co-opt the Swedish dream?

In the mid-seventeenth century, rather few Swedes proved willing to emigrate, and even the Dutch produced only a few thousand real settlers. The great majority of those who came to America intended to strike it rich in a hurry and then return. Seeing the Swedish success on the Delaware River, the Dutch came to conquer Fort Christina in 1655. They, in turn, were conquered by the English, who arrived in force in 1664. From that year forward, it was clear that Delaware would remain English, and it was perhaps around

On the site where Swedish settlers first landed on the banks of the Christina River is a monument designed by Carl Milles.

this time that the state obtained its name (Delaware comes from *De La Warr*, name of an English nobleman whose career was in Virginia, rather than the First State).

How important was the Duke of York and his conflict with William Penn?

James, the Duke of York, sent the English naval forces that subdued New Netherland in 1664, and for some time he was the proprietary owner of a large section of North American coast, including Delaware. James handed over his rights to the Delaware area when William Penn obtained his very large land grant in 1682, however, and though James did not fight for his rights, the people of Delaware did. Consisting of three counties, known as the Lower Counties, these settlers resisted being taken over either by Pennsylvania or Maryland.

How did Delaware develop during the late colonial period?

The boundary issue festered, and was only completely resolved when Charles Mason (1728–1786) and Jeremiah Dixon (1733–1779) ran their famous boundary drawing in 1767–1769. Delaware was, by this time, commercially successful. The colony had some tobacco farms, but the greater amount of its wealth came from trans-Atlantic trade. The merchants of Delaware did not gain an outsized reputation, such as those of Newport, Rhode Island, but their commercial success was almost as significant.

When the Thirteen Colonies moved toward revolution, Delaware was among the forefront. Only a few settlers, almost all of them fronting directly on the Atlantic Ocean, threw in their lot with the crown. Delawareans remember, and occasionally reenact, Caesar Rodney's famous ride to Philadelphia, where he cast a vote that broke the tie in the Delaware committee, and allowed the Declaration of Independence to move forward in the Second Continental Congress.

I seldom hear of Delaware statesmen in the years of struggle leading up to the American Revolution. Was the state too small to play an important role?

Delawareans seldom even remember his name, but John Dickinson was their most distinguished representative to the Continental Congress. Seven years before the war began, Dickinson penned *Letters from a Farmer in Pennsylvania to the Inhabitants of the British Colonies*. Printed in a Philadelphia newspaper, they were subsequently reprinted many times and formed some of the soundest arguments for America's need for greater economic freedom within the British Empire. One reason Dickinson seldom gets his due is that when the Revolution came, he was in favor of remaining part of England's empire, albeit under conditions that were favorable to America.

What role did Delaware play in the Revolutionary War?

A rather large one. Pennsylvania gets more of the attention, in the history books especially, but Delaware was the key to the Delaware River and, therefore, to any British moves up that river. The Battle of Brandywine River, in September 1777, was fought on

Delaware soil, and in its immediate aftermath, the president (rather than governor) of Delaware, was captured by the British. By then, the Delaware section of the Continental Line had already developed a powerful reputation, thanks to its relentless fight at the Battle of Long Island, in August 1776.

Delaware also saw some of the most intense battles between American privateers and British warships. By the end of the war, Delaware skippers had captured numerous British merchant vessels, but the state had taken a beating, thanks to partial British occupation of its coastal areas. If Delaware was strong for the patriot cause before the war began, it emerged from the Revolution with an enhanced reputation. It's no surprise that Delaware was the first state to approve the brand-new Constitution, entering the Union in December 1787.

What is significant about the Battle of Cooch's Bridge?

The Battle of Cooch's Bridge, also known as the Battle of Iron Hill, took place near Newark, Delaware, on September 3, 1777. It pitted the Americans versus German and British soldiers. What is best known about the battle may actually be a myth. It is claimed by some that it marked the first time that the American flag—the famous Betsy Ross flag—was raised in battle. Historians have not been able to prove or disprove the claim, but the legend lives on.

DELAWARE IN THE LIFE OF THE NATION

Was there ever a chance that little Delaware might be swallowed up by one of the larger states?

Although it was a very real fear on the part of the people of Delaware, discussions and debates at the Constitutional Convention in 1787 put an end to this. In Philadelphia it was decided that each of the original thirteen states—no matter how large or small—would be treated as equals with all the others. Equally important was the decision that all states that subsequently entered the Union would also stand on an equal basis.

Who were the du Ponts and how did they become so successful?

Éleuthère Irénée du Pont (note that when it comes to the company's name there is no space in DuPont when there is one in the actual family name) was a Frenchman who settled in Delaware in 1802. A student of the famed chemist Antoine Lavoisier, he experimented with different types of powder and eventually hit upon one of the best formulas. DuPont powder was present wherever the Civil War was fought, but when World War I came along, the company switched its energy to the making of explosives. In 1912, an antitrust case resulted in DuPont having to break into three separate companies: DuPont, Hercules, and ICI Americas.

The du Ponts began their success in America by producing gunpowder. Shown here is one of their early gunpowder wagons that was used at the company's mill in Wilmington.

Other du Ponts made a name for themselves as well: for instance, Pierre (1870–1954) was the chairman of General Motors and Pierre IV "Pete" (1935–) was governor of Delaware in 1977–1985 and briefly ran for president in 1986–1987.

How did Delaware fare during the War of 1812?

It seemed likely that Delaware would suffer punishment, or revenge, from the British Royal Navy during the War of 1812. Plenty of British ships did cruise the area, capturing privateers when possible, but most of their efforts were directed against Baltimore, Maryland, and Washington, D.C. Delaware did not play an important role in the defense of Fort McHenry at Baltimore, in 1814, and when the war ended, the people of the state breathed a big sigh of relief. They had dodged a powerful bullet.

Did Lincoln, and other Northern leaders, fear that Delaware would join the Confederacy?

They did. The First State is long enough—geographically speaking—that there were people in the southern counties that favored the Confederate cause. Slavery, too, was an established part of life in Delaware. But the institution had faded enough that rather few state residents were willing to stick their necks out to rescue the Confederate cause.

Delaware voted against Abraham Lincoln in the presidential election of 1860, and there was an obvious disdain for the new president. On the other hand, Delaware never seriously considered seceding from the Union. Maryland, which had much stronger ties to the Southern States, stayed in the Union—if only by a thread—and it made no sense for Delaware to go out on a limb. Slavery, too, had never been a big issue or concern for most white Delawareans. There still were some slaves, who were emancipated in 1863, but the state's economy was never driven by slave labor, as was the case with Maryland and Virginia.

How did Delaware become part of the so-called "Solid South"?

The Solid South refers to the fact that since about 1870, the Southern states have voted in concert. Between 1870 and about 1965, they tended always to vote for the Democratic Party. In the wake of the Civil Rights Movement, these states made a complete about-face and became regular supporters of the G.O.P ("Grand Old Party").

Delaware would, by all logic, have been with the Republicans. But in the immediate aftermath of the Civil War, small groups of federal troops were garrisoned on Delaware soil; some of these soldiers acted as if Delaware were a conquered and defeated state (this certainly was not the case). They did enough damage to Delaware's relationship with the federal government that right up to the 1930s, Delaware voted as part of the Solid South.

When did Delaware begin to receive immigrants from the other side of the Atlantic Ocean?

The state had been founded on immigration, of course, but as late as 1880 the Delaware population looked very much as it had one century earlier. This changed in the last two decades of the century, however, as Germans, Irish, Italians, and Poles began to arrive. They came to the industrial section, around Wilmington, in search of factory jobs. Perhaps it is mere coincidence that the African American population of Delaware began to decline at that same time, dropping to as low as 15 percent by the beginning of World War II.

How important are bridges to Delaware and its economy?

There aren't as many bridges as some of the locals would like, but those that exist are of great importance. The Delaware Memorial Bridge, which spans the Delaware River, connecting New Jersey with Delaware, was one of the marvels of mid-twentieth century construction. Commissioned in 1946 and completed in 1949, the Memorial Bridge is almost two miles long, and it carries a total of eight lanes of very busy traffic

Almost two miles long, the Delaware Memorial Bridge connects New Jersey with Delaware.

between the two states. The Baltimore and Chesapeake Canal, completed in 1829, played a similar role in the nineteenth century, allowing for commercial development.

How did Delaware fare during World War I and World War II?

The state benefited in both cases, thanks to its proximity to Philadelphia and Baltimore. A large number of American soldiers passed through Delaware, on their way to training camps elsewhere, and some of those young men later played important roles as policy-makers. In the aftermath of World War II, Dover Air Force Base was established, allowing many younger people to gain their first look at the First State.

Over 30,000 Delawareans served in World War II, and their contributions—as well as those of the state's many industries—changed the state irrevocably. One can still find plenty of peaceful spots in the First State, but the northernmost of the three counties—New Castle—became thoroughly urbanized. The single largest shipyard was owned by the Dravo Corporation, and Dover Air Force Base was established during the war.

What was life like in the immediate aftermath of the Second World War?

Many white Delawareans expressed content at the state's condition, and that of their families, while many blacks expressed frustration that sometimes erupted in anger. Blacks had been leaving the First State for more than a generation, heading to the Midwest, but those who remained felt both out of touch with events and ignored by the Anglo majority. As a result, there were race riots in Wilmington in 1967. These became even worse in April 1968, when the population learned of the assassination of Martin Luther King Jr. The National Guard was brought in, and it remained in Delaware for more than a year.

When did Delaware make the decision to become extremely friendly to corporations?

The decision was made in the late 1970s, and by 1985, Wilmington was the address of choice for numerous financial institutions. Favorable terms extended to credit card companies meant that the great majority of Americans, round the nation, saw a Delaware address when they opened the envelope containing their credit card statements.

What was life in Delaware like at the turn of the twenty-first century?

Some Delawareans lamented the loss of the northern third of the state to industry and commerce, but others pointed out that much of the state's natural beauty remained. Delaware was as tied as ever—perhaps even more so—to the fortunes of Washington, D.C., and Baltimore, where many of its residents worked. Those who did not go to the urban megalopolises, however, tended to live rather quiet lives in the countryside and to be quite pleased.

How important was the rise of Joe Biden to the vice presidency?

Born in Delaware in 1935, Joe Biden has consistently been one of the most thoughtful and articulate of American public servants, though, at the same time, he has a remarkable tendency to insert his foot in his mouth. Ever since he became a youthful U.S. senator in 1973, Biden was seen as a potential national candidate, but his run for president in 1988 seemed to remove him from contention. Not only was he capable of verbal gaffes, but he seemed to lack the seriousness necessary for national leadership.

Much of this changed when Biden was tapped as the Democratic vice presidential nominee by Barack Obama, following another brief and unsuccessful presidential run. Deep into his second term as the number-two man in the Oval Office, Biden was known as "the sheriff," the one who kept everyone else on track.

What will Delaware look like a generation from now?

The chances are that the present trends will continue, and that Delaware will be a bifurcated state, with strong urban and rural values expressed in the same population. Whether Delaware will ever find a way to win cultural independence from Baltimore and Washington, D.C., remains to be seen.

FLORIDA

Nickname: "The Sunshine State"
Capital: Tallahassee
Statehood: March 3, 1845; 27th state

AT A GLANCE

Where does Florida get its nickname?

From the fantastic sunlight that bathes the area ten months out of the year (the other two months are the rainy season).

What are the major symbols of the Sunshine State?

"In God We Trust" is the state motto. The mockingbird is the state bird, and the orange blossom is the state flower. The sabal palmetto palm is the state tree.

How large, or small, is Florida?

Comprising 58,976 square miles (152,747 square kilometers), Florida is twenty-first among the states in geographic size. As of the year 2010, there were 18,801,310 Floridians, placing it at fourth among the states in terms of population.

How did Florida ever become such a multicultural place?

In a sense, it has always been a rich mixture of isolated and cosmopolitan. Right from the time of the Spanish conquest, there was an international presence in Florida; at the same time, however, Florida became known as an inbred place, composed of people who seldom went elsewhere. Today, Florida is one of the most multicultural of all the states, with numerous languages spoken in school systems that positively dwarf their Northern and Midwestern counterparts. But move fifty miles in from the urban centers, and you can still find that distinctive Florida accent, and people who declare that they love nothing in the world so well as their own front porch.

Is there any one scene, or physical area, that exemplifies the best of what is Florida?

Cape Kennedy, where numerous rockets were fired as astronauts made their way into outer space, remains the single most iconic place in Floridian culture, but the space program no longer has the powerful lure it did in the 1960s. Greater Miami, therefore, especially when seen from the air, is the new Florida: miles upon miles of beach-front condominiums, streets that fairly soak up the sunlight, and a vista that seems to go on forever. Greater Miami, too, is where the natural scene and the ethnic mixture really come into focus: one can see the old and the new along the same avenue.

Does it ever get cold in Florida?

On those rare occasions when this happens, the orange crop is threatened. And given the importance of oranges to Florida's economy, that's no small matter. Most of Florida experiences broiling summer heat, followed by some relief in autumn, which is followed by a damp and rainy season in winter. Floridians like to claim that they are immune to changes in the weather; some old-timers make it a point to get in the ocean water every day of the year, rain, shine, or light snow!

Is Florida primarily old-line Anglo-Saxon? Primarily second-generation Hispanic? Or both?

In terms of natural increase, the Hispanic community seems certain to outdistance the old-line Anglo-Saxons and all other ethnic groups. It's possible, however, that enough of the early Floridian culture will endure that its mark will still be seen in future years. But Florida contains multitudes, and a third great group is composed primarily of retirees. Known as "snowbirds," they fly from their Northern and Midwestern towns in the mid-autumn and remain in Florida till early spring. Then they return north.

It's the rich mixture of the old and the new, the old-fashioned and the modern,

A harvester picks fruit from Florida's most famous orchard crop: oranges.

that makes Florida so endlessly diverse. In the same day, perhaps even the same afternoon, one can converse with old-style Floridians who almost never leave home and with Cuban exiles who left their beloved island nation two generations ago. One thing's for certain: Florida is never dull.

How did Florida, or Key West, become the haven for so many Hemingway lookalikes?

Ernest Hemingway actually grew up in the Midwest, but by the 1940s he was identified with Florida in general and Key West in particular. Today, simply by strolling the streets of Key West, one sees any number of bearded, middle-aged men who are doing Hemingway impressions. Not all of them are fully conscious of the effect, but a majority are seeking to cash in on the legendary literary figure.

EARLY HISTORY

How many Native Americans lived in what we now call Florida?

Perhaps as many as 200,000. This "guesstimate" comes from the records of the first Spanish explorers and conquerors, who arrived in the 1530s and fought many of the Indians of present-day Florida. To the best of our knowledge, the Indians of Florida lived in larger settlement groups, and perhaps larger tribes as well, than the Native Americans of almost any other East Coast state.

The Florida Indians, too, seem to have enjoyed a richer, more well-developed cultural life than many of their contemporaries. Not only did they have more hands to accomplish the work required, but they also seem to have had more fun, evidenced by testimonials, and the occasional artistic rendition, by early French and Spanish explorers. Of course the entire story is not one of good fortune. The Florida Indians also seem to have had more tyrannical leaders than their contemporaries: this was made possible by the larger population groups.

How much do we know about the expedition of Hernando de Soto, in 1538–1541?

The Spaniards who survived (de Soto did not) left plenty of records, and we gather that the expedition had a nightmarish aspect, both for the would-be conquerors and the people who fought, or resisted them. The 500-odd Spaniards possessed many advantages, including those conferred by horses, swords, and even dogs, but the Indians fought with great fierceness. On almost every occasion, the Spaniards triumphed, but it was a bloody, and rather miserable, affair for everyone concerned. And even when de Soto and his men departed, the native peoples were stung by a vicious aftermath. No one knows precisely how many Indians died from smallpox, measles, and mumps in the years that followed, but we suspect the number is large.

We usually hear about the Spanish influence. But were there French involved as well?

A group of Huguenots (French Protestants) arrived on the east coast of Florida in 1562, looking for a place to practice their faith in peace. That first group did not remain long, but it was followed by a much larger settlement group that arrived in 1564. The French established a colony in the neighborhood of St. Johns, Florida, but they were attacked, and virtually annihilated, by a Spanish expedition in 1565. The victorious Spaniards set about building Saint Augustine, known as the oldest continuously occupied place in the United States.

SPANISH RULE

How long did Spain rule Florida?

If you ask the Indians and their descendants, the Spaniards only ruled a narrow edge of coastline, and the Native Americans were the real governors of Florida. On Spanish maps, however, most of present-day Florida appeared as part of the Spanish Empire, between about 1580 and 1763. During all that time, the Spanish population never exceeded 6,000, and sometimes it was a good deal less. The military and political presence never blossomed, but Spain left its imprint thanks to the monks and friars, particularly of the Franciscan Order, who established mission settlements in northern Florida.

Spanish rule came to an abrupt end in 1763, when Great Britain, having won the Seven Years War, took possession. That occupation lasted only twenty years, and at the conclusion of the American Revolutionary War, Spain once again took possession of Florida. The second round of Spanish rule was no more successful than the first, however, and by 1819, the year of the Adams-Onis Treaty, it was apparent that American settlers would become the majority. Spain made a graceful exit, and Florida became first a territory, and then a state, in 1845.

What kind of people moved to Florida before the Civil War?

They tended to be adventurers, and the great majority of them came overland, passing through South Carolina and Georgia, rather than arriving by sea. Then too, there were quite a few U.S. military personnel, who arrived to fight the Seminole Indians and to take possession of the southernmost parts of Florida. The Seminole proudly claim that they are the only people in the world ever to defeat the U.S. military. It's closer to the truth to say that they fought the United States to a draw.

The people who came from Georgia were primarily known as "crackers," an expression that defies all attempts to be nailed down. Some claim that cracker comes from the sound of wagons rolling over country roads, while others assert that its foundation is in the cracking sound made as early Southern pioneers made their morning breakfast. Whatever the original derivation, there is no doubt that cracker was—for many decades—a useful stereotype.

FLORIDA IN THE LIFE OF THE NATION

I seldom hear about Florida in the lead-up to the Civil War. Why is that?

Florida produced no outstanding statesmen during the antebellum era. The Sunshine State entered the Union in 1845, and it seemed decidedly third place to states such as Georgia and South Carolina. Only when the move toward secession gathered strength did Florida become important in the considerations of North and South, and this was due primarily to the large number of federal installations—forts especially.

How eager was Florida to join the Confederacy?

Not nearly as eager as its neighbors. Florida had a very small population in 1861, and its people knew they would be among the first to be targeted by a Union naval blockade. The vote taken in Tallahassee was, therefore, only lukewarm in favor, and Florida entered the Confederacy as the least populous and weakest state of the new nation. Floridians sent plenty of young men to fight in the Confederate armies, but Florida regiments did not earn the accolades of, say, their Alabamian neighbors.

The Civil War retarded Florida's development, but it did not inflict heavy casualties or destruction to the landscape. One thing is for certain: the U.S. Army and Navy became much more prevalent in Florida in the years following the war, and Floridians never entertained thoughts of secession again.

What was the role of Fort Zachary Taylor during the Civil War?

Fort Zachary Taylor, named for the U.S. president who died in office in 1850, is located in Key West. Despite Florida being a Confederate state, the fort remained in Union hands and acted as headquarters for a naval blockade squadron. This resulted in many Confederate supply ships being unable to leave or arrive at Confederate ports. The site never saw any battles, but many historians believe that the fort helped ensure that the war didn't last longer than it did.

How long did it take the long coastline of Florida to become fully tied, or knit, together?

Given the incredible length of coastline, it happened with rather good speed. The culminating move came in 1910, when Henry Flagler completed the railroad line that went all the way from Miami to Key West. Once the Florida Keys were firmly tied to the mainland, Florida became more valuable as a strategic asset of the United States, and more attractive to outsiders, in terms of real estate deals. The first Florida land boom took

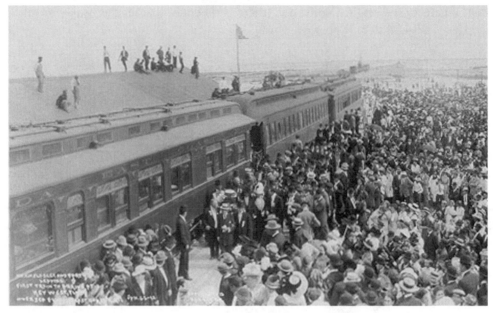

This historic photo was taken in 1912 as the first train linking mainland Florida to Key West prepared to depart on its maiden trip.

place in the early 1920s, and pretty soon, all sorts of Northern types—ranging from the Connecticut Yankee to the Indiana Hoosier—wanted their piece of Florida real estate.

When did the real estate boom come to an end?

The market was red-hot in 1925, with people traveling from the northern states by the thousands, and it remained pretty decent well into 1926. At the beginning of 1927, a cargo ship sank at the entrance of Miami Harbor, making it nearly impossible for more travelers to arrive; this, coupled with weakness in the local banks, led to a precipitate crash in the summer of 1927. Floridians who had been well-to-do on paper suddenly found themselves thrown back by many thousands of dollars, and even the wealthy who had managed the boom sometimes fell on hard times. This was the first, and by no means the last, time that a Florida real estate boom turned into a bust.

How did Florida fare during the Great Depression?

In a word, badly. The state was just beginning to recoup its losses from the real estate crash when the Great Depression hit, with full force, in the autumn of 1929. Many Floridians spent the next decade, sometimes more, just trying to survive.

The New Deal programs of the Roosevelt administration did little for Florida: the southern states that benefited most tended to be Tennessee and Kentucky. Not until the beginning of World War II did Florida begin to recover, and that recovery started strong and lasted a long time. For the first time, a sustained economic development was seen.

How did Florida do in the decades following World War II?

Two developments spell the difference: refrigeration and air-conditioning. Anyone who examines the news magazines of 1945 is struck by the frequency of the ads for air conditioning systems, and refrigeration, which was pioneered by a Georgian, really took off in the decades after 1945. As a result, many people who previously declared Florida as too hot, changed their minds, and another exodus from the northern states commenced.

Young college graduates, including those who had seen service in World War II, flocked to northern Florida in the three decades after 1945. They tended to be well-educated, and to come from solid middle-class families in the northern cities. These Northerners coming to Florida came from all over New England and the Midwest, but for some reason they were named the Cincinnati indwellers, and years later something like the Cincinnati syndrome was described.

What other development in the 1940s was relevant to Florida?

Miami Beach pharmacist Benjamin Green developed a suntan cream in 1944. He had devised a concoction to protect himself from the sun when he served in World War II. But after he got home, he improved it by mixing cocoa butter and coconut oil with other ingredients and applied it on his bald head until he got it right. This was, no doubt, a welcome invention to many Florida beachgoers!

When did Disney World come to Florida?

Walt Disney, best known as the man who created Mickey Mouse, established Disneyland in Anaheim, California, in 1955, and seeing its success he built Disney World just outside of Orlando, in northern Florida in 1971. Disney World was an immediate hit, drawing families from all parts of the Eastern and Midwestern states. Disney World also heralded Florida's appearance as part of the "New South," later replaced by the "Sunshine South."

What was the great dividing point so far as culture and language are concerned?

In 1980, the United States opened its doors to refugees from Fidel Castro's regime in Cuba. Quite a few Cubans had already come, but about 125,000 arrived in 1980, and they quickly established what Floridians refer to as "Little Havana" in the streets of Miami. The

Did people from other countries come to Florida?

They did indeed. After about 1965, there was a marked uptick in the number of Germans choosing to live in Florida for at least part of the year. Closer to home, quite a few French Canadians chose to spend part of the winter in southern Florida. *La Floride* (Florida) is a popular Quebecois film that depicts the saga of a Montreal family fleeing the snow and bitter cold for life in the condominiums of greater Miami.

The center of Calle Ocho in Little Havana is a buzzing hive of Cuban American activity.

Cuban exiles were an unusual ethnic group. Right from the start, they emphasized their own culture and the need to use their newfound status in America to liberate Cuba.

Little Havana became more noticeable to the wider world in 1983, when the movie *Scarface*, starring Al Pacino, was released. While it sensationalized the drug culture—especially that involving cocaine—*Scarface* was a good delineation of the racial and ethnic tensions of Greater Miami, showing corrupt cops, desperate Cuban exiles, and a scramble for existence. Seldom has one film done so much to describe an ethnic culture in the United States.

Given all the tensions, how it is that so many snowbirds kept coming south?

The same years that saw the influx of Cuban exiles—the early 1980s—also witnessed much colder winters than normal in the New England and Midwestern states. Many northerners, who had previously shrugged at the idea, packed up and moved south, where they found relief from the terrible winters. Ironically, the pattern changed dramatically in 1987–1988, with the summers becoming much hotter (this is when the expression *global warming* was first used). Some of the recent arrivals cursed their luck, declaring they had jumped out of the frying pan and into the fire, but others, especially those who went back north in springtime, could hardly believe their good luck.

94

Then too, Florida developed policies that kept wages and prices relatively low, meaning that retirees and others could come south and live better than anticipated. This policy resulted in another Florida boom, but this time it was primarily a boom in actual buildings, rather than land. The late 1980s and early 1990s saw Florida's population rise to roughly 14 million, a number that no one would have anticipated two decades earlier.

What was the most controversial moment in Florida's recent history?

Beyond a doubt, this was in November 2000, when the presidential election between Republican George W. Bush and Democrat Al Gore was contested. The margin between the two men was thin nationwide, but was razor-thin in Florida, which had, at that moment, Jeb Bush—younger brother of George W. Bush—as its governor. At 4 A.M., Gore conceded the election; but he soon took this back, and the stage was set for roughly six weeks of agonizing recounts.

The votes were counted and recounted numerous times, with laypersons serving alongside experts in attempting to determine exactly which ballot had been cast for whom. Expressions like "hanging chads" became part of the political lexicon during the recounts, which grew closer and more difficult to determine on each occasion. Finally, a U.S. Supreme Court decision brought the process to an end, and Florida's electoral votes were awarded to George W. Bush, who received enough electoral votes to be elected president.

When did the new building boom commence?

Between about 1995 and 2005, Florida underwent staggering growth, both from old and settled communities and newcomers. The Sunshine State led the economic boom that ran across the nation, but it also led the way into the so-called Great Recession that began in 2008.

Will Florida continue to grow at a rapid pace?

The economic recession that began in 2008 marked a slowdown of real estate prices, and the liquidation of quite a few big estates, but the number of people desiring to move to Florida was at an all-time high. The chances are good that Florida will surpass New York as the nation's third most populous state.

What is a hanging chad?

When a voter punches his or her choice in paper ballots, holes are created that are meant, of course, to reflect the voter's selection. Sometimes, however, either the voter does not deliver a strong enough "punch" or the paper ballot has been misaligned, with the result being a "hanging chad." It was the difficult, sometimes painful, task of people doing the recounts to determine whether the voter had made a true, valid, or complete selection.

GEORGIA

Nicknames: "The Peachtree State"; "Empire State of the South"
Capital: Atlanta
Statehood: January 2, 1788; 4th state

AT A GLANCE

Which of the two nicknames is more commonly used?

People say Peachtree State far more often than Empire State of the South. There is a connection between the two, however; Georgia's abundant agricultural output is what led it to become the Southern equivalent to New York State.

What are the major symbols of the Peachtree State?

"Wisdom, Justice, Moderation" is the state motto. The brown thrasher is the state bird, and the Cherokee rose is the state flower. The live oak is the state tree.

How large, or small, is the Peachtree State?

Comprising 58,921 square miles (152,605 square kilometers), Georgia is twenty-second among the fifty states in physical size. The Peachtree State had 9,687,653 residents as of the year 2010, placing it ninth among the states in terms of population.

Is there any one place from which one can see the best and the worst that Georgia contains?

There is indeed. Ten miles west of downtown Atlanta is Stone Mountain, an immense hunk of granite that looms up like a giant (only the thick tree cover prevents it com-

On the immense rocky surface of Stone Mountain the Danish-American artist Gutzon Borglum chiseled the images of Jefferson Davis, Robert E. Lee, and Stonewall Jackson. The site marks the spot, too, of the founding of the second Ku Klux Klan in 1915.

pletely dominating the scene). This is where the Ku Klux Klan was suddenly reborn, in the summer of 1915, but it is also the heart of what one can call the reconciliation of the races in modern, twenty-first-century Georgia.

Thanks to the immense sculpture of Robert E. Lee, Stonewall Jackson, and Jefferson Davis, Stone Mountain seems like a memorial of the Confederate past, but as one climbs to the top (hopefully before the noonday heat), he or she observes as many blacks as whites, and just as many foreign-born—as in Indian, Pakistani, and others—as native-born Americans. If ever a monument to racism and ethnocentrism has been altered to one of inclusiveness, it is Stone Mountain.

How much beauty can be found in Georgia?

A great deal. While only a small percentage of it is of the stunning kind that we identify with places such as Niagara Falls and the Grand Canyon, Georgia slowly unveils its charms to the beholder, rather than overwhelming him or her all at once. From the Chattahoochee State Forest in the north to Providence Canyon in the southwest, Georgia is filled with surprises. Of course there's the man-made element, too, such as the highways that seem to stretch on forever, winding their way through the green and blue of the hills, and the natural red clay of Georgia soil.

What is the tantalizing legend that accompanies the lushness of Blackbeard Island?

Blackbeard Island—all 5,618 acres of it—was named after pirate Edward Teach, better known as Blackbeard. In the late 1800s and early 1900s, the island was used as a quarantine site for yellow fever victims. A crematorium—for those who died of the disease—was built but was reportedly never used. It was later used as a site for the processing of yellow pine timber. Currently, it is a national wildlife refuge—home to migratory birds. But legend has it that Blackbeard buried his pirate treasure on the island. Alas, it has never been found!

Can one ask an old-time Georgian about the weather—and get any type of response?

The answer usually comes in the form of a chuckle. Georgians are justly proud of the sunshine that lights up their state nine or ten months out of the year, but they sometimes complain of the excessive heat. And when cold, ice, or snow strike, all bets are off. Georgia experiences the occasional snowstorm; the one that came in February 2014 was so severe that highways were shut down for days, and thousands of motorists were stranded. One thing Georgians do not suffer, on average, are the potholes that come from extended icy conditions; Georgia's highways, therefore, tend to be smooth as silk.

Who are some of the best-loved of Georgia's sons and daughters?

Margaret Mitchell, the insightful author who penned *Gone with the Wind*, remains one of the perennial favorites, but Flannery O'Connor has come a long way in the past twenty years or so. Martin Luther King Jr. is surely the best-known of all Georgia movers and shakers, but Jimmy Carter is the only Georgian ever to occupy the Oval Office.

Is the typical Georgian of our time close to the twentieth-century caricature or the nineteenth-century stereotype?

In both cases, the Georgian was seen as male, middle-aged, and rather simple in his tastes and habits. While James Earl ("Jimmy") Carter served as the thirty-ninth president of the United States, his younger brother Billy was seen as the personification of the half-ignorant, half-ridiculous rural white Georgian. But the very fact that this man's elder brother rose to become president tells us something about the nature of siblings, and about how far Georgia has come. It was during Jimmy Carter's political time that Georgia began to shine as one of the finest examples of the New South.

Plenty of old-time Georgia residents remain. They are best-known to outsiders, at least, as the people who spend much time at

Margaret Mitchell, the famous author of *Gone with the Wind,* is shown here in a 1941 photograph.

the local country store, and who seldom seem in a hurry for anything. Whether they will remain the stereotype of the state is difficult to say. Georgia demonstrates more cultural variety—between its old-timers and newcomers—than almost any other Southern state.

EARLY HISTORY

Who were the first inhabitants of what we now call Georgia?

Their names are unknown to us, so we label them the Mound Builders. They were part of a mound-building culture that stretched, at its height, from central Illinois to southern Mississippi, and from western Louisiana to northwestern Georgia. When we examine the size and solidity of their earthen mounds, we marvel that anyone would spend this time and effort; the chances are that they used the mounds for religious and ceremonial purposes. Like nearly all the Mound Builders, those of northwest Georgia moved away centuries before the first white settlers arrived, leaving us to marvel and to ponder. Were they the ancestors of today's Cherokee and Creek tribes? DNA evidence may unlock the answer at some point.

When did the first whites begin to arrive?

The expedition of Spaniard Hernando de Soto came through a section of Georgia in 1541, but virtually no traces of his activity remain. We know, from the records, that de Soto fought and killed many Native Americans, but the diseases he inadvertently spread may have killed far more Indians than his men ever did.

Following de Soto, the Spaniards stayed away for centuries, and it was not until the early eighteenth century that both England and Spain looked on this area with interest. The English wanted a buffer zone between their budding colony in South Carolina and the Spaniards in Florida; the feeling was met with complete reciprocity. Georgia was, for many years, the route by which escaped black slaves made it from slaveholding South Carolina to Florida, where they became free persons.

Who was James Oglethorpe, and how did he leave so deep a mark on Georgia?

Oglethorpe (1696–1785) was born to wealth and prominence. From an early age he demonstrated an altruistic attitude that culminated in his receiving a charter from King George II in 1732. The charter allowed Oglethorpe to found Georgia as a trustee colony and to establish it as a haven for men in debtor's prisons. Oglethorpe never truly succeeded in making Georgia a place of refuge for debtors because the need for defense— from the Spaniards in Florida—took precedence over his personal ideals for the colony.

What difficulties did the Georgia colony face in its early years?

The threat of Spanish power, directed from Florida, was a consistent danger. In 1743, Spain sent a powerful expeditionary force, intended to wipe Savannah off the map. James

Can a parallel be drawn between James Oglethorpe and James Earl Carter?

Yes indeed. Both men were true idealists and both men were also deeply practical. Neither achieved great success during his time as chief executive, but both are well-remembered by those who came later. Jimmy Carter is almost universally recognized as the finest former president the nation has ever had (witness his work for Habitat for Humanity, for instance), while James Oglethorpe retired to live in London, where he was the friend and confidante of Samuel Johnson, the greatest literary figure of the Georgian era.

Oglethorpe met and defeated the Spaniards at the Battle of Bloody Marsh, on St. Simons Island. From that year forward, Georgia was relatively safe from external threat.

How did Georgia respond to the crisis that was the Revolutionary War?

Georgia was the youngest of the Thirteen Colonies in 1775 and the one that maintained the strongest ties to the British motherland. Even so, Georgia ejected its royal governor swiftly, and the colony moved, like its fellows, to becoming one of the original Thirteen States. The reason Georgia is not well-known for its revolutionary history is that few military heroes came from the Peachtree State. Button Gwinnett was important in the Second Continental Congress, but Georgia proved unable to hold off the British when they arrived, in 1778. As a result, South Carolina grabbed nearly all the glory associated with the struggle of 1775–1783, so far as the southernmost colonies were concerned.

Was the cotton gin as important as we usually hear?

Beyond a doubt. When Massachusetts-born Eli Whitney came south to visit the plantation of Catharine Greene, he was told of the many difficulties Georgia planters experienced in separating the cotton from its seeds. In a matter of weeks, the ingenious Whitney designed the world's first cotton gin (short for engine). Using a hand crank, one person could separate as much cotton from the seeds as fifty people previously. As a result, the cotton industry boomed, and the need for African American slaves increased.

When was it apparent that Georgia was, and would remain, one of the strongholds of the peculiar institution, as slavery was often called?

By the time William Crawford became U.S. secretary of state in 1815, Georgia was thoroughly identified with the production of cotton and the slave system. Crawford was, perhaps, the finest diplomat and statesman Georgia produced during the antebellum period, but even he could not halt, or alter, the trend that made the Peachtree State into a one-crop economy.

The invention of Eli Whitney, the cotton gin (a 1940s model is shown here) revolutionized cotton harvesting, making it much more profitable and less labor-intensive.

Georgia also witnessed the first genuine gold rush in U.S. history. In 1828, gold was discovered in northeastern Georgia, and a flood of white settlers spilled over from South Carolina and Tennessee. The resulting land changes effectively pushed the Cherokee Indians out and made the terrible "Trail of Tears" nearly inevitable.

I've heard of the Trail of Tears but don't know much about it. Was this event restricted to what happened in Georgia?

The Trail of Tears started in Georgia, but its ramifications were obvious to people—white and Indian alike—throughout the Deep South. In 1830, Congress passed the Indian Removal Act, and President Andrew Jackson, no friend to the Creek and Cherokee, began its implementation. By 1838, virtually all the Creek and Cherokee had been forced off their lands and relocated to present-day Oklahoma, then known as Indian Territory. The worst part of this truly heart-rending process was the Trail of Tears, when roughly 4,000 Cherokee perished during their relocation. The federal government blamed the supply wagoners, who in turn blamed the state governments. Everyone was blamed, but virtually no one took responsibility, and the Trail of Tears remains, today, one of the worst blots on the reputation of the United States.

What was Georgia's role in bringing on the Civil War?

By 1860, Georgia had replaced South Carolina as the Deep Southern state with the largest population and most booming economy. Unlike South Carolina, the people of Georgia were deeply divided on the subject of secession: the measure passed the special legislative session by the slim margin of thirty votes. Once the war began, however, Georgia was destined to be one of the mainstays of the Confederate war effort.

How bad was the Civil War, so far as Georgia and its people were concerned?

It was the greatest of calamities, the worst of times. Georgians subscribed to the widespread but mistaken belief that the Northern men were not up to a long war, when, in fact, the Yankees proved to have the greater staying power. And when General William T. Sherman led a major Northern army through the heart of Georgia, in 1864–1865, he made good on his boast, to "make Georgia howl."

Was Georgia the land of magnificent mansions and gallant men, as portrayed in *Gone with the Wind*?

Margaret Mitchell was a native Georgian who lived in Atlanta. She may have based "Tara," the home of the heroine, Scarlett O'Hara, on a mansion twenty miles to the northeast. The short answer, however, is no: the great majority of Georgians—white and black alike—lived rather simple, unadorned lives. Perhaps it was that very knowledge that led this gifted novelist to go in the other direction and make the antebellum South seem more wonderful than was really the case.

There were perhaps 100 families in antebellum Georgia who lived the sumptuous lifestyle so much admired by novelists and Hollywood filmmakers, but nearly all of them emerged from the Civil War in bad shape. The economy was wrecked by the Union men commanded by General William T. Sherman, who famously predicted that he would "make Georgia howl" as he passed through.

How long did it take Georgia to get back on its feet?

Roughly forty years. Cotton came back strong in the 1880s and 1890s but was then subjected to the invasive worm known as the boll weevil. Tobacco production had never

What was so special about cotton grown in Georgia?

The climate was about 99 percent perfect for the growing and harvesting of cotton. The first major effort was made in 1785, just after the American Revolution, and it was the appearance of the famous device known as the cotton gin—ironically, developed by a Northerner—that allowed Georgia cotton to become famous worldwide. Along with the "white gold" grown in the uplands, Georgia also became famous for its short-staple cotton grown on the Sea Islands.

How did Stone Mountain gain so negative a reputation?

In 1915, the film *Birth of a Nation* was released to the cinema (it was a silent film, not a "talkie"). Millions of viewers—one of them being President Woodrow Wilson—saw the film and pronounced it real, declaring that the short time when blacks had the vote, whites in the Southern states were treated like second-class citizens. To prevent any return to those times (imagined or otherwise), the Ku Klux Klan was reborn, with the opening ceremonies held at Stone Mountain. The next year, 1916, a group of sculptors came to Stone Mountain, their intention being to create the greatest memory to the Confederate South that has ever been attempted. It was not by accident that in one of his greatest speeches, Reverend Martin Luther King Jr. called for freedom to ring, at places like Stone Mountain.

been strong, and the state therefore came to rely on its lumber and timber industry. During the decades in which Georgia made the economic transition, its politics were poisoned by racial overtones. One popular state governor—Tom Watson—started his career as a genuine populist, but, finding it impossible to win election any other way, turned into a race-baiting segregationist. Some of the ugliest episodes of Georgia history belong to the early twentieth century, when blacks were no longer enslaved, but when their lives were endangered and made difficult on a daily basis.

Cotton was big in the 1880s, but what was invented during the same time that became an international hit?

In 1886, Atlanta pharmacist John Pemberton invented Coca-Cola. He concocted the syrup, which was then paired with carbonated water at local soda fountains, where they typically sold the beverage for a nickel. Pemberton's bookkeeper, Frank Robinson, came up with the name and the distinctive script. Pemberton sold his interests just two years later, shortly before his death.

How did Georgia's economy change in the early twentieth century?

After the boll weevil did its terrible work, destroying several harvests in a row, Georgia farmers began to diversify. They raised hogs and planted soybeans, as well as cotton. The state's economy took years to recover, but the results were generally well-liked. At the same time, Georgia became well known for its lumber industry. The white pine trees of southern Georgia were highly desired for pulp, newsprint, and other wood sources; as a result, a new industry was born.

Which U.S. president died in Georgia?

President Franklin D. Roosevelt, afflicted with polio, often travelled to Warm Springs, Georgia, to enjoy the medicinal quality of the local hot springs. He purchased a home there in the early 1930s and occasionally stayed there as president. The home became known as the Little White House. It was there, on April 12, 1945, that Roosevelt, having been elected to his fourth term the previous November, suffered a fatal stroke.

Was the Civil Rights movement born in Georgia?

There is truth in the proposition, but it isn't the full truth. Most of the former Confederate States had deeply unsatisfied black populations, and there was enough discontent to go around, but Georgia, Alabama, and Mississippi, between them, saw the most anger and the loudest protests. The reason Georgia is so prominent in discussions of the Civil Rights era is that Martin Luther

U.S. President Jimmy Carter grew up on a Georgia peanut farm.

King Jr. came from Atlanta. He did his most important work in Alabama, but he could not avoid paying attention to his home city.

When did Atlanta become the prototypical New Southern city?

The movement started in the 1970s, and really gained strength when Jimmy Carter was elected to the White House in 1976. Atlanta gained steadily in popularity, particularly for people from New England and the Midwest, eager to avoid any more winters. Atlanta grew in concentric rings, with one fine-looking suburb piled atop the other. The result was that Atlanta came to possess 4 million-plus people, without a sense of feeling crowded. Its suburbs, especially, had far more land than was typical of other major American cities. The price, however, was paid by the morning and late afternoon commutes, which came to be legendary. It was claimed that in no other city in the nation were the people so downright friendly and hospitable … *until* they got in their automobiles, and from that moment it was every person for him or herself.

How and when was CNN founded?

Until the year 1979, the typical American news broadcast was thirty minutes in length. The Iran Hostage Crisis of 1979–1981 showed the need for more extensive coverage, and Atlanta entrepreneur Ted Turner launched Cable Network News (CNN) in 1981. Within one decade, CNN was the leader in the new cable news industry, and its rivals were forced to extend their coverage. By about the year 2000, most Americans had the opportunity to watch news and politics 24/7, if they so desired.

How important were the Summer Olympics of 1996 to Atlanta and to Georgia?

The Olympics can hardly be overstated: they were the moment at which the nation came to fully embrace the Peachtree State. Atlanta constructed new housing, added greenspace, upgraded its sports facilities, and saw an increase in tourism. Tragedy struck the games when a pipe bomb exploded, killing two and injuring more than 100 people. But Atlanta persevered.

What was life in Georgia like at the turn of the twenty-first century?

It was about as bifurcated as in any state in the Union. Atlanta and its seemingly endless suburbs were almost as cosmopolitan as New York City, while the countryside seemed as bucolic.

Where will the Peachtree State be a generation from now?

At the time of this writing, in 2015, Georgia continues to boom as never before in its history. Atlanta has one of the largest airports in the world, and the city continues to expand in ever-larger concentric rings. There seems to be no limit to how much more expansion Georgia can handle.

HAWAII

Nickname: "The Aloha State"
Capital: Honolulu
Statehood: August 21, 1959; 50th state

AT A GLANCE

Where does Hawaii get its nickname?

From the native Hawaiian language. "Aloha" means "hello" or "goodbye."

What are the major symbols of the Aloha State?

"The Life of the Land Is Perpetuated in Righteousness." This, the official state motto, dates from the time when Hawaii was a kingdom, ruled by a native dynasty. The nene is the state bird, and the yellow hibiscus is the state flower. The kukui is the state tree.

How large, or small, is the Aloha State?

Comprising 6,468 square miles (16,752 square kilometers), Hawaii is forty-seventh among the states in geographic size. As of the year 2010, there were 1,360,301 residents, making Hawaii fortieth among the states in terms of population.

What makes Hawaii so different from the rest of the United States?

Just about everything. Unlike the East Coast, which was settled largely from a religious impulse, Hawaii was settled first by Polynesian Islanders, and then by people of European descent, including Americans. Unlike the West Coast, which thrived as a result of gold and silver rushes, Hawaii was settled by people who wished to live happily, rather

107

than on the road to wealth and fame. And, unlike virtually all the rest of the nation, Hawaii is a set, or chain, of islands, gently rocked by the Pacific Ocean.

How can so small an area comprise so many different mini-climates and ecosystems?

This marvel is produced by the volcanic lava that periodically spews from the two major volcanoes (both of them on the Big Island). Additionally, Hawaii is nearly at the center of the famous trade winds, first described by British captain James Cook. The combination of lava in the soil and moisture brought by the winds allows for an amazing diversity of plant life on the Hawaiian Island.

Though Hawaii has plenty of automobiles and motorcycles, the area tends to be sheltered from extreme noise. Hawaiians are big believers in physical fitness, and they often choose occupations or lifestyles that allow them relative freedom from cars and motorized conveyances. Hawaii is not, perhaps, for everyone, but it is a rare tourist who does not like most aspects of the lifestyle.

Can the casual tourist see much of the best that is Hawaii?

The great majority of tourists see The Big Island and Oahu, and pass the other seven leading islands by. It makes good sense, given that these two islands are set up for tourism, but it means that many visitors never see the whole that makes up Hawaii. To have a truly enlightening journey, one should try to arrange for local guides.

Hawaii is essentially a series of volcanoes that long ago thrust up from the sea. There is some danger as one comes close to these, but rather few people come to any harm.

This 2014 photo of the Hawaiian islands was taken from the International Space Station.

Rather than the land of difficulty and danger, Hawaii has traditionally been known as the place of relaxation and contentment.

HAWAII

How many islands are there?

There are 132 in all. Only seven of these are in the main part of the chain that is inhabited, however, and most of them remain uninhabited to this day. The Hawaiian Islands lie far to the south of what we ordinarily think: they are about parallel to the middle part of Mexico, and they form the southernmost part of the United States.

Do Hawaiians discuss the weather very much?

Only to grin and express how lucky they are. Of all the places in the entire United States, only southern California and southern Florida come close to Hawaii in terms of temperate weather during the winter and marvelous summers. Then too, the Floridians and Californians sometimes have to put up with extreme heat: this is not the case in Hawaii.

Of course the scene is not truly perfect: some small things emerge as flies in the ointment. The trade winds of the region blow very hard, and Hawaiians sometimes have to put up with severe winds. These seldom last for very long, however.

Can the Hawaiian be told apart from the tourists who flock to his or her shore?

No longer. Today there are so many different culture groups within Hawaii, ranging from Koreans, Chinese, and Japanese to Samoan, Anglos, and native Hawaiians that the difference is no longer obvious. But in terms of personal ease, the Hawaiian often stands out from those who come to visit. Hawaiians do not have to hurry in order to see the major sites: they expect to have a lifetime to do so.

Who are some of the best-loved Hawaii sons and daughters?

Daniel K. Inouye, who parlayed admirable service in World War II into a congressional and senatorial career, was, throughout his long lifetime, one of the most admired of all Hawaiians. Going back to the late nineteenth century, one finds great appreciation for Father Damien of Molokai, the Belgian-born Catholic priest who ministered to the lepers. And in recent times, much has been made of the fact that Barack Obama, the forty-fourth president of the United States, was born in Hawaii.

Have mainlanders always been so fond and appreciative of traditional Hawaiian clothing and dance?

No. The missionaries, who formed an important nineteenth-century group, tried to discourage traditional dance and dress, and they even prevented some Hawaiians from surfing. The last of these prohibitions was the first to change, as surfing spread from Hawaii to the mainland Forty-Eight, and by about 1950, mainlanders professed their liking for traditional Hawaiian festivities. Though it was a stereotypical television program in

109

many respects, the success of *Hawaii Five-0,* the police show of the 1970s, indicated how far Hawaii had come in gaining acceptance by the nation as a whole.

EARLY HISTORY

For how long have humans lived in what we now call the Aloha State?

Only for about 1,500 years. To the best of our knowledge, Hawaii had no human inhabitants until about 500 C.E., when a group of Polynesians arrived: they are the descendants of virtually all the native Hawaiians of today. These Polynesians brought an extensive culture and religious background, including the belief in a number of gods and goddesses, as well as curses and blessings that could be extended by these divine beings. Native Hawaiian culture may have been gentle in many respects, but the word of the priests appears to have been law.

When did the first people of European descent arrive in Hawaii?

Spanish sailors may have sighted the islands in the sixteenth or seventeenth centuries, but Captain James Cook—one of the first Englishmen to circumnavigate the globe—appears to have been the first European to land in Hawaii. Arriving in January 1778, he struck up a wary friendship with the local tribes, who appear to have considered him a type of spirit being: somewhere between human and divine.

The British government learned of Hawaii in due time, and the name Cook gave the area—the Sandwich Islands—stuck for almost three generations. In the meantime, both British and American missionaries, as well as merchants, considered how to take advantage of this new find.

Who was King Kamehameha?

There were actually five different kings of that name. Kamehameha I was a powerful tribal chieftain who was in his twenties when Captain James Cook arrived. Perhaps Kamehameha gathered from Cook that Europeans lived in kingdoms and principalities rather than tribal groups; then again, he may have come to the idea on his own. In either case, however, Kamehameha was the first native Hawaiian to unify the islands; he accomplished this through a long series of wars and much bloodshed. His cause was assisted by the fact that various European merchants

There are many statues of King Kamehameha I in Hawaii. This one stands in front of the Hawaii State Supreme Court building in Honolulu.

brought guns, and that his people were among the first to use them on the Hawaiian Islands. By 1820, the islands were fully unified under the monarchy he established, and it must be said that his monarchical style, while heavy-handed, was very effective.

When did the United States first become aware of the Hawaiian Islands?

Small numbers of merchant ships paid call on the islands between 1810 and 1820; by the latter date, the area was well-described on maps in Washington, D.C. There was little need to be concerned about the area until victory in the Mexican War brought California to the U.S. flag; from then on, American policy makers watched Hawaii with ever-increasing interest.

American missionaries first arrived in Hawaii around 1820, and they soon made their presence well-known. Though few in number, the missionaries were influential. They attempted to convert the Hawaiian natives to Christianity and were not above performing the occasional parlor trick in order to do so. It helped the missionaries' cause that the native population was decreasing in size, because of the inadvertent introduction of a number of European diseases.

Right up to the time when the Civil War ended, Hawaii was still far off on the map, and it attracted little attention among the American public. But in the three decades that followed, sugar merchants and pineapple growers pointed to the islands, declaring that they needed to come under the Stars and Stripes.

How did the native Hawaiian monarchy come to an end?

In 1893, a coup was carried out, and Queen Lili'uokalani was deposed. She had long been aware of the danger and done her best to thwart it, but the pressure exerted by sugar, coffee, and pineapple merchants became too much to handle. One year later, the Hawaiian Republic was declared, but it was obvious that the government was under the thumb of British and American merchants. In 1898, Congress voted for the annexation of Hawaii, and President William McKinley, who was right in the middle of the Spanish-American War, signed the order. Two years later, Hawaii become a U.S. territory.

What you can tell me about the Dole family?

There were a number of prominent Doles associated with Hawaii. Sanford Dole (1844–1926) was a member of the Supreme Court of the Kingdom of Hawaii beginning in December 1887 and four years later was appointed to Queen Lili'uokalani's Privy Council. Following the end of her monarchy in 1893, Dole became president of the provisional government of Hawaii, a position he held until he became the first governor of the Territory of Hawaii in June 1900. At the same time that Dole was governor (1900–1903), his cousin, Edmund Pearson Dole (1850–1928) was attorney general. Another Dole, James Dole (1877–1958) founded the Hawaiian Pineapple Company, which later became the Dole Food Company, a giant in the pineapple industry.

HAWAII IN THE LIFE OF THE NATION

How long and arduous was the process toward statehood?

To many Hawaiians, it seemed as if this never would happen. There was considerable cultural prejudice against the native Hawaiians, on the part of many mainlanders, and the idea that the nation should not be "tainted" by taking in too many foreigners. It seemed quite possible that Hawaii would remain a territory for centuries.

Adding to the sense of imperialist control, the U.S. Navy established one of its most important bases on the island of Oahu in 1900. From small beginnings, Pearl Harbor eventually became the center of the U.S. Pacific Fleet, and today it is the headquarters of a unified system of command for Army, Navy, Air Force, and Marines in the Pacific.

How did Hawaii fare during World War I and the Great Depression?

If the Japanese had not been so effective in snapping up German islands in the East Pacific, Hawaii might well have been attacked. But World War I passed without any substantial danger to Hawaii, and the Great Depression hardly affected the islands at all. Americans continued to purchase pineapple and sugar, and the massive influx of U.S. Navy personnel meant that plenty of money flowed over the counters at Hawaiian shops.

The advent of the Second World War was a whole different matter, however. Suddenly, Hawaii, and the naval base at Pearl Harbor, became the front line of what could become a shooting war between the United States and Imperial Japan. All sorts of warnings and drills were issued, but none of them made any difference in the end.

How did Japan manage to pull off so large an operation and maintain the advantage of surprise?

Anyone who studies the attack on Pearl Harbor comes away with a grudging respect for the Japanese. They sent a huge task force all the way from their home islands to within 300 miles of Pearl Harbor without being detected. The task force launched over 300 planes that attacked Pearl Harbor on Sunday, December 7, 1941. Nearly 2,500 U.S. ser-

Did any Americans come as tourists in the early twentieth century?

Very few. Hawaii was so far distant that only the wealthy could afford the trip, and many of them returned home to say that the islands were nothing special (perhaps they wished to discourage others from experiencing the beauty they had found). Commercial air flights from the West Coast to Hawaii were established in 1935, and from that year forward, an increasing number of mainlanders ventured out to Hawaii. Most of them returned to report that they had the time of their lives!

An aerial view of Pearl Harbor taken on October 30, 1941, just weeks before the Japanese attack.

vicemen were killed, and most of the seven battleships either were sunk or were severely damaged. At the same time, most historians believe the Japanese also committed a cardinal error by not following up with a third aerial assault, and in their failure to attack the strategic oil reserve. Had this been destroyed, American efforts in the Pacific would have been held up by at least six months, perhaps even longer.

How did the Hawaiian Islands fare in the immediate aftermath of the Japanese attack?

Hawaii boomed! Hundreds of thousands of U.S. servicemen passed through the area on their way to fight the Japanese in all parts of the Pacific. Millions of mainland Americans became much more conscious of Hawaii as a result of the war. The Hawaiian economy soared as a result.

What role did Hawaii play in the remainder of World War II?

Given that it was a U.S. territory, and not a state, Hawaii did not have to send any men into the U.S. Armed Forces (although some volunteered). Hawaii was vitally important to the flow of men, aircraft, and machines across the Pacific, however, and the Hawai-

Did James Michener, author of the epic novel *Hawaii*, come from Hawaii?

Not even close. He was a New York City boy, but his writing sometimes makes it seem as if he were a native Hawaiian Islander, or perhaps a native of Tahiti. No other American of the 1950s and 1960s wrote so convincingly about the pleasures of the South (and Central) Pacific as Michener, and he continued turning out books on Pacific themes right up to his death.

ian Islands looked like a war zone between 1941 and 1945. When the war ended, some U.S. servicemen elected to remain on the islands, while others went home to tell family and friends that the Hawaiian Islands were one of the best places to be found. But tourism did not commence until the arrival of passenger aircraft.

Was there any chance things would go back to normal in Hawaii once the war ended?

Not one in ten. Too many Americans had seen Hawaii, and the stories they told friends and family meant that the area received a major influx of tourists in the five years following the war. The high-rise hotels along Waikiki Beach—later made famous by the camera angle in scenes of the TV show *Hawaii Five-0*—arose during the early 1950s, and there was no way Hawaii could go back to its calm and placid past.

What kind of ethnic mixture did Hawaii have by about the year 1960?

The Aloha State finally achieved statehood in August 1959. President Dwight D. Eisenhower signed the bill that brought in Hawaii as the fiftieth state. By that year, Hawaii was one of the most racially and ethnically diverse places in the United States. Native Hawaiians had fallen in population, while Chinese, Japanese, Samoans, and Koreans had increased in number. Anglo-Americans from the mainland began settling in Hawaii, leading to what sometimes seemed like an experiment in multicultural democracy. One of the first Native Hawaiians to rise to prominence was Daniel K. Inouye, a veteran of World War II who became the first of his people to serve in the U.S. Congress.

When did Hawaii become the surfing capital we know today?

Hawaiians had surfed for generations, but the missionaries discouraged the practice, and it was not until about 1910 that surfing came back into style. One of the major Hawaiian heroes of this period was Duke Kahanamoku (1890–1968), who won a gold medal in swimming at the 1912 Olympics. He helped popularize the sport, which soon became a favorite in southern California.

How many programs—educational and otherwise— have been filmed in Hawaii?

It's a long list, and little wonder: people do not tire of seeing sunny beaches and happy tourists. The single most famous of all the television programs was *Hawaii Five-O*, which premiered in 1968 and remained on the air for twelve years (and returned as a remade series in 2010). Something wonderfully incongruous was shown when the hard-working detectives of the Honolulu police department tracked down desperate criminals in places that looked fit only for tourist fun. And the second best-known of all the programs was *Magnum P.I.* (or Private Investigator). This program, which ran during the 1980s, starred the handsome and tanned Tom Selleck.

How did the cost of living in Hawaii ever grow so high?

The problem of today is the same one encountered by mainlanders a century ago: virtually all the goods of Hawaii, including automobiles and building materials, must be shipped from the mainland. While the U.S. Navy was the single largest employer, some of these costs were cushioned, but these days the consumer pays the full freight. As a result, Hawaii is certainly one of the nicest places to live, but it is also one of the most expensive.

I seldom hear anything about the politics of Hawaii. Why is this?

It's because Hawaii is about as close as one can find to a "one-party state." The Democratic Party has ruled in Hawaii ever since the 1970s, and there is no reason to believe this will change. Hawaiians believe the Republican Party hardly knows they exist, and they believe they are better off with the Democrats on almost any occasion. On the local level, too, Hawaiians tend to be gentler about their politics than mainland Americans.

Where will the Aloha State be a generation from now?

The chances are that it will be even more diverse, in terms of ethnicity. Hawaii's economy is less easy to predict. The state either will flourish, with even more investment from the outside, or it will run into serious trouble. In either case, however, the people of Hawaii have demonstrated their capability and creativity so many times that it seems likely they will weather any storm.

IDAHO

Nickname: "The Gem State"
Capital: Boise
Statehood: July 3, 1890; 43rd state

AT A GLANCE

What is the origin of the state nickname?

Gem State was an obvious choice for the people of Idaho, because it was precious minerals that brought most of the early settlers.

What are the major symbols of the Gem State?

"It is Forever" is the state motto. The mountain bluebird is the state bird, and the syringa is the state flower. The western white pine is the state tree.

How large, or small, is the Gem State?

At 83,569 square miles (216,443 square kilometers), Idaho is larger than it sometimes seems. The Gem State is thirteenth among the states in geographic size. As of the year 2010, there were 1,567,582 residents, placing Idaho thirty-ninth among the states in terms of population.

So little is known about Idaho, at least at first glance. Does the state suffer from an identity crisis of some sort?

Not at all. The people of Idaho are very conscious of who they are, and they are perfectly willing to remain in the background, allowing others to discover them and their wonderful state at leisure. One thing about Idahoans that is quite noticeable, right from the start, is that they are not in a hurry.

Why is this so?

Perhaps it's the result of so many Basque shepherds coming to Idaho over the last century. They bring a relaxed style, both to work and their lives in general. Then again, it may be because the people of Idaho have seen that being in a hurry doesn't pay. Each time they indulged in a "rush," usually one in pursuit of silver or gold, it ended up leaving people, in general, poorer than before. But whatever the reason, the people of Idaho move at a slow pace, except when they are skiing.

Is there any state that contains as much variety as Idaho?

Except for the dryness that afflicts about 70 percent of the state, Idaho has just about everything and anything that one could wish for. Tall mountains allow for backpacking and skiing; fast-running rivers bring out the best in whitewater experts; and the sheer rugged beauty of the land—its sunsets most especially—has become the stuff of legend. Was it merely by chance that Ernest Hemingway spent his last years in Idaho? Probably not.

Fittingly, there's a giant potato in front of the Idaho Potato Museum.

Is the weather much of a topic of conversation in Idaho?

Only during the really cold spells of winter, and they don't last very long. Idaho is sheltered from the worst of the cold that comes from Canada by its mountains, and large amounts of warm Pacific air reach all the way to the western part of the state. Summer can be quite hot, but given that 40 percent of the state is forested, there's usually a place to find refuge. Most Idahoans consider themselves blessed where the weather is concerned.

When did Idaho potatoes became so well-known?

Southern Idaho is nearly ideal for the cultivation of potatoes, thanks to its varied climate, with long summer days but cool spring evenings. Idaho was already known for potato production by 1941, but World War II proved decisive. The federal government purchased vast amounts of Idaho's potato crop for the war effort, and millions of American servicemen became accustomed to the idea that their potatoes came from Idaho.

Can the Idahoan be told apart from his or her neighbors in Washington and Montana?

Not really. The people of these mountain states have much in common. The northernmost part of Idaho is actually closer—both by road and as the crow flies—to eastern Washington State than to the southern part of the state. What these people—those of western Montana, eastern Washington, and most of Idaho—have in common is a great love of freedom. They love the United States, and are pleased to serve under the Stars and Stripes, but they wish the federal government would learn how to leave well enough alone.

EARLY HISTORY

For how long have humans lived in what we now call the Gem State?

For thousands of years. Descendants of the first Americans—those who came across the Land Bridge between Siberia and Alaska—filtered their way into Idaho pretty early on, but they never settled there in great numbers, because there were more open and accessible areas to the south and southwest. Idaho, therefore, had a rather small Native American population, and even when the first people of European descent arrived, they found the landscape not too different from what it had been thousands of years earlier. The snow-capped mountains; the gushing rivers; and the all-too-infrequent meadows were as beautiful then as they are today.

Most of the Paleo-Indians of Idaho are anonymous to us: we do not know their tribal names. But when the first Anglo-Americans appeared, early in the nineteenth century, the Kutenai, Salish, Nez Perce, and Coeur d'Alene tribes predominated. Some of these names are truly Native Americans; others were imposed by the first explorers and settlers.

These early explorers—what were they looking for?

Lewis and Clark operated under orders from President Thomas Jefferson; their goal was to cross the continent and comment on the flora, fauna, and people they encountered. Wilson Price Hunt and his group were out to enlarge the fortunes of John Jacob Astor, the New York businessman who sent them west to penetrate the fur trade. But the people who came after both of these exploring groups were primarily interested in converting the Native Americans to their religion.

Who were the first Anglo-Americans in Idaho?

Captains Meriwether Lewis and William Clark led the Corps of Discovery right across the midsection of the state in the early autumn of 1805. This was actually one of the most difficult parts of their journey, and they still weren't certain they would make it to the Pacific Coast before winter. But once they found the Snake River, Lewis, Clark, and company built canoes and continued their epic journey, which brought them to where the Columbia River meets the ocean.

Lewis and Clark were amateur ethnologists, deeply interested in the lifeways of the Indians they met, but they reserved their best, most insightful comments for the Native Americans they met in Oregon and Washington State; we learned little from them about the Indians of Idaho. So it was also with the second major group of explorers who came through in 1811–1812. Wilson Price Hunt and his men had a terrible time on the Snake River; most of their canoes capsized in Devil's Canyon, which, at 7,000 feet, is the deepest in the Lower Forty-Eight. Hunt and his men did reach the mouth of the Columbia, where they built Fort Astoria.

These explorers all seem to have been transient. Who were the first real settlers of Idaho?

They make an interesting story. In 1836, two couples set out from New York State, with mission-making on their mind. Marcus and Narcissa Prentiss Whitman went all the way to Washington State, to become the first permanent settlers there, while Henry and Eliza Spalding settled near present-day Lewiston, Idaho. The two couples had the same motives, and both were in earnest, but they seem to have preferred to remain 150 miles apart. Quite possibly this is because one of the husbands had become too friendly with the other man's wife! Tragically, the Whitmans were killed in a massacre by the Native American Cayuse tribe on a mission near Walla Walla, Washington.

Did people on the East Coast, or even in St. Louis, Missouri, know the name Idaho?

Not yet. They learned that there was a great stopover place between the Bitterroot Mountains on one side and the rivers that fed into the Columbia River Basin. In these early years, Idaho did not seem to have any great attraction, but the mineral finds in Colorado (1858) and then Nevada (1859) brought so many miners to the Far West that it was natural they would begin to investigate. The first silver was discovered in Idaho in 1860, and the number of permanent settlers picked up immediately.

Idaho became a U.S. territory in 1863, but it played no part or role in the American Civil War. Not only was the scene of action a long way off, but there were enough Southern men among the miners that it seemed wise to leave the whole matter alone. This doesn't mean Idaho was spared from conflict, however.

What was the worst day of Idaho's history?

From the perspective of the Anglo-American white person, it may have been any one of a number of natural disasters, including enormous floods. To the Native American, though, the worst day was certainly on January 15, 1863. A group of U.S. soldiers had come into southeastern Idaho, intent on obtaining revenge for Indian attacks on settler groups. Whether the Shoshone had in fact committed the transgressions is hard to say; what is abundantly clear is that the white soldiers took a deadly revenge. Almost 400 Indians, including women and children, were killed in the Bear River Massacre.

How did things like this happen without provoking the moral outrage of Americans on the East Coast?

A lot of it has to do with the fact that the Civil War was being fought in deadly earnest. In the same month that the Shoshone were massacred, tens of thousands of Union soldiers were recuperating from the terrible licking they had taken at the Battle of Fredericksburg, Virginia, one month before. National attention—the newspapers especially —went to the Civil War struggle, not to what happened in the Far West. To take a conversation a bit further, however, the majority of Anglo-Americans were not very sympathetic to the plight of Indians. Not until the Indians were almost entirely penned up on reservations did white Americans begin to express regret. And that brings us to one of the great—though sad—stories of Indian resistance.

Was Chief Joseph a native of Idaho or of Washington State?

These are primarily the definitions assigned by white people. To Chief Joseph, it was apparent that he lived on the edge between these two states, and that he and his people enjoyed the great natural bounty of

This monument to the Bear River Massacre was constructed by the Daughters of Utah Pioneers. It is a National Historic Landmark.

the area (salmon fishing especially). Therefore, when the federal government declared that he must move to a reservation, Joseph led his people on one of the great migrations—with a military flavor—of the nineteenth century.

Through the summer and early autumn of 1877, Chief Joseph and his band of Nez Perce dodged federal soldiers in northern Idaho, eastern Washington, and western Montana. The battles that were fought were small, but the Indians often prevailed. In October 1877, Joseph and his group came almost within sight of the border with Canada. It was their intention to cross over to the more friendly people of "Mother Victoria." Joseph and his people were caught at Bear Mountain, however, and he did go onto a reservation, where he spent the rest of his life. It was at this time that white Americans began to express sympathy for the defeated Indians.

IDAHO IN THE
LIFE OF THE NATION

How difficult was it for Idaho to attain statehood?

The process took longer than expected, but there was little conflict over the matter. By 1890, Idaho had nearly 90,000 inhabitants, more than enough to apply for statehood, and the Gem State entered the Union on July 3 of that year.

Did things begin to settle down once the Indians were all on reservations?

No. The next set of conflicts, and perhaps an even more severe set, was between miners and the owners of the mines. Gold, silver, and quartz were all found in Idaho, and perhaps one-tenth of all the male residents were miners by the year 1900. Just one year prior to that, Governor Frank Steunenberg called in federal troops to assist in preventing disorder during a series of miners' strikes. And five years after, the governor—who had recently left office—was assassinated when someone rigged a bomb to the front gate of his home.

I never knew that the Gem State had such a violent history. Why isn't it more publicized?

Perhaps because there are no great or visible heroes to the situation. Most of us, naturally, sympathize with the miners rather than the mine owners, but there were desperadoes and hooligans among them as well. The International Workers of the World (IWW) seem like heroes in retrospect, but at the time they were viewed as dangerous people—and possible communists. The great story of the miners and their long battle for better working conditions is therefore little known.

How did Idaho fare during the First and Second World Wars?

The Gem State definitely benefited from World War I. The National Guard was quickly mobilized, and Idaho sent more than 20,000 men to fight in the Great War. World War II provided even greater opportunities for service (perhaps 50,000 Idahoans served), but the state's record was marred by the presence of several internment camps. These were built to house Japanese Americans whose loyalty was questioned. Considering it better to remove these people from the West Coast, the federal government built a number of camps, among them the Minidoka Camp in Idaho. But if the world wars were boosts to the economy of Idaho, the same cannot be said for the Great Depression of the 1930s.

How hard-hit was Idaho by the Great Depression?

We believe that all forty-eight of the American states (Alaska and Hawaii had not yet entered the Union) suffered, but there are some states where matters were much worse than others. Idaho was perhaps in the top half-dozen of states that suffered the most. Work in the mining camps practically ceased. Many young men took to the road as hobos, and it was often years before they returned. It was at this time that Idaho began to sport a number of ghost towns, which had once been prosperous mining communities. Silver City, Idaho, only has a dozen or so residents these days.

What is remarkable about the city of American Falls?

The town of American Falls was founded in 1800 near the west bank of the Snake River. Its centerpiece is a dam that was completed in 1926. To accommodate the construction of the 94-foot-high, 5,277-foot-long dam, the entire town moved in 1925! According to the city's website, 344 residents, 46 businesses, three hotels, one school, five churches, one hospital, six grain elevators, and one flour mill were moved to higher ground. The dam was completed sixty days ahead of schedule.

Did the federal government make a concerted effort to better living conditions for the people of Idaho?

Yes. President Franklin D. Roosevelt was especially interested in the Gem State. Though he did not live to see the result of his work, Idaho benefited from a number of federal agencies being located in Idaho over the next decade. One of the most significant of these was the National Reactor Testing Station, established near Arco in 1952.

Basque shepherds had already been coming to Idaho for two generations, and by the 1950s, they formed the second largest minority group in the state. Hispanics came in greater numbers during the 1970s and 1980s. But the single biggest change—so far as Idaho's pocketbook was concerned—was the influx of outdoorsmen.

How did Ernest Hemingway end up in Idaho? And has his family remained there?

Renowned author Ernest Hemingway is shown here typing his book *For Whom the Bell Tolls* in a Sun Valley, Idaho, lodge in 1939.

Hemingway was a tormented soul on several levels, a torment that he beautifully concealed by means of an ultra-masculine exterior. Born in Illinois, he'd lived in several parts of the country and had found some brief happiness in Key West, Florida. But by his mid-fifties, Hemingway was desperate to get away from the mad rush of civilization and to find solace in the great American interior. He settled on Idaho and spent his last years in Ketchum. His family remained there after his death from suicide, in 1961.

Hemingway has many imitators, even today, in Key West—long-bearded men who shuffle about as if they were the great man of letters. He has even more admirers in Idaho, but these are the rugged outdoors sort who believe—as he did—that man must live the strenuous life in order to become his best self. Even today, a half century after Hemingway's death, one can still find hikers, backpackers, and wildcat miners who claim they are doing what Hemingway did.

The strenuous life may have its benefits, but don't the people of Idaho already face enough challenges from the natural world?

That's what most of us—the less-rugged of people—believe. Idaho experiences flash floods and terrible forest fires. Ninety-one people died at the cave-in of the Sunshine Silver Mine in 1972. The state also suffers from frequent droughts. None of this deters the typical Idahoan, however. He or she knows the risks and chooses to disregard them.

From aerial photographs, the southern part of Idaho seems extremely dry. How did it ever become so well-known for its potatoes?

Tubers can thrive under many conditions, but they are especially successful in areas that combine brilliant sunshine with cool nights, and Idaho has this particular combination. Irrigation was needed—it is true—to maximize the potential of Idaho's agriculture, and the completion of the Minidoka Dam in 1906 was a big step forward. At about the same time, the lumber industry thrived in Idaho, and there was plenty of work available right up to the start of the Great Depression.

The completion of the first paved road, connecting the northern and southern parts of the state, was a major landmark, but Idaho struggled throughout the Great Depression. Not until World War II put a premium on the delivery of foodstuffs did the potato industry recover from the depths to which it had sunk.

What was life in Idaho like at the turn of the twenty-first century?

It was much calmer than in the past. There were some survivalist groups, usually tucked away in the mountains, but the Gem State had taken on a more "normal" appearance than in previous decades. Outdoor sports continued to be the rage.

Where will the Gem State be a generation from now?

Idaho passed the one million mark in population just in time for its 100th anniversary, in 1990, and the population has been growing steadily. The chances are that Idaho will hit two million by the census of 2030. As to the quality of life there, the chances are that these will be the same rugged, cheerful, and adaptable folk that we know today.

ILLINOIS

Nicknames: "The Tall State"; "The Prairie State"; "Land of Lincoln"
Capital: Springfield
Statehood: December 3, 1818; 21st state

AT A GLANCE

Which of the nicknames is used most commonly?

The Land of Lincoln remains a popular favorite. The people of Illinois like to be connected with the image of Abraham Lincoln, especially in the early and middle sections of his career. For his part, Lincoln clearly loved the city of Springfield; he made a memorable speech to its residents before leaving for the White House, in 1861.

What are the major symbols of the Tall State?

"State Sovereignty, National Union" is the state motto. The cardinal is the state bird and the native violet is the state flower. The white oak is the state tree.

How large, or small, is Illinois?

At 56,354 square miles (145,956 square kilometers), Illinois is twenty-fourth among the fifty states in geographic size. As of the year 2010, there were 12,830,632 residents, making Illinois fifth among the states in terms of population.

Is there any one place from which one can view the grandeur that is Illinois?

Actually there are two. The first is a soaring tower and the second is a crowded city area. Between them, the visitor or tourist can take it all in.

The Willis Tower, still commonly referred to as the Sears Tower, in downtown Chicago, was once the tallest building in the entire world. As of 2016, it was the fourteenth tallest in the world (but second in the United States), but that doesn't detract from the amazing view one enjoys from the observation deck. Standing up there on a cloudless day, one can see all the way to Evanston in the north, and the entire metropolitan sprawl lies at his or her feet. Lake Michigan beckons to the right, or east. And if this is not sufficient, one can travel to Springfield, the capital, in just a few hours' time, there to see the streets and even the home of Abraham Lincoln before he became the twelfth president of the United States.

What makes Illinois different from its neighbors, such as Indiana and Wisconsin?

Illinoisans like to think of their state as the center of the American Heartland, and they are not far mistaken. Illinois lies at the juncture, or meeting place, between the soft rolling hills of the Midwest and the bigger, wilder country that lies on the west side of the Mississippi River. Long before present-day Illinoisans gained their vanity, quite a few Native Americans may have felt the same way. It is no accident, surely, that the largest of all Indian ceremonial mounds is in Illinois, or that some of the oldest artifacts from prehistoric Indians are located in the region.

The natural beauty is obvious—anyone can appreciate it—but Illinois holds several dangers, both for the casual tourist and the longtime resident. The first is tornadoes, which strike the state with great frequency during the summer months. Downtown Chicago does not experience many tornadoes, but most summer mornings one awakes to massive rolls of thunder and the occasional rain shower, due to Chicago's proximity to where warm air from the south collides with cool air coming off Lake Michigan. The second major hazard is posed by flooding, which tends to occur in the spring months. The Mississippi River has overflowed its banks many times; the most dangerous floods were in 1927 and 1993.

Is the weather a big topic of interest to people in Illinois?

It is. During the summer, some of the hottest of all temperatures are recorded in and around Chicago. The summer of 1995 was notorious for hundreds of deaths, mainly among the elderly. And wintertime, if possible, is even worse. There's nothing like Chicago during a blizzard, and the locals eventually run out of places to put the snow. So even though they are veterans at handling the weather, Illinoisans discuss it a great deal.

What are the highest and lowest temperatures ever recorded in Illinois?

On July 14, 1954, the mercury rose to 114 degrees F (47 degrees C) at East St. Louis. The locals swore that it was even hotter. And on January 5, 1999, the temperature sank to –36 degrees F (–38 degrees C) at Congerville.

Is the city of Chicago really a state unto itself?

This has long been asked. There are recent immigrants who know a great deal about downtown Chicago but who have never strolled a farm field in the state. Likewise, there

Chicago, one of the nation's most populous cities, has a flavor all its own compared to the rest of Illinois.

are natives of small towns who have never been in the big city. Unlike its East Coast counterparts, such as Boston and New York, Chicago grew up as a "farmer's town," and it has never entirely lost its agrarian connections. The stockyards of Chicago used to be the center for the meat industry in the United States; today the area is just as likely to be populated by well-coifed stockbrokers, dealing in agricultural futures.

It's safe to say that the people of Illinois have a love-hate relationship with the metropolis. They know, of course, that it provides much of the wealth and energy that makes their state hum; they are also aware that many of their tax dollars fund its lavish projects. Theirs is a relationship not made in heaven, but one that makes sense on earth, meaning the rich farmland of Illinois.

EARLY HISTORY

For how long have humans inhabited what we call the state of Illinois?

For roughly 12,000 years. This number has to be provisional, because future archeological discoveries might be made. But we are quite confident that Illinois is one of the longest-settled of all the states, and that its early inhabitants were more successful in   129 creating a lasting culture than many of their contemporaries. The best evidence for this exists at Monk's Mound, in East St. Louis.

Undiscovered by white peoples until 1811, Monk's Mound is named for a group of Roman Catholic friars who stumbled on the earthen structures in East St. Louis. Slowly, they unraveled the mysteries, and eventually they realized that the central mound occupies nearly fourteen acres. Cahokia—as we moderns call it—could have housed up to 20,000 people, but we suspect that they never gathered there for very long, that Cahokia was a ceremonial center to which various Indian peoples from the Midwest came during the months of high summer.

Why were these mounds abandoned?

We aren't certain, but the best evidence available suggests that the Native Americans left the area during a period of prolonged drought; dendrochronology—or the study of tree rings—provides much of our evidence in this regard. Cahokia probably went through a lengthy period of gradual decline and was completely abandoned by about 1450 c.e. It then lay empty for centuries, until the Trappist monks discovered the place.

No less an authority than Thomas Jefferson was thoroughly flummoxed when he got the news. The Indians he met during his lifetime seemed incapable of organizing and building on a massive scale. Jefferson, therefore, believed that Cahokia was probably built by some early race of super-folk, who disappeared. Today's explanation is much more prosaic. The Indians who built Cahokia melted away, leaving their descendants in ignorance about how the mounds were built.

When did the first Europeans arrive, and what did they find?

The Spaniards, in all their early explorations, never made it to Illinois, and it was Frenchmen, fur trappers, and traders primarily who first arrived in the Tall State. They came from Quebec and Montreal, on canoe journeys that totaled around 1,200 miles. Arriving at the site of what is now Chicago, they recognized its importance and value but were eager to press on.

Father Jacques Marquette and Louis Joliet led the first organized mapping expedition in 1673. They were the first Europeans to see the northern section of the Mississippi River. They were followed by René-Robert Cavelier de La Salle, who canoed down the length of the Mississippi in 1682, and, upon arriving at the Gulf of Mexico, grandly claimed the land and all the waters that drained into it for France.

Could Illinois have become the center of a real French empire in North America?

Given time, France might have sent enough settlers to make a go of it. But the very speed and rapidity that brought the dauntless fur traders all the way to the American Heartland also trapped them there in the center of the continent. Their connections to Quebec and Montreal were tenuous at best. Even so, if the Louisiana colony, which began to develop around the year 1718, had come on strong and fast, there is a chance that France would have established a great ring through the American Heartland, and that many of us today would speak French!

Up until about 1750, France enjoyed a tenuous monopoly on the fur trade in the Midwest, but the English and their Indian allies, who included the Six Nations of Iroquois, were eager to break it. The French and Indian War—the final of the four conflicts—ended in 1763, with complete victory for England, and all the regions of Canada and the Midwest passed, on paper at least, to the British crown. Just to make sure everyone understood he was sovereign, the young King George III issued the Proclamation of 1763, prohibiting his white American subjects from crossing the crest of the Appalachian Mountains. Few people paid him much attention.

How much of a role did Illinois play in the American Revolution?

Though it was far from statehood, and there were only a few hundred setters at most, Illinois was important: it proved the linchpin in the fight for the American Midwest. The British started with the advantage, possessing several forts in the region, but the American revolutionaries struck hard and fast. Led by Colonel George Rogers Clark, American forces captured Vincennes, Indiana, and Kaskaskia, Illinois, in the summer of 1778. The British made a counterattack, and repossessed Vincennes, but Clark led a daring late winter campaign that culminated in the repossession of the fort. As a result, the Peace of Paris, in 1763, gave most of the American Heartland—on paper—to the Americans.

When did Anglo-Americans start coming to Illinois?

The area was part of the Old Northwest Territory, sectioned off by the U.S. Congress in 1787, but it was not until about 1810 that many settlers went as far as Illinois. Those who did had to take extra care during the War of 1812, but when that conflict ended, the way toward Anglo settlement of the Heartland was assured. Numerous chroniclers report that 1816 and 1817 were the critical years, in which pioneers went farther and faster than ever before; some of this was in response to the terrible "Year without a Summer," as 1816 is called, a time of unseasonably lower temperatures.

What did the Native Americans think about all these changes in sovereignty, from French to British to American, and so forth?

Most of them were blissfully unaware that the European powers claimed sovereignty. It seemed ludicrous, on the face of it, that a power so distant as Great Britain could possess Illinois. But if they had to choose between the three major groups, the Indians generally preferred the French, who, on the whole, took up less room and changed the landscape less than the others.

Quite a few of them are. That he was an immensely strong young man, a superior wrestler, and something of a local wit are all well-testified to. That he split rails for a living remains in doubt. There is no question, however, that Lincoln was, at the time of his election in 1860, the roughest, toughest frontier person elected to the presidency since George Washington pulled off the same feat, many decades earlier.

Most of us know that Abraham Lincoln became the quintessential man from Illinois, but he was actually born in Kentucky and spent his adolescence in Indiana. As a young man, Lincoln moved to Illinois and never looked back. He spent some years in Salem, and then moved to Springfield, the up-and-coming territorial capital.

When did Lincoln become known nationally?

Although Abraham Lincoln served in Washington, D.C., as a U.S. representative from Illinois's Seventh District, he served only one term, in 1847–1849. After his term was up, he worked as a lawyer, but he started to gain prominence nationally in subsequent years, albeit in unsuccessful attempts for higher office. He lost as a Whig candidate for the U.S. Senate in 1854, and he came in second place in his attempt to be the new Republican Party's vice presidential nominee in 1856. But it was in 1858 that Lincoln's fame spread nationally, when he ran as a Republican against incumbent Democratic senator Stephen A. Douglas. The two of them participated in seven debates—arguably the most famous debates ever in American politics. Lincoln lost to Douglas, but his grasp of the issues of the day led to him being his party's nominee—and eventual victor—in the 1860 presidential campaign.

How important is Lincoln, and the memory of the Civil War, to the identity of Illinois?

The two can hardly be exaggerated. Lincoln was, and remains, the greatest of all Illinois heroes, and the Civil War was the furnace in which Illinois tested its greatness. Many

While President Abraham Lincoln was actually born in Kentucky, he spent much of his early life, as well as legal and political career, in Illinois and is forever associated with this state that calls itself "The Land of Lincoln."

thousands of Illinoisans served in the War Between the States, and they generally gave better than they received. Cairo, Illinois, located right where the Ohio and Mississippi rivers come together, was a prime location, and Ulysses S. Grant seized it while he was still only a colonel. The Civil War never saw battle in Illinois, but a Confederate prison was located in Rock Island. Almost 2,000 prisoners and guards from the prison are buried in the nearby Rock Island National Cemetery. The Tall State did powerful work in the war, and by 1865, Illinois was the third most prosperous of the industrial states. Eighty percent of the state's lands were still used for farming, but the great metropolis of Chicago was on its way to becoming the giant of the region.

An 1871 photo showing destruction at the corner of Dearborn and Monroe Streets after the Great Chicago Fire.

What was the worst day in Illinois history?

Beyond a doubt this was September 9, 1871, the date of the Chicago Fire. Early and Victorian America were filled with city fires, but the one that lay parts of Chicago in ashes was perhaps the worst of all. We believe that the fire began in Mrs. Catherine O'Leary's barn (indicating the continuing connection between urban and rural) and we know that it spread fast, fueled by lively breezes coming off Lake Michigan. Hundreds of acres of city buildings were destroyed, and roughly 300 people died, in one of the greatest of all municipal disasters. Those who viewed the wreckage believed Chicago would never rise from the ruins, but the city proved them wrong in record time.

When was the high point for Chicago, the time when it became known as the City of the Big Shoulders?

The poet Carl Sandburg gave it this title in 1915; by then, Chicago was one of the fastest-growing cities in the entire world. The stockyards held the beef cattle from five surrounding states, and the many trains entering and exiting carried vast amounts of produce. Lake Michigan was filled with ships of all sizes, most of them bringing goods or carrying them away. Chicago was a magnificent, sprawling sight, but there was plenty of filth alongside the wealth. Were it not for the Chicago School of Architecture, the city might have languished.

We naturally associate skyscrapers with Manhattan, but Chicago is actually the birthplace of the modern skyscraper. Early on, Chicago architects learned how to build tall and lean, and to pitch the buildings so the terrible winds from Lake Michigan would not shatter the glass windows.

When did Chicago become the center for market retail?

Sears, Roebuck and Co., Marshall Field, and numerous other department stores flourished toward the end of the nineteenth century. Many of the great Chicago fortunes were made by outsiders, like Marshall Field, who then spent lavishly on making Chicago gleam. The Art Institute of Chicago and the Field Museum date from the early twentieth century.

Chicago was the pioneer in mail order catalogs, whereby the consumer could shop from the convenience of his or her living room. Though some East Coast elite persons continued to favor their local stores, there was a time when Chicago seemed ready to take over the entire retail clothing industry.

How did Illinois fare during World War I and World War II?

Both world wars were boom times for the Tall State, both because of the army training camps and thanks to the demand for foodstuffs. Chicago became better-known to the American public as well. But in-between the two world wars was the Great Depression, and it was a truly terrible time for many people in Illinois.

Farm prices fell steadily for almost five years, and many family farms went bankrupt. Matters inside the great metropolis were, if anything, even worse, with numerous bank failures and store closings. This was also the period when greater Chicago was known as the worst of all cities, where mobs and gangs were concerned. The Federal Bureau of Investigation (FBI) grew out of the intense need to keep up with the gangsters.

How easy, or difficult, was it to make a living in Illinois in the 1950s and 1960s?

For many people, suburban whites especially, it seemed like a dream. The suburbs expanded out from Chicago in one concentric ring after another, and new shopping malls and department stores opened all the time. These were good times on the farm as well, and the Tall State prospered as never before. Only by around 1968 did it become apparent that many people, especially African Americans in the inner city, were being left far behind.

When did Chicago become the number-one city in the nation, as far as the African American population was concerned?

The 1920s saw a major migration of African Americans from the Deep South to the Midwest. Detroit, Michigan, and Gary, Indiana, received the greatest numbers at first, but by the late 1930s, Chicago was the destination of choice. The blacks who arrived found better-paying jobs than almost anywhere else, but their living conditions were mediocre at best, and in many cases these became worse as the century progressed. By about 1965, Chicago was a thoroughly segregated city, with the African American sections suffering from a lack of reliable housing and public transportation.

What was the worst single event in Illinois's political history?

In the summer of 1968, the Democratic National Convention, held in Chicago, resembled a circus, and at times a riot, rather than orderly proceedings. Army helicopters hovered overhead, and police fired tear gas as youthful protestors shouted, denouncing the whole event. Three people were killed—far fewer than could have been—but the event was, beyond a doubt, the most disgraceful in Chicago history.

When did the Chicago comeback begin?

As recently as 1975, Chicago seemed like a disaster zone. Apartments could be found on the cheap, because so many well-to-do people had fled the city. Ironically, this was the very period when the rock group Chicago sang of the wonders of growing up in a congested urban environment, with songs such as "Saturday in the Park." The turnaround began around 1985, with more people moving into the city than out, and the miracle that brought about the transformation began one year later, when *The Oprah Winfrey Show* broadcast for the first time. Never in American history has the fate of one great city been so intimately tied to the fortunes—nearly all of them good—of one person.

Born in rural Mississippi, Oprah—as she is known to hundreds of millions around the globe—had a hard-luck life till her mid-twenties. Finding her way into broadcasting, she became the center of her own show, and it's safe to say that neither popular culture nor the discussions about what constitute American culture have ever been the same. It helped that Oprah was African American, but it was her unusual blend of intelligence and warmth that made her a winner on television, just about every single afternoon. Her fans knew that *The Oprah Winfrey Show* was broadcast in Chicago, and the city suddenly became fashionable once more.

How important was Barack Obama to early twenty-first century Illinois?

To some Illinoisans, he was the second coming of Abraham Lincoln. Like Lincoln, Obama was a lawyer, keenly interested in the well-being of his clients. Like Lincoln, Obama came out of nowhere to become the nominee of a major party for the American presidency, and his election was seen as a watershed moment in American politics. And like Lincoln, Obama came into office at a time of national crisis (Lincoln faced the Civil War; Obama faced a financial crisis that rocked Wall Street to its very foundations).

Once in office, Obama displayed a more cautious, even conservative, side, meaning that he was more intent on preserving the good that existed than in taking major chances in order to create something new. Many Americans recognized him as a good steward, a leader who shepherded the nation through the financial crisis that began in 2008, but some were disappointed that his presidency took on a rather formal tone once he was in the White House.

We've mentioned Lincoln and Obama; what other American president has a connection to Illinois?

Popular contemporary Republican president Ronald Reagan was born in Illinois and lived there until after he graduated from college. He was born in Tampico, lived many years in Dixon (his boyhood home is open to the public), and received his college degree at Eureka College. From there, he moved to Des Moines, Iowa, to become a radio baseball announcer, and then he moved to California where he soon became an actor. His involvement in the Screen Actors Guild led to his interest in politics. He was the governor of California in 1967–1975 and he was U.S. president in 1981–1989.

Where will the Tall State be a generation from now?

The chances are that Illinois will do quite well. The state has an excellent balance between industry and agriculture, and its entertainment industry is beginning to grow. One of the key benchmarks to watch is the price of farm products. If rising populations around the world continue to produce increased demand, Illinois is likely to thrive.

INDIANA

AT A GLANCE

What are the most prominent signs and symbols of the Hoosier State?

"The Crossroads of America" is both the nickname of and the motto of the Hoosier State. The cardinal is the state bird, and the peony is the state flower. The tulip poplar is the state tree.

How large, or small, is the Hoosier State?

Comprising 36,184 square miles (93,716 square kilometers), Indiana is thirty-eighth among the fifty states in geographic size. Its population, as enumerated in 2010, of 6,483,802, places it fifteenth among the states.

What is the most spectacular sight to be seen in Indiana?

Natural enthusiasts can point to sections along the shore of Lake Michigan, and farming devotees can point to the rolling farmland of the central part of the state, but the nation as a whole identifies Indiana primarily with the Indianapolis 500, the most dramatic and intense of all automobile races. Run on the Sunday before Memorial Day, the Indy 500 has seen amazing feats, as well as some terrible failures and deaths. It's the American Dream gone wild, the desire to move at almost insane speeds, and to do so time and again, in the town called Speedway.

Indiana is a heartland state, and it also forms the dividing line between the various sections of the Midwest. To its east lies Ohio and to its west is Illinois. Indiana has, quite likely, seen more people pass through its fields and over its roads than have settled there: not for nothing is it called the Crossroads of America. There is yet another way in which Indiana is the center, however, and this has to do with geography and water tables. At a subtle, easily missed point in the northern part of the state, a water divide takes place, with the rivers in one direction turning to Lake Michigan and eventually the St. Lawrence River, and those in the other heading toward the Ohio River, the Mississippi, and the Gulf of Mexico.

Indianans are extremely proud of their Hoosier basketball team.

Do Hoosiers talk about the weather very much?

It's one of their favorite topics of conversation, with Big Ten Basketball not far behind. Indiana has warm but not unbearable summers; its winters, likewise, are moderate. A major degree of difference can be seen in the amount of snowfall, with northern sections receiving about forty inches of snow, and southern ones getting one-fourth that amount. Indiana is also known for its tornadoes, but they are not, generally speaking, of the devastating type known on the western side of the Mississippi River. The hottest day ever recorded was July 14, 1936, when the mercury rose to 116 degrees F (47 degrees C) at Collegeville. The coldest was at New Whiteland, where the temperature fell to –36 degrees F (–38 degrees C) on January 19, 1994.

Where does the term "Hoosier" come from?

We really don't know. At least a dozen different explanations have been offered over time, and while all of them have some strength and solidity, none has ever been shown conclusively to be the source. Perhaps the most appealing of the possibilities is that when a person entered an Indiana log cabin the occupants called out "Who is there?" and did so in a dialect that eventually shortened it to "Hoosier."

Who are some of the best-loved sons and daughters of Indiana?

William Henry Harrison and his grandson, Benjamin Harrison, each served as U.S. president. Though neither was born in Indiana, both lived there. The Hoosier State is sometimes called the Land of Vice Presidents. Schuyler Colfax served as Ulysses S. Grant's number-two man during his first term (1869–1873). Thomas A. Hendricks was elected vice president with Grover Cleveland in 1884, but he died not quite nine months into his term. Charles W. Fairbanks was elected vice president in 1904; he served one term, under President Theodore Roosevelt. And in 1912, Thomas R. Marshall was elected on the ticket with Democratic nominee Woodrow Wilson and went on to serve two terms. In modern times, Dan Quayle was elected vice president in 1988 under George H. W. Bush. These five men were all active in Indiana politics before becoming vice president; only Marshall and Quayle were born there.

Is the Hoosier a recognizable type? Can he or she be picked out of the crowd?

Not these days. A century or so in the past, however, the Hoosier was quickly identified. He or she was the country person in the mix, showing little sign of sophistication. Along with this went an undeniable charm, a naiveté that appealed to most observers. We often forget that Abe Lincoln spent his teenage years in Indiana, and that the mix of intelligence and awkwardness he brought to the White House was as much Indiana as Illinois.

EARLY HISTORY

For how long have humans lived in what we now call the Crossroads of America?

Perhaps 12,000 years. Their names are unknown to us, but they left evidence in the burial grounds and ceremonial sites that crop up around the Hoosier State. These early Native Americans, almost certainly descendants of those who crossed the Bering Land Bridge, farmed a bit, but lived more by hunting and fishing, and they had plenty of sustenance.

When the first European explorers arrived, they found at least half a dozen tribes in the Indiana region, but some of these were transitory groups, migrating south in winter. The French fur trappers and traders who came in the 1680s were not in search of farmland—they wanted to strike it rich quick—but they soon realized the potential of the Indiana area, where almost everything grew faster and matured better than in other parts of the Midwest.

Was there any chance Indiana could have become part of a French empire, stretching over the American Heartland?

The energy and drive of the fur merchants and the missionaries suggests that it was possible, but France's reach exceeded its grasp. The single biggest difficulty was that rather few French men or women wished to leave the homeland, and the stories they heard of the terrible winters in Quebec and Montreal disinclined even them. The French enjoyed the glory of being the first travelers and settlers, but they never came in large enough numbers. Had they done so, the history of North America might have been rather different.

Who were the first English, or Anglo-Americans, to see this region?

The people of the Thirteen Colonies seemed unbearably slow compared to the French. While La Salle was canoeing down the Mississippi River, in 1682, the Anglo colonies hugged only a narrow section of the East Coast. The English settlement pattern proved superior in the end, however, and this is because they really took over the land, transforming it. This is one reason that the Native Americans, in many places at least, preferred the French.

When did Indiana become part of the struggle between England and France?

Not until the French and Indian War (1754–1763), and even then almost no battles or skirmishes were fought in the Hoosier State. The Peace of Paris, in 1763, transferred the area, at least on paper, from France to England. King George III promptly issued the Proclamation of 1763, prohibiting his Anglo-American subjects from crossing the Appalachians into the Midwest, but few people paid much attention. The stories they heard about the soil in the Midwest were just too good.

What role did Indiana play in the Revolutionary War?

The British were all-too-aware of the importance of the region. Colonel Henry Hamilton, based out of Detroit, became known as "Hamilton the Hair-Buyer" because of the money he paid Indians for American scalps. But in 1778–1779, George Rogers Clark led American militia forces to victory at Kaskaskia and Vincennes. Clark's victories ensured that most of the Midwest would be American territory when the war ended.

The first trickle of American settlers arrived in the 1790s, and in 1800 Indiana was sectioned off from the Ohio Territory and given territorial status. The Virginia-born William Henry Harrison served as the first territorial governor.

Who were Tecumseh and Tenskwatawa?

They were Shawnee Indians and brothers, born to the same parents. Both grew up in the time when Indiana seesawed between Indian and white control, but they came to maturity at the time when the latter had the upper hand. Tecumseh, the elder brother, seemed the more likely leader, but Tenskwatawa, whose name means "Open Door," experienced a series of religious revelations around the year 1803, and he became known as The

How did Virginia get to play so large a role in the development of other states, particularly in the Midwest?

It has much to do with Virginia's population, largest of the original thirteen colonies. Virginia also fostered a large number of daring frontiersmen, ranging from the young George Washington to George Rogers Clark and his younger brother, William Clark, of Lewis and Clark fame. During the first decade of the nineteenth century, Virginians were the most active and most recognized of all frontier Americans, and their actions had consequences that went well beyond the Old Dominion State.

Prophet to the Shawnee. Though he had previously been an alcoholic, and considered a lost cause, Tenskwatawa now became the hope of the Shawnee. Unlike many other Indian leaders, he considered a tribal confederacy the only answer. He also taught that the Indians should refrain not only from the white man's goods, but from all forms of contact. Tecumseh had previously been the leader of the family; he and his brother now became coequals.

How did the Battle of Tippecanoe come about?

In the summer of 1811, Tecumseh embarked on a journey to the Southeast, visiting all the tribes that remained in that region. To all, he preached the message of

Tecumseh was a great Indian leader of the Shawnee.

his brother and of the necessity to form a powerful Indian confederacy. Tecumseh strictly enjoined his younger brother not to engage in conflict while he was on this mission, but Tenskwatawa had no choice. Territorial governor William Henry Harrison, learning that Tecumseh was gone, gathered a militia army and marched on Prophetstown, in present-day Lafayette, Indiana. Tenskwatawa's warriors gave battle on November 11, 1811, and though the battle was not a clear-cut victory, Harrison was able to burn Prophetstown in the aftermath. As a result, Tecumseh returned from the Southeast to find that the tribal alliances in the north were in disarray, to say the least.

What happened to the Shawnee brothers?

Tecumseh joined the British cause during the War of 1812 and was made a brigadier general. He fought valiantly but was defeated and killed at the Battle of the Thames River (in Ontario) in October 1813. His younger brother lived many years afterward, but he never again played a leading role among the Midwest Indians. With the death of Tecumseh, the best hope of the Midwest Indians faded, never to return.

INDIANA IN THE LIFE OF THE NATION

How did Indiana fare in the antebellum years, the decades prior to the start of the American Civil War?

Indiana was one of the big success stories; each successive U.S. Census recorded another significant rise. The number of farms and farm animals grew as well. And as late as 1859, one could still describe Indiana as the heart of the heartland, the center of the Midwest. Just one year later, however, when Chicago hosted the second Republican national convention, that honor shifted to Illinois.

Once the Civil War began, Indiana showed its stuff, providing nearly 400,000 young men to the Union cause. Indiana did not have as many generals or outstanding heroes as its eastern neighbor, Ohio, but at the regimental level, Indiana was second to none.

What makes the University of Notre Dame unique, and who put the university's football team on the map?

Notre Dame is one of the great anomalies in American higher education—a thoroughly Roman Catholic university set right in the middle of the Protestant heartland, a school that prides itself to the max on academics, but which has perhaps the most crazed fans of any university, anywhere. Notre Dame began quietly enough, as a place for young men to learn about the world while concentrating on the unseen hand of God. But in the 1920s, led by legendary coach Knute Rockne, Notre Dame became known for its football team, and the Fighting Irish have been successful ever since.

How did Indianans fare in the decades that followed the Civil War?

This was a period of slow decline. Indiana had already become third-place—to Ohio and Illinois—in population; its fine agricultural fields continued to produce wonderful products, but the state itself languished toward the end of the nineteenth century. Of all the Midwestern states on the east side of the Mississippi River, Indiana was the one that came closest to a farmer's revolt in the 1890s, making it more akin to Nebraska and Kansas than its close neighbors. But the real surprise, as far as observers of the Hoosier State were concerned, was the rather sudden rise of the Ku Klux Klan (KKK).

I don't think of the KKK in connection with the Midwest. How did this happen?

Indiana, in the years immediately following World War I, became the center of a new KKK, one that directed its anger as much at foreigners, Catholics, and Jews as it did at African Americans. For a time, there were 4 million members of the new KKK, and a great many of them lived in Indiana. When the Grand Wizard of the KKK was arrested on charges of having sex with a minor, the phenomenon faded, but Indiana did not regain its good name for many years.

How did the city of Gary get established?

The great majority of American cities—perhaps as much as 98 percent—have evolved over time, in response to different needs, demands, and waves of immigrants. Gary is one of the few exceptions to the rule: it was an entirely planned city, with U.S. Steel Corporation acting both as the benefactor and as the likely recipient of the wealth that could be generated when it built a new plant.

How important is the Indy 500 to the economy—and the identity—of the Hoosier State?

Very few people predicted its emergence, but it makes sense in retrospect. Some of the first automobiles were produced in the Midwestern states, which also had some of the finest mechanics and engineers (Purdue University turned out many of them). So when the Indianapolis 500 was run for the first time, in 1911, it's not surprising that the fans went pretty crazy. That first surface was very much where the present one is today, with the difference being in the speed of the vehicles. The first Indy 500 was won with a racing time of 6 hours and 42 minutes.

What happened to the railroads that once crisscrossed Indiana?

They are still there, but they carry more freight than passengers. Indiana benefited from the early part of railroad history because so many trains came through the state. But over time quite a few Hoosiers began to complain that the trains brought as many problems as they solved. There have been a number of environmental clean-ups, for example.

What else crisscrosses Indiana?

Highways! More major highways intersect in the Hoosier State than in any other state in the union. There are also more interstate highways (14) per square mile in Indiana than anywhere else.

One of the most famous races in the world, the Indy 500 is a great tourist draw and economic boon to the state.

Who is the best-known of all entertainment personalities from the Hoosier State?

Michael Jackson, beyond the shadow of a doubt. While still only six, he was practicing every day, urged on his by steel-making father and his older siblings. Jackson's voice was a winner from the very beginning (many fans still remember "I'll Be There," for example), but as he matured, he brought a new, aggressive style of dancing that became the rage during the 1980s.

Jackson entered a long period of decline around 1997. He went into seclusion and lived a mysterious life, far from the public view, until his death in 2009. His brothers and sisters, on the other hand, kept the music going, and continued to win praise for America's "first family of popular music."

What was the worst day in Indiana history?

In May 1974, Indiana was struck by a series of tornadoes that killed forty-eight people and caused more than $200 million in property damage. These tornadoes came at a time when the state was already in rather rough shape and they compounded the misery for many of the people involved.

How important was Dan Quayle to the image of the people of Indiana?

When he first appeared on the national scene in 1988, Senator Quayle seemed like the embodiment of Hoosier values; he had an excellent opportunity to present homespun values and virtues to a national audience. Quayle did not weather well, however; he often seemed poorly informed in policy debates, for example. Those who liked him at the beginning clung to him, however, and as the twentieth century came to an end, he was still the more recognizable Hoosier on the political scene.

On the Democratic side, Senator Birch Bayh had a long and distinguished career. Many Democrats hoped he would be their standard-bearer in 2004 or 2008, but he backed away from the national scene.

What other Hoosier became a famous television personality?

David Letterman was born in Indianapolis, went to Ball State University, was a race car enthusiast, and was a radio talk show host and television weatherman in his native city, before he headed to California to go into show business. He turned to comedy writing, then caught the eye of Johnny Carson who had him fill in as his occasional guest host. Letterman got his own morning show on NBC before becoming a late-night host on NBC and CBS. He retired in 2015. Throughout it all, his love for Indiana always shone through, as he frequently rooted for Ball State on his show and became part owner of an Indianapolis 500 racing team.

What was life in Indiana like at the turn of the twenty-first century?

The Hoosier State had its critics, who alleged that nothing had changed, and the state
was doomed to suffer from cultural paralysis. Admirers pointed to the state's bountiful

agricultural land and declared there would always be a place for states such as this one. The truth probably lies somewhere between the two extremes. Like other Midwestern states, Indiana has lost population, not in absolute terms but relative to the national average. Indiana has often found ways to reinvent itself, but the needs are more pressing than ever before.

Where will the Hoosier State be a generation from now?

The chances are that the Hoosier State will squeak through, but the chances it will flourish are remote. Indiana experienced much economic dislocation and relocation over the past century, and this seems likely to continue. Indianans like to remain loyal to their home state, however, and it's likely there will always be people proud to call themselves Hoosiers.

IOWA

IOWA

Nickname: "The Hawkeye State"
Capital: Des Moines
Statehood: December 28, 1846; 29th state

AT A GLANCE

What are some of the most important signs and symbols of the Hawkeye State?

"Our liberties we prize and our rights we will maintain" is the state motto. It suggests the importance of states' rights. Even as states fought for the Union in the Civil War, quite a few states wished to stand for their rights. The eastern goldfinch is the state bird, and the wild rose is the state flower. The oak is the official state tree.

How large, or small, is Iowa?

Comprising 56,273 square miles (145,746 square kilometers) Iowa is twenty-fifth among the states in geographic size. The population of 3,046,355, as enumerated in the census of 2010, places Iowa at thirtieth among the states in terms of population.

Why does Iowa receive so little attention from the rest of the nation?

It has a lot to do with the time that Iowa achieved statehood. If the Hawkeye State had entered the Union even a decade earlier, it would have received a lot of attention, as the first state to be formed on the western side of the Mississippi River. Then, too, Iowa would have been hailed as the bounteous place from which the nation's corn supply later would come. But Iowa entered the Union in 1846, when the Mexican War was six months old. Much more attention went to the war with Mexico than to the admission of the Hawkeye State. And, just two years later, California suddenly became big news thanks to the discovery of gold near Sacramento. As a result, Iowa lost its "big" moment, and the same can be said through much of its subsequent history.

Where does the state nickname come from?

This remains a subject of considerable debate. There are those who claim Hawkeye derives from Chief Black Hawk, who led the Sauk Nation in one last fight against the white settlers in 1832. Others believe Hawkeye comes from the protagonist of James Fenimore Cooper's novel *Last of the Mohicans*. Given that many Americans were reading *Last of the Mohicans* around the time Iowa was first settled, the second explanation seems the more likely.

When did Iowa become so important in the selection of the American president?

Until the 1950s, the candidates of the major political parties were primarily selected by small groups of powerful and influential men, most of whom resided in big cities such

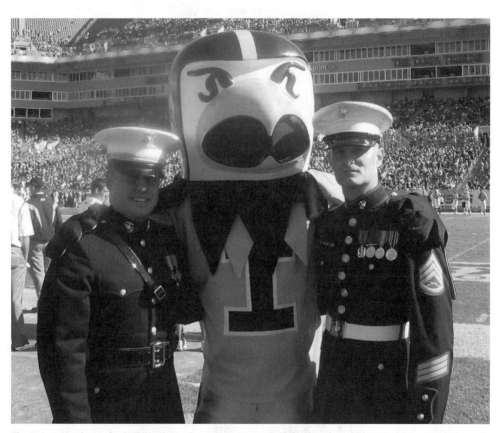

The University of Iowa football team's Hawkeye mascot poses with U.S. Marines. Although the Iowa nickname probably either came from a character in a James Fenimore Cooper novel or from Chief Black Hawk of the Sauk, as a mascot he is a hawk.

as Chicago and New York. When the primary system—in which the voters cast direct ballots—became popular in the 1960s, New Hampshire became the state that always holds the nation's first primary. Not to be outdone, the people of Iowa fought to have their party caucuses take place two weeks before the New Hampshire primary. Caucuses are different from primaries in that the voters caucus with one another, and then—when all the debates are finished—the people in that town hand all their votes, or delegates, to one candidate.

Will Iowa ever be known for something other than the long rows of cornfields that are featured in virtually all advertisements and descriptions of the state?

It already is. Not only do Iowa voters carry out the first caucuses of the national election year, but Iowa is known as the home of the Iowa Writers Conference, perhaps the most influential of all such programs. And while on the subject of art, one cannot omit naming one of the most popular of all American paintings. Iowa native Grant Wood's *American Gothic* displays a middle-aged farmer and his twenty-something daughter standing in front of their farmhouse. Both hold pitchforks, and they are unsmiling. Precisely what Wood intended this to achieve remains somewhat mysterious, but *American Gothic* has been commented upon and imitated almost since it first appeared in 1932.

EARLY HISTORY

For how long have humans lived in what we now call the Hawkeye State?

For perhaps 15,000 years. Most of the early Paleo-Indians are unknown to us, but we can say something about their descendants, the people who lived in Iowa when the first white explorers arrived. The first person of European descent to meet and describe them was Father Jacques Marquette, who, along with Louis Joliet, arrived in what is now Iowa in June 1673. The two Frenchmen quickly noted the difference as well as the rivalry between the Indians who lived along the Mississippi River and those who lived in the hinterlands. The Sauk and Fox Indians were most numerous among the former, and the Sioux predominated among the latter. Neither of these groups had yet acquired

Father Jacques Marquette was the first European to encounter Indians in what is now Iowa.

149

horses (that occurred two generations later), but the Sioux were already known as one of the most aggressive of all tribal groups.

Why don't we—today—see more signs of the years when Iowa was a French territory?

Marquette and Joliet arrived in 1673, and René-Robert Cavelier de La Salle claimed the entire area for France in 1682, but very few Frenchmen—and almost no women—came to back up the claim. France had its hands full with the Louisiana and Illinois areas, neither of which it could truly populate. An aggressive policy on the west bank of the Mississippi River was therefore out of the question.

France maintained a very loose hegemony for more than fifty years, but the end of the French and Indian War, in 1763, spelled the end of its rule. The entire Louisiana area, including Iowa, then passed to Spain, which maintained an even looser and less vigorous command of the region. It was during the Spanish era that Iowa saw its first true settler, as compared to explorer. Julien Dubuque settled on the west side of the Mississippi River in 1788 and commenced to establish a series of lead mines. He prospered over the years, selling the lead to merchants in St. Louis.

Was the name Iowa even known to the men who effected the Louisiana Purchase in 1803?

The Americans who purchased the vast Louisiana area from France may have seen Iowa on a map or two, but it meant nothing special to them; the real prize was the Louisiana Territory itself. But to anyone who studies the treaty, it seems incredible that Napoleon Bonaparte would part with so vast an area, for the trifling sum of $15 million.

Iowa started to see a handful of settlers during the 1820s, but the area did not carry the name by which we know it today. What we call Iowa was first part of the Louisiana Purchase, then part of the Missouri Territory (1812–1821), and then part of the Territory of Michigan (1834–1836). Not until 1838 was the Territory of Iowa established, and it took another eight years before Iowa achieved statehood.

Didn't anyone realize the incredible fertility of this state, which now possessed one-quarter of all the Grade 1 agricultural land in the United States?

They did not. Other areas—in Illinois and Indiana—possessed such fine soil that very few people paid attention to Iowa in these early decades. It took the Black Hawk War to bring that fact to people's attention.

In April 1832, Chief Black Hawk led Sauk and Fox warriors across the Mississippi, from Iowa into Illinois and Wisconsin. Black Hawk achieved considerable success for a season, but his victories had the result of galvanizing the militia of all the nearby states (the young Abraham Lincoln was one of many men who later claimed the Black Hawk War as the time when they gained a national consciousness). Defeated, Black Hawk sur-

> **Is this how the typical white American viewed Black Hawk—as a noble person fighting for a lost cause?**
>
> That is how he was perceived by the people of Washington, D.C., and New York City, who had little, if any, reason to fear the Native Americans. The closer to the frontier one got, the more disliked Black Hawk was, and books written, even a half-century later, referred to him as just one step removed from barbarism.

rendered a good-sized chunk of what is now eastern Iowa. He was taken prisoner to Washington, D.C., where he became perhaps the first of all the great fighting chiefs to receive sympathy from the white American population. His portrait was painted by George Catlin, the foremost painter of men and women on the frontier.

Was there ever a chance Iowa would become one of the states where slavery was permitted?

Not one chance in ten. It cannot be said that the white people of Iowa were terribly sympathetic or friendly to African Americans. But the Missouri Compromise of 1820 was abundantly clear. No territory or state that allowed slavery would be permitted in any area north of 36 degrees, 30 minutes north latitude. And by the time statehood was achieved, many white Iowans prided themselves on being against the institution.

Statehood was achieved on December 28, 1846. Ansel Briggs was the first state governor. Iowa became the twenty-ninth state of the Union, and the fourth to be carved from the Louisiana Purchase. It was also the first state to come from the Louisiana Purchase that specifically forbade slavery.

IOWA IN THE LIFE OF THE NATION

How important was the Civil War to the people of Iowa?

Some of them, to be sure, did not care very much, and hoped only to avoid its effects. The majority of Iowans were enthusiastic for the Union cause, however, and they enlisted in significant numbers, in order to demonstrate their loyalty. Perhaps 40,000 men from Iowa served in the Civil War.

When did Iowa acquire the reputation it has today: as the land of rows of corn?

Iowa was a big producer of corn by the 1880s, but the nation did not catch up with Iowa till the 1920s. It was then that photographs of those long rows began to appear in national magazines. Much of that corn was shipped to Battle Creek, Michigan, and turned into breakfast cereal, and as Americans became ever keener for cereal, they became more aware of the Hawkeye State.

We all associate Iowa with corn, but what is it about Iowa and apples?

Oregon produces more apples, but Iowa is forever identified with the fruit, thanks to the new variety that appeared on Jesse Hiatt's farm, near East Peru, in the 1880s. He entered the new variety in a local contest, and it soon won the title of "Hawkeye." Years later, it was renamed the Delicious apple, and ever since it has been one of the most popular of American fruits.

Amidst the imagery of miles of cornfields, people might be surprised to learn there is an "Island City" in Iowa. Where is it?

Sabula is a small city on the Mississippi River on the Illinois border, about midway between Dubuque and the Quad Cities. Founded in 1835, it became an island city in the 1930s when a lock and dam was constructed, leading to the flooding of the lowlands area of Sabula. The city was once the site of a pearl button factory; fishermen would catch clams and sell the clams to hog-slaughtering businesses as feed and the pearls to the button factory. Plastic buttons ended the pearl button industry, but Sabula is now a tourist town, with nearby parks and camping.

Who is the only American president to come from the Hawkeye State?

Born in West Branch, Iowa, in 1874, Herbert Clark Hoover was the son of farmers. Orphaned at the age of nine, he spent time with a number of relatives in Iowa before moving to Oregon in his teen years. Throughout life, Hoover wore the clothing of the Quakers, the faith of his parents.

Hoover attainted stunning success in his twenties and thirties. He graduated from Stanford University, married a woman who majored in geology, and together they became successful mining engineers, as well as millionaires. By the time he became U.S. food administrator in World War I, Hoover was recognized as something of a genius; as secretary of commerce, he was called the "Wonder Boy." But all this success came crashing down when he became president of the United States in 1929.

Why was Hoover such a failure as president?

It was not due to hard-heartedness or personal meanness. Having lifted himself so spectacularly in life, Hoover found it diffi-

President Herbert Hoover was the only native Iowan to serve in the White House.

cult to understand the plight of millions of Americans, during the Great Depression. Then, too, he believed the federal government should play a small role in the economics of the nation. Hoover, therefore, did not combat the Great Depression, and when he left office in 1933, there were more unemployed than when he entered the White House.

Americans did not, generally speaking, blame the Hawkeye State for Hoover's failures. There were times in the 1930s, however, when Americans from far-off states heard of the plight of Iowa farmers and shrugged their shoulders, saying that they owed it to the man from West Branch.

Two first ladies were from Iowa; who were they?

President Hoover's wife, Lou Henry Hoover, was born in Waterloo in 1874. The wife of President Dwight D. Eisenhower, Mamie Doud Eisenhower, was born in Boone in 1896. Following a restoration in the late 1970s, the former first lady's house opened as a birthplace museum.

How did the Hawkeye State fare during World War I and World War II?

In both cases, Iowa was called upon to raise more corn and hogs than ever before, and both times the people of Iowa rose to the challenge. Among the states of Iowa, Nebraska, North Dakota, and South Dakota, they raised almost enough agricultural products to feed the U.S. Army.

What was the single biggest moment for Iowans during World War II?

Given that the Hawkeye State sent 261,000 men and 4,000 women into harm's way, there are doubtless thousands of individual stories from World War II. The heroism and patriotism of the state are best reflected, though, by the truly incredible sacrifice of Thomas and Alleta Sullivan. In 1943, they learned that all five of their sons—George, Francis, Joseph, Madison, and Albert—who ranged from twenty to twenty-nine years of age, were dead. All of them died when the cruiser *Juneau* sank, during the Battle of Guadalcanal. Thomas Sullivan went to work on the railroad that day; he later commented that for a person who had lost everything, work could be some solace.

The five Sullivan brothers had rushed to the naval recruiting station in the days immediately following the Japanese attack on Pearl Harbor. Remarkably, their sister, Genevieve, enlisted soon after it was discovered that the five brothers were dead.

How did Iowa fare in the decades that followed World War II?

The state experienced a mixture of up-and-down, but the signature story—one that appalled most observers—was the shrinking number of family farms. In 1940, there were more than 200,000 family farms in Iowa; this number was cut in half by 1970, and the decline only continued. The Hawkeye State continued to churn out even more agricultural product than in the past, but it was primarily achieved by large companies, which bought up family farms at an alarming rate.

153

What made one Iowa county famous?

The Bridges of Madison County was a best-selling novel written by Robert James Waller in 1992 that was made into a movie starring Clint Eastwood (who was also the director) and Meryl Streep. One of the key characters in the story is a photographer who is in Madison County to take pictures of its famous covered bridges. While the book and movie were fictional, the bridges really existed. There were once nineteen bridges; only six remain.

Madison County is also known as the birthplace of actor John Wayne, who was born in Winterset. His home and a museum are tourist attractions.

What was the worst overall experience Iowans had in modern times?

Beyond a doubt it was the summer of 1993, which saw flooding, both along the Mississippi and its many tributaries, to such an extent that observers called it "biblical" and a "once-in-a-century" event. The winter of 1993 was quite cold, with a good deal of precipitation, but it was the early spring rains that really upped the ante. Iowans were already tense by the Fourth of July, but it was the ten inches of rain that fell north and west of Des Moines, on July 8, that really spelled disaster. One levee after another was broken, and flood waters gushed not only into farm fields, but also right into small towns, sometimes carrying away entire houses.

Iowans worked as only they can, forming bucket brigades and long lines of men and women moving sandbags, but the effort could not keep up with the destruction. President Bill Clinton hastened to Iowa, but he could do little other than offer moral support. The flooding was beyond anything he—or any longtime Iowan—had ever seen.

How long did it take to "clean up" after the great floods of 1993?

The cleanup was effected within six months, but the long-term results were little short of disastrous. People who had planned to move to the Hawkeye State changed their minds, and insurance companies enacted whole new sets of provisions that virtually cancelled out what might be called flood insurance. In many cases, a major flood throws off one industry or sets back one or two counties; in this case, virtually the entire state was affected.

What was the biggest surprise associated with Iowa in the early twenty-first century?

The writer Dagoberto Gilb expressed it this way in *State by State: A Panoramic Portrait of America* (2008): "What I do visualize when I think of Iowa, like everyone, a cartoon image of it: corn and pigs and big farmers who eat hearty American food." On his first trip to the Hawkeye State, Gilb met plenty of those big farmers, but he also encountered far more Hispanics, Mexicans especially, than he ever anticipated. Writing in 2007, Gilb described the endless rows of corn, *and* the endless number of trucks that carried migrant workers to the fields. Though he found plenty of Cumberland Farms and Dunkin' Donuts, Gilb found even more Mexican businesses, with names like Aztec, Los

154

Pinos, and Fiesta Cancun. He soon realized that it was difficult to find Americans to perform the long hours of planting and harvesting, and that the Hawkeye State had a deep Mexican imprint.

What are some of the most dramatic moments associated with the Iowa caucuses?

Iowa has had a caucus system since the 1940s, and it sometimes seems like a throwback to a much earlier time. Unlike New Hampshire voters, who go to the polls to vote in secret, Iowans gather in their respective caucuses for several evenings in December and January of each general election year. The Iowa straw poll—as it is called—has been a favorite of political pundits for more than a generation. Surely, however, the caucuses of 2004 and 2008 were the most surprising.

In January 2004, Vermont governor Howard Dean seemed primed to secure the Democratic presidential nomination. Ahead in the polls for months, he began to slip during the days leading to the Iowa caucuses, and on the critical night, Dean learned he had come in third, with Massachusetts senator John F. Kerry in the lead. Dean gave a rousing speech that seemed just fine to his supporters in the room, but which played very badly on national television. At the end of his speech, Dean gave something like a war whoop, which spelled the end of his candidacy.

One bad move can ruin an entire campaign?

If one were to name all the campaigns that have been sabotaged by one bad move, it would make a long list. Dean did himself in in January 2004, and Barack Obama surged to the top of the group of Democratic contenders when he did the opposite, in January 2008. Front-runner Hillary Rodham Clinton—wife of former president Bill Clinton—seemed assured to win the Democratic nomination, but she stumbled badly in Iowa. Some observers declared that Iowa voters—who are about 98 percent white—would never select an African American candidate, but they were proven wrong. Obama came out of Iowa with momentum, and even though Hillary Clinton won the first primary, in New Hampshire, he secured the nomination in 2008.

What will the Hawkeye State look like a generation from now?

The chances are excellent that Iowa will remain what it is: the greatest of the Heartland states, meaning that it produces the most food. No matter how inexpensive the rent might be, it is difficult to imagine large corporations using sections of prime Iowa land for call centers or data processing. Wal-mart, too, may aspire to take over sections of Iowa, but it will never have the number of consumers necessary to fill the stores. Barring some truly unexpected event, Iowa will continue to be the state that seems most predictable—to the casual tourist—and which has some surprises up its sleeve.

KANSAS

Nickname: "The Sunflower State"
Capital: Topeka
Statehood: January 29, 1861; 34th state

AT A GLANCE

Where does the state nickname come from?

Almost all the early explorers and settlers commented on the abundance of sunflowers. When the time to choose a nickname came, it was an easy selection.

What are the most popular signs and symbols of the Sunflower State?

"To the Stars Through Difficulties" is the state motto. The truth of this was self-evident during the tumultuous 1850s, but it has been echoed in more recent times by the difficulties small-time farmers face. The western meadowlark is the state bird and the sunflower is the state flower. The cottonwood is the state tree.

How large, or small, is the Sunflower State?

Comprised of 82,277 square miles (213,099 square kilometers), Kansas comes in at fourteenth among the fifty states in geographic size. The state population of 2,853,118, as enumerated in 2010, places Kansas at thirty-third among the states.

Why is Kansas sometimes referred to as the "middle of the middle"?

Geographically, the center of the United States is in Kansas, but the expression means more than that. Kansas has, almost since the time of its founding, been one of the centers of public opinion, meaning that he or she who can persuade the voters of Kansas can often accomplish the same with the voters nationwide. Over time, this "middle of the middle" mentality became solidified. Of course there were exceptions to the rule, as when the Populist movement of the 1890s threatened the entire social fabric of the state, but Kansas then and Kansas now tends to stand for stability, a stability that leans more to conservatism than liberalism.

Is Kansas really anything more than endless rows of cornfields?

Don't talk down those cornfields: they've fed millions, perhaps even billions of people across the globe. But yes, Kansas is not as geographically uniform as we think. The northeastern part of the state has many rugged bluffs, on the western side of the Mississippi River, and there are more uplands in the central part than expected. It's true, however, that there are sections of the Sunflower State where the horizon seems to go on forever, exposing just one cornfield after another.

Is the weather a topic of major conversation in Kansas?

It has to be. A large number of Kansans still work family farms, and they, like Dorothy, have to watch the sky at all times. Even the urban Kansan, however, tends to be more interested in and opinionated on the subject of the weather than his or her counterpart in other states. Since about the year 2005, a number of cable television programs have developed with Midwestern weather—tornadoes especially—high on their list.

Kansas temperatures, too, can swing wildly. The warmest ever recorded was at Fredonia, where the mercury rose to 121 degrees F (49 degrees C) on July 18, 1936. The coldest was –40 degrees F (–40 degrees C) at Lebanon on February 13, 1905.

Can the man or woman of Kansas be told apart, or identified separately, from other Midwesterners?

No longer. Until about 1950, Kansans were readily identifiable, both by their clothing and attitude, but they now might just as well come from Iowa or Illinois. It's ironic that this change happened at the very time when the most famous Kansan of them all— Dwight D. Eisenhower—served as president of the United States.

EARLY HISTORY

For how long have humans lived in what we call the state of Kansas?

For perhaps 10,000 years, but during most of that time they left very little in the way of material culture. The Native Americans may have planted some corn and beans, but Kansas was better known to them as a hunting region, for the hunting of bison most especially. When the first European settlers arrived, they found Osages, Comanche,

> ## How could Major Long ever have gotten Kansas, and much of the American Midwest, so wrong?
>
> Anyone who examines the list of agricultural products that issue from the Midwest realizes how mistaken Long was, but he was no one's fool. More likely, Long saw no rapid success from agriculture, and he may have encountered too many of the high winds and tornadoes for which Kansas is infamous.

Cheyenne, Crow, and Pawnee in what is now Kansas. What these Indians had in common was that virtually all of them had recently been liberated and seen their lives improved by the appearance of the horse.

Who were the first Europeans to see Kansas?

Spanish explorer Coronado and his people came through in 1541 and claimed the land for Spain. They noted that the climate was not dissimilar to the Spanish motherland and predicted it would one day be rich in lemon trees. Only small groups of Spaniards followed, however, and most of Kansas was decidedly Indian country when the first French explorers and fur merchants arrived in the eighteenth century. Unlike the Spanish, the French did not see either the agricultural or commercial potentials of Kansas, perhaps because they had already devoted so much attention to Illinois.

Kansas was part of the ill-defined Louisiana Territory, which Napoleon, the emperor of France, sold to the United States in 1803. The first explorers to see parts of Kansas were Captains Meriwether Lewis and William Clark, of the Corps of Discovery, which went west in 1804. Other explorers followed, and in 1821, Major Stephen H. Long described sections of Kansas—as well as parts of Nebraska—as the Great American Desert, an area unfit for cultivation or human habitation.

When did the nation as a whole suddenly become enlightened about Kansas?

The first wagons rolled over the Oregon Trail in 1843, and the reports were encouraging. While the landscape was hot and flat, there were plenty of places where agriculture might succeed. It was the passage of so many people over the Oregon Trail that awakened East Coast Americans to the potential of what existed in the middle of the middle.

Early in the 1850s, a trickle of settlers became a stream, with two competing sources. Southerners, primarily from Missouri, wished to ensure Kansas would eventually become a slave state and add its strength to the slaveholding ones, while Northerners wished to be certain that Kansas would be a Free Soil state. Competition between these groups resulted in the Kansas-Nebraska Act, which passed Congress in 1854, opening both of the brand new territories to white settlement.

Was John Brown as important to the history of Kansas as he was to that of the nation?

For several years, John Brown (1800–1859) was almost entirely identified with his actions in Kansas. Long a drifter, and a rather confused person on the emotional level, Brown was dead-certain about one thing: slavery was wrong, and he must do something about it. Arriving in the Kansas Territory in 1855, Brown gathered a militia group and called himself captain. No one opposed this.

How terrible were the events at Pottawatomie Creek in 1856?

To label John Brown a terrorist, as many historians do, is to apply a twenty-first-century term to a nineteenth-century phenomenon. Brown was a messianic figure who genuinely believed that the slaves must be freed. Toward that end, he was willing to undertake almost any action.

Abolitionist John Brown led an 1859 armed rebellion that began with the Battle of Black Jack and Battle of Osawatomie in Kansas and ended with his loss at Harpers Ferry in West Virginia. He was tried, convicted, and killed for treason.

And so we should not be surprised to learn that he, several of his sons, and several of their friends kidnapped five proslavery men at the Pottawatomie settlement and butchered them ruthlessly. This was done to avenge the recent deaths of five Free Soil men, in the nearby town of Lawrence.

How could such a person—a cold-blooded killer—ever have won so much public approval?

At the time of the killings in Kansas, Brown was either looked down upon or hated by a majority of Americans. Three years later, however, he became a huge popular hero as the result of his courageous performance at his trial. Wounded, captured, and put on trial

---

Did Brown get his hands dirty or red with blood?

To the best of our knowledge, he did not. Most accounts declare that Brown looked on while his sons and their friends accomplished the terrible deed. There is not the slightest doubt that he was the architect of what happened, however.

for his attempt to seize Harpers Ferry, in what is now West Virginia, Brown came across as a truly noble presence. Unable to stand, he lay on a cot and made no attempt to defend himself; he accepted it as a given that he would die as part of the struggle to free the slaves. He was not our current idea of a fine man or great hero, but there was something undeniably noble about his attitude at the time of his death, in December 1859.

KANSAS IN THE LIFE OF THE NATION

Was there any chance that the American Civil War would commence in Kansas?

Not really. Kansas was pointed in the right direction, meaning that it was a transition zone to the Far West, but rather few men—North or South—wished to spill their blood in defense of a land they had never seen. What Kansas showcased, however, was the increasingly nasty nature of the division between proslavery and Free Soil groups.

How did Kansas achieve statehood?

Throughout the late 1850s, all moves toward statehood were blocked, and for a time there were not one but two territorial capitals: one at Lawrence and the other at Lecompton. The proslavery movement in Kansas began to slacken, however, and the election of Abraham Lincoln, from nearby Illinois, spelled the death knell for that movement. In January 1861, just two months before the outbreak of the Civil War, Kansas entered the Union as the thirty-fourth state. While it was not necessary for Kansas to join in order for the Union to win the war, the morale effect was considerable.

How did Kansas fare in the decades following the Civil War?

Like most of the Midwestern states, Kansas experienced one period of boom, followed by bust, after another. It wasn't really the fault of the Kansans themselves; they were victims of the price of agricultural goods, and those prices varied a great deal. International pressures on food prices began in the late nineteenth century, making matters even more difficult.

The Populist Movement spread like wildfire through the central and southern parts of the Midwest, as well as large sections of the Old South. Populist reformers like Mary Lease urged Kansans to "raise less corn and more hell." Protest marches, sometimes on the state capital and sometimes even towards Washington, D.C., became ever more frequent. But the energy that Kansans and other Midwestern farmers displayed toward the powers-that-be faltered as the result of the presidential election of 1896.

When were the wild days of Kansas, when it was the center of the Wild West?

These were the 1870s, a rather lawless decade during which many Kansas towns fell under the spell, and control, of outlaws. Some of these were rather colorful characters,

Ranchers from states like Texas brought their livestock to Kansas in the 1870s (as shown in these antique postcards) because the railroads were completed there first, connecting Kansas to markets in the rest of the United States.

who lent a certain charm to their activities, while many others were mindless brutes, who enjoyed wreaking terror on the inhabitants. A number of prominent lawmen—some of whom had less than stellar pasts themselves—arose to combat the thugs. Wyatt Earp, Bat Masterson, and Wild Bill Hickok are some of the best-known.

In what way was William Jennings Bryan such a crushing disappointment?

At first he seemed tailor-made. Born near Omaha, Nebraska, and raised in the difficult circumstances Kansans had become accustomed to, Bryan declared his run for president in 1896. Bryan knew a good deal about the Populist Movement, and he sympathized with aspects of its platform, but he did not wish to become completely identified with it. The "Boy Orator," as he was known, possessed a magnificent speaking voice, and he believed he would one day be president, even if this first attempt, in 1896, did not succeed.

At the Democratic National Convention—held in Chicago—Bryan disappointed his strongest supporters by speaking not about the price of corn, or wheat, but by waxing about the need for a currency based on two metals, not one. He gave a magnificent speech, concluding with the memorable words, "You shall not press down upon Man this Cross of Gold," but all the talk of a bimetallic standard distracted the voters from the main concern: the price of farm goods. Bryan gave it a spirited effort, but he lost to Ohioan William McKinley, in what was perhaps one of the most important of all presidential elections.

Why did Texas cattlemen drive their merchandise to Kansas?

Because the railroads arrived there first! Had a direct railroad link existed, Texans would surely have loaded their beef cattle aboard trains. Lacking this, however, they drove their animals north to towns like Abilene and Dodge City.

How might things have been different if Bryan were elected?

His election would have shifted the center of American politics from the Buckeye State of Ohio, 300 miles east of the Mississippi, to the Sunflower State of Kansas, well west of the big river. As a result, agricultural issues would have been much more important. William McKinley was a fine man, much-loved by those who knew him best, but he was not the person to lead the nation in a redefinition of its core issues.

Bryan ran again, in 1900, in 1908, and 1912, drawing less support on each occasion. His one "golden" moment had been the election of 1896. Bryan showed up on the national stage at a later date, however, serving as one of the prosecutorial attorneys in the famed Scopes Monkey Trial (see Tennessee).

Is there any truth to the idea I sometimes hear that L. Frank Baum's novels of the Kingdom of Oz were based on late nineteenth-century American politics?

The only person who could conclusively answer this question was Baum himself, and he is long dead. When one surveys the Oz books, however, he or she is often struck by the importance of gold, of magic, and of all sorts of pledges and promises. There are those who say the Cowardly Lion is based on Nebraska politician William Jennings Bryan but, again, there is no proof.

How important was the Temperance Movement in Kansas?

It was one of the most noteworthy of all movements of the late nineteenth and early twentieth centuries. Led primarily by women, the Temperance movement was spearheaded by calm and quiet reformers such as Susanna Salter (1860–1961) but also dramatic, even fear-inspiring, persons such as Carrie Nation (1846–1911). The former was the first woman ever elected as a mayor in the United States (the town of Argonia, Kansas), and the latter was an Ohio-born radical reformer. Nation began by praying outside saloons, but she later employed her famous hatchet to break down the doors and intimidate patrons. Both types of reformers were, quite likely, needed, and it is clear that alcohol use declined in Kansas by about the year 1920. This does not mean the use of alcohol disappeared, however.

How did Kansas fare in the first half of the twentieth century?

The First World War was a minor plus for Kansas, in that the demand for foodstuffs increased nationwide. Farm prices dropped soon after the war's conclusion, however, and when the Great Depression arrived in 1930, it found the Sunflower State already in an economic funk. Numerous Kansans lost their farms, and the situation looked as dire, if not worse, than the great crisis of the 1890s. This was small, however, when compared to the disaster of the Dust Bowl.

Was the Dust Bowl as horrific as people often claim?

Imagine life on the Kansas prairie, an endless succession either of sun-filled days or of watching for twisters or tornadoes. Then add to the mix an enormous cloud of dust that seems to follow the person—or animals—right across the landscape. Add to this a powerful wind, and you have the makings of something even worse than the famous tornado in *The Wizard of Oz*.

Had the Dust Bowl lasted a week or even a month, Kansans today would still remember it. But the drought that made the Dust Bowl possible lasted for almost three years, and in that time the lives of most Kansans were profoundly affected. How many Kansans abandoned their farms and headed to California is not known, but it may have been one-tenth of the total state population. And for those who remained, life after the Dust Bowl had a precarious aspect that had never before been seen.

How did Kansas fare during World War II?

There was great pride that the Allied commander-in-chief in Europe was Dwight D. Eisenhower, a native of Abilene. There was satisfaction, too, that so many young men from Kansas acquitted themselves well in battle. The single most important effect, however, was an increase in the need for foodstuffs and a consequent rise in the price of

A dust storm swarms over a small Kansas town in this 1935 photo. The Dust Bowl wiped out agriculture in the state and much of the American heartland.

farm goods. Some Kansans who had abandoned their land in the 1930s returned to the Sunflower State. Others, who had hung on during the bad times, did rather well in the 1940s and 1950s.

When did the U.S. military become a noted presence in Kansas?

This happened in the 1950s and 1960s, when the Strategic Air Command looked for sites for missile silos. It turned out that sites in Kansas and Nebraska were better locations than other states because of the number of farms and the widespread openness of the landscape. Numerous U.S. military installations were established between about 1955 and 1970.

Did countercultural events such as those of the 1960s have any play in Kansas?

Very little. Kansas was—and remains—a very conservative place in the best sense of the word, meaning that its residents wish to preserve that which already exists. Kansas saw few, if any, peace marches during the Vietnam War. To be sure, this attitude did not win applause from all directions. In 2005, political author Thomas Frank wrote *What's the Matter with Kansas?* Not quite an indictment of Kansas and its people, the book explains how the Republican Party hoodwinked the voters of rural Kansas, persuading them to vote against their own best interests.

What was life in Kansas like at the beginning of the twenty-first century?

In some ways it was the worst that native Kansans had ever seen. There was no Dust Bowl, and everyone was grateful for the fact. But farming produced less money than ever before, and numerous families simply gave up the fight, usually moving out of state. The situation was so dire that some communities offered free land to whoever would come and make a go of it, usually for a period of five years!

Is there any chance that the Sunflower State will simply fold, because so many people have left its farmland?

This has been asked many times, and it has to be admitted that it seems a possibility. As long as people need food, there will be the need for places like Kansas. And its people, too, are not the type to quit easily.

KENTUCKY

Nickname: "The Bluegrass State"
Capital: Frankfort
Statehood: June 1, 1792; 15th state

AT A GLANCE

What are the major signs and symbols of the Bluegrass State?

"United We Stand, Divided We Fall" is the state motto. The cardinal is the state bird, and the goldenrod is the state flower. Though little known outside the Bluegrass State, the The tulip poplar is the official state tree.

How large, or small, is the Bluegrass State?

Comprised of 40,411 square miles (104,664 square kilometers), Kentucky comes in at thirty-seventh among the fifty states in geographic size. The population of 4,339,367, as enumerated in 2010, places Kentucky at twenty-sixth among the states.

What does bluegrass mean?

It's the name of a distinctive type of grass that appears in certain parts of north-central Kentucky, and the name eventually spread to encompass the entire state. Don't go looking for the bluegrass, though: let it find you!

Do Kentuckians discuss the weather?

Old-timers do, and they usually have opinions as to whether hot and humid or cold and damp days are better for various types of activities, but the newcomer to Kentucky finds **167** the Bluegrass State a pleasant combination of the two. Summer heat can be oppressive, but it often leads to a spectacular fall. And winters are mild in the Bluegrass State.

Can the Kentuckian be distinguished from his or her neighbor in Ohio?

Certainly. It was Alexis de Tocqueville, one of the first great observers of the American cultural scene, who noted that the Ohio River established a severe line of demarcation. Today, of course, there is no slavery or slave system to differentiate the people of the Upper South from those of the Lower Midwest; even so, one can readily spot the difference. The Kentuckian tends to speak in longer, slower sentences, while the Ohioan is rapid in speech. In clothing, too, the Kentuckian looks much more "country" than his or her neighbor on the north side of the river.

What's the only national park in Kentucky?

Mammoth Cave National Park is located in the southwestern part of the state, near Bowling Green. There are approximately 400 miles in this system of caves, making it the longest cave system in the world. It is made up of limestone and sandstone.

EARLY HISTORY

For how long have humans lived in what we call the Bluegrass State?

For thousands of years. The inhabitants of early Kentucky were mound builders; the state has its share of sloping mounds that puzzled the early white settlers. Kentucky was, to the best of our knowledge, superb for a combination of hunting, fishing, and farming, so much so that various Native groups fought for possession. When the first white explorers and settlers arrived in the eighteenth century, they found the Shawnee in possession of much of the north, while Creek and Cherokee competed for the southern part.

Why did it take so long for the Anglo-American settlers to make their way across the Appalachian Mountains and into Kentucky?

The Appalachian Mountains are formidable without being severe, and the modern-day backpacker can make his or her way through them in ten days. In the eighteenth century, however, the English settlers of the East Coast had a healthy respect, and some fear, for what lay on the other side of the mountains. Life along the coast was much safer, so it seemed, and the majority of them therefore remained. Not until the incredible, almost insatiable, desire for land manifested did a handful of explorers begin to make their way to the other side.

Dr. Thomas Walker, of Virginia, was the first white American to make the trip. He entered the Cumberland Gap—right about where North Carolina, Kentucky, and Tennessee come together—in 1750, and named it in honor of the Duke of Cumberland.

Had the French and Indian War not started in 1754, the settlement of Kentucky would have come earlier; as it was, many of the most adventuresome of the early pioneers were teamsters and scouts, who made their name in that war.

Was Daniel Boone as important as we so often hear?

Beyond a doubt. There are, of course, some misconceptions about Boone, the first of which is that he carried a "Kentucky Rifle." It was really a "Pennsylvania Rifle," made by German immigrants to the Keystone State. Boone, too, was born in Pennsylvania, but he spent much of his early life in Virginia. Boone was not the only Anglo-American who wished to move to Kentucky. James Harrod, for whom Harrodsburg is named, led the first group of permanent settlers over the mountains in 1771; Boone followed a few years later. To Boone goes the honor of pioneering the Wilderness Road through Cumberland Gap, however, and he soon became a legendary figure, thanks to his many encounters with the Native Americans. It's not too much to say that Boone was the Captain John Smith of Kentucky.

The Shawnee resisted the first white encroachment on their lands, and the commencement of the Revolutionary War, in 1775, meant that they could often get muskets, rifles, and gunpowder from the British, located in their forts in the Upper Midwest. The Shawnee carried out a desperate struggle against the white pioneers, knowing that time and numbers were both against them. Daniel Boone was captured by the Shawnee early in 1778. He spent several months among them, and was, apparently, adopted into the tribe. After making his escape, he returned to Boonesborough, and led the defense of that fortified town against the Shawnee in the autumn of 1778.

Frontier woodsman and hero Daniel Boone was best known for exploring the lands that are now Kentucky.

When did the tide turn in favor of the American settlers?

Skirmishes raged in 1782 and were repeated throughout the 1780s. By the end of that decade, however, the whites had the upper hand. The Shawnee withdrew across the Ohio River (they later made their last stand under Chief Tecumseh). White settlers than began pouring through Cumberland Gap, establishing towns and forts throughout Kentucky. Fur trapping is what brought Daniel Boone and the other early pioneers; tobacco farming sustained their children and grandchildren.

Kentucky remained very much part of the frontier well into the nineteenth century, but its advocates, on the national level, made certain that the area achieved statehood. This was the first area west of the mountains to enter the Union, and it was a key test, to see whether the newly developed states would enter as real equals. Kentucky achieved this, entering the Union in 1792.

How important was slavery to the early founding and development of Kentucky?

Most white Kentuckians will proudly tell you that slavery had little to do with the settlement of Kentucky, and the assertion is correct to that point; Kentucky would not have thrived without slave labor, however. The white settlers, coming from Virginia and North Carolina, were well-accustomed to slavery, and they brought their slaves with them. It's true that early Kentucky was not the land of large plantations; rather, it was a place of small-scale slavery, with yeoman farmers sometimes owning two or three slaves. Did the small numbers make any difference to the African Americans who had to labor to plant and harvest the tobacco and corn? Of course not.

At what point did the image of the Kentucky rifleman become that of the American soldier?

As we've seen, the Kentucky Rifle was actually from Pennsylvania, but it's true that Kentucky and Tennessee, between them, formed the basis for the national self-image where military preparedness is concerned. As the War of 1812 commenced, former president Thomas Jefferson gave his opinion that the riflemen of these two Western states could conquer British Canada all on their own. Daniel Boone was the progenitor of this irregular military style, but he was followed by many others. And in Tennessee, the image of the bear-hunting Davy Crockett came to equal that of Boone.

The War of 1812 actually demonstrated the weakness of the American military system. Canada was not conquered, and the United States was lucky to emerge with a "draw" on its hands. The image of the Kentucky frontiersman remained powerful, however, right up to the time of the Civil War.

How important is Henry Clay to the history and culture of the Bluegrass State?

Though he's not quite as significant as Daniel Boone, Henry Clay stands just one rung beneath him. Born in Virginia, Clay spent most of his life in Kentucky and most of his career representing the Bluegrass State in the U.S. Congress. During the War of 1812,

Clay was one of the so-called War Hawks—eager for a confrontation with England—but in the years that followed, Clay became known as the Great Pacificator, or Great Compromiser—eager to find common ground between North and South. It's thanks to his many efforts that the Union did not split apart in 1820, the year that Missouri's quest for statehood nearly wrecked the balance of power in the U.S. Senate. Clay was also well-known as a lover of horses and an owner who raced his in numerous competitions. Part of the Bluegrass tradition of horse-racing derives from him.

THE CIVIL WAR

What was life in Kentucky like during the "antebellum" years, those just prior to the Civil War?

Kentuckians had a sad sense that the world was passing them by. For two generations, they had been the pioneers, and one generation earlier they led the way in crossing the Mississippi River. But by 1860, the scene of action had passed to the Far West, and neither Kentucky nor Virginia (which can almost be called its parent state) possessed their earlier importance. For white Kentuckians, life in 1860 did not quite have the charm it held for their grandparents. For black Kentuckians, things had become much worse. Slavery had spread to nearly all parts of the Bluegrass State.

Did Kentucky ever join the Confederate States of America?

Confederate leaders were anxious for it to do so. One of the earliest, and most optimistic, of Confederate flags had fifteen stars, the last of these intended for Kentucky. But the Bluegrass State was too deeply divided, and there never was a strong movement for secession. Resistance to Yankee aggression was a whole other matter, though. We often forget that Southerners sometimes call it the War of Northern Aggression. That is how many Kentuckians felt about the Civil War. Whether or not they supported slavery, white Kentuckians were outraged at the invasion by Federal troops, and this drove many of them into the Confederate camp.

There never was a time when Kentucky was ripe to fall into Confederate hands, however. The land and waterways conspired to give the Union the upper hand, all

How did Abraham Lincoln feel about the Bluegrass State?

With his usual great skill, Lincoln, who was born in Kentucky and lived the first five years of his life there, foretold that the state would be vital to the cause of the Union. In one of his most prescient letters, Lincoln declared that he hoped the good Lord was on his side, but that he knew he *must* have Kentucky.

throughout the contest. Union steamboats patrolled the Ohio River; rich harvests in Ohio allowed the North to feed its soldiers far better than their Confederate counterparts; and Kentucky slowly fell into Union hands. Plenty of white Kentuckians resisted to the last, and many of them moved south into Tennessee to prolong the contest.

What was life in Kentucky like in the decades that followed the Civil War?

The state was not on its knees, as was the case with Virginia and Tennessee, but many Kentuckians maintained long, and negative, memories about the Yankees and the North. The Kentucky economy recovered within a decade, and the Bluegrass State made a clear choice to continue in the economic ways of its forebears, rather than turn to industry. Kentucky remained the land of tobacco, of corn, and of thoroughbred horses. Moonshine, or the making of hard liquor, was already part of Kentucky culture, but it boomed in the decades of the late nineteenth century.

What Kentucky did not possess, in these years, was a leader on the national scale; it had no new Henry Clay. The state languished, therefore, where national politics was concerned, and when Kentucky was spoken of as a national presence, the expression was almost always in the past tense.

When did the Kentucky Derby first become part of American culture?

The Run for the Roses—as many call it—is a true Kentucky icon. It first was run in 1875, and it is traditionally held on the first Saturday in May. The "most exciting two minutes in sports," as some refer to it, has seen all manner of surprises and upsets. Oliver Lewis, riding Aristides, won the first race in 1875 in a time of 2:37:75. Victor Espinoza, riding American Pharaoh , won the 2015 race, in a time of 2:03:02. American Pharaoh went on to win the Triple Crown. The Kentucky Derby is the first leg of the American Triple Crown; the other two races are the Preakness Stakes and the Belmont Stakes.

Thoroughbred racing at Churchill Downs in Louisville is a tradition that goes back to 1875.

When did Kentucky become aware of the long arms of the federal government?

Kentuckians were distrustful of the federal government ever since the Civil War's conclusion, but they suddenly became more aware of its strength in the 1930s. Led by President Franklin D. Roosevelt, the government wished to change the lives of millions of people living in Appalachia, to bring them into the modern world. One of the best ways to accomplish this was by providing them with electricity, and this meant the damming of numerous rivers in Kentucky and Tennessee.

The resistance of old-timers in Tennessee is better-known, but there were plenty of counterparts in Kentucky, people who claimed the lives they lived were perfectly all right, and they did not want the federal government's interference. Heart-rending stories have been told—most of them accurate—of retirees forced off their land by federal agents to make way for the new bridges and dams. If this was progress, and the modern world, many Kentuckians wanted nothing to do with it.

How did Kentucky ever become the home of Thomas Merton?

Born in France in 1915, Thomas Merton grew up in the United States and was educated in England. A cynical man in youth, he became an ardent follower of the Roman Catholic Church and a member of Our Lady of Gethsemane, in north-central Kentucky. The Trappist Monks had long searched for remote rural areas, and they were pleased with what they found in Kentucky. What no one expected was that Merton would become a worldwide celebrity.

During the twenty-nine years he was at Our Lady of Gethsemane, Merton penned dozens of books, thousands of journal entries, and thousands of letters. One of the most prolific writers of the twentieth century, he gave his readers great insight into what it meant to be a Roman Catholic during the tumultuous time of change known as Vatican II. Merton wrote with such surpassing skill that some of his readers mistakenly believed him a cosmopolitan, living in one of the great American cities. No, he was as rural as they come, living in Kentucky, the land of Protestants and Bible thumpers.

What's the story behind Kentucky Fried Chicken?

In 1930, Harland Sanders opened up a small diner in Corbin, Kentucky, where he served fried chicken and other food. Over the next few years, he expanded his restaurant, added tables, and built on to the location. He added his "Original Recipe" to his chicken and obtained the honorary title of "Colonel." Originally known as Sanders Court and Café, Sanders went on to franchise his business as Kentucky Fried Chicken (KFC), and the chain became very successful.

How did Kentucky become the guardian of the nation's supply of gold?

In 1933, at the height of the Great Depression, President Franklin D. Roosevelt took steps to ensure the safety of the nation's money supply. He declared a bank holiday and used his personal charm and persuasiveness to stop Americans from emptying their

The U.S. Gold Bullion Depository building at Fort Knox.

bank accounts. As part of this program, Roosevelt determined that the country needed a secure place for its precious metals, and Fort Knox, in south-central Kentucky, opened in 1937.

Who became the major Kentucky poet of the late twentieth century?

Born in Henry County, Kentucky, in 1934, Wendell Berry was a talented poet who was also a farmer. When people asked him about the contradiction between these vocations, he scornfully replied that they were meant to go together—that a love of words is on the same level as a love of the land. While he farmed, Berry penned dozens of books and hundreds of essays, usually on the same theme: the loss of connection to the soil.

The Kentucky Wendell Berry grew up in had lost some closeness to the land, but the landscape in which he found himself late in life was bewildering to him. One of his books, *What are People For?*, explored the many ways in which modern society seemed determined to make humans obsolete. Both critics and admirers found it necessary to visit Berry on his farm, because he seldom went to the big cities, which he saw as signposts of the decline of civilization.

How did NASCAR become so important to Kentucky?

The National Association for Stock Car Auto Racing was established in 1947, and development moved along much more rapidly than anyone expected; prior to this, most racetracks had, and made, their own rules. Kentucky, with its sporting population, seemed perfect for the expansion of NASCAR, and the sport boomed in the 1980s and 1990s.

A television program had a lot to do with the increased popularity of NASCAR. *The Dukes of Hazzard*, which ran from 1979 to 1985, was filmed in Louisiana, but the scenes of Southern backcountry life could easily be transplanted to most other Southern states.

Kentucky and Tennessee, especially, were identified with *The Dukes of Hazzard*, the heroes of which continually outran the hapless police with their high speed car.

Where will the Bluegrass State be a generation hence?

That's one of the great questions, because Kentucky is presently split between its rural past and semi-urban future. There still are plenty of unspoiled areas of Kentucky, but urban creep continues to assert itself, especially in Louisville and along the Ohio River. The chances are that the Bluegrass State will have to make some firm decisions about whether to remain one of the great natural wonders, or to continue to move in the direction of industry and modernization.

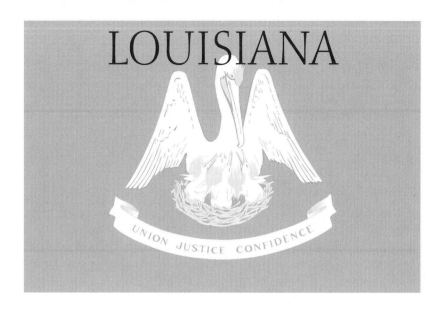

LOUISIANA

Nickname: "The Pelican State"
Capital: Baton Rouge
Statehood: April 30, 1812; 18th state

AT A GLANCE

Where does the state nickname come from?

This remains a matter of some debate. There is no doubt that the pelican was a common sight in southern Louisiana, when the first settlers arrived. At the same time, it's clear that the first French settlers arrived aboard *Le Pelican*, the ship captained by Pierre Le Moyne d'Iberville.

What are the most important signs and symbols of the Pelican State?

"Union, Justice and Confidence" is the official state motto. The brown pelican is the state bird, and the magnolia is the state flower. The bald cypress is the state tree.

How large, or small, is Louisiana?

Comprised of 47,752 square miles (123,366 square kilometers), Louisiana is thirty-second among the states in terms of geographic size. Its population of 4,533,372, as enumerated in the census of 2010, placed it twenty-fifth among the states.

Is there any one place from which one can see the best that is Louisiana?

Yes indeed, but sad to say, it's also become one of the places from which the worst disaster can also be viewed. Until 2005, the year of Hurricane Katrina, the port of New Orleans and the lower wards of the city were seen as one of the marvels of the United States, a place where industry, commerce, and culture all came together to produce something nearly unique. One can still maintain this position, but it has to be balanced by the recognition that New Orleans, and Louisiana, suffered one of the great catastrophes of recent American history, and that the perils of living in lower Louisiana are much more evident today.

Is Louisiana more than an endless line of bayous?

Of course! Nearly three-quarters of the state is high and dry. Many of the most notable events and occurrences of Louisiana history have taken place in the lowlands, however, and it's natural that those areas receive more attention. Louisiana, 300 years ago and today, is essentially formed by the lower Mississippi River, which carves its way south, altering the landscape as it goes. The Mississippi is a dynamic presence in the lives of most Louisianans; they know that the great river often changed course, and that when it does so the lives of humans and the life of the landscape are deeply affected.

Do the people of Louisiana discuss the weather very much?

As a general rule they don't. Native-born Louisianans know what to expect: heat and more heat throughout the summer months, and mild but rainy seasons in the winter. The one thing that can make them perk up their ears in a hurry is any discussion of hurricanes, however, and this was true long before Katrina slammed into the coast in 2005. Louisiana and its people have been hit by dozens of major hurricanes in their history.

The temperature moves up and down to a greater extent than one might imagine. The single hottest recorded day of Louisiana history came on August 10, 1936, when the mercury hit 114 degrees F (45.5 degrees C) at Plain Dealing. Few people are surprised by this figure. Many are surprised, even stunned, to learn that the lowest recorded temperature was -16 degrees F (-26.7 degrees C) at Minden on February 13, 1899.

Can the Louisiana person be detected from his or her neighbor in Mississippi?

Definitely. The two people share many attributes, but the Louisianan is more dramatic, in speech and gestures. Ethnically, too, the people of Louisiana are more diverse than their Mississippi neighbors.

EARLY HISTORY

For how long have humans lived in what we call the Pelican State?

For thousands of years. We don't know when the first Paleo-Indians arrived, but their descendants became Mound Builders, part of the Mississippian culture—as we call it— that spread throughout the South and parts of the Midwest. When the first people of European descent arrived, they found a great number of tribes in Louisiana. One of the first names for the place that became New Orleans was Chumash, which means alligator.

Who were the first Europeans to come to Louisiana?

Members of the expedition of Hernando de Soto came through Louisiana on their way to Mexico City, following the death of their leader somewhere in present-day Missouri. But the first people to lay a good claim to the region were French explorers, led by René-Robert Cavelier de La Salle. He and his group came down the Mississippi in canoes, and on April 9, 1682, he claimed all the lands and waterways of the region for King Louis XIV of France, thereby giving Louisiana its name.

La Salle intended to return to Louisiana, but when he came from a different direction—in 1685—his pilots missed the mouth of the Mississippi River, and he ended up in Texas instead (the sad story of La Salle's colony is told in the Texas entry). It was therefore left to another Frenchman, Pierre Le Moyne d'Iberville, to lead the first French settlers up the mouth of the Mississippi River. He achieved his breakthrough, finding his way into the river, on Mardi Gras ("Fat Tuesday") of 1699, and the holiday has been celebrated with vigor in modern-day New Orleans.

What happens during Mardi Gras?

Mardi Gras occurs on the day before Ash Wednesday, which is the first day of Lent. A parade with floats is held; attendees dress up in different Mardi Gras colors (purple meaning justice, green meaning faith, and gold meaning power), wear masks and beads, drink and eat, and choose a king; and, when all is said and done, the city of New Orleans sees over $1 billion spent by revelers.

Why did the French colony develop so slowly?

It's the same story as in French Canada: the motherland never sent people in large enough numbers. No one has ever quite puzzled out the reason, but neither France nor Spain ever gathered, or sent, enough colonists to make their colonies thrive. England, by contrast, had lots of unemployed people or displaced farmers to send.

New Orleans was laid out in 1718, with Iberville's younger brother, Jean-Baptiste Le Moyne, as the first governor. French Louisiana was slow going, but most people could see the potential that lay in the thick soil, as well as the amazing set of waterways. One event that had negative consequences for Louisiana was the "South Sea Bubble," a stock market boom and bust back in France. Many investors soured on the idea of colonies and colonization entirely.

Louisiana was named for the king of France. So how did it end up in Spanish hands?

In 1762, France—knowing it would lose the French and Indian War—ceded Louisiana to Spain. It seemed better that a fellow nation, with a monarch from the same Bourbon fam-

These balconies in the French Quarter are actually Spanish in style, as are the windows.

ily, should hold the region. Spain did not do very much with New Orleans, or Louisiana, during its tenure, but the mix of French and Spain culture that one finds in Louisiana today is a product of this period. Louisiana was also enriched by an ethnic infusion from Nova Scotia, the Acadian exiles who became known as Cajuns in the South. And after the French colony in present-day Haiti was overthrown by a black revolution, many French Haitians migrated to New Orleans, making it one of the most diverse places in North America.

How then did France manage to sell all this land, which it had previously given to Spain?

In 1800, Napoleon Bonaparte, the dictator of France, quietly forced the king of Spain to retrocede the entire Louisiana area, which meant something much larger than the present-day state of that name, to France. Napoleon considered making New Orleans the center of a new French empire in America, but he changed his mind, and in April 1803, his representatives sold the entire area to the United States for about $15 million.

This, surely, was one of the best land bargains ever, from the American point of view, and a rather sad one for France. As a result, Louisiana came under the Stars and Stripes, first as a territory, and then, on April 30, 1812, as the eighteenth state of the Union.

What role did Louisiana play in the War of 1812?

At the war's beginning, the action was almost entirely on the East Coast and the Canadian border. Late in the conflict, however, the British decided to capture New Orleans,

> ## We all know that there is a French Quarter in downtown New Orleans, and that some of the famous spots have French names. Where is the Spanish feel?
>
> It's much more subtle, nearly below the surface, but it can be found. Quite a few restaurants in the Garden District present Spanish-language menus, for example. But in truth, the French presence, in the culture and life of New Orleans, is much stronger than its Spanish counterpart.

either to hold it in perpetuity or for use as a bargaining chip at the peace table. The people of lower Louisiana had plenty of warning; they knew the British were coming. Even so, there was great concern because Louisiana had not yet developed a military tradition. Some observers questioned whether the multicultural community of greater New Orleans could band together and form a strong defense.

Andrew Jackson, major-general of the Tennessee militia, came to the rescue. Having defeated the Creeks in a six-month Indian war, he was the logical candidate to lead the defense of New Orleans. Arriving in December 1814, Jackson placed the city under martial law. He proceeded to gather a truly interesting and diverse group pf fighters, which included merchants, people of the streets, Louisiana planters, and even a group of pirates from Barataria.

How sensational was the American victory at the Battle of New Orleans?

Americans had won the Revolutionary War through patience and self-discipline; with French assistance, they won the climactic Siege of Yorktown in 1781. The end of the War of 1812 was very different. Andrew Jackson and his rather motley crew won an astonishing victory over the British attackers on January 8, 1815. Roughly 2,000 British were killed, wounded, or missing that day, while American losses were in the neighborhood of 60. Two things soured the victory, however.

First and foremost, the Battle of New Orleans was fought two weeks after the Treaty of Ghent, which officially ended the conflict (news of the treaty did not arrive in time to prevent the battle). Second and just as important, Jackson earned the reputation of a tyrant in the weeks that followed his victory. New Orleanians were by no means sad when Jackson returned to Tennessee.

How did the Pelican State fare in the decades prior to the outbreak of the Civil War?

Louisiana boomed as never before, but these were uneven boom times, with a small minority at the top enjoying most of the gains. The city and port benefited from enormous

181

amounts of foodstuffs that were shipped down the Ohio and Mississippi rivers, with New Orleans serving as the great staging port for merchandise on its way overseas.

The plantation system of lower Louisiana probably hit its peak around 1845. By then, the Pelican State was exporting 4 million bales of cotton per year, and New Orleans was one of the wealthiest places in the nation, on a per capita basis. At the same time, the lives of the African Americans of New Orleans moved in one of two directions. For a small number, life got decidedly better, and there were whole sections of the city where free people of color lived well. For the majority of African Americans, things got much worse, with slaveholders demanding more work than ever before.

Was there any doubt Louisiana would join the Confederacy?

Virtually none. The Pelican State was so deeply involved in slavery and the cotton trade that one could hardly imagine it existing without them. Louisiana seceded from the Union in January 1861, and it supplied General P. G. T. Beauregard, who ordered the first shots to be fired, against Fort Sumter, on April 12, 1861.

For a time, Louisianans were jubilant, anticipating an easy victory over the North. But the war came to their doorstep in the spring of 1862, when a Union flotilla forced its way past the twin forts seventy-five miles downstream from New Orleans. Once this was accomplished, the Union fleet came directly to New Orleans, and one look at the big black guns aboard those ships was sufficient to persuade New Orleans to surrender. The city soon came under martial law.

This 1862 illustration from *Harper's Weekly* shows panicked New Orleans residents scrambling for food after the Union had effectively blocked it off from the rest of the Confederacy.

Might the story of the Civil War have been different if New Orleans had not succumbed in 1862?

The chances are about 2 percent in favor and 98 percent against. But if New Orleans had successfully resisted the Union fleet, the war might have lasted longer. As it was, news of New Orleans's fall spread rapidly throughout the South, causing consternation and dismay.

How do the people of New Orleans, and southern Louisiana, remember the military occupation?

To them, 1862–1865 was the worst of times. President Lincoln installed Benjamin "The Beast" Butler as military governor of Louisiana, and many people complained that the state was turned into the North in miniature. In reality, Lincoln used Louisiana as a test, an example of how a Southern state could be turned around in order that it might be readmitted to the Union. And this happened in record time.

What was life in New Orleans, and Louisiana, like in the decades that followed the Civil War?

The city actually made a rather smooth comeback. Cotton was still important, but many other crops were now grown in the Deep South, and New Orleans continued to be the shipping port. The great fortunes of the antebellum era did not return, but lower Louisiana had a good-sized middle class by the turn of the twentieth century. Sadly, the same cannot be said for the lower and working classes, who fell deeper into poverty with each passing year. Sharecropping on the fields that belonged to wealthy men was the doom of many rural Louisianans; holding down two or even three jobs in a desperate struggle to keep afloat was the story for many people in New Orleans. The city, too, saw an increase in racial violence.

How long did the people of Louisiana languish in poverty?

For many, it was the case of three generations, with each one coming off poorer than the previous. The great change appeared to come in the early 1930s, when Huey Long, a populist called "the Kingfish," was elected governor of Louisiana. That Long was a demagogue, and only marginally trustworthy, is indisputable; it also cannot be argued that he was very interested in making life better for the common people. More miles of roads were built in his short tenure than in the thirty preceding years.

Long was a skillful politician but he overplayed his hand, making enemies both of many locals and of President Franklin D. Roosevelt. Long sometimes compared himself to the president, making it seem as if he was the superior of the two. This was a bad error but not a deadly one. It was Long's foes in Louisiana who brought him down. He was shot and killed in the capitol, at Baton Rouge, on August 18, 1935.

How did Louisiana fare during World War II?

Many young men were mustered for the war, and many others passed through the Pelican State on their way to military camps. Louisiana benefited, both as a transportation hub, and because quite a few servicemen later decided to settle in the Pelican State. New Orleans and its port were more important than ever before. What Louisiana did not see, however, was an uptick in its economy in the years that followed the war. Housing remained pretty much as it had for half a century, and even sections of New Orleans looked downright shabby. Outsiders liked the fact that prices in New Orleans were low; locals cursed the tourist trade.

What is the longest continuous bridge over water in the world?

The Lake Pontchartrain Causeway holds that honor. It is a nearly twenty-four-mile-long bridge that spans over Lake Pontchartrain from Metairie to the south to Mandeville to the north.

A National Guard helicopter works to repair a broken levy in New Orleans in this photo taken not long after Hurricane Katrina devastated the city.

For how long has Louisiana been the victim of hurricanes?

Almost from the time when the French first came to settle. Perhaps there were plenty of hurricanes in the seventeenth century, but we don't know about them. Once lower Louisiana became well-settled, the pattern of major hurricanes was established, however, and it seemed that each one was worse than the last. By the 1950s, the Army Corps of Engineers had designed the answer, a levee system so complex and developed that even major spillovers would merely spill into predesignated areas. The system was excellent, and even Hurricane Camille, in 1969, lashed the coast without harming the Crescent City.

How bad was Hurricane Katrina?

New Orleans and lower Louisiana had been spared so many times that locals ignored some of the early warning signs. People who should have fled the area did not do so, and forced evacuations did not begin until it was too late. Those people who could escape the New Orleans area did so, primarily by driving out of the city in SUVs. This left perhaps 80 percent of the population stuck in the greater New Orleans area, with nowhere to go. That seemed all right, because the Superdome was opened for the public. But when the storm hit, on August 30–31, 2005, it was much worse than anticipated. Perhaps Katrina was not a Category Five hurricane, but it was close enough.

Thousands of people were trapped in the Superdome, which became a death trap in the heat. Nearly 3,000 other people died outright in lower Louisiana. Tens of thousands of homes were reduced to rubble. And in all of this, it was obvious that neither the state nor federal government was up to the task.

How could the federal and state governments—with all their resources—fail the people in an emergency such as this?

That question has been asked many times, and it requires a two-part response. First, no one anticipated that the levees would fail, as they had held up well, time and again. Second, the state government was too late to the scene, and a truly inept group of leaders of the Federal Emergency Management Agency (FEMA) handicapped the federal government. Even so, it was shocking to witness the weakness of the response and the way Mother Nature humiliated the governments while wrecking the lives of so many people.

How long did the cleanup, and restoration, take?

As of 2016, the cleanup is about 98 percent complete, but restoration is only at the 50 percent level. Whole wards of lower New Orleans were virtually destroyed, and there was some question as to whether the areas even should be rebuilt, because of the concern they would be wrecked yet again. In most cases, the decision to rebuild was made, and there are plenty of hero stories, both on individual and group levels. But New Orleans, and lower Louisiana, have not yet returned to where they were in the weeks prior to Hurricane Katrina.

Where will the Pelican State be a generation from now?

Very likely it will be thriving. The trouble, however, is that lower Louisiana, the most prosperous part of the state, will always be at the mercy of the newest, and most dangerous, hurricane.

MAINE

Nicknames: "The Pine Tree State"; "Vacationland"
Capital: Augusta
Statehood: March 15, 1820; 23rd state

AT A GLANCE

Which of the nicknames is more commonly used?

It depends on the age of the person. People over the age of fifty tend to use "Pine Tree State," and those younger than fifty tend to employ "Vacationland."

What are the most important signs and symbols of Vacationland?

"I Direct" or "I Guide" is the official state motto. The chickadee is the state bird, and the white pine cone and tassel is the state flower. The white pine is the official state tree.

How large, or small, is Maine?

For New England, Maine is a very large state. Comprised of 35,380 square miles (91,634 square kilometers), it is almost four times the size of Massachusetts. But when measured against the nation as a whole, Maine turns out only to be thirty-ninth among the fifty states in geographic size. The population, as enumerated in 2010, of 1,328,302, places Maine as forty-first among the states in terms of population.

How did such a hard-working state ever gain the name Vacationland?

Maine is, quite likely, the hardest working state in the entire Union. Its people are computer-savvy, but they generally prefer to do things by hand, and many of the finest of all American handcrafts come from Vacationland. The odd juxtaposition between the state's

187

proclivity and its nickname comes from the fact that Mainers learned—about a century ago—that they needed to diversify in order to succeed. The majority of the state's residents continued to build boats, pick blueberries, and walk the Appalachian Trial, but a significant minority entered the tourist trade and have been there ever since. As a result, Maine blends hard-working artisans with soft-selling tourist managers like no other state.

Is there one single spot from which the casual tourist can see the best that is Maine?

There are two in fact. The first is from the summit of Mount Katahdin, the highest point in the state. Relatively few tourists go there, however; it's almost as if the mountain is reserved for those who have completed walking the Appalachian Trail. By contrast, Cadillac Mountain, in Acadia National Park, located on Mount Desert Island, attracts tourists by the hundreds of thousands each summer, and it would be difficult to compile a number for all those who have gone there in the last hundred years. Standing atop Cadillac Mountain—which is named for the same French explorer who lent his name to the famous car—one has a 360-degree view of coastal Maine and a significant look at the interior. The granite formations atop Cadillac Mountain are quite special, and many a tourist loses his or her footing while exploring the mountain (relatively few disasters or tragedies have taken place, however). Once one goes atop Cadillac Mountain, there is a place in his or her heart for Vacationland, and the chances are that he or she will return.

Do real Mainers talk about the weather?

No, they groan about it. For four months of the year, Maine is a feast of sunlight mixed with occasional fog, and of blueberries ripening, just asking to be picked. For another three months of the year, Maine is pretty decent, an okay place to be. And for a solid five months of the year, Vacationland is a frozen wilderness, where ice-cutters are required, and where it seems winter will never end. It's the combination of the extreme cold sweeping down from Canada, *and* the dampness that comes from the North Atlantic; between them, these two can drive even a seasoned New Englander pretty crazy. But spring has always followed winter, and the locals can always hope that the coming winter won't be as bad as the one they've just endured.

Can the person from Maine be detected or told apart from his or her neighbor in New Hampshire?

They share many qualities, including a real grittiness, but the Mainer is the more talkative of the two. He or she employs the famous Down East accent that has identified Mainers for almost two centuries, and when asked for directions, he or she replies with those infamous words: "You can't get there from here! (which is actually pronounced "Yu caaant get thar from here!").

Is it true that Maine is the whitest state in the nation?

Maine, Vermont, and New Hampshire vie for that dubious title, but it isn't really their fault; when African Americans escaped slavery in the South, they tended to migrate to

Boston, New York, or Philadelphia, or even all the way to Canada, rather than settle in the northern New England states. Portland has a sizeable black population, but once one goes inland, the population looks lily white.

Why is Maine so seldom heard from in national politics?

Over the last twenty years, Maine has been well-known for the number of women who serve in the U.S. Senate, and they tend to be moderate, regardless of which side of the aisle. But in terms of national influence, Maine is overshadowed by its smaller neighbor, New Hampshire, which holds the first primary in the nation. The last time a son of Maine contended for the

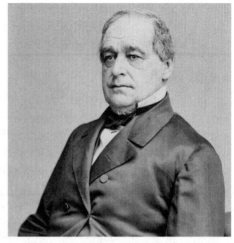

Hannibal Hamlin was President Abraham Lincoln's first vice president before Andrew Johnson. No Maine resident has made it further in politics than he did back in the 1860s.

presidency was in 1976 when Edmund Muskie sought the Democratic nomination. Prior to that, in 1964, Republican senator Margaret Chase Smith was the first woman to seek the presidential nomination in one of the major parties.

The closest any son of Maine has come to the presidency was in 1860, when Republicans selected Hannibal Hamlin as the vice presidential running mate. Hamlin was a man of fine quality, but he was, of course, completely overshadowed by Abraham Lincoln, who ran at the top of the ticket. And when Hamlin was dropped from the ticket in favor of Andrew Johnson in 1864, Maine faded into obscurity where major party alliances are concerned.

EARLY HISTORY

For how long have humans lived in what we now call Vacationland?

For thousands of years. Most of their names—and lifeways—are unknown to us, because the Maine climate is not kind to artifacts. If the Indians had built mounds in Maine, these would have disappeared thanks to erosion. But we can say that when the first people of European descent arrived, they found Maine well-populated with Indian peoples, with tribal names that are reflected in the names of such rivers today as Androscoggin and Kennebec.

Who were the first white people to see, and map, the coast of Maine?

A Frenchman, Samuel de Champlain, came along the coast as early as 1604. He gave Mount Desert Island its name, and he mapped and charted large sections of the coast.

Champlain was followed by Captain John Smith—of Virginia fame—who first arrived in 1614. Like Champlain, Smith was a first-rate cartographer, and it's from his early maps that we know the Indian names of many of the locations. Neither of these two left a deep imprint on the inner part of the state, however; that remained a mystery for some decades to come.

The first English settlers began drifting into Maine in the 1640s. They tended to live far apart from each other, on separated islands or inlets. Some made it a few miles inland, and it was to one of these families that Maine's first real hero was born. Sir William Phips (1651–1695) grew up in what is now Wiscasset. A farmer and a fisherman—most Mainers combined the two—Phips displayed great ambition. By the age of thirty he had moved to Boston and become a minor merchant. By forty, he'd discovered the wreck of a Spanish treasure galleon and become rich, as well as receiving a knighthood from King James II. Phips later served as the first royal governor of Massachusetts, and by sheer bad luck, his tenure coincided with the Salem Witch Trials.

Is there a way for us to go back in time and experience how truly rugged, and frightening, early Maine must have been?

There is. The paintings of Winslow Homer are an extraordinary re-creation of early Maine, complete with fishing boats, lobstermen, and widows who walk on lonely beaches, hoping their husbands will magically return. Homer was not a Maine native, but he came to understand the state better than any other visual artists, and his many works—available in museums and in all sorts of reproductions—form one of the finest of all our looks at Early America. Homer was followed by photographer Eliot Porter, whose many books on Maine—its wilderness especially—give us a second look at the magical but dangerous world that the people of Maine experienced.

How did Maine ever come to be part of the Massachusetts colony (and then the state)?

It happened as a result of the French and Indian Wars. When these commenced in 1689, Maine was still an independent colony, or rather a group of small independent colonies. Both the people of Maine and their would-be protectors in Massachusetts believed it would be better for Maine to be absorbed into the Bay colony, and this happened around the end of the seventeenth century. For the next 120 years, Maine was part of Massachusetts, meaning that the Bay State was, geographically speaking, much larger than it is today.

How did Maine make it through the long period we know as the French and Indian Wars?

The people of Maine suffered plenty, from attacks by the French and their Indian allies, but they gave back plenty too. By about 1750, the coast of Maine was swept almost entirely clear of Indians, and by 1800 it was rare to find Native Americans in any part of the state. This was not the result of genocide—the systematic extermination of a people—but rather was created by the Indians fading into the background, and—for many years—passing themselves off as whites. When Maine's Native Americans reemerged, in the mid-twentieth century, they displayed great pride in their heritage, but this was not possible during the long struggle over who would own and possess the land.

Did Maine play any part in the Revolutionary War?

More than we might expect. When the Revolution began in 1775, men from Machias, Maine, seized the *Margaretta*, a British sloop; their descendants claim this was the first such capture of the war. And throughout the Revolutionary War, the British showed a keen interest in the waters of Penobscot Bay, just about at the mid-part of the long Maine coast. As a result, the Massachusetts Bay colony sent a large fleet in the summer of 1779, intending to recapture the area. The Penobscot Bay expedition was one of the truly unmitigated disasters of the war for the Americans, however. Just about every ship that went north either was captured or was forced aground (and then burned by the British). Paul Revere, who had already done the most sensational action of his long life (the ride that warned the colonists that the British were coming to the countryside), was court-martialed for his part in the Penobscot Bay expedition.

Who is the single most famous woman from Maine during this early period?

Very few people knew her story until historian Laurel Thatcher Ulrich brought out *A Midwife's Tale*. Ulrich's book takes the reader through the rich, complex, and daunting

This painting by Dominic Serres (1719–1793) depicts the Penobscot fleet on its way to its fateful encounter with the British in 1779.

world that Martha Ballard faced during the late eighteenth and early nineteenth centuries. A native of Massachusetts, Ballard came north to Maine with her family soon after the Revolutionary War. While her husband and sons cut trees, sawed lumber, and attempted to make a home in the wilderness, Ballard tended first to her family and then her neighbors. Over the course of a long career, she was present as midwife at the birth of more than 1,000 babies, and lost very few of them. We would know none of this information today except for her remarkable diary, which still exists.

How did Maine finally become its own state?

Massachusetts actually was weary of administering so large a territory, and the Bay State leaders were not dismayed when they learned that numerous Mainers ached for independence. The right moment came when the events of 1819–1820 disturbed the nation as a whole. Missouri applied for statehood, and it was obvious that the Show Me State would enter the Union as a slave state, one in which slavery was permitted. The trouble was that this would throw off the balance between slave and free states in the U.S. Senate.

Many arguments were made, and the tone of the national debate became unpleasant enough that many historians see 1819–1820 as the first harbinger of the American Civil War. In the end it was agreed that Missouri would enter as a slave state, and that Maine, spliced off from Massachusetts, would enter as a free one. The balance of political power was therefore preserved, and Maine took its place as the twenty-third state.

How did Maine fare in the antebellum years, the decades leading to the Civil War?

Maine flourished. Its population remained relatively small, but its arts and handcrafts became known everywhere. Maine's single largest contribution to the nation—in those years—was in the building of ships. The oak and pine trees of Maine were already legendary for their strength and consistency (this is one reason the British Royal Navy had been so keen on Maine), but Mainers now displayed special skill in building the best schooners, sloops, and even yachts of the time. It was during these years that the coast of Maine gained the upper hand on the interior, in an economic sense, and that disparity is still seen today. Many of the fine homes and estates along the coast were first built in the years leading up to the Civil War.

Was there any doubt that Maine would be with the Union, when the Civil War came?

Not in the slightest. Mainers had been around for more than two centuries, but they had only been allowed statehood forty years earlier. It was, therefore, especially important for them to demonstrate a powerful loyalty to the Union, and this they did.

The action for which Maine is most famous is the defense of Little Round Top on July 2, 1863. On the second day of the Battle of Gettysburg, Lieutenant Colonel Joshua Chamberlain and his men from Maine fended off eleven separate attacks by Confeder-

Which state has the largest number of Civil War monuments?

In the South it is Virginia, but in the North it is a tie between Ohio and Maine. And, given the great disparity between the populations of those states (with Maine much the smaller), it is clear that Mainers treasure their connection to the Civil War. It was during that great conflict that they matured as a people and claimed their identity.

ates, many of whom were from Alabama. The 250-odd men from Maine withstood each attack with great coolness, and when he was out of ammunition, Chamberlain ordered a bayonet charge down the hill. He led the charge in person, and the exhausted Confederates were swept from the field. The fight at Little Round Top—brilliantly shown in the 1993 film *Gettysburg*—was a turning point in the war, as observers realized Union men could fight just as brilliantly, and with as much passion, as their Southern opponents.

What was the single worst day in the history of Maine?

Some cynics might declare that every Maine winter has a host of such days, and that it's a lucky person who survives any of them. In truth, however, Mainers are so well-prepared that they seldom meet with real disaster. And the great irony is that the worst disaster ever to befall the state came at the warmest time of year.

On July 4, 1866, Portland hosted a major celebration of the national holiday. Thousands of people, both from Portland and the hinterland, were present. Somehow, someone cast a firework into a bale of hay, and a truly disastrous fire ensued. A few dozen people were killed in the fire, but roughly 12,000 were rendered homeless. These two figures, plus the fact that the disaster happened at a time of celebration, makes July 4, 1866, the worst day in the state's history.

How did Maine fare in the decades that followed the Civil War?

It was a time of great growth. The lumber and shipbuilding industries kept right on moving (there is a four-mile section of the Maine coast where the people claim more ships have been launched than any comparable area in the world), but it was the beginning of the tourist trade that pointed in the direction of Maine's future. In the 1870s and 1880s, many wealthy families of Boston, New York, and Philadelphia discovered Maine, its cool summer breezes most especially. In a time before air conditioning was even invented, the coolness made all the difference, and the Vanderbilts, Morgans, and Eliots moved north to Mount Desert Island for the summer months. Acadia National Park was not yet formed, but the actions of these wealthy people led to large sections of land being preserved in a pristine condition. Bar Harbor became the village of choice for many of these outsiders, and they brought much wealth to the region.

What role did Maine play in the First and Second World Wars?

The world wars were a definite boon to Maine, helping along its economy. The First World War ended a little too soon, from the perspective of some Mainers, but the Second World War created an immense demand for products from Maine. Portland, the major port that was closest to the European front, saw an enormous U.S. Navy presence during World War II. Quite a few of the GIs who shipped out from Portland liked what they saw and later returned to the area to settle.

When World War II ended, Maine was in good shape economically, and the state soon advertised itself as Vacationland, the place where other New Englanders came to enjoy the simple pleasures of sailing, fishing, and long walks along the beach. Within a decade or two, the tourist promotions were spread to other states, and Maine began to develop the reputation as *the* vacation spot of choice on the East Coast.

Was lobstering always a big part of life along the Maine coast?

Not in the early years. Maine's fishermen used to concentrate on cod and salmon, but as the fishing stocks depleted, they turned their attention to lobstering and made this another of the great successes for the tourist industry. Many people from Boston and even Connecticut do not consider their summer complete unless they've had lobster from Maine.

Lobsters are a big part of the fun and culture of Maine.

It was during the 1960s and 1970s, too, that Maine won attention as one of the "cleanest" states, meaning that a person could stroll through the woods and feel close to nature in its natural, primary sense. The Appalachian Trail won widespread popularity during these years, and Acadia National Park, which is largely (but not entirely) on Mount Desert Island, became one of the most visited of all national parks.

What is notable about the city of Eastport?

Several things. Eastport is the easternmost city in the United States (nearby Lubec is the easternmost municipality). Eastport is made up of several islands. And, as a result of a dispute during the War of 1812, in 1814 the British claimed that Eastport was part of New Brunswick (which was not yet a Canadian province) and occupied it until 1818, making it the only U.S. municipality ever under foreign rule.

What is meant by "windjamming"?

Maine has always been a place for sailors, but the 1980s and 1990s brought a renewed interest in the windjammer fleet, meaning the sloops and schooners that carry tourists out into the Atlantic for five- or six-day tours. Those who love the windjammers—and there are many—prize the fact that the tourist gets to perform some of the sailing activities, and that he or she comes away enriched from the experience.

Can anyone predict where Vacationland will be a generation from now?

Where Maine is concerned, conservative predictions tend to be better than extravagant ones. The chances are that Maine will continue to display that nearly unique combination of handcrafts and pleasure advertising that has made the state so successful. The winters will continue to be hard and long, and Mainers will continue to gripe, knowing all the while that the hardest winters tend to bring forth the most beautiful springs and summers.

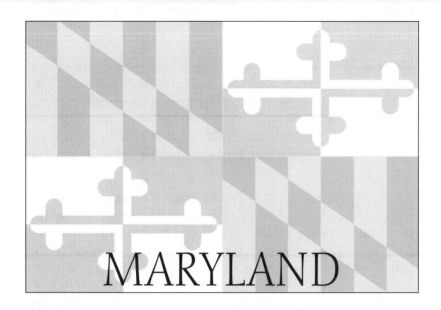

MARYLAND

Nickname: "The Old Line State"
Capital: Annapolis
Statehood: April 28, 1788; 7th state

AT A GLANCE

Where does the state nickname come from?

"Old Line" comes from the fact that Maryland soldiers played a heroic role in the last stages of the Battle of Long Island during the Revolutionary War. Fought in August 1776, the battle was a loss for the Americans and a terrible discouragement to General George Washington. Late in the battle, he witnessed a section of Maryland soldiers fighting to prevent the British from cutting off the main body of retreating Americans; Washington dubbed these men his "Old Line" soldiers, and the name stuck.

What are the most important signs and symbols of the Old Line State?

"Manly Deeds, Womanly Words," the official state motto, comes from the coat of arms of the Calvert family, Anglo-Irish aristocrats who wanted to establish a colony in North America to serve as a haven for Roman Catholics; King Charles I granted them title to the area we now call Maryland. The Baltimore oriole is the state bird, and the black-eyed susan is the state flower. The white oak—one of the most popular of all trees nationwide—is the official state tree.

How large, or small, is Maryland?

In the early period of its development, Maryland seemed large to the pioneers, the men and women who established the first plantations. Over time, they began to run out of 197 room, however, and Maryland—at 12,406 square miles (32,132 square kilometers)—is forty-second among the fifty states in geographic size. The population of 5,928,814, as enumerated in the census of 2010, places Maryland nineteenth among the states in terms of population.

Why is Maryland so less-known than Virginia? Wasn't it settled at about the same time?

Virginia actually came first by a full generation, but this isn't the reason why Maryland is so often slighted. Maryland and Virginia had reasonably similar histories through the colonial period, but Virginia had a larger population, and it gained most of the attention. And when the American Revolution came along, Virginia seized almost all the glory, so far as the states along Chesapeake Bay were concerned. Though it often lives in the shadow of its larger, more populous neighbor, Maryland has been the home of many inventors and innovations, and the chances are it will continue to be a quiet success on its part of the Atlantic coast.

Maryland is one of the oddest-shaped of all the states, but the result is that the visitor can experience all sorts of natural variety in a short distance. From crowded Baltimore, one can journey south along the east side of Chesapeake Bay, and from the northeast corner one can journey straight west, with an extremely skinny spot in the state, at the town of Hancock. Maryland's coastline is quite short, but it's memorable. And throughout the tour, one finds all sorts of rolling countryside, which is pleasing to the eye.

Do Marylanders talk about the weather very much?

Not really. They know what to expect: mild winters and very hot summers. Maryland tends to escape most of the perils we expect from our twenty-first century weather. Hurricanes tend to pass over the state, and tornadoes are rare. Summer temperatures can be extreme, and Marylanders look for relief on Chesapeake Bay, one of the most frequented of all waterways in the nation for amateur boating.

Can the Marylander be told apart from his neighbors in Virginia and Pennsylvania?

One used to be able to detect the difference right away; the Marylander stood out as a rural person, trying to find his way in a conglomeration of urban areas. Today, though, the Marylander is likely to be just as sophisticated as his Washington, D.C., neighbor.

EARLY HISTORY

For how long have humans lived in what we call the Old Line State?

For thousands of years. Most of their names and tribal occupations are unknown to us, however, as Maryland is not rich in archaeological remains. About the most we can say is that when the first European settlers arrived, they found the Leni-Lenape, whose name means "The People," living in much of present-day Maryland.

Who were the first Europeans to settle in the region?

Some Swedish merchants may have skirted the coast, but English men and women, who began arriving in the 1630s, primarily settled Maryland. The *Ark* and the *Dove* are their equivalent to the *Mayflower* of Massachusetts fame. The first arrivals came to St. Mary's City, almost at the southern tip of the inner part of Maryland. Henrietta Maria, the French-born queen of England, named the area, and the hope of Lord Baltimore was that

A replica of the Maryland *Dove* is anchored at historic St. Mary's City.

Maryland would become a haven for English and Irish Catholics. King Charles I agreed, and Maryland was, for a brief time, the only American colony with a substantial number of Catholics, even though they never formed the majority.

What were the early years of the Maryland colony like?

They were very contentious, with Protestants and Catholics vying for power. Some outright fighting occurred, with Virginia colonists lending support to the Protestants of Maryland. And in 1689, upon learning that William and Mary had overthrown King James and established a new government in the motherland, Maryland went through a revolution of its own. Maryland attempted to demonstrate its allegiance to the Protestant cause and removed the Catholics from all places of authority. The dissension was so sufficient that King William later took away the charter previously given to the Calvert family and made Maryland a royal province. From that time forward, the colony was more secure.

How and when did tobacco become the basis for Maryland's economy?

Maryland started a generation after Virginia. In the 1660s, tobacco became the leading export, and a hilarious novel, *The Sot-Weed Factor* was published in Old England. The view from the motherland was that Maryland had nothing but tobacco and that its people were little better than opium addicts! Of course there was much exaggeration and poetic license in the book, but it remained in print a very long time and helped to shape popular conceptions of life in Maryland.

In fact, however, life in colonial Maryland was rather tough, for the African American slaves most especially. Many sensational stories have been told of hair-raising escapes from slavery in Maryland, and the slaveholders of that colony—and later state—went to remarkable efforts to recapture their "people" and return them to slavery.

For whom is Annapolis named?

The city is named for Queen Anne, during whose reign (1702–1714) Maryland began to prosper. A genteel style of life developed in the Maryland plantations during this time, and life in the colony was more stable than at any previous time. This continued through the mid-colonial period, and the anticipation of the British crown was that Maryland would remain one of the most contented of colonies. It's true that there were no outbreaks against British government during the 1760s, but when the American Revolution began in 1775, Marylanders proved quite ready to step up to the challenge.

Maryland did not produce any outstanding political leaders during the Revolution. Here, as so often, Virginia overshadowed Maryland. But Annapolis played host to a meeting of delegates that could have led to the writing of the new Constitution, but, once again, the Old Line State was upstaged, this time by its Pennsylvania neighbor!

How important was the Mason-Dixon Line?

Run by two Englishmen in the 1760s, the Mason-Dixon Line was vital for an understanding of where Pennsylvania ended and Maryland began. Beyond that, however, the Line also became a symbol for the division between North and South. Even today, we still speak of events that happen north or south of the Mason-Dixon Line. Running this boundary was necessary because King Charles I's grant to Maryland often conflicted with King Charles II's grant to William Penn and the colony of Pennsylvania.

How did Maryland fare in the National period, meaning the early nineteenth century?

Neither Maryland nor its neighbor Delaware gained much population in the early decades of the 1800s, because so many state residents picked up and moved west. The price of tobacco declined, making Maryland farms less profitable. But the episode for

What is Francis Scott Key's connection to a less noble aspect of Maryland history?

It was not Key's fault that he married into the family of Roger Taney, who later became the chief justice of the U.S. Supreme Court. But when Taney handed down the Court's decision in the infamous case of Dred Scott in 1857, the family name was tainted. In the ruling, the Supreme Court declared that the Founding Fathers had never seen blacks as in any way equal to whites, and that African Americans were not citizens in any sense of the word.

which Maryland is best known, its moment of shining glory, came in 1814, during the latter part of the War of 1812.

Having already burned Washington, D.C., the British were on a roll, and when they came to assault Baltimore, in September 1814, the odds seemed stacked in their favor. Knowing they would come, the commander of Fort McHenry, in Baltimore's harbor, asked the ladies of the city to stitch the largest American flag yet seen. When it was complete, he hung it over the battlements and declared this was one outpost that would not fall.

Is this where the National Anthem comes from?

It is the very moment. Throughout the night of September 13–14, 1814, the British fleet assaulted Fort McHenry with cannon shots and bombs, as well as the new Congreve rockets that had proved so effective in the capture of Washington, D.C. All night, American Francis Scott Key, who was aboard a British warship to conduct an exchange of prisoners, awaited the result, and when the first light of morning came, he rushed up on deck. Somewhat to his surprise, and much to his delight, the huge American flag still waved over Fort McHenry. Key immediately penned his words, which were later attached to a British song called "To Anacreon in Heaven"; the title was eventually changed to "The Star-Spangled Banner." It officially became the National Anthem in 1931.

> O, say can you see
> By the dawn's early light
> What so proudly we hailed,
> At the twilight's last gleaming.

How did some Maryland residents fool the British during the War of 1812?

The town of Saint Michaels, Maryland, was the site of a militia battery that was used to defend the town's shipyards. Anticipating an attack, the townsfolk dimmed their lights and hung lanterns in trees and masts of ships. As a result, many British cannons shot too high, resulting in minimal damage to the town. A house that did get hit still remains and is known as the Cannonball House.

Who was one of the first African American heroes to come from Maryland?

Many of Maryland's black heroes are anonymous to us, meaning that they were slaves who escaped and made their way north, never entering the history books. One of the few prominent exceptions to the general rule was Benjamin Banneker, a black slave who gained his freedom and became an outstanding inventor.

How did Maryland fare in the years just prior to the American Civil War?

These were the worst of times for the majority of Marylanders. White slaveholders showed no sign of releasing their many slaves. Black Marylanders suffered under a legal system that, if anything, had become even worse with the passage of time. And virtually

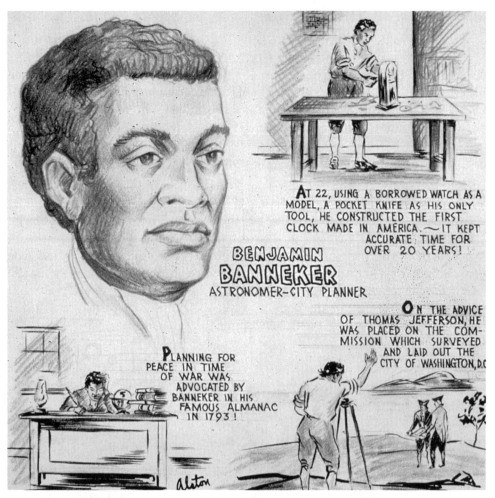

Benjamin Banneker was a naturalist, surveyor, farmer, and almanac author who also created an accurate clock when he was only twenty-two.

all Marylanders suffered from a long economic depression, caused by the continuing slide in the price of tobacco.

Maryland seemed less important than in the past, both in economic terms and in the politics of the nation. But when the Civil War commenced, Maryland was important because of its location. Washington, D.C., stood on land Maryland had once released to the national interest. If Maryland joined the Confederacy, the federal capital would almost certainly fall to the Confederates.

Was there any moment when Maryland seemed likely to go to the Confederate cause?

Virginians ardently hoped it would. In September 1862, as they crossed the Potomac into the Old Line State, soldiers of the Army of Northern Virginia sang, "Maryland, my

> ## Could the North—and the Union cause— have withstood the loss of Washington, D.C.?
>
> **V**ery likely, yes. But the setback would have been enormous, and the chances are that the Civil War would have lasted much longer. President Abraham Lincoln understood the importance of Washington, D.C., and the fact is he needed to keep Maryland in the camp of the border states.

Maryland!" which later became the state's anthem. This was an earnest effort to convince Marylanders that their fortunes were tied to tobacco and to the interests of the slave-holding Confederacy. Much to the surprise of observers, Maryland did not make any move. In fact, only a few dozen Marylanders even joined the Army of Northern Virginia. And when Robert E. Lee lost the Battle of Antietam—also known as the Battle of Sharpsburg—it was a certainty that Maryland would remain one of the border states.

Who was—and remains—the most infamous of all Marylanders?

Beyond a doubt this was John Wilkes Booth, the misguided stage actor who shot and killed Abraham Lincoln on April 14, 1865. Booth came from a famous family of actors who lived in rural Maryland, and from the very beginning his sympathies lay with the Confederacy (this was *not* true of his elder brother). On learning that Lincoln intended eventually to enfranchise the slaves, Booth made his mind up, and he snuck into Ford's Theatre, in Washington, D.C., to shoot and kill the president. Booth then escaped across the border to Maryland and led federal troops on a long chase. When they finally ran him down in Port Royal, Virginia, they shot and killed him on the spot.

How did Maryland do in the last third of the nineteenth century?

The Civil War ended, the slaves were freed, and tobacco finally came to the end of its long run. Some tobacco farms remained, but most Marylanders saw the need to diversify. Major manufacturing did not come to the Old Line State until the early twentieth century, but the late nineteenth century saw a major increase in the number of schools and colleges, and, the founding in 1876 of the world-famous Johns Hopkins University.

Baltimore, meanwhile, saw some of its worst days, as what had once been a beautiful colonial town turned into a serious urban slum. The Progressive Era, starting around 1890, witnessed the cleanup of Baltimore. The city also produced one of the great social critics of the era. H. L. Mencken, a Baltimore native, became the acid-tongued reporter and essayist who skewered many aspects of American society (attacking the ignorance and bigotry that existed in the Southern states was one of his favorites).

How important was—and is—the Chesapeake Bay Bridge?

To the people of Maryland and to commuters to and from Washington, D.C., it could not be more important. For two generations, automobile traffic had to go all the way "up"

203

to northern Maryland in order to approach Washington, D.C., and numerous Marylanders simply moved to the nation's capital, rather than make that effort. In 1952, the Chesapeake Bay Bridge, roughly six miles long and twenty-four feet above the bay, was completed. For two years, it held only westbound traffic. This was altered in 1954, when it opened to traffic in both directions. Less known than other great American bridges, such as the Golden Gate Bridge, the Bay Bridge, as it is most commonly known, is as important to the economy of the Chesapeake region as the Golden Gate is to its section of California.

The U.S. Naval Academy at Annapolis.

When did the U.S. Naval Academy become so prestigious an institution?

Established in 1845, the Naval Academy was important right from the outset, but only naval officers and their families knew of it until the mid-twentieth century. The Academy then became better known for its cutting-edge programs in the sciences, and many young people attended, even though their final goal was not to serve in the U.S. Navy. Among the academy's most famous graduates are Jimmy Carter (class of 1946), who later became president of the United States, and John S. McCain (class of 1958), who later served as a senator from Arizona and ran for the presidency.

What was life in Maryland like during the Civil Rights era?

Maryland was not—like North Carolina and Alabama—rocked by a decade-long series of protest marches or changes. Plenty of racial and ethnic tension existed, however. There were riots in the late 1960s, especially in Baltimore.

Maryland native Thurgood Marshall rose to become the first African American justice of the U.S. Supreme Court. Marshall's presence on the high court became a powerful influence, helping to remind white Americans both of how far blacks had come and how much the laws of the nation needed to reflect a new, color-blind society.

How did Baltimore get cleaned up in the 1970s?

The waterways around Baltimore are some of the most congested, and consequently polluted, in the nation. This is the inevitable result of so much manufacturing and the passage of so many ships. In the early 1970s, however, concerned Baltimoreans made a major effort to clean up the Inner Harbor, and within a decade they turned it into a model for historic preservation and defense of the environment. Today, the visitor strolls through colonial-era homes and walks cobblestoned streets that have almost no equal for beauty and ease of use.

What was life in Maryland like at the turn of the twenty-first century?

The look of the state continued to be rural, but its feel was decidedly urban and suburban. Nearly three-quarters of all Marylanders lived in close proximity either to Washington, D.C., or Baltimore, and some critics alleged that the entire state was a vast bedroom community.

ODDS AND ENDS

How many people come to see the wild horses on Assateague Island?

The thirty-seven-mile-long island—two-thirds of it in Maryland, one third in Virginia—has other attractions, of course, including its long beaches, but the wild horses are surely the most popular. No one knows precisely how or when these horses arrived, but it seems possible they are the descendants of a group that came ashore after a shipwreck. One thing is for certain: these wild horses provide a magnificent sight for the tourist.

The wild horses of Assateague Island.

Where will the Old Line State be a generation from now?

Maryland will continue to receive less attention than Virginia and Washington, D.C. This is part of the state's fate, and it cannot be avoided. On the other hand, the lack of attention sometimes allows Maryland to make advances that surprise, and even confound, the people of other states. Expect that Maryland will continue to move along at a slow and quiet pace and that it will have sudden moments of unexpected glory.

MASSACHUSETTS

Nickname: "The Bay State"
Capital: Boston
Statehood: February 6, 1788; 6th state

AT A GLANCE

What is the origin of the nickname, and what is the state motto?

The coast of Massachusetts contains a great bay that extends all the way from Province-town to Cape Ann. The early settlers called it the Bay colony, and the nickname transferred to the state. The state motto is "By the sword we seek peace, but peace only under liberty."

What are the most important signs and symbols of the Bay State?

The one that has endured the longest is the image of an Indian, on the state seal, who implores with the words, "Come over and save us." These words came from the Puritan founders of Massachusetts, who believed it their task to come and civilize, as well as Christianize, the Native Americans. The black-capped chickadee is the state bird, the mayflower is the state flower, and the American Elm is the state tree.

How large, or small, is the Bay State?

Compared to midwestern and far western states, Massachusetts is very small. Comprised of 8,262 square miles (21,398 square kilometers), Massachusetts places forty-second among the fifty states in geographic size. The population of 6,692,824, places Massachusetts as fourteenth in population.

Fenway Park is home to the Boston Red Sox.

Is there a center to the widespread cultural life of Massachusetts?

If so, it is found in the one square mile that surrounds Fenway Park. The famous CITGO sign is close by, as are Huntington Avenue and Northeastern University. College professors rub shoulders with bricklayers, who in turn hail taxicab drivers who come from far-off lands. There's an excitement to this part of downtown Boston and a real multiculturalism that makes the city, and state, one of the most vibrant of places to be.

Is there more to Massachusetts than Boston, Worcester, and Provincetown?

People have been asking this question for more than a century. Boston devotees often give the answer in the negative; they think the only worthwhile things are found within the big city. But in fact, Massachusetts has a broad array of wonders, some of which have nothing to do with the urban experience. Just ask anyone who lives in the Berkshire or Hampshire Hills.

It's true that Cape Cod, Nantucket, and Martha's Vineyard are hard to beat, but there are many scenic wonders, often on a smaller scale, to be found. Bish Bash Falls in the extreme southwestern part of the Bay State is one example; the Chesterfield Gorge is another. The Potholes of Shelburne Falls have drawn oohs and aahs from visitors for decades, and that area is well-known for the skill of its craftspeople. If one looks for one true scenic wonder, however, one that really encapsulates what the Bay State has to offer, it might well be the sunset over Provincetown, with all eyes looking to the west.

How can so small a state as Massachusetts provide so much conversation—and debate—where the weather is concerned?

The answer lies in the number of Massachusetts Yankees who have kept diaries over the centuries, and who therefore provide us with a wealth of knowledge about Bay State weather. We know, for example, that the winter of 1697 was the worst of the seventeenth century and that 1740 was the worst of the eighteenth century. Massachusetts has, over time, provided more weather data than almost any other state, and it should come as no surprise that some of the loudest voices about the dangers of global warming come from there. What they should add, however, is that if Massachusetts weather is a good example, then we stand an equal chance of freezing to death!

How many artists, writers, poets, and sculptors have lived in the Bay State?

It makes for an incredible list, ranging from Robert Frost and Emily Dickinson to Robert Francis and sculptor Daniel Chester French. The many colleges and universities of Boston produce more than their share of Nobel Laureates, and the little hill towns of the western part of the state shelter a simply amazing number of visual artists. Pottery and glass-blowing are among the most numerous.

Perhaps all this cultural activity takes place simply because Massachusetts is locked in by snow and ice four months a year, forcing people to use their internal resources to create something new. Very likely, however, it also has something to do with the Puritan work ethic, which came to the United States via the Puritans and Pilgrims of 1620 and 1630. Slackers do exist in Massachusetts, but they are not much in favor. Even the most antiestablishment writer or artist in the Bay State tends to hold himself or herself to a strict schedule, and to therefore turn out an impressive body of work.

Who are some of the favorite sons and daughters of the Bay State?

It makes for a very long list, running from John Adams and his son John Quincy Adams to John F. Kennedy and his younger brothers Robert and Ted. The people of Massachusetts are also very fond of cultural heroes too, people like Annie Sullivan, who went south in order to teach the young Helen Keller. Quite a few leading Massachusetts people actually performed their most important work out of state, such as Johnny Appleseed, for example, who left Massachusetts for Ohio.

Poet Robert Frost was among a number of renowned authors and poets from Massachusetts.

The Bay State has produced a number of social activists, people who see it as their task to reform some area of society. Among the best known are Dorothea Dix, who singlehandedly reformed aspects of the prison system, as well as treatment of the insane, in the nineteenth century. Massachusetts also has had a number of countercultural heroes, such as Abbie Hoffman.

EARLY HISTORY

Why was it so easy for the Pilgrims and the Puritans to take over eastern Massachusetts?

In a physical sense, it wasn't easy: they battled fierce winters, along with hunger and deprivation. In terms of Native American resistance, however, it was easy because so many Indians died in the smallpox epidemic of 1616–1617, three years before the Pilgrims arrived on the Mayflower. The Indians never knew what hit them. The white settlers rejoiced that there was so little resistance. Only later did it become apparent that European disease accomplished most of the work.

Is there any real difference between the Pilgrims and the Puritans?

Not in a religious sense: both groups dissented from the Anglican Church (Church of England). The difference is in terms of social status. The Pilgrims were rather humble, working-class folk, who were pleased, and then delighted, to establish a small colony. The Puritans, on the whole, were middle- and upper-class, and they were extremely ambitious. One imagines that if a Puritan from, say, 1650, could arrive in Massachusetts today, he or she would be thrilled by the cultural and economic advancement, while lamenting the backslide in terms of religious feeling.

By 1692, the Puritans overshadowed the Pilgrims to such a degree that William and Mary—the only joint monarchs of English history—folded the Plymouth colony into the Massachusetts Bay establishment, and the success of Massachusetts was assured. It's important, too, to remember that all of Maine came within the Massachusetts fold, and remained there until 1820.

What else happened in Massachusetts in 1692?

The Salem Witch Trials occurred in Salem Village. Several young girls claimed they were possessed by the devil and accused some local women of being witches. This led to hysteria and a trial that resulted in the hanging of nineteen women and more than one hundred others being accused of participating in witchcraft.

How many French and Indian Wars were there?

If one counts King Philip's War, which raged in Massachusetts between 1675 and 1676, there were a total of five. King William's War (1689–1697), Queen Anne's War

(1702–1713), and King George's War (1744–1748) were all draws, meaning that neither side imposed its will on the other. But the final conflict, known appropriately as the French and Indian War (1754–1760) ended in complete success for the Anglo-American forces. From that point, there was no doubt that the Puritan ethic would dominate New England, and it was increasingly apparent that New England was going to dominate the other northern and middle colonies.

Why is Massachusetts so important to the story of the Revolution?

Perhaps it's because so many of the leaders of that struggle came from Massachusetts. One thinks immediately of Samuel Adams and his second cousin John Adams, but John Hancock, Joseph Warren, Paul Revere, and many other Massachusetts men played important roles. And of course, the early fighting almost all took place in Massachusetts.

Lexington Green and Concord Bridge were the scenes of the first skirmishes, on April 19, 1775, and Bunker Hill, right across the Mystic River from downtown Boston, was the scene of the first big battle. George Washington arrived in Cambridge on July 3, 1775, to take command of the forces now called the Continental Army. Washington's first major success came in March 1776, when his placement of cannons on Dorchester Heights forced the British to evacuate Boston (the state still celebrates Evacuation Day on March 17 each year).

How much did the Bay State change in the decades following the American Revolution?

Massachusetts was a frontier state, and a fairly rough place until about 1820; after that year, it became increasingly refined. Bostonians, especially, were known for their easy charm and social grace, and the capital city took on a truly elegant demeanor. People began calling Boston the Athens of America, as its many cultural, educational, and philanthropic institutions thrived. Harvard College, known for its graduates becoming men of the cloth, turned into Harvard University, known for its scientific, medical, and legal experts.

Architecturally, too, the Bay State took on a new look. Charles Bulfinch, a noted architect, started the Federalist style in Boston; many of his buildings remain today. And pretty, and sometimes elegant, churches and town halls fill the Massachusetts countryside. By then, too, Massachusetts had fully evolved its special contribution to American democracy: the New England town meeting. Usually held in May, the town meeting is where the moderator, selectmen, town clerk, assessors and so forth present their business to the town voters, for approval or rejection.

When did the Irish come to Massachusetts?

They had already been there to a small degree, but the 1840s was the decade in which they really arrived. Almost at once, Boston became a city divided between its Anglo and Irish sections, with rather few people able to cross the lines between. Experiencing ethnic distrust, even enmity, the Irish struggled for a long time, but by the early twentieth century they had practically taken over the post office and fire departments of the towns of eastern Massachusetts. Today the difference between the Anglo and Irish contingent is usually shown by whether they choose Sam Adams beer or Guinness ale to celebrate Evacuation Day, which, by sheer coincidence, also falls on Saint Patrick's Day.

What role did Massachusetts play in the Civil War?

Not nearly as large as it did in the American Revolution. By 1861, Massachusetts had fallen behind numerous other Northern states in population, and try as it might, it could not field nearly as many men. But in moral terms, Massachusetts was important. It was here that the first two regiments of African American soldiers (led by white officers) were raised, and it was in the Bay State that the most eloquent spokesmen for abolition delivered their speeches.

After the Civil War, Massachusetts fell even further behind the more populous states, but it retained its leadership in the arts and sciences. Even though Alexander Graham Bell was a native of Scotland, and though he migrated to Canada, it was in Boston that he developed the world's first practicable telephone. And when the Massachusetts Institute of Technology (MIT) opened its doors in 1871, Massachusetts became a magnet for inventors of all kinds.

When did the Kennedys get their start in politics?

John F. Kennedy, the thirty-fifth president of the United States, was born in Brookline, Massachusetts, a descendant of successful Irish politicians on both sides of his family.

President John F. Kennedy poses with his children and other relatives' children at the Kennedy Compound in Hyannis Port, Massachusetts.

His grandfather, John F. "Honey Fitz" Fitzgerald was mayor of Boston. Even so, it took a combination of Fitzgerald political skill and Kennedy money to launch the dynamo that became the Kennedys of Hyannis Port and Washington, D.C.

Joseph Kennedy Jr. (1915–1944) was expected to be the standard-bearer. Following his death in World War II, leadership passed to the second-eldest son, John, better known as Jack. He ran for a U.S. congressional seat from Cambridge, won it handily, and then reached the U.S. Senate in a serious struggle with Henry Cabot Lodge. From there, Jack Kennedy employed his charm and good looks, as well as those of his wife, Jackie Bouvier Kennedy, and in 1960 he was elected president. He was assassinated in Dallas, Texas, on November 22, 1963.

How many American presidents have hailed from Massachusetts?

First came John Adams, who was in the White House from 1797 to 1801. His son, John Quincy Adams, was elected in 1824, and he served one term. In 1923, Vice President Calvin Coolidge, who was Vermont-born but a Massachusetts citizen by choice, was suddenly elevated to the presidency by the untimely death of President Warren G. Harding. Next came John Kennedy, in 1960. The most recent president from Massachusetts is George H. W. Bush, who was born in Milton and served from 1989 to 1993. This totals five Massachusetts residents who have reached the White House. Incidentally, all but Coolidge were born in Norfolk County.

Could the Kennedys have gone on to send more sons (and daughters) into national politics?

For a time it seemed that nothing could stop the combination of Irish descent and Boston money. Robert F. Kennedy became a U.S. senator from New York and appeared to be on his way to winning the Democratic presidential nomination in 1968, when he was struck down by an assassin. The fourth and youngest brother, Edward M. Kennedy, made a run for the Democratic nomination in 1980, but he lost to incumbent Jimmy Carter. Kennedy remained in the U.S. Senate for the rest of his life, however, and some claim his fingerprints are all over the most important liberal legislation of the late twentieth century.

The second and third generation of Kennedys have produced a few members of the U.S. House of Representatives, but no outstanding stars. John F. Kennedy Jr., who repeatedly declared he had no wish to follow in his famous father's footsteps, died tragically in a plane crash in the summer of 1999, leading many to declare that there was a curse on the family.

How many other Massachusetts persons have come close to the presidency, without attaining it?

It's a long list. In recent years, there were several men who made the attempt. Senator Paul Tsongas ran in 1988, but Michael Dukakis, at that time the governor of Massachusetts, won the nomination. Dukakis lost the election of 1988 in a rout to Vice President George H. W. Bush, but this did not prevent other Massachusetts sons from making the attempt. In 2004, Senator John F. Kerry—who was Austrian by ethnicity, rather than Irish—captured the Democratic nomination but lost the general election to incumbent George W. Bush. In 2012, former governor Mitt Romney won the Republican nomination but lost the election to Barack Obama.

What was the Bay State's economy like at the turn of the twenty-first century?

The Massachusetts economy was a fascinating mixture of technical and technocratic, while plenty of residents continued to earn their money the old-fashioned way: by the sweat of their brows. Commercial fishing was much smaller than in previous years, but it still had a strong appeal. Computer programmers were a dime a dozen in the Boston area, and Highway 128, which covers Boston in a concentric ring, was filled with computer companies. The western part of the state continued to produce a mixture of loggers, farmers, poets, and college professors. Only the northern middle of the state was suffering in 2000, as it had not developed a specialty.

SPORTS

How important are the Boston Red Sox to the city of Boston?

Bostonians live or die with the Red Sox every season, but the same is true of millions of other people around the Bay State; in fact, Red Sox loyalty runs so deep that there are sections of southern Connecticut where towns are split right down the middle: half Red Sox and half Yankee fans. Legend has it that the Red Sox suffer from the curse of the Bambino (meaning Babe Ruth). In 1918, the Red Sox traded Ruth, who was then primarily a pitcher, to the Yankees, where he became one of the greatest, and surely the most famous, of all baseball hitters.

What are the worst of all the Red Sox failures?

Bay State residents will never forget Yankee shortstop Bucky Dent's pop fly that magically turned into a home run in October 1978; it spelled the end of one of the better Red Sox seasons. In 1986, the Red Sox reached the World Series and played quite well, only to be outdueled by the New York Mets (at least it was not the Yankees *this* time, fans said). Red Sox fans also lament the seasons of 1967 and 1975. On both occasions, the Red Sox won the pennant, only to falter in the World Series. And fans of Ted Williams—the last ballplayer to hit the magic batting average number of .400—lament that he never had a World Series ring.

Boston finally pulled it together in 2004, when the Red Sox defeated the St. Louis Cardinals in the World Series. The curse of the Bambino was finally lifted, after eighty-six years. They went on to win the World Series in 2007 and 2013 as well.

How did the Boston Marathon become the premier event of its kind?

The Ancient Greeks actually did not run marathons, but the modern Greeks began the practice with the Olympics of 1896. A number of track and field men from Boston and Cambridge were present, and on their return home, they organized the first Boston marathon in April 1897 (fifteen men ran that first year). Within a decade, there were 100 times as many runners, and the number of spectators grew so large that it could only be estimated.

Marathon enthusiasts remember Bill Rodgers, who won four times in the 1970s, but since 1990 outsiders have primarily won the Marathon, with men from Kenya holding most of the trophies. The all-time favorite of the true Boston Marathon fans, however, is John "the Elder" Kelley, who ran the Marathon sixty-one times, and won

The Boston Marathon is one of the most famous foot races on the planet. Thousands flock to the city each year to participate or watch this premier endurance event.

it twice. When asked where his enthusiasm came from, Kelley replied that it was a natural high. Anyone who watched him agreed.

Why don't we hear more about the Boston Celtics?

Year after year, especially in the 1960s, the Celtics performed magic in Boston Garden, winning one National Basketball League (NBA) championship after another, and producing some of the greatest men in the sport. Bill Russell was perhaps the most famous. And yet it never mattered to the same degree. Bay State residents take for granted that the Celtics have won nearly 20 NBA championships, but they concentrate instead on the painful fact that the Red Sox have won only three World Series since 1918.

How has the Boston Marathon coped with the disaster of 2013, when two terrorists set off a number of bombs near the finish line?

Remarkably well. In 2014, just to make sure the spectators turned out, the organizing committee adopted the slogan "Boston Strong." So far, this slogan has done its work, and it seems likely that the Boston Marathon will continue to be *the* marathon, worldwide.

Where will the Bay State be in, say, the year 2050?

The chances are it will not be a political powerhouse; those days are now gone. That it will continue to have millions of devoted fans, men and women devoted to their sports   215

What was the scariest day in Massachusetts history?

One can point to the terror bombing at the Boston Marathon in 2013, or to the Dark Tide (a flood of molasses that killed twenty people in Boston) of 1919, but the single most frightening event came on November 18, 1755. An enormous earthquake, which caused almost 2,000 chimneys to collapse immediately, awoke Bostonians and their country cousins at 4 A.M. Fortunately, the quake was centered off Cape Ann, to the northeast, and Boston escaped what could have been a complete disaster. Bostonians remembered that day for many years, however.

teams and to the commonwealth itself, is beyond doubt. But the single most likely prediction we can make is that Massachusetts as a whole, and the Boston area in particular, will be the number-one draw where high school seniors and their parents are concerned. Harvard, MIT, the Berkeley School of Music, Northeastern University, and all sorts of other places of higher education will continue to attract the best and brightest from around the nation.

MICHIGAN

Nickname: "The Great Lakes State"
Capital: Lansing
Statehood: January 26, 1837; 26th state

AT A GLANCE

What are the most important signs and symbols of the Great Lakes State?

"If You Seek a Pleasant Peninsula, Look About You" is the official state motto. Many forests blanket Michigan. The robin is the state bird, and the apple blossom is the state flower. The white pine—one of the most popular of all trees, nationwide—is the official state tree.

How large, or small, is Michigan?

It's larger than many people first think, because they forget that the Upper Peninsula adds so much in terms of size. Comprised of 58,692 square miles (152,012 square kilometers), the Great Lakes State is twenty-third among the fifty states. The population of 9,883,640, as enumerated in the 2010 Census, places Michigan at eighth among the states.

What happened to Detroit around the turn of the twentieth century?

During the heyday of the American automobile industry, Detroit was the fourth-largest metropolitan area in the United States, and one of the wealthiest per capita. As the American auto industry reeled from Japanese and German imports, Detroit experienced a major economic decline. Some observers claim that the "rot" in Detroit's economic system was seen as early as 1985, while others claim that the city did reasonably well for another decade. There is no doubt, however, that Detroit entered the twenty-first century in sad shape.

217

The General Motors headquarters was still in Michigan, but the jobs were either outsourced or much reduced in terms of wages and benefits. The city as a whole suffered from a shrinking tax base. Areas of Detroit looked like bombed-out zones, and little business was conducted within the city. But for every person who wrote off Detroit, there was another who vowed that the city would recover one day. And the most positive recent signs were shown by residents who have reclaimed areas of the city, sometimes even growing gardens on rooftops. Also, some businesses (notably, Quicken Loans) have moved into Detroit.

Why is Michigan's natural beauty so little known and appreciated?

To anyone who drives through the Great Lakes State, it's a mystery that Michigan is not better known. There are long stretches of beautiful farms and fields, more lighthouses even than in Maine, and to top it all off, Michigan is divided into the Upper Peninsula and the Lower Peninsula, which showcase quite different scenery. Knitting it all together is the "Mighty Mac," the bridge of the Straits of Mackinac. Then again, Michigan—in its heyday—advertised its industrial and commercial strength to such a degree that many Americans forgot about the natural surroundings.

Do the people of Michigan talk about the weather very much?

For six months of the year they don't have to. Spring and summer bring plenty of sunshine and heat, but these are ameliorated by the fine breezes coming in from Lakes Huron, Erie, Michigan, and Superior. Those same breezes, in winter, however, can turn into something truly fierce. Michigan has not witnessed many natural disasters, but a great number of ships—large, small, and in-between—have been lost in storms on the Great Lakes. Canadian singer Gordon Lightfoot serenaded about the loss of one of them—in Lake Superior—in the 1976 song "Wreck of the Edmund Fitzgerald."

Can the man or woman of Michigan be told apart from his or her Midwestern neighbors?

The difference is not profound. A Michigander can often be mistaken for an Indiana Hoosier, and the same is true in reverse. It's when one begins to talk either about the great days of the automotive industry or the great years of Motown recordings that the Michigander shows his or her pride. There's a memory, too, of how the state led the way in numerous social and economic improvements, until the downturn that commenced in the 1980s.

Michigan is well known for its natural beauty, which attracts tourists who enjoy the great outdoors from all over the world.

EARLY HISTORY

For how long have humans lived in what we now call the Great Lakes State?

For thousands of years. Their names and tribal affiliations are not known to us, but it's reasonable to assume that the Ojibway, Fox, Sauk, and others who greeted the first settlers of European descent are among their descendants. Michigan does not have very much in the way of relics from the Paleo-Indian days; our knowledge becomes much more clear and certain when the first French fur traders arrived in the 1660s and 1670s.

It often seems strange that France was able to penetrate so far into the continent at so early a time. How did they leave the English behind?

France did not come to the broad coast of the eastern seaboard; rather, French explorers and settlers came down the Saint Lawrence River to enter on the Great Lakes. Once they passed Niagara Falls, the French moved with speed on to the lakes and the Midwestern lands that surround them. In most of this movement, the French were assisted by Native Americans, who taught them the art of canoe travel, and they were in pursuit of animal fur, particularly that of the beaver. Many historians declare that the humble beaver inadvertently did more for the exploration of North America than any other animal.

When was the first permanent settlement established in what is now Michigan?

The French settled Michilimackinac, right on the Strait of Mackinaw, as early as 1690, but Detroit, first established in 1702, was even more important. The city gains its name from the French word for strait. The founder was Antoine de La Mothe Cadillac, a rather unscrupulous fellow who has lent his name to Cadillac Mountain in Maine, as well as the justly famous car that used to be the standard for luxury.

The French never arrived in great numbers, but they held on to most of Michigan for over fifty years. Not until the end of the French and Indian War in 1763 did they lose their power in the region, and they were replaced by the British, who possessed the string of forts previously held by France.

Who was Pontiac?

He was a chief of the Ojibway tribe who lamented the departure of the French and intended to drive the British from the Midwest and Great Lakes. Quite a few Native American leaders laid plans like his, but very few ever came close to success. Pontiac, too, was doomed to disappointment, but for a solid six months he and his confederated Indian warriors created a very tense scene on the western frontier. All the forts between Detroit and Fort Pitt, the latter in western Pennsylvania, fell to the Indians. Only the long holdout by the garrisons of those two remaining forts ensured British victory. In 1764, Pontiac made peace with the British (he was killed by a fellow Indian in 1769).

What role did Michigan play in the Revolutionary War?

The British still held all the forts when the Revolutionary war commenced, and Colonel Henry Hamilton—based out of Detroit—became known as "the Hair-Buyer" because of his eagerness to pay Indians for American scalps. The British were stunned, however, when Colonel George Rogers Clark led Virginia militiamen all the way across the mountains and into the Midwest. Clark captured most of the British forts and ensured that the United States would gain title to most of the lands of the American heartland.

The Treaty of Paris (1783) granted the title to most of the Midwest lands to the brand new United States. Great Britain did not withdraw from the forts of the Upper Peninsula until 1794, however, and tensions between the two nations remained high. When the War of 1812 began, the British and their Indian allies captured Fort Detroit, and it remained in British hands until 1813. Once the Americans accomplished the reconquest, however, they made certain that Detroit and the surrounding area remained under the Stars and Stripes.

How and why did Michigan boom?

The answer can be put succinctly: lumber and immigration. In the two decades following the War of 1812, immigration to Michigan soared, partly as a result of the completion of the Erie Canal, which linked Buffalo with Albany, and thereby New York City. For the first time, recently arrived immigrants could take an all-water route that brought them rapidly to the very edge of the frontier, where they took advantage of low prices for land. Immigrants came from many Western European nations, but the Norwegians and Swedes showed a special interest in Michigan, because of its forests. Many lumberjacks of Michigan first learned their trade in the Old World.

What role did Michigan play in the American Civil War?

A large one. The Great Lakes State was young enough that its residents felt a need to prove themselves in battle. That the war was far away, geographically speaking, did not lessen their patriotism, and Michigan sent over 100,000 men to the battlefields. No outstanding leader of Michigan troops emerged during the war, however, and the Civil War is not strong in Michigan memory, as it is with, say, the state of Maine.

When the Civil War ended, Michigan was in good shape economically and was poised to take advantage of the combination of railroad and steamboat connections that now plied the Upper Midwest. Detroit competed with Chicago for a time, but the latter was greatly assisted by the fact that the first transcontinental railroad was routed through its area; as a result, Detroit fell behind Chicago.

What brought so many mechanics and entrepreneurs to Michigan during the late nineteenth century?

It's hard to say with certainty. Michigan was already known as a place for the rural handyman, but by around 1890, Detroit gained the reputation for being a great city for mechanics. They tinkered with all sorts of changes and inventions, and the city was ahead of nearly all its Midwestern neighbors in street lighting and the spread of telephone wires. The really amazing change, however, the one that determined much of Michigan's future, was the advent of the automobile industry.

Henry Ford (1863–1947) is, of course, the best known, but he had competitors such as Ransom E. Olds (1864–1950) and others. Ford was not among the first people to develop an automobile; rather, he was the first to demonstrate that autos could be made on an assembly line. He established the first medium-sized automo-

Henry Ford helped revolutionize the auto industry with products such as the Model T, a mass-produced car that was affordable for many Americans.

bile factory in Detroit, and it soon became Ford, the number-one company in the industry. Ford pioneered the way both with his Model T and in relations with his workers. Unlike many "robber barons" of the early twentieth century, Ford treated his workers well. There was method behind his choice: he wanted his workers to be able to afford the automobiles he produced!

When did Detroit go from being a city that produced cars to become *the* Motor City?

During the 1920s. The Model T was the breakthrough. Its relatively low price meant that millions of Americans could purchase automobiles, and Americans took to the open road in a way never before seen. The pioneer impulse remained in the cultural DNA of the nation, and millions of people drove for the sheer fun of it. Ford's assembly lines, meanwhile, turned out one Model T after another, winning fame and riches for the inventor, the company, and the state.

Michigan was one of the most prosperous states of the nation during the 1920s, and it weathered the Great Depression better than most of its neighbors. By now Ford, General Motors, and a handful of smaller companies were in direct competition, but this never seemed to hurt the profits for any of them. Detroit received a new wave of immigrants in the 1920s and 1930s, as well as African Americans who moved from the South. As a result, there were plenty of hands to perform the important work.

Did Detroit—and Michigan—diversify its economic base during these good years for the economy?

They didn't need to. The times were so good. Then too, Michigan had little else to offer other than lumber and the mining of iron ore. It made perfect sense for the Great Lakes

State to continue on the established path: to be first in the production of automobiles not only in the nation but the *world*. As good as the times were, they were about to become even better.

How good was the Second World War to Detroit and Michigan?

World War II generated an economic boom so large that it seemed it would never go away. The orders for millions of autos, jeeps, and personnel carriers came direct from the federal government, along with the promise of paid overtime for virtually all the workers. All the major manufacturing companies of Michigan benefited from the boom, and Detroit was awash in cash during the 1940s.

If the 1940s saw government orders and contracts, the 1950s witnessed the culmination of all that the automotive industry had ever promised. Detroit now churned out millions of autos each year, attempting to satisfy the insatiable demand of the American consumer. What once had been the land of the Model T now turned into the place that turned out long, tail-finned autos that cruised over all parts of the nation. That many of these were gas-guzzlers was ignored, because the price of a gallon of gasoline had never yet reached fifty cents. By about 1965, the innovations in Detroit seemed stalled, however. The major automakers continued to turn out a wide variety of cars, but they suddenly had competition from overseas.

How important was the year 1973 to the story of Detroit, Michigan, and the nation?

It can hardly be overemphasized. In 1973, the nations of the Organization of the Petroleum Exporting Countries (OPEC) began a short-lived oil embargo against the United States and other allies of the nation of Israel. The price of gasoline doubled that winter, and millions of Americans scrambled, looking for energy alternatives. The autos that had been so successful, and popular, for almost two generations were suddenly scrapped

Why did Americans—who had grown up with stories of Henry Ford and Ransom Olds—begin to purchase cars made in Germany and Japan?

It's one of the oddest turnarounds of the twentieth century. Germany and Japan were the great enemies in the Second World War, the people who Detroit factories worked to defeat. Both of those nations cottoned on to the idea of automotive success right after the war, however, and Japanese and German engineers developed an enviable reputation for automotive reliability. The first Americans to purchase these foreign cars doubtless did so as a novelty, but they were followed by millions of others, especially after the price of gasoline shot up to a dollar a gallon and beyond.

(many of them rusted in backyards) while Detroit's manufacturers attempted to produce more efficient cars. But when the oil embargo stopped, and prices dropped a bit, Americans went back to buying large, heavy, energy inefficient vehicles.

What else did Michigan give to the rest of the nation (during the boom years of the automobile)?

A distinctive sound came from the record companies of Detroit. In the mid-1960s, people called it Motown, in honor of the music label that produced many of the biggest stars. The list of recording artists and their creations is a long one. Gladys Knight and the Pips, The Temptations, Diana Ross and the Supremes, and many others sent out music that was played across the nation. That Motown had an African American sound was inarguable; that it was usually a soothing presence was equally apparent. It's possible that some Americans were slowly cured of racist feelings against blacks by listening to so much music made by black recording artists.

How important was the "Mighty Mac" to the future of the Great Lakes State?

In 1957, one of the marvels of American engineering was opened for all the world to see. The Mackinac Bridge, connecting the Upper and Lower Peninsulas, took years to construct, but when it was completed, millions of people came, to drive or even to walk across the five-mile span. This was as important to the fortunes of the Great Lakes State as the Brooklyn Bridge was to the people of Lower Manhattan, and as significant as the completion of the Golden Gate Bridge in California, a generation earlier. Mighty Mac al-

The impressive Mackinac Bridge, completed in 1957, connects the two peninsulas of Michigan.

lowed the Upper Peninsula to receive far more tourists than ever before, and it brought the disparate parts of the state together. Even so, there remains a certain cultural prejudice, with some people of the Upper Peninsula acting as if there were no Lower one!

When did things begin to go wrong for Detroit and Michigan?

As late as about the year 1979 Michigan was still known as a "high wage, high tax, high services state," meaning that people paid a lot to the state government and received a lot from it. But a sink in automotive profits and a certain stubbornness on the part of the major automakers meant a dip in state revenues, and Michigan never recovered from the downturn. The gasoline crisis of 1979 helped bring on the situation, but it only became worse in the 1980s. By 1990, Detroit was losing population, and sections of the city were in sad repair.

A certain type of blindness made matters worse. Many Michiganders continued to believe that the good days would return, that what they experienced in the 1980s and 1990s were only a temporary downturn. As a result, the state did not diversify its economy to any great extent, and by about the year 1999, Michigan was known as a "medium wage, medium tax, and no services state."

What was life in Michigan like at the turn of the twenty-first century?

Many rural sections of the state were doing just fine. Farm products earned a decent return, and Michigan was able to promote tourism because of its large areas of unspoiled land (many came to see the Sleeping Bear Dunes National Lakeshore on Lake Michigan). The story of urban Michigan was quite different, however. Detroit was in the worst shape by far, but Grand Rapids, Ann Arbor, and other localities were struggling. What was most appalling was the indifference shown by much of the rest of the nation. If Detroit, which was the birthplace of the auto and twentieth-century mass production, should simply collapse, what did that say about the future of the rest of the United States?

Will Detroit make a comeback? Will the Great Lakes State again play a major role in the national economy?

This is one of the great questions regarding Detroit and Michigan, but it also has implications for the so-called Rust Belt as a whole. As recently as 1960, the industrial states of Ohio, Michigan, Indiana, and Illinois were still doing reasonably well, but the introduction of so many foreign automobiles—Japanese especially—brought about a long, slow, and painful demise. The state is still seeing some major setbacks, such as the water crisis in Flint in which the drinking water was poisoned by lead; a scandal arose in which many people in 2016 have been demanding the resignation of Governor Rick Snyder for his handling of the situation.

Whether Michigan can find a new way to prosperity remains to be seen.

MINNESOTA

Nickname: The North Star State
Capital: St. Paul
Statehood: May 11, 1858; 32nd state

AT A GLANCE

What are the most popular signs and symbols of the North Star State?

"Star of the North" is the official state motto. The common loon is the official state bird, and the pink and white lady slipper is the state flower. The red pine is the state tree.

How large, or small, is Minnesota?

Comprised of 84,402 square miles (218,601 square kilometers), Minnesota is twelfth among the states in geographic size. The population of 5,420,380, as enumerated in 2010, places Minnesota at twenty-first among the states.

Is Minnesota the land where the women are strong, the men are good looking, and the kids are all above-average (as radio personality Garrison Keillor once famously described the fictional Minnesota town of Lake Wobegon)?

Sometimes it seems that way. Thanks to its Norwegian and German influences, the North Star State is known for hard-working, thrifty, and good-humored people. Most importantly, Minnesota does not provide the means, or method, for a number of vices. Though there doubtless are quite a few dropouts and misfits in Minnesota—past and present—they don't receive much attention. And, for that matter, we don't hear about the amazing superstars either. Perhaps that is what Keillor meant by the children being "above-average." 225

Does Minnesota live up to its name, which means "Land of Sky-Blue Waters"?

At least 80 percent of the time it does. The remaining 20 percent, however, air pollution shames the state, reducing its natural beauty. And to Minnesotans, the condition of the natural world is usually number one on the list.

Ever since the first French fur trappers arrived in the seventeenth century, the North Star State has been known for its rivers, streams, and lakes; one of its unofficial titles is "Land of Ten Thousand Lakes." Minnesota has much to offer the nature lover, including long sections of summer when canoeing is popular, and even longer sections of winter when cross-country skiing and snowmobiling are major attractions.

Do Minnesotans discuss the weather very much?

Again, Garrison Keillor proves to be our best guide. During the ferocious winter of 1993, he spoke at length about how winter turns men and women into better people than they previously were. Concluding one radio broadcast, Keillor declared that this particular winter made him a better person than he wanted to be.

How important is Garrison Keillor to the image of Minnesota?

He may not be its face, but he is surely its voice. For over four decades, Keillor has hosted *A Prairie Home Companion*, an iconic radio program that pokes gentle fun at the Midwest and the United States in general. Why do we care so much what our neighbors think? Will we survive the seemingly end-less stretch of middle age, where all we do is pay the bills and feed the pets? Keillor provides more answers—with tongue in cheek—than anyone else. He recently an-nounced that the show's 2015–2016 sea-son would be its last.

How important are the German and Scandinavian cultures in present-day Minnesota?

To an outsider, the folk of the North Star State seem much like those of any other, but they don't see it that way. A majority of them are descendants of hardy pioneers who left Germany and Scandinavia and came in search of areas in North America that re-sembled what they knew back home. They found it in Minnesota, where the forests, lakes, and eventually the iron mines re-minded them of life back in the old country.

Raconteur and author Garrison Keillor has brought the charm and whimsy of the Minnesota people to the world with his radio show *A Prairie Home Companion*.

What kind of politics did those European immigrants bring?

Germany and its Scandinavian neighbors had plenty of internal difficulties during the mid-nineteenth century, when so many of their sons and daughters found their way to Minnesota. The Germans, especially, were concerned about the failure of the liberal revolution of 1848. The new immigrants, therefore, brought a concern about politics and political finance that has lasted to the present day.

German and Scandinavian contributions have made Minnesota a more vibrant place in which to live: numerous festivals that celebrate the Old World influence attest to this. But the German and Scandinavian influence is also seen in Minnesota politics.

Can the Minnesotan be differentiated from his or her counterpart in Wisconsin?

They are a whole lot alike. One difference is that Minnesota has, from its earliest days, been a bit wilder, and it shows more of the frontier influence.

EARLY HISTORY

For how long have humans lived in what we now call the state of Minnesota?

For at least 10,000 years. Those who came may have found life here to resemble what their ancestors had known in Alaska, just after crossing from Siberia. The Ice Age had faded, but Minnesota was—and remains today—a rather cold place, with some of the lowest temperatures found in the nation. These early Native Americans came too late to hunt the woolly mammoth, but they found plenty of fox and deer. Fishing was also, doubtless, the source of much of their food.

When the first Europeans—most of them French—appeared, they found the Dakota and Ojibway in large numbers. Both of these tribes became allies of the French, but they were too far from the main scene of action to influence the outcome of the French and Indian Wars.

It seems like a long way from Montreal to Minnesota. How did the French make that long trip?

Primarily by canoe. Of all the Europeans who came to North America, the French adapted to Native American techniques the best. Learning the art of building and then paddling birch bark canoes, French explorers reached the Great Lakes by the late 1660s. Duluth is named for Daniel Greysolon, Sieur Du Luth, who arrived there in 1679. Mistakenly believing he was close to China, Du Luth donned a robe before going ashore. Once there, he realized that while the Great Lakes were indeed a passageway across part of America, they would not carry the traveler all the way to China.

Other Frenchmen followed, but Minnesota was not like Illinois, a section that France felt bound and determined to colonize. Only a few dozen fur trappers and soldiers were there during the late colonial period, and when Britain won the area—through the final French and Indian War of 1754–1763—very few Frenchmen cried any tears. As the philosopher Voltaire expressed it, these northern regions were merely thousands of acres of snow and ice.

Did the British take a real interest in Minnesota?

No. There were so many other colonial areas for them to expend energy and money on. What Minnesota had, in great abundance, was timber (for which the British had no immediate need) and beaver furs. Independent fur merchants gathered the latter more profitably, and the government of King George III therefore spent very little time or attention on the area just west of the Great Lakes. To the Americans, it was another matter, however.

When did the United States become aware of Minnesota and its potential?

The area came under the American flag in 1783, but there were no settlers, or even explorers, for nearly two decades. Those Americans who came to Minnesota did so primarily for the trade in furs, and as Minnesota was increasingly "trapped out," it seemed there was no need for any further expenditure of energy. The federal government had Fort Snelling built in 1819, as a precaution, however, and the completion of the Erie Canal, six years later, meant that thousands of new settlers and pioneers could more easily reach Minnesota. What had previously been a three-month trip by horse or wagon (or both), now became a three-week trip from Albany, New York, over the Erie Canal, and then the Great Lakes. Many of the new settlers got off the boat in Duluth.

Was there any other way to reach the wilderness that was then Minnesota?

In 1823, the first steamboat came up the Mississippi River. The *Virginia* made it all the way from St. Louis, Missouri, to Fort Snelling, and its arrival spelled a new era for opening the northern parts of the Midwest. What had been a trickle of settlers now became a small flood, and in 1849, Congress made Minnesota a territory. Only 6,000 people were counted in that first census, but by 1858, the number had climbed to 150,000, and Minnesota entered the Union as the thirty-second state.

When did the name of Henry Schoolcraft become well-known?

In the summer of 1832, Schoolcraft, an explorer and ethnographer, came to a tiny little stream coming out of Lake Itasca, in north-central Minnesota. This, Schoolcraft declared, was the ultimate origin of what became the mighty river known as the Mississippi.

Today, a sign in Lake Itasca State Park tells the viewer that here, at 1,475 feet above sea level, is the commencement of the Mississippi, and that the great river runs 2,552 miles from this spot to the Gulf of Mexico. Given the importance of the Mississippi River and its many tributaries, it's not too much to say that this—little Lake Itasca—is about as close as we come to nailing the geographic center of the North American heartland.

Was Minnesota's path to statehood easier or harder than most?

The process took longer, but it was not especially difficult. Many congressmen and senators were keen to bring in more states from the Upper Midwest, knowing they would come in as free states, rather than as places in which slavery was permitted.

What role did Minnesota play in the American Civil War?

Given the long distance from Washington, D.C., it seems as if Minnesota could have kept out of the action. Just the opposite was the case, however. Roughly 20,000 Minnesotans served in the Civil War. It's true that no major leaders came from the Gopher State (the unofficial nickname that came from an 1859 newspaper cartoon). But Minnesota was determined to demonstrate its allegiance to the Union and its opposition to slavery.

Some people claim that Minnesota had a civil war of its own during the Civil War years. Is there any truth to that?

There is, indeed. During the 1850s, the federal government bought up nearly all the land in Minnesota belonging to the Dakota Sioux. During the severe winter of 1862, the federal government did not deliver its promised supplies of food and merchandise to the tribe, and many of the young warriors went on the warpath. Chief Little Crow knew better, but members of his tribe persuaded him to take the leadership. Several Minnesota towns were attacked and burned, and nearly 500 white settlers were killed.

The federal government exacted a severe retribution. Colonel Henry Sibley led the United States and militia forces that defeated the Dakota in battle, and they took many prisoners. Nearly 150 were sentenced to death, but President Abraham Lincoln required that the cases be sent to his desk. Carefully examining each in turn, Lincoln upheld the death penalty in 38 cases, resulting in hangings in 1863. The rest of the Dakota had, by then, been pushed out of Minnesota.

How and when did the railroad come to Minnesota?

Born in Canada in 1838, James J. Hill came to St. Paul as a young man. He founded the Great Northern Railway, which eventually connected Duluth with Seattle, Washington. Other railroad barons followed his example, and by 1885, railroads virtually crisscrossed the state. As a result, Minnesota farmers were able to get their produce to market, primarily in Chicago, and wheat production increased on the Minnesota plains.

Lumber, too, made its appearance as a distinctive Minnesota product in the 1880s. Great numbers of lumberjacks went into the Minnesota forests and emerged with trees so large that some people could not believe the photographs. Not all of this development was even-handed, or free from pain, however. A giant forest fire struck eastern

Minnesota in 1894, destroying the town of Hinckley. More than 400 people died in the Great Hinckley Fire, one of the worst natural disasters seen in the Upper Midwest.

What was the crowning glory, as far as economic development was concerned?

It was the discovery of iron ore in the Vermilion Range and then the Mesabi Range. When the U.S. government negotiated with Great Britain, and drew the line between America and Canada, its delegates had no way to know just how important that line would be. Just by chance, most of the best deposits of iron ore and coal lay on the southern side of the boundary, affording even greater material wealth to the United States.

Railroad executive James J. Hill brought the Great Northern Railway to Duluth, connecting Minnesota to Seattle, Washington.

The Merritt brothers—seven in all—led the way in discovering the iron ore of the Mesabi Range. By 1900, that range supplied a majority of the nation's iron ore. And, as a result of the timber and iron ore industries, large numbers of Germans, Norwegians, and Swedes began migrating to Minnesota. The cultural environment of Minnesota changed at the same time as its economic circumstances.

How did Minnesota fare during World War I and World War II?

The First World War was a definite shot in the arm to Minnesota's industry; employment of miners far outstripped that of loggers, for example. Roughly 123,000 Minnesotans served in the First World War, and they acquitted themselves well on the battlefield. Many of them, and their compatriots back home, were dissatisfied with economic conditions at the end of the war, however. The Farmer-Labor Party was formed in Minnesota in 1918.

World War II, likewise, provided economic stimulus to Minnesota, but the time between the wars, the Great Depression especially, was a very difficult time in the North Star State. Many miners lost their jobs, and the state did not benefit greatly from the New Deal programs, which were oriented more to the Far West than the Upper Midwest. Like most of the nation, Minnesota found World War II, and the commensurate need for soldiers in uniform and workers in the mines, to be a great improvement over the previous decade.

How and when did Minnesota become known as the state with "clean" politics?

It actually shares this distinction with neighboring Wisconsin, whose governor, Robert "Fighting Bob" La Follette, led the way in the early twentieth century. In both states, the

Why is the German influence so keenly felt in Minnesota?

During the early twentieth century, Minnesota had more newly arrived Germans than any other state in the Union. Their presence is still felt today, but Poles, Norwegians, and Swedes blend with them as well, all of whom together give this northern state a rather Nordic feel. The Germans of Minnesota have never been anti-American, or opposed to the federal government, however; on the contrary, they are some of the best-adjusted of all immigrant groups.

voters demanded, and eventually received, political reforms that included the use of the referendum, meaning that voters could demand the legislature act on a certain issue. Minnesota and Wisconsin have continued this tradition, and their state legislatures are known as among the thriftiest and the most socially conscious of any to be found in the United States.

How did Minnesota fare in the decades following World War II?

The iron industry continued much as before, but a decline in the price of iron meant lower wages for many Minnesota workers. Forestry continued to be important, but Minnesota also saw a sharp rise in its service industries, including tourism.

One of the biggest moments for the state was the opening of the St. Lawrence Seaway in 1959. Ships had long made the difficult and dangerous passage over part of the Great Lakes, but the entire waterway was now connected. This made commerce for Minnesota, for the port of Duluth most especially, much more feasible.

Who were some of the most important Minnesotans in public life?

That Minnesota has provided a vice president, in Hubert Humphrey, is well-known. Less-known is the remarkable friendship between two Supreme Court justices. Harry A. Blackmun was born in Illinois but raised in St. Paul, and at an early age he became good friends with Warren E. Burger, who was born and raised in St. Paul. The two young men did not plan on intersecting careers, but they eventually both served on the U.S. Supreme Court—Blackmun as an associate justice for 24 years, and Burger as chief justice for 17 years. The Burger Court helped reshape many aspects of law in American society during the 1960s and 1970s.

Given the strong-minded quality of Minnesota voters, is it surprising that none has ever reached the presidency?

No. The two upper Midwestern states of Minnesota and Wisconsin are different in numerous ways but united in their approach to Progressive politics (the political style that dominated much of the nation between 1890 and 1910). It would be quite a feat for any politicians from these states to rise to the presidency, because their constituency is so defined.

231

The Mall of America not only has the biggest enclosed shopping grounds in the country, it also includes an amusement park, aquarium, comedy club, the Universe of Light displays, and much more for the whole family.

How about Hubert Humphrey? Did he stand a chance?

After serving as vice president under Lyndon B. Johnson (1965–1969), Hubert Humphrey made a run for the White House on his own. He narrowly prevailed at the 1968 Democratic National Convention in Chicago and then made a spirited run for the White House against Republican Richard M. Nixon. Humphrey came close to success, but narrowly lost to Nixon by less than one percentage point.

Another Minnesotan, former vice president Walter Mondale, was the Democratic nominee in 1984 but lost to incumbent president Ronald Reagan in a landslide.

How about iconoclasts such as Jesse Ventura?

Almost no one expected Jesse Ventura (a very successful professional wrestler) to go anywhere in politics. Ventura chose the right moment, however. In 1999, he ran as the Reform Party candidate for governor and prevailed against both his Republican and Democratic opponents. Ventura came into office in an outburst of enthusiasm, mixed with skepticism by many of the voters. He performed reasonably well in office but did not run for a second term.

What is the largest shopping center in the United States?

The Mall of America opened in Bloomington in 1992. It has sixteen movie theatres and over 400 stores. Owned by the Triple Five Group (a Canadian concern), the Mall of America was intended to be supreme, right from the very conception. Over 11,000 people work at the Mall, and roughly 13,000 work there during peak seasons. Approximately 42 million people visit the mall each year—ten times the population of the state of Minnesota.

How will Minnesota fare in the future?

Like many of the Upper Midwestern states, Minnesota faces an uncertain future. The industries that once brought prosperity to the region are now in rough shape. One should never count the people of Minnesota out, however: they've faced adversity before.

MISSISSIPPI

Nickname: "The Magnolia State"
Capital: Jackson
Statehood: December 10, 1817; 20th state

AT A GLANCE

What are the most popular, and significant, signs and symbols of the Magnolia State?

"By Valor and Arms" is the official state motto. The mockingbird, famous for disrupting all sorts of evening conversations, is the official state bird, and the magnolia is the state flower. The magnolia also doubles as the official state tree.

How large, or small, is Mississippi?

Comprised of 48,432 square miles (125,438 square kilometers), Mississippi is thirty-second among the states in geographic size. The population of 2,991,207, as enumerated in the census of 2010, places Mississippi at thirty-second among the states.

Is there any one spot, or place, from which one can take in all that is Mississippi?

No, the state has too much variety for that to be possible. But if one looks for the quintessential Mississippi, he or she finds it in the small towns, places of roughly 3,000 to 5,000 in population. It is in these towns that the Old South, as opposed to the New South that rose in the 1970s, can be found.

It was in towns like these that singer Elvis Presley grew up, and where talk show host Oprah Winfrey spent six formative years of her childhood. It was in places like these   235

This is the restored home that was the birthplace of singer Elvis Presley in Tupelo, Mississippi.

that writers William Faulkner and Eudora Welty obtained their strongest inspiration. And it was in the smallest of the small towns—places that barely appear on the maps— that the blues, perhaps the most distinctive of all American music, began.

Is there any one place in which one can see the ruin of the so-called Cotton Kingdom?

There are perhaps half a dozen places where the Cotton Kingdom—which flourished from about 1820 to 1860—can be viewed, but the single best is almost certainly the Windsor Ruins. Here, on the east bank of the Mississippi River, are twenty-two towering columns of stone, each capped by a huge cast-iron Corinthian capital. This is all that remains of the Windsor Plantation, one of the richest places in all the Confederate South.

During the Civil War, Windsor became an army hospital, and many locals attest that ghosts from those times inhabit the area. A terrific fire brought down the structure in 1890, and the ruins have stood ever since, as a testament to that earlier time.

Is there ever a time when it is not hot in Mississippi?

The occasions are rare, but they do occur. Ninety-five percent of the time, the weather in Mississippi is predictable: hot, muggy, and with a chance of showers. When a major hurricane blows in from the Gulf, all bets are off, however, and the same holds true for major tornadoes. Despite all the heat, and attendant dangers, there are those who love Mississippi so dearly they would never choose to live anywhere else. This loyalty is sometimes expressed with great resolve, and at other times involves a certain surrender, a willingness to let the Magnolia State be what it is.

Do Mississippians tend to discuss the weather?

No. They already know what to expect: hot, muggy, and humid. Of course there are the occasional variations, the magnificent rainfall that produces a few cool days in summer. Then, too, Mississippi can be hit with some cold days in winter. On average, however, the Magnolia State is smack in the middle of nearly tropical weather, thanks to warm air coming in from the Gulf of Mexico.

Who are some of the favorite sons and daughters of the Magnolia State?

Mississippi has many heroes and heroines, but they tend—like the state itself—to have many sides to them. Jefferson Davis, for example, was a self-made man who exhibited many fine personal qualities, but whose stubbornness helped bring on the Civil War, and whose stint as president of the Confederate States made that war an even worse experience than would otherwise have been the case. William Faulkner, almost certainly one of the truly great American novelists, loved Mississippi as only an insider could.

EARLY HISTORY

Who were the Mound Builders?

Their tribal names are unknown to us, and even the chronology of when they built their earthen mounds is somewhat shaky; what we do know is that the people who left their mark across the South and Midwest were amazing builders. Lacking the means to transport stone, they moved earth in prodigious amounts. So it is that today we can still see signs of their presence, pyramid-like structures that still rise from the flat Mississippi alluvial plain. Why were they built? Like the people who built the ancient Stonehenge, the Mound Builders were a highly ceremonial culture; almost certainly they built these earthen structures for various forms of ceremony and worship.

Were the Natchez Indians direct descendants of the Mound Builders?

We really aren't certain. DNA evidence may answer that question someday. All we can say for sure is that the Natchez lived close to the mounds that had been built centuries earlier, and that the first Europeans to arrive, mostly French, believed the Indians incapable of building anything so elaborate. Like other theorists, especially those who think the Egyptian pyramids were raised by aliens, the early European explorers declared that there must have been some earlier super-race, because the Indians could not have accomplished it.

When did the French arrive, and why is their presence not felt more strongly today?

France sent out thousands of truly great explorers and adventurers, but not that many true colonists. Anyone who speaks to a native of France will hear of the wonders and glory of his or her native land, and it was difficult, in the eighteenth century, to persuade many of these natives to emigrate. Mississippi, which was an adjunct of the Louisiana colony, therefore had only a sprinkling of merchants and farmers, nothing like the number required to colonize this land.

Spain, which received the area from France in 1762, also proved unable or unwilling to make the major investment required; it was not until Mississippi started to be settled by Anglo-American farmers that the incredible potential of the black earth, particularly within the Delta, was really used. Mississippi came formally to the United States through the Louisiana Purchase of 1803, which settled the land titles once and for all. This would be part of the United States.

Was there any chance, in the early years, that Mississippi would not be part of the slaveholding culture that arose in the South?

Perhaps there was one chance in ten. But the amount of labor necessary to raise cotton in Mississippi appalled the white settlers, and the only answer, from their point of view, was to bring in more black slaves. Adding further to their difficulties was the fact that Congress formally ended the slave trade from overseas in 1808. This meant that the white farmers of Mississippi had to find their slaves from within the United States, and it probably led to the infamous expression, to be "sold down the river." A forced migration began, under which slave masters in Virginia and Kentucky sold numerous African Americans and brought them downstream or overland all the way to Mississippi and Louisiana. Of course, it was also possible to outrun the law and continue to bring in slaves from Africa or the Caribbean, but it became more difficult and dangerous all the time.

Why does race slavery in Mississippi seem different, on the face of it, from that known in North Carolina or Tennessee?

Perhaps it's a matter of feeling, brought on by the fact that Hollywood producers tend to display slavery in Mississippi as different than elsewhere (witness the 2014 film *12 Years a Slave*). But geography also plays a major role. A slave in North Carolina or Virginia could dream about the North, and perhaps learn enough about it to make escape a possibility one day. The typical slave in Mississippi might hear about the Northern states and potential freedom, but they were just too far away.

How many real mansions and antebellum fortunes were founded?

Not nearly as many as we have been led to believe. When the Civil War began, the typical Mississippi white farmer had perhaps 300 acres but only three to four slaves. His life, while free, was not materially much better than theirs. But the few families who really succeeded did so in a spectacular fashion, and it is their lavish lifestyle that the movie producers have sold us on.

To be sure, there was more to Mississippi than cotton and slavery. The town of Natchez, which developed a sinister reputation as a place of ill repute, might, over time, have evolved into an industrial powerhouse. Roughly 80 percent of the wealth of Mississippi was built on cotton; however, the white gold that came off the fields was sold in New Orleans.

Was there any chance Mississippi would not join the Confederate States of America?

Almost none. A leading member of the Mississippi delegation to Congress was Jefferson Davis, whose plantation was just a few miles south of Vicksburg. Davis was as conciliatory as any Southern statesman could be, but when the tide turned, with South Carolina's secession, he became the *de facto* leader of his state. Mississippi was the second state to depart the Union; its legislature made that move on January 9, 1861.

Did white Mississippians understand the North? Did they realize the magnitude of their decision to secede from the Union?

They really didn't. Even the best-educated of white planters in Mississippi misjudged the North; they believed its people would grow tired of war and allow the Confederate States to go their way. And the early fighting in the Civil War was in Virginia and Tennessee, far removed from the cotton fields of Mississippi. A major shock came in May 1862, however, when the Union Navy seized New Orleans and then progressed up a long section of the Mississippi River. The war, quite suddenly, hit home.

Vicksburg, Port Hudson, and a handful of other Confederate stations, all of them in Mississippi, were all that held out from that original Yankee invasion. And when President Abraham Lincoln looked at the situation, he placed his finger on the map and declared that Vicksburg was the key. As long as that Confederate stronghold remained, the Confederacy was still joined. If Vicksburg fell, the Confederacy would be cut in two and the different sections would eventually collapse.

How terrible was the Vicksburg Campaign?

To the whites of Mississippi, it was the worst of all calamities. For many of Mississippi's blacks, the campaign was the first ray of light, the sign that slavery would one day come to an end.

Union general Ulysses S. Grant crossed the Mississippi from Louisiana, capturing Port Hudson, and then, in a lightning campaign, the state capital of Jackson. Grant's men burned much of Jackson. They then moved on Vicksburg, and, after a forty-seven day siege, the town fell to Union forces on July 4, 1863. From that moment, the Confederacy was cut in two, severed by the Mississippi, which now was in Union hands. Mississippi suffered from deep physical scars that took decades to heal, but the psychological ones ran deeper.

How bad was life during the sharecropping era?

To the average white person, down on his or her luck in the Civil War's aftermath, the sharecropping era was bad enough; to the typical African American, sharecropping resembled slavery, minus only the whippings. Of course there were exceptions to the rule, such as black Mississippians who prospered toward the end of the nineteenth century, but they were probably no more than two out of every hundred.

Cotton remained king until the infamous boll weevil, an invasive insect, destroyed the crops of 1921 and 1922. From then forward, Mississippi had to diversify, and the state learned how, by tending to pork, soybeans, cattle, and grain. What no one anticipated was how important music would become to Mississippi.

Where do "the blues" come from?

This can be debated almost endlessly, because most of the early composers are unknown. But by the 1920s, a distinctive new sound was coming out of Mississippi, and it found its way to places like St. Louis and New Orleans. Jazz had come just a bit earlier; the blues now took over as the soulful export from the Mississippi Delta region.

The Delta, poised between the Mississippi on the west and the Yazoo to the east, has long been Mississippi's most productive farmland; it now became home to the finest of Southern musicians.

How did Mississippi fare in the mid-twentieth century?

The Magnolia State did well during World War II, thanks especially to the U.S. Army training camp at Biloxi, but almost immediately after, the state's economy went again on hard times.

How bitter were the social battles during the Civil Rights movement?

Fewer people were killed in Mississippi than in Alabama, but the nation was appalled and shocked by what was shown on television screens. When James Meredith attempted to enroll at Ole Miss, the University of Mississippi at Oxford, angry crowds barred his

Blues musician and songwriter John Primer was born in Camden, Mississippi. Though his fame came from playing in Chicago, his musical heart stems from his birthplace.

entrance to the school. Meredith did manage to enroll, but he later participated in a famous civil rights march, where he was shot and wounded.

Who was Medgar Evers, and why does his name come up so frequently?

The murder of Medgar Evers on June 12, 1963, was one of the most horrific episodes of the long African American struggle for civil rights in the South. Evers was a U.S. Army veteran who served in the Normandy campaign, graduated from college, and was working as a salesman when the civil rights struggle commenced. He was also a field secretary for the National Association for the Advancement of Colored People (NAACP). On this particular June afternoon, he came home, parked his car in his driveway, and emerged, wearing a shirt that declared "Jim Crow must go." Seconds later, Evers was shot in the back.

Years, and then decades, passed before justice was finally served. Through the civil rights struggle and beyond, most white residents were unwilling to testify against their neighbors. But in 1994, Byron De La Beckwith (1920–2001), a leading member of a white supremacist group, was convicted of Evers's murder.

What was life in Mississippi like at the beginning of the twenty-first century?

For perhaps one-third of the population, things were better than ever before. Mississippi had come a long way since the struggles of the Civil Rights era, and improved race relations seemed the harbinger for other good things to come. For another third of the population, things were about the same, and for those in the bottom third, Mississippi continued to be—on the statistical average—just about the worst place in the nation to live. This comes from a number of statistical studies, regarding health care, education, and average yearly income.

What was the single worst day in Mississippi history?

Civil War buffs point to the Battle of Vicksburg. And civil rights participants would very likely point to a group of murders, carried out in the 1960s, and those who remembered the days of sharecropping would declare that the 1880s were the worst of times. But natural disasters have done almost as much to harm the people of the Magnolia State. Old-timers would probably vote for the summer of 1927, when the Mississippi River flooded its banks and wiped out the entire crop in the Delta—a flood of near-biblical proportions. In more modern times, Hurricane Katrina, which struck during the final week of August 2005, was the single biggest tragedy ever to hit the state. A twenty-mile section of the Mississippi coast was ruined, with hardly a building left standing close to the shore. The oil industry was hard hit.

How important is the casino industry to the Gulf Coast of Mississippi?

It is hard to overstate its importance. More than a dozen casinos are near the shoreline, and most of them took direct hits during Hurricane Katrina. It's easy to criticize the negative aspects that come along with these casinos; it's tough to recognize that without them, though, the Mississippi Gulf Coast would be in rather bad economic shape.

Could anything be worse than Hurricane Katrina?

No, but the British Petroleum oil spill of April 2010 did its best to draw equal to it. Deepwater Horizon, the oil rig that blew a sudden hole, spilled millions of gallons of oil into the Gulf before it was finally capped, and the Mississippi coastline, which was just beginning to recover from Hurricane Katrina, suddenly witnessed tragedy all over again. Teams of volunteers worked furiously to clean up the coast, but a solid three years passed before tourists returned, and in the meantime the state lost billions of dollars.

Will Mississippi ever escape the vicious combination of factors that make it one of the poorest of states?

It's certainly possible. The trouble is that expectations keep rising, and each time Mississippi does make substantial progress, the rest of the nation moves further ahead. Does this mean there will one day be a mass exodus from the Magnolia State? Don't bet on it. Mississippians love their state.

MISSOURI

Nicknames: "The Show Me State"; "The Crossroads State"
Capital: Jefferson City
Statehood: August 10, 1821; 24th state

AT A GLANCE

What are the most popular signs and symbols of the Show Me State?

"The Welfare of the People Shall Be the Supreme Law" is the official state motto. The bluebird is the official state bird, and the hawthorn is the state flower. The dogwood is the state tree.

How large, or small, is the Show Me State?

Comprised of 69,707 square miles (180,540 square kilometers), Missouri comes in at twenty-first among the fifty states in geographic size. The population of 6,044,171, as enumerated in the census of 2010, places Missouri at twenty-first among the states.

Is there any single spot from which the best of Missouri can be viewed?

Almost certainly it is from the top of the 630-foot Gateway Arch, in St. Louis. This magnificent monument, completed in 1963, honors the vast number of pioneers who passed through Missouri on their way to the Great Plains and the Far West. No other monument has ever surpassed the Arch as an example of the connection between all of the United States that leads to this point and also that lies beyond.

Are any parts of Missouri still as wild as when the pioneers first arrived?

Very few. Missouri does have plenty of open space, but it shows the hand of humans. Then too, the urban environment continued to creep on the rural. Missouri is best seen as a great landscape that continues to evolve.

Do Missourians talk about the weather?

All the time! Summer heat does not frighten them, and the occasional winter cold does not disturb them. They are terrified of tornadoes, however, and with good reason. Throughout its history, the Show Me State has experienced tornadoes, but they seem to have become more severe since around 1990. The single worst was on May 22, 2011, when an EF5 tornado struck the town of Joplin, killing 158 people and injuring another 1,150. The property damage came in at $2.8 billion, making it the most costly single tornado in American history.

Can the Missourian be told apart from his Southern and Midwestern neighbors?

The impressive St. Louis Gateway Arch stands 630 feet (192 meters) tall on the banks of the Mississippi River.

He or she can. There is an expansiveness to the Missourian, a tendency to exaggerate in the best sense of the word, that is sometimes a dead giveaway. Missourians are rightly proud of their state history, but they are also keenly aware that they are now one of the pivotal swing states, indicating the political mood of the nation as a whole.

EARLY HISTORY

For how long have humans lived in what we now call the Crossroads State?

For thousands of years. Little is known about the early Paleo-Indians of Missouri, but like their kin on the eastern side of the Mississippi River, they built large earthen mounds, most likely for ceremonial purposes. When the first people of European descent arrived, they found any number of Indian groups and tribes—including the Wachita, Osage, Sauk, and Fox—indicating that Missouri was already a crossroads.

Did Hernando de Soto and his men really make it all the way to Missouri?

The journey of Hernando de Soto and his 600 Spaniards is one of the great—though not always attractive—stories of early American history. Landing in western Florida in 1539, de Soto and his Spaniards wandered through parts of Florida, Georgia, Alabama, and Mississippi, before crossing the Mississippi River to arrive in Missouri. They did not

How different might Missouri be if the Spaniards had followed up the de Soto expedition?

It's possible that large sections of the Midwest and South would now be filled with Spanish speakers. But the very scope and daring of the de Soto expedition reveal one of the weaknesses of the Spanish form of colonization. Like Hernán Cortés in Mexico, de Soto was able to travel great distances and—from his point of view—accomplish great things. What this heroic style of travel and conquest did not involve was the patient, laborious process of real colonization, which at that time inevitably required the work—and sacrifices—of many peasant laborers and farmers.

spend much time in the Show Me State, but it is likely that de Soto was buried on Missouri soil. The remaining Spaniards built rafts, floated down the Mississippi River, and returned to Mexico City, concluding one of the great odysseys of American history. Several of de Soto's men left journals of the expedition, from which we gather that the Spaniards fought almost endless battles against the Indians and generally gave great injury to those they encountered.

Who came after the Spaniards?

The French came from almost completely the other direction. From their base in what is now Quebec, the French sent fur trappers and merchants to the Great Lakes. Under the leadership of Father Jacques Marquette and Louis Jolliet, and then René-Robert Cavelier de La Salle, French explorers found their way all the way down the Mississippi River, arriving at the river's mouth in April 1682. La Salle claimed the vast river and those waterways that flowed into it for King Louis XIV, thereby giving Louisiana its name.

The French were more able than the Spaniards to follow up their initial discovery, and in the early eighteenth century, French fur traders established posts in southern Illinois and western Missouri. St. Louis was a going concern by about 1750, and neighboring posts such as Ste. Genevieve are today among the oldest of all European-built towns in the Midwest. Slavery was a regular feature of life in Missouri right from the beginning. The first census, taken in 1773, shows that there were 444 whites and 193 African Americans in St. Louis. Ste. Genevieve had 400 whites and 276 slaves.

If the Spaniards failed to follow up their exploration, why does the area not show a stronger French connection today?

This is largely because of the series of battles that we call the French and Indian War. The last of these, known in Europe as the Seven Years' War, ended in 1763, and France chose to cede the Louisiana area, including Missouri, to Spain rather than lose it to

Britain in the peace treaty. And so, without fully intending it, and without any time to prepare for the role, Spain again became the top European power in this part of America, where the South and Midwest meet.

One does not think of Missouri in connection to the American Revolution, but British agents stirred up trouble with the local Indian tribes, and there was something very close to a major battle near St. Louis in 1780. Foreknowledge on the part of the Spaniards, however, warded off British efforts, and Missouri remained part of the Spanish empire till it was retroceded to France in 1800.

I get kind of dizzy seeing the changes on the map. Did anyone at the time think it was strange for Missouri and Louisiana to keep moving about in terms of possessions?

They didn't. Europeans took for granted that imperial expansion involved the movement of peoples and possession of areas. The Anglo-Americans, who had won their independence from Britain in 1783, were fans neither of the French nor the Spanish, and it was immaterial to them which colonial power possessed Missouri. What changed the scenario, however, was the movement of common, everyday folk from Tennessee and Mississippi, across the big river and into Missouri.

So if Missouri was Spanish—according to de Soto—then it became French, according to La Salle. France then ceded it to Spain—was there one more change?

Actually there were two. In 1800, Napoleon Bonaparte, the leader of France, forced Spain to retrocede Louisiana, including Missouri, to France. And in 1803, Napoleon made one of the worst deals in real estate history, selling the vast Louisiana country, as it was then called, to the United States for about $15 million. Realizing the great historical importance of this transaction, Americans in St. Louis and New Orleans conducted a ceremony in May 1804. The Spanish flag was respectfully hauled down and replaced by the French, which hung only for a few hours before being taken down and replaced by the

I usually think of Daniel Boone as the ultimate, or archetypal, Kentuckian. How did he end up in Missouri?

Several states actually lay a claim to Boone. Born in Pennsylvania, he spent much of his life in Virginia, and then led some of the first settlers into Kentucky just as the Revolutionary War commenced. Boone spent twenty-four years in Kentucky, but he eventually complained of a lack of "elbow room" and made the final move of his life, to eastern Missouri. The famed painter Chester Harding arrived at Boone's home and made a painting of him, just a few days before he died in 1821.

How "big" was the New Madrid earthquake of 1811?

On December 16, 1811, Missouri and the neighboring region was hit by an earthquake so large and devastating that the same quake, if it happened today, would have rendered millions of people homeless. Centered at New Madrid, in southeastern Missouri, the quake was so powerful that the Mississippi turned and ran in the opposite direction for several days. Few people were killed because the population was dispersed in frontier towns.

Stars and Stripes. In this fashion, the commercial transactions finally came to an end, and all of what is now the Show Me State came under American sovereignty.

Is this when Missouri really began to become populated with white settlers?

Yes, they now arrived in large numbers. Just the knowledge that Daniel Boone had crossed the Mississippi and now lived in Missouri was enough to persuade some people to make the move; new maps that showed large sections of open territory, just begging to be settled, convinced others. The War of 1812 could have acted as a deterrent, but when it ended in 1815, there was no holding people back. Missouri, which was part of the Louisiana Territory until 1812, now moved towards statehood.

It seems incredible that these events could happen so quickly. Are Missourians today aware of what their ancestors accomplished?

They are indeed. Missourians believe that they are among the most important of all the frontier Americans, and that the pioneer settlements in the Show Me State are as significant to the growth of America as the landing of the Pilgrims at Plymouth in 1620! This pride is one reason why Missourians say people have to prove or "show" something in order for them to take it seriously. This is, after all, the Show Me State.

MISSOURI IN THE LIFE OF THE NATION

What was the path toward statehood like?

It was one of the most tumultuous of them all. Numerous states had previously come into the Union without much difficulty, but the circumstances of the year 1819, when Missouri applied for statehood, were such that it could not be so in this circumstance. In 1819, there were eleven free states in the Union—states where slavery was prohibited—and eleven slave states (states where slavery was permitted). Given that each state sends two senators to Washington, D.C., this meant that the admission of Missouri as a slave state would upset the political balance of power in the nation's capital.

247

All sorts of amendments and agreements were considered. There were efforts to bring Missouri in as a slave state, but as one where no new slaves could be added. Other efforts involved drawing a line through the state and allowing slavery on one side and prohibiting it on the other. In 1819–1820 the nation faced its first truly serious internal dissension, and there were some, including the retired Thomas Jefferson, who feared for the nation's future. In the end, the Missouri Compromise brought in Missouri as a slave state and Maine—which had previously been part of Massachusetts—as a free state.

How did Missouri fare in the years between the Missouri Compromise and the beginning of the American Civil War?

One can almost ask: how did the city of St. Louis fare? In the first generation of statehood, Missouri boomed as a whole, but St. Louis was the pacemaker, setting the trend. Thanks to its magnificent location on the Mississippi River, St. Louis received river traffic from as far north as Ohio, and as far south as New Orleans. Flat-bottomed boats, keelboats, canoes, and eventually steamboats all came to St. Louis, making it one of the most successful of all places in the American Midwest.

St. Louis also had one of the most interesting ethnic mixtures in the young nation. There were French and Spaniards, as well as a majority of Anglo-Americans. After about 1848, St. Louis had a large number of Germans, who emigrated after the failed revolution in their homeland of that year. Of course there were also African American slaves, the number of which continued to increase.

Is it during this period that Missouri became known as the Crossroads of America?

Yes. Anyone who studies the list of journeys of exploration in the nineteenth century is struck by how many of them departed from Missouri. Lewis and Clark were in St. Louis before they departed from St. Joseph. William Becknell departed from Independence, Missouri, as he pioneered the route that became the Santa Fe Trail. And the most famous of them all, the Oregon Trail, commenced either in St. Louis or Independence, depending on the choice of the individual pioneer.

Given all this activity, I imagine that Missouri boomed in a financial sense. Is that true?

Yes. The Show Me State was one of the most prosperous of all the states during the decade that led to the American Civil War, though the state did go through some difficult times, the most prominent of them being the Panic of 1837, during which most of the banks failed. Thomas Hart Benton, the longtime U.S. senator, was the biggest hero of Missouri during these years. Known as "Old Bullion," he castigated the bankers and the money system for the failures that harmed the lives of so many common folk.

Was there any chance Missouri would join the Confederacy when the Civil War came?

That's one of the truly great questions, and it can only be answered by speaking from the perspective of two different constituencies. If the average farmer of Missouri in 1861 was asked, the answer was "of course." The native Missouri farmer remembered the South from his parents' time and naturally sympathized with South Carolina, which started the Civil War by attacking Fort Sumter in April 1861. But if one asked the typical urban dweller of the city of St. Louis, the reply was "absolutely not." Born in Germany, or perhaps New York City, the typical St. Louisan had many cultural prejudices, but he or she was dead-set against slavery and would view joining the Confederacy as the worst of all possible choices.

And so the stage was set for a major showdown. In May 1861, a young U.S. Army colonel seized control of the federal armory at St. Louis, denying its muskets, rifles, and cannon to the Confederate cause. The common people of St. Louis made no bones about their full support for the Union. And the typical country dweller vowed to have his or her revenge on the people of St. Louis, regardless of how long it took.

How many battles and skirmishes were fought in Missouri during the Civil War?

Many people have attempted to establish a final count but none have been successful. There were just too many of them. The first real battle was at Wilson's Creek in June 1861. Dozens of other battles and hundreds of skirmishes followed. Missouri remained one of the border states throughout the Civil War, never giving its allegiance to either side, but the Show Me State suffered more than almost any other. Long after the wounds had healed in South Carolina and Georgia, Missourians remembered the pain of the Civil War.

What was life in Missouri like in the decades that followed the Civil War?

Because it never departed the Union, Missouri was not conquered territory, and there was never an armed occupation by the Union. But Missouri felt like a disaster zone to the people who emerged from the Civil War's conclusion. Large sections of the coun-

How important is Mark Twain to the history of Missouri?

Not very. Twain was born and raised in the town of Hannibal, and his boyhood there provided the stuff for many of his best writings. But after brief service as a riverboat pilot, and an even shorter time in the Confederate army, Twain picked up and moved first to Nevada and then California. He returned to Hannibal on only a few occasions, and it is perhaps more accurate to say that Missouri assisted Twain's writing more than Twain ever assisted Missouri.

tryside had simply been devastated, with towns and villages on the brink of ruin. Long-festering animosities remained for generations, and the economy did not pick up for a long time.

One of the few jobs that did not suffer in the economic downturn following the war was a riverboat worker. Pilots, seamen, cooks, and other workers were needed on these waterwheeled vessels that continued to travel down the Mississippi.

How big was the St. Louis World's Fair of 1904?

Held to commemorate the one-hundredth anniversary of Lewis and Clark's departure, the St. Louis World's Fair was the biggest seen in the United States to that time. Roughly 20 million people attended, between April 30 and December 1, 1904. Many new technologies and gadgets were displayed, with the brand-new automobile holding center stage.

What is unique about the state capital in Missouri?

First off, Jefferson City is the third site of Missouri's capitol. The first two state capital locations were in St. Louis; the third was in St. Charles. The fourth location (and third city) was in the more centrally located Jefferson City (named after the third U.S. president, Thomas Jefferson). The first capital in this city burned in 1837; the second Jefferson City capital also burned, in 1911, after being struck by lightning; the third, and current, structure was completed in 1917.

How did Missouri fare in World War I?

The Show Me State was as ready for World War I as any state in the Union. The National Guard mobilized there immediately, and Missouri sent many young men to the battlefields in France, including a young Harry S. Truman. Most gratifying to the people of Missouri was that the commander-in-chief of the American forces was General John J. Pershing, a native of the town of Laclede.

When did the rise of Harry Truman begin?

Born in Lamar, Missouri, in 1884, Truman came from a middle class family. Demonstrating steadiness rather than brilliance, he served in World War I, and then began a rise in Missouri politics. Some people claimed he was tainted by his association

President Harry S. Truman is shown here signing the declaration of war against Korea.

with Tom Pendergast and the political machine that ran Missouri politics, while others lauded Truman for his loyalty to his former "boss" at a time when Pendergast could do nothing more for him. Truman was elected to the U.S. Senate in 1934, where he compiled a good to excellent record, and in 1944, he—and millions of others—were surprised when Franklin D. Roosevelt asked him to be his running mate on the Democratic ticket. Elected vice president in 1944, Truman expected he would have a rather boring time in Washington, as the number-two man to a very colorful and popular president, but Roosevelt's death, on April 12, 1945, completely changed the equation. Suddenly the Man from Missouri was in charge of the United States and was the leader of the free world.

Did Harry Truman display a "Missouri style" while in the Oval Office?

He never used that expression, but Truman was about as Missourian as one could be: plain-spoken, hardworking, and impatient without vanity or ostentation of any kind. He had long before overcome the deficiencies of his rural education, reading widely in history and biography, and he was one of the most conscientious presidents the United States has ever known. Truman had the heavy burden of deciding on how to use the atom bomb; he alone made the momentous decision to use the bomb against Japan in 1945. This was the single biggest decision of his presidency, but it was followed by many others.

Should the United States intervene in Korea? Should it do so as a sovereign nation, or as part of the United Nations? To what extent should the United States face down the Soviet Union? How trustworthy were American allies in Western Europe? All these and more were questions Truman faced while in the White House, and to his credit he never shirked the task. Many people—then and now—have questioned his decisions, but *very* few have ever cast aspersion on his sincerity. When Truman departed the White House in 1953, he retired to Independence, Missouri. Late in life, he delighted in giving short piano recitals to visitors to the Truman Library.

What was life in Missouri like at the turn of the twenty-first century?

By 2000, Missouri was known as one of the most important of the "swing" states, meaning that it could go either way in the general election. Republicans held the edge at the state level, but the two parties were almost evenly divided in the state as a whole, and the way Missouri went often indicated the mood of the nation.

Where will Missouri be a generation from now?

The chances are that the Show Me State will be just about where it is today: a place filled with pride over its past accomplishments, but without a clear path to the economic future. This does not mean Missouri is doomed; the same can be said for at least a dozen other of the fifty states.

MONTANA

Nickname: "The Treasure State"
Capital: Helena
Statehood: November 8, 1889; 41st state

AT A GLANCE

What are the most popular signs and symbols of the state?

"Gold and Silver" is the official state motto. The western meadowlark is the official state bird, and the bitterroot is the state flower. The ponderosa pine is the official state tree.

How large, or small, is the Treasure State?

Montana is the fourth largest of the fifty states. Comprised of 147,042 square miles (380,837 square kilometers), Montana sprawls across the northwestern part of the nation in a fashion that is unparalleled. Only when one looks all the way south to Texas does one see a comparable dominance in terms of geographic size. The state population of 989,415, as enumerated in the census of 2010, reveals that Montana is only forty-fourth among the states in terms of population.

What makes Montana so different from its neighbors and the rest of the nation?

No one has ever been able to answer this definitively, but there's no doubt that Montanans are different. One of the times this was expressed well on film was in the 1992 movie *A River Runs Through It*. The younger brother, portrayed by Brad Pitt, turns to the elder one with a quizzical expression. The elder brother urges the younger to move with him and his fiancée to Chicago and start a brand-new life. The brothers have suffered equally from the domineering attitude of their preacher father, and this seems like

253

the heaven-sent opportunity they've both longed for. But the younger brother turns and says quietly, "Oh, I'll never leave Montana, brother." What he leaves unspoken is that incredible passion Montanans feel for their native state. Regardless of what happens—good, bad, or indifferent—they prefer to live under the wide-open skies and to gaze at the Rocky Mountains.

Is there any one spot, or vantage point, from which one can see the best that is Montana?

To native Montanans there might be a hundred such spots, and all of them together would not do complete justice to the beauty that exists. But to an outsider, a casual tourist, the best place was surely from the higher level of an Amtrak train—the so-called Dome Car—as the train gets close to the Rocky Mountains. As one travels from east to west, the Rockies start out as specks on the horizon, and then, during the long afternoon, they grow into formidable giants. The Amtrak schedule usually carries the tourist into the mountains just as darkness begins, and morning finds them on the other side, coming down the west side of the Cascade Mountains. More recently, the Dome Cars have been replaced by full-length viewing cars that have floor-to-ceiling windows.

This 1972 photo shows the Empire Builder (or Dome Car) train passing by the Montana Rockies (the dome cars are seen toward the back).

What most observers struggle with is the attempt to convey the scene to the folks back home. One can hold a cell phone and attempt to narrate, but about 98 percent of everything is missed. One can attempt to write a long letter, and while this is better, it still misses a great deal. This is why Montana really should be experienced, rather than described.

Do Montanans discuss the weather to any great degree?

No. They know precisely what to expect: a short summer filled with the most amazing colors and light, followed by a long winter with howling winds and enormous snowdrifts. They might exchange some anecdotes about winters of the past, or about how a friend or relative struggled through twelve feet of snow during one winter, but most of the time they are quiet on the subject.

Montana can surprise the casual tourist with its summer heat. The single highest temperature ever recorded was 117 degrees F (47 degrees C) at Glendive on July 20, 1893. The single coldest recorded was –70 degrees F (–57 degrees C) at Rogers Pass on January 20, 1954

Is Montana one of the whitest states in the Union?

It is indeed. The Anglo majority are mostly third- and fourth-generation descendants of rugged pioneers who came from the Midwest during the heyday of the mining boom, and they are not easy to get to know. But touch their hearts in some way, and Montanans become the most faithful of friends.

A substantial Native American minority exists in Montana, but the Crow, Shoshone, and Northern Cheyenne mostly stick to the reservations, which are vast in size. One of the largest controversies of recent years is whether the Northern Cheyenne will allow mining rights to natural gas companies. If they do, it's likely that every member of the tribe could quickly become a millionaire. But the Cheyenne, like other Indians of Montana, have seen money come and go before; the only thing that holds permanent value is land.

EARLY HISTORY

For how long have humans lived on the plains and in the mountains of Montana?

For thousands of years. Long before the current tribes—whose names we know—appeared, there were significant numbers of Paleo-Indians in Montana. Like Montanans of today, they admired the vast landscape; like them, they also found it difficult to earn a living. The numbers of Indians never grew that large, therefore, and so much room existed that they did not trouble each other very much. The chances are that when Lewis, Clark, and company came up the Yellowstone River, many of the Indians may have thought them merely another tribal group, albeit a strange-looking one.

255

By the time the first Anglo-Americans arrived, the different Indian groups of Montana had formed into distinct tribal groups. The Cheyenne, Blackfoot, Crow, Assiniboin, Flathead, and others gave each other wide distance, because there was so much room in the area. Horses came to the various Indian groups just a generation or so before the arrival of the first white people; even so, the Indians appeared—to those first pioneers—as if they had possessed horses since time immemorial.

What did Lewis and Clark think as they crossed the vastness of what is now Montana?

Happily, we have their journals, and we know that they were quietly in awe of the landscape, as well as the animals; for example, this is where they met their first grizzly bear. Lewis and Clark were in haste; they needed to get over the Rocky Mountains and into the Columbia River Basin before winter arrived. They moved quickly across the plains, therefore, and when they entered the mountains, they had the extreme good luck of running into Sacajawea's elder brother, a chief among the Shoshone. Obtaining horses from him, Lewis, Clark, and the Corps of Discovery then made their way across Idaho to find the Snake River, and finally the Columbia.

On their way back to St. Louis, the following spring, Lewis and Clark split up for a time, and Lewis was attacked and nearly scalped by a group of Blackfeet warriors. This was but the first of many times that white explorers and settlers would run afoul of the Blackfoot, who were some of the finest horsemen on the Northern Great Plains.

How long did it take before settlers followed in the footsteps of the explorers?

Nearly fifty years. The major reason is that the Mormon and Oregon trails were just south of the paths that would have taken the settlers to Montana. Once one arrived in the Willamette Valley of western Oregon, there seemed no need to return to the great interior. The Native Americans therefore had the run of Montana for another generation, and they do not seem to have feared the white people to any great extent. The magnitude of their error was revealed when the Civil War ended, allowing thousands of settlers and U.S. soldiers to move to the Far West.

How important is George A. Custer to the story of Montana?

He is usually more closely identified with North and South Dakota—which then formed the Dakota Territory—but his final battle, Custer's Last Stand, was fought in southeastern Montana. Custer had angered the Sioux and Northern Cheyenne by his aggressive promotion of the area, as well as his own reputation. Led by Sitting Bull and Crazy Horse, the Sioux and Cheyenne laid a clever trap for Custer, and he stumbled right into it. On June 25, 1876, the year of America's centennial, Custer and his men were wiped out at the Battle of the Little Bighorn. There were no survivors.

The Indians were, of course, elated by their victory, but in the blood and death of that

afternoon lay the ruin of their people. The Sioux and Cheyenne did not realize that this was the year America turned 100, or that the American public would demand the extermination of the Indians who killed Custer. Within twelve months of the Battle of the Little Bighorn virtually all the Indians of Montana had been captured or had escaped to British Canada. Many of those who crossed the international boundary later came back, claiming that "Mother Victoria" was not as good a host as they anticipated.

Was there any more fighting with the Indians after 1876?

Only to a small degree. Chief Joseph brought the Nez Perce into western Montana in 1877, but his tribe was from Washington State and Utah, and their quarrel with the federal government did not spread to Montana tribes. Montana soon changed from the land of Indian fighters to that of railroads and mining camps.

How big was the mountain just outside of Butte?

The city is named for the mountain from which more iron ore was extracted than any similar mountain in North America. Mining began at Butte in the 1870s, and every year brought more miners.

How long was Montana a U.S. territory?

Montana became a U.S. territory in 1864 and remained so until becoming a state in 1889. Montana Territory's first capital was Bannack, unusual in that it was located in the far southwestern part of the territory. Bannack was capital for a little over eight months, before being replaced by Virginia City in 1865 for about ten years. Helena was the last capital of the territory—and the first and only capital of the state. The original capital of Bannack is now a ghost town, though the original dwellings of Bannack are now part of the Bannack Historic District. A state park is also located there, and every July the locals celebrate Bannack Days, harkening back to the gold mining days.

How did Montana evolve immediately after achieving statehood?

Montana achieved statehood in 1889. Over the following decade, thousands of settlers poured into the Treasure State. These tended to be solid citizens who erected homes and created townships. There were plenty of conflicts between cattlemen and sheep barons, but Montana was headed in the right direction as the nineteenth century came to its end.

MONTANA IN THE LIFE OF THE NATION

Why did so many strong—even overpowering—women come from the Treasure State?

A novelist perhaps can answer this question better than an historian. Our best guess, however, is that the very conditions that made life so difficult for the early pioneers also helped develop some very strong-willed individuals of both genders. Montana was one of the earliest states to allow women to vote; it also produced the first female member of the U.S. Congress.

Elected in 1916, Jeannette Rankin was a Montana rancher's daughter. She, along with forty-nine other members of the U.S. House of Representatives, voted against American entry to World War I, and she paid a stiff price: the voters rejected her in 1918. By the oddest of chances, Rankin was elected again to the House in 1940, and she was a member when President Franklin Roosevelt asked for a declaration of war against Imperial Japan. This time the vote was 388–1, with Rankin casting the only negative vote. She received death threats, and again she failed in her reelection bid. But she stuck to her (pacifist) guns and led peace marches at the time of the Vietnam War.

Voted to the U.S. House of Representatives in 1916, Jeannette Rankin was the first woman in America to have a seat in Congress.

When did the Great Depression strike the Treasure State?

About eleven years earlier than the rest of the nation. When the United States entered World War I, Montana was pleased to supply its quota of young men, and these restless soldiers proved their worth during the Great War. But the same year that saw the declaration of war—1917—witnessed the commencement of a terrible drought on the Northern Plains. At the same time, the demand for foodstuffs and for mining materials dropped, and Montana entered desperate economic circumstances. Many families who had arrived in the 1890s fled the Treasure State, heading south and southeast. Most of those who had arrived in the 1870s and 1880s hung on, but they endured some very grim years before things improved. Even the New Deal programs did not make much difference in the lives of the people of Montana; it took the advent of the Second World War for them to start to come out of the Great Depression.

What was life in Montana like in the two decades that followed World War II?

Economically, conditions were much improved. The Treasure State had lost many of its most valuable citizens during the terrible drought period, however, and overall recovery was uneven. The census of 1960 revealed that Montanans were now about evenly split between rural and town dwellers, even though the size of those towns did not resemble East Coast towns.

Did the 1960s ever come to Montana?

Surprisingly they did. The Montana system of higher education was much-expanded during the 1950s, and when the Sixties came along, there were plenty of young college and university students willing to listen to radical ideas. The expression "Generation Gap" was not coined in Montana, but perhaps it should have been, because the political separation between those young people and their parents was truly severe.

How did the Native Americans of Montana feel about the Sixties and a generally more liberal approach throughout the nation?

Nine times out of ten, the Indians distrusted the liberal views espoused by advocates of the youth movement. Numerous films attempted to see the other side of the story, including the truly fine film *Billy Jack*, but the truth is that most Indians of the Great Plains had heard the federal government make and break plenty of promises. There was no need, they said, to give credence to yet another set of pledges by the white people.

Is Montana, then, one of the states where Indian–white relations are still pretty tense?

A lot of the time there aren't any relations! The Indians of Montana mostly live on large reservations and have no need to communicate with the white people, who often live as far as fifty miles away. Of course there are some heartwarming exceptions to the rule, when white people go out of their way to learn about Native American culture and slowly win the trust and affection of those they approach.

Is Black Elk a good example of a successful symbol of Indian–white relations in Montana?

Born in northern Wyoming, Black Elk (1863–1950) was a Sioux medicine man who had a powerful spiritual experience around the age of eleven. For the rest of his life, he remembered and related the story of how medicine spirits—male and female—came to instruct him about his people, the whites, and how they should relate. In his sixties, Black Elk converted to Roman Catholicism. Just how seriously he took this conversion is not well-understood, but many Native Americans, believing in a multiplicity of gods and goddesses and spiritual powers, did not find it difficult to accept the Christian god as another important member in their religious view.

When did things get better for miners and worse for the state as a whole?

The Anaconda Copper Mining Company began closing its Montana mines in the late 1970s, and the price of copper shot upward as a result. This severely harmed the Montana economy, and many people lamented the ill effects of Anaconda's decision. Environmentalists pointed to the immense scars the major copper companies had left on the land and, therefore, declared that the closings were worth it, regardless of the price.   259

A 1968 photo of an Anaconda Copper Mining Company operation in Deer Lodge County, Montana, not long before the mines closed in the state and sent the economy reeling.

Montana could, quite possibly, have fallen into another period of terrible economic recession, but two separate events rescued the state: the discovery of oil, and the influx of wealth from the outside.

Montana had oil wells almost from its first decade as a state, but the U.S. energy crisis of 1973 prompted new efforts to uncover oil, and Montana was one of the states that benefited the most. Numerous Montana farmers said that the price of oil and gas didn't matter any longer, because they could produce all that they needed right in their own backyard (it's important to remember that a Montana backyard is often five or six hundred acres). Certainly there was some conceit and braggadocio involved, but Montana came closer than most states of the Union to energy self-sufficiency. This would not have been sufficient without money coming from other states, however.

When did the outsiders arrive?

They started coming around 1985, and they haven't stopped yet. Ted Turner, founder of Cable Network News (CNN), was perhaps the most famous, but hundreds more followed him. At about the same time that survivalist groups began to migrate to Montana, claiming they would outlast the terrible disasters on their way, many wealthy men and women moved to Montana, primarily to enjoy the natural beauty. Simply by purchasing land and showing up at the local grocery to buy products, these wealthy outsiders bettered economic conditions in Montana. Of course they weren't welcomed by everyone.

What national park in Montana connects with a foreign national park?

Glacier National Park, located in the northwest part of the state, adjoins Waterton Lakes National Park, located in the very southwest part of the Canadian province of Alberta, to form the Waterton-Glacier International Peace Park. The governments of Canada and the United States bonded together and created this park in 1932 to commemorate the peace and goodwill the two nations share with one another. The international park is massive: 1,720 square miles (4,556 square kilometers). Waterton-Glacier was the world's first so-called peace park; today there are approximately 170.

What was life in Montana like at the start of the twenty-first century?

It was, quite likely, the best it had ever been. All the same variables—including the long winters—still existed, but Montanans had adjusted so well that they seemed well-positioned for the new century. Some communities still witnessed occasional anger and distrust between those who had been there for three generations and the newcomers, but even this phenomenon began to fade. The rising price of oil benefited many Montanans, and the state looked to ways to diversify its economy, which had been based for so long on cattle and mineral products.

Where will the Treasure State be a generation from now?

It may well have a new name! Treasure State echoes of the past, when mining was the number-one generator of wealth. Mining still has its place, but it is no longer the preeminent way to earn a living.

Montanans will remain who they are, one of the most resourceful groups of people to be found in the United States, and, down deep, one of the most generous groups as well. They know what it is to endure hard times, and if you listen to them, the state and the nation will always come through.

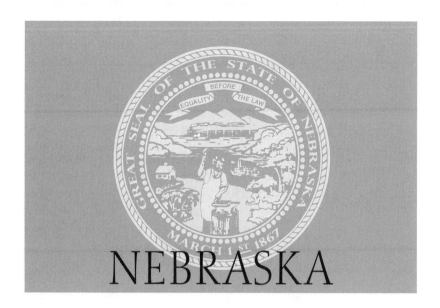

NEBRASKA

Nickname: "The Cornhusker State"
Capital: Lincoln
Statehood: March 1, 1867; 37th state

AT A GLANCE

What are the most important signs and symbols of the Cornhusker State?

"Equality Before the Law" is the official state motto. The western meadowlark is the state bird, and the goldenrod is the state flower. The cottonwood is the official state tree.

How large, or small, is the Cornhusker State?

Comprised of 77,349 square miles (200,333 square kilometers), Nebraska is fifteenth among the fifty states in geographic size. The population of 1,826,431, as enumerated in the census of 2010, places Nebraska at thirty-eighth among the states in terms of population.

Why is Nebraska so little-known to people from other parts of the nation?

Like Oklahoma, Nebraska suffers from a false image, one created in the late nineteenth century. Because Nebraska was settled at a time when very exciting things were happening in other areas, people often overlook the Cornhusker State. Natives of Nebraska know this and are not surprised when outsiders display ignorance about the state.

Is there anything Nebraska can do to correct the mistaken image so many people hold?

Only by pointing to maps and using them to describe certain specifics. The outsider typically believes, for example, that Nebraska is flat as a pancake; only the experience of the Great Plains can persuade him or her otherwise. Some outsiders think Nebraska is the land of violent summer thunderstorms, while others believe it is the land of winter blizzards, when in fact it is both.

Do Nebraskans discuss the weather very much?

They do indeed. "Never turn your back on the sky" is practically a proverb in Nebraska, where mild weather can change to severe conditions in a matter of hours. It's the amazing openness of this part of the Great Plains that produces such change and volatility.

EARLY HISTORY

How much do we know about the various peoples who have lived in what we now call Nebraska?

Not as much as we would like. The Paleo-Indians may have been in Nebraska as many as 20,000 years ago, but they did not leave much material culture for us to examine. The first Nebraska natives of whom we have certain knowledge were villagers, who harvested corn and lived in fixed locations. Later came the Pawnee, the most numerous of all the Native Americans of Nebraska.

At the time white people started settling Nebraska, the Pawnee were the most numerous tribe in the state (from a c. 1859 painting by Alfred Jacob Miller).

Why do the Pawnee have such a bad name in history books and movies?

This is due to the fact that George Catlin—most famous of all painters of the American Indians—painted a great many Sioux and Cheyenne, both of whom were perennial enemies of the Pawnee and Crow. Early American writers took Catlin's work at face value, attributing all sorts of noble qualities to the Indians of North and South Dakota, and ascribing many vile characteristics to those of Nebraska. By the time the movie *Dances with Wolves* was released in 1990, most students of the American West had fallen prey to the long-told stories of the negative qualities of the Pawnee, and the film continued to perpetuate the stereotype.

Who were the first people of European descent to cross Nebraska?

Francisco Vásquez de Coronado and his men walked across sections of Nebraska in the early 1540s, which technically brought Nebraska under Spanish rule, but none of the Spanish kings made any effort to back up the claim. Few people came to the region again until small groups of French fur traders entered the area in the mid-eighteenth century.

When did the first American fur trappers and merchants begin arriving in Nebraska?

The Spanish-born Manuel Lisa established the first trading posts along the Missouri River, but it was Captains Meriwether Lewis and William Clark and their Corps of Discovery who gave a definite American imprint to the land, during their epic journey of 1804–1806. Lewis often walked the west bank of the Missouri River while the keelboats moved upstream, and he was one of the first travelers to describe the rich mixture of scrub brush and marshy swamps that predominated at that time. Lieutenant Zebulon M. Pike followed Lewis and Clark in 1806, and then Major Stephen H. Long in 1820–1821. It was Long who described the area as the "Great American Desert," discouraging an entire generation of Americans from settling in Nebraska.

In his official report, Major Long branded most of Kansas as part of what he called the "Great American Desert," a landscape so hostile to humans and agriculture that he believed it would forever remain the domain of the coyote and grasshopper. Many people who have studied Long's report marvel at his mistake, because he certainly was not a fool. Is it possible that he crossed Nebraska at a period of unusual drought? Or was he—like so many other white Americans—so accustomed to thinking of timber as one of the foundations of civilization that he simply wrote off an entire area that had little in the way of trees? One thing is for certain: more corn has been harvested on those "barren" plains than almost anywhere in the United States.

During the 1830s, the stories of land in Oregon sounded much more promising than those in Nebraska, and the Cornhusker State therefore became a way of passage. Fur trader Robert Stuart pioneered the Oregon Trail in 1812–1813, but it was not until the 1840s that settlers learned how to handle wagons in the Nebraska area, much less to use them to cross the Rocky Mountains. Nebraska was one of the longest sections of the Oregon Trial, and many would-be settlers arrived in Oregon to declare how happy they were to have made it all the way.

What role did Nebraska play in the lead-up to the American Civil War?

Even though there were only a few thousand people in Nebraska, the newly formed territory helped bring about the tensions that eventually culminated in the guns being fired at Fort Sumter. In 1854, the U.S. Congress approved the Kansas-Nebraska Act, which opened those two areas to white settlement. Of the two, Kansas played the better-known role—thanks to the actions of John Brown—but Nebraska was actually the larger piece of land; in fact, the Nebraska Territory was much larger than the present-day state.

How important was the fur trade to the development of Nebraska?

Nebraska would surely have been developed at some point—thanks to the quality of its soil—but the fur traders and trappers accelerated the process. On the early maps of the Midwest, regions of Nebraska featured prominently because so many trappers had been through the area. Whether they were French-Canadians or Scots-Irish, the fur trappers and traders were primarily interested in profits, rather than national expansion. They unwittingly advanced the growth of the United States.

Was it essential that the Oregon Trail cut through what is now Nebraska?

Pretty much. Once one crossed the wide Missouri and proceeded either on horseback or in a covered wagon, Nebraska was the best way to cross. The River Platte formed the left-hand, or southern, side of the Oregon Trail for hundreds of miles, and visibility ranged from good to excellent. One of the enduring signposts of Nebraska is Chimney Rock, an unusual rock formation that juts up sharply from the plain, and which served as a landmark for hundreds of thousands of people who passed. But the excellent stories told about the Oregon Trail often leave off one important part: the storms.

The circulation of air over Nebraska, which contains a curious mixture of warm and cool, leads to serious volatility, and the Oregon Trail pioneers often saw storms well in the distance. The veterans among them persuaded everyone to circle the wagons, and everyone got very low, in order to avoid both the pelting rain and the sand that it kicked up. Few people died in these storms, but they were a defining element of passing the Oregon Trail, and many emigrants admitted they were more frightened of the storms than they were of Indians.

Has Nebraska always been a place that people visit while on the road to somewhere else?

That is part of what Nebraskans live with. First came the fur trappers, and then came the Oregon Trail emigrants. Then, in the 1850s, the Kansas-Nebraska Territory was formed, with a distinct emphasis on Kansas. Kansas endured being in the national news, while little was heard of Nebraska. This was not necessarily harmful, but it reminded Nebraskans that no one tended to take them, or their part of the territory, very seriously.

It was the transcontinental railroad that made settlement of Nebraska possible. The Central Pacific Company built its end of the railroad through Nebraska and Wyoming on the way to its junction with the Union Pacific Company, which built east from Sacramento. And when the Golden Spike was driven in northern Utah in 1869, Nebraska was among the first beneficiaries.

In modern times, Interstate 80, which begins on the East Coast in New Jersey and ends on the West Coast in the Bay Area of California, passes through or near the big cities of Nebraska—Omaha, Lincoln, and Grand Island—acting as a crossroad for the traveler heading across the United States.

How did Nebraska attain statehood?

In the 1850s, all the attention was on Kansas, because there were many Southerners in the region trying to turn Kansas into a state that permitted slavery. This was never an issue in Kansas; one early census showed less than a dozen slaves in the entire area. But there were plenty of legislative battles, especially over how prominent the railroad companies would be and how the land would be settled. Congress passed the Homestead Act in 1862, and many Nebraskans, witnessing how the act benefited Iowa and Kansas, were eager to get into the action.

The final area of contention was over black suffrage: should the handful of African Americans in Nebraska be given the right to vote? President Andrew Johnson vetoed one bill that would have allowed this, but Congress overrode him, and in March 1867 he signed a proclamation, making Nebraska the thirty-seventh state.

NEBRASKA IN THE LIFE OF THE NATION

How many people came to Nebraska after statehood, and where did they come from?

Nebraska had fewer than 50,000 residents at the time it became a state; less than a decade later, the population had increased by 250 percent. Three-quarters of the newcomers were native-born, and they tended to come from nearby states. Even so, there were plenty of folk who came from far away, and Nebraska's early censuses show plenty of people from various parts of Western Europe. What was lacking, in comparison to states like North and South Dakota, was a major influx by people from Eastern and Northern Europe.

What was the single best decade of Nebraska's early history?

The 1880s were good for the Cornhusker State. Immigrants continued to arrive; workers used new types of machinery on the plains; and Nebraska also benefited from cattle drives. The economy did not boom, but it was healthy enough to provide work for nearly everyone who wanted it. For Nebraska, the great change—and it was rather shocking—was the bad economic times that came in the 1890s.

Drought was the single most important cause, but Nebraska also suffered from a lack of "hard" money. Many Nebraskans complained that they were victims of the railroad companies, which were almost able to set the price of farm goods. It comes as no surprise that Nebraska was part of the Populist Movement, which began in the 1890s, or that one of the great populists of the era, William Jennings Bryan, hailed from the Cornhusker State.

Who was William Jennings Bryan, and how did he rise to such sudden prominence?

Born in Nebraska in 1860, Bryan was a farmer's son who worked as a journalist before going into politics. Blessed with a thick mane of black hair and a magnificent voice, he became the leading speaker on behalf of the oppressed farming community of the Midwestern states. In the mid–1890s, Bryan stole the attention from other Populist speakers and absolutely captivated the Democratic national convention in Chicago with his "Cross of Gold" speech. Arguing that gold was one of the worst vices of the American economy, Bryan promoted the free coinage of silver as the primary issue of his 1896 presidential platform.

Midwestern farmers did not realize that Bryan had already shot his bolt. Having taken aim at gold, he was compelled to give that one speech a hundred, if not a thousand, more times, and he soon began to sound tired and old. He barnstormed magnificently during the presidential campaign of 1896 but lost to Republican William McKinley of Ohio, in what many believe to be one of the most important of presidential elections. Historians consider the election of 1896 one of the most pivotal of modern American history because the potential revolt on the plains and prairies was thwarted by the interests of railroad companies and banks.

Was Nebraska important to World War I?

The Cornhusker State was far from the scene of action, but its people turned out bumper crops during World War I, helping to create the impression of the American soldiers as "doughboys." The French gave them this name; they marveled at the physical size and well-being of the American infantrymen.

Nebraska son William Jennings Bryan was a U.S. congressman and, from 1913 to 1915, secretary of state. Though he ran for president three times, he never won the high office.

One area in which Nebraska was spared was the terrible epidemic of influenza that spread around the nation in the months immediately after the war ended. Because it had no major military base to which soldiers would return, Nebraska escaped one of the great epidemiological disasters of modern U.S. history.

How did Nebraska fare during the Great Depression?

The Wall Street stock market crash of 1929 did not harm Nebraska very much; it was the consequent drop in the price of many farm goods that did the damage. The price of corn declined 80.6 percent between 1929 and 1933, and wheat fell by 73 percent. Nebraska was among the six states that farm prices most powerfully affected, and its people suffered accordingly. Many Nebraskans hit the road early in the Great Depression, heading for all sorts of places, but the Dust Bowl that struck the Midwestern states in 1935 and 1936 set the state reeling. Some counties lost as many as a third of their population during the 1930s.

What is unique about Nebraska's state government?

Nebraska is the only state in the union that meets as a unicameral (meaning "one house") body. There is no separate House of Representatives or Senate (though the forty-nine members are commonly referred to as "senators"). Members officially run for election as non-partisan candidates (though their party affiliation is typically known), and the two candidates who tally the most votes in the primary move on to the general election. The first unicameral legislature met in 1937.

How important was Nebraska to the American effort in World War II?

It would be difficult to overstate Nebraska's role. Not only did the Cornhusker State turn out vast amounts of agricultural products, which became loaves of bread and K-rations for the American G.I., but Nebraska also began to figure in the policy-making decisions of leading American Army generals. When World War II ended, some of these generals remembered the key position of Nebraska, nearly at the center of the Continental United States, and they considered the area when looking for new air bases. As a result, the Strategic Air Command was located very close to Omaha, providing a much-needed shot in the arm to the local economy.

How did Nebraska come to play so large a role in the Cold War?

First came the Strategic Air Command, then the missile silos. Not only is Nebraska nearly dead-center geographically, it also commands a fine view—and aerial path—toward the Soviet Union. All sorts of U.S. nuclear missiles were, therefore, placed underground in Nebraska, something that gave the Soviet policy-makers fits. Of course the Russians had their own missile silos, but they lacked an empty space as strategically located as Nebraska.

How did Nebraskans feel when the Cold War came to an end?

The majority of them had never fully admitted their vulnerability, meaning that they went about their daily lives without much thought of the incredible dangers of potential nuclear war. But when it was revealed just how many bomb and missile sites had been placed in Nebraska and other parts of the Great Plains, some people breathed an enormous sigh of relief, grateful that they—as well as their Russian counterparts—had gone unscathed.

THE WARREN BUFFETT PHENOMENON

Nebraska's location in the center of the United States made it a good choice for placing nuclear weapon silos during the Cold War.

How did America's single most successful investor get his start?

Born in Omaha in 1930, Warren Buffett was a young man with an extraordinary mind for mathematics. By the age of fifteen, he took deductions on his U.S. tax return, and by the age of twenty-five, he had saved the equivalent of nearly a million dollars in today's money. His father persuaded him to attend the Wharton School of Business at the University of Pennsylvania, but he left after two years and finished up his bachelor's degree at the University of Nebraska–Lincoln, followed by a business degree at Columbia University. And once he began investing, the sky was the limit.

Possessed of great thrift as well as acumen, Buffett has spent most of his life in the modest home he purchased in the 1950s. He became the great investor of the late twentieth century, and as chairman of the board of Berkshire Hathaway, he came to be worth something in the neighborhood of $60 billion, making him one of the wealthiest people on the planet—indeed, in all of human history.

How did the image of the investor from the Midwest become so prominent?

In their attempts to imitate Warren Buffett's success, many investors' groups sprang up in Midwestern states. Often these were composed of retirees, eager to make their dollars stretch. Quite a few of these groups recorded real success, but none came anywhere close to the man best known as the "Oracle of Omaha."

Where will the Cornhusker State be a generation from now?

With many of the Midwestern states, one feels relative confidence in predicting more of the same. This is not the case with Nebraska. The state and its people have been more vulnerable to sudden economic shifts than the great majority of states.

NEVADA

Nicknames: "The Silver State"; "The Battle-Born State"
Capital: Carson City
Statehood: October 31, 1864; 36th state

AT A GLANCE

What are the most important signs and symbols of the Silver State?

For many outsiders, the skyscrapers of Las Vegas are the number-one vision that brings Nevada to mind. "All for Our Country" is the official state motto. But the mountain bluebird is the state bird, and sagebrush is the state flower. The single-leaf pinyon and the bristlecone pine are the state trees.

How large, or small, is Nevada?

Comprising 110,572 square miles (286,367 square kilometers), Nevada is seventh among the fifty states in geographic size. The population of 2,790,136, as enumerated in the census of 2010, reveals that Nevada had the thirty-fifth largest population.

How did Nevada, and Las Vegas specifically, become "Sin City" of the United States?

It happened over time, with various legislative decisions contributing, but the elements of Nevada history were there from the very beginning: risk, chance, opportunity, and the threat of violence behind the scenes. From its earliest days, the Silver State was a place where people got rich quickly and lost their winnings even more rapidly.

Is Nevada primarily a land of desert? Or of mountains?

Both. Nevada is the driest of all the states; it averages less than four inches of moisture per year, at the lower elevations. At the same time, the state has many mountains, some of which remain snowcapped for much of the year.

Nevada has one of the loneliest stretches of highway in the nation, the single biggest "strip," and it receives more than 50 million visits per year! Though some elitists spurn Las Vegas and what it stands for, there is no doubt that "Vegas" is the single most-popular destination in the nation, and among the most popular in the entire world.

Besides the terrain of Nevada's land, what else is unusual about it?

About 85 percent of the land in Nevada is owned or managed by the U.S. government, making it the state with the highest amount of government-owned land (compare that with the lowest: less than 1 percent in Connecticut, Iowa, and New York). This includes defense sites and natural acreage.

Do Nevadans discuss the weather very much?

No, because they are, to an astonishing degree, people who live indoors. The advent of air conditioning came about the same time that Las Vegas rose to prominence, and virtually all residents of the Silver State have some form of it. Given the extreme high temperatures that sometimes occur, many Nevadans remain indoors. Of course there are exceptions, such as those who ski in nearby mountains and Nevadans of all social types who flock to Lake Tahoe. But, like Arizona, Nevada is a highly urban state.

Can the Nevadan be told apart from her or his Southwest neighbors?

No longer! As recently as 1960 this was possible, both as a result of a slight accent and the type of clothing. Since about 1970, however, the local Nevadan "look" and attitude have been altered, and even replaced many times, due to the immense number of people who pass through.

Risk, or games of chance, do appeal to the Nevadan, however. Perhaps it's the legacy of being founded as a result of a silver rush. Then again, it may come from so many gangsters relocating to the area from Chicago in the 1940s. There's no doubt that Nevadans relish risk and turns of the dime more than most Americans.

EARLY HISTORY

For how long have humans lived in what we call the Silver State?

For thousands of years, but they did not live in any great numbers. The earliest Native Americans to reach Nevada may have arrived in time to see some of the enormous glacier-created lakes begin to disappear; chances are, however, that it wasn't very long before Nevada turned into the cauldron of heat and sunshine we know today. Petroglyphs do exist in Nevada, and we suspect humans have long attempted to make a go of settling the area, *and* that they met with little luck until recent times.

When did East Coast Americans first become aware of Nevada?

The name—which means "snow covered"—did not yet exist, but handfuls of American fur trappers and explorers, such as Jedidiah Strong Smith (1799–1831), came through in the 1820s. Others, like federal exploratory leader John C. Frémont, came in the 1840s. In both cases, however, the travelers were on their way to California and only stumbled by accident on what we call the Silver State. It took the arrival of the Mormons in neighboring Utah, and the successful conclusion of the War with Mexico (1846–1848), for Nevada to receive any attention.

West Coast Americans were, naturally, more conscious of Nevada, but they considered it northing more than a punishing way station on the trail to the Golden State—until silver was discovered in 1858.

What brought so many miners to the western states in the mid-nineteenth century?

The California Gold Rush had a lot to do with it, but it does not provide the full answer. Mining was off to a great start on the East Coast, with Pennsylvania leading the way. At certain times, many miners were laid off, and it made good sense for them to pick up and move elsewhere. Of course not all of them headed for the West Coast, or the Rocky Mountains, but when the news arrived that silver had been discovered in Nevada, many of them packed their bags.

Is it really fair, or accurate, to call the discovery of silver in Nevada the "Comstock Lode"?

Like so many great discoveries of human history, the finding of silver in western Nevada came as something of a fluke, and only a few dozen men (no women) were involved in the earliest strike. Henry Comstock (1820–1870) does not appear to have done much of the digging or work; he seems to have been a rather sharp fellow who purchased other miners' shares and then popularized the find with his name.

The find, in the area of present-day Virginia City, was nothing less than sensational. Silver lay under the enormous mountain of the same name, and prospectors began coming from all directions. Oregonians dropped everything and rushed south; Californians rushed east; and quite a few East Coast Americans sold everything and packed up to move west.

Why is Virginia City so well-known, even today?

A good question. We don't speak of Sutter's Fort, in present-day Sacramento, with anywhere near that same level of interest. Perhaps it's because Virginia City rose faster than

An 1870 photo showing a mining town near Virginia City, Nevada.

almost any other American place, and when it fell, it did so dramatically. In a matter of months, Virginia City went from a place of a few dozen to one of 5,000, and at the height of the silver boom it was up to 25,000. But today Virginia City has about 1,500 residents. Virginia City gained fame, too, when one of the most famous of all American writers, Mark Twain, lived there for a time and wrote for the *Territorial Enterprise*.

Was this also the time of the Pony Express?

It was indeed. The first Pony Express riders charged across the Nevada desert in 1859, and their importance peaked in March 1861, when one brought Abraham Lincoln's first inaugural address. Not all Nevadans were keen for the Union, and Lincoln did his utmost to reach those who were on the fence.

The matter became even more pressing as Lincoln sought congressional votes in order to pass the Thirteenth Amendment, which would abolish slavery. Anxious to have the support of Nevada, both for the amendment and the presidential election of 1864, Lincoln rushed the process. Some Nevadans were delighted to oblige, and—learning that the issue was imminent—they sent a telegram that listed all their voters and the entire text of the new state constitution (this cost $3,744 at the telegraph office, the single largest amount yet paid for one message). Lincoln's efforts bore fruit, and Nevada came in as the thirty-sixth state on October 31, 1864.

How necessary was Nevada to Union victory in the Civil War?

The state, with its relatively small population, was not terribly important, but the mineral wealth was. Gold and silver from Nevada, shipped across the Sierra Nevada and then sent by steamship from San Francisco, was vitally important to the Union cause. Had Lincoln lived longer, he doubtless would have found some way to display his gratitude to the Silver State. After his untimely death, however, Nevada became less important in the eyes of the federal government.

Did anyone ever question whether it was a good idea to settle in such an arid landscape?

Plenty of people did so. But they tended to be those who moved on rather rapidly, establishing themselves in California or Oregon. Those who remained in Nevada declared they would tough it out and make the desert bloom, one way or another.

Even today, they have not really succeeded in changing the topography, or making it gentler. Nevada is an incredible story of human success, enabling millions of people to live in that harsh landscape, but the land itself remains much the same as when the first pioneers came through.

How did Nevada fare toward the end of the nineteenth century?

The state's population was growing, but it had no major urban center. Reno was the largest place, but it did not exceed 50,000. The rise of Las Vegas was necessary to transform the Silver State, and this began, albeit slowly, soon after the start of the twentieth century.

Even the earliest settlers, the Mormons sent by Brigham Young (1801–1877) in the 1850s to guard a section of the Mormon Trail, recognized that Las Vegas—which translates as "the meadows"—was a special place. Las Vegas still had only a few hundred people in 1900, however, and it was not until the 1920s that the population began to rise. Right from the beginning, there was a spirited debate as to whether gambling should be legalized.

What crisis prompted Nevada and the town of Las Vegas to alter their laws and statutes?

The Great Depression hit Nevada especially hard; many people picked up and left. In 1931, the Nevada state legislature passed a bill that legalized gambling. Another, passed that same year, liberalized the divorce laws of Nevada. A six-month residency requirement was reduced to six weeks, and throughout the 1930s many American couples—from all social classes—began flying to Reno in order to get a quick and easy divorce.

Nevada had made a deal with the devil, as it soon learned. The legalization of gambling brought all kinds of unsavory types to the Silver State. And when the brand-new Federal Bureau of Investigation (FBI) proved expert at rooting out crime in Chicago, many of the gangsters moved to the Far West.

How did the federal government assist Nevada during the 1930s?

The plan to build an enormous dam on the Colorado River was already in the works
when the Great Depression hit; to their credit, federal planners did not abandon the
idea of so costly an endeavor. Between 1931 and 1936, Hoover Dam was built on the
Colorado, just twenty-five miles from Las Vegas.

On October 9, 1936, the lights were turned on, revealing that something truly amazing had taken place. This enormous structure held back the Colorado River, creating the
115-mile-long Lake Mead, which would provide water and electrical power not to one
but to three states: Arizona, Nevada, and California. It was also during the construction
of the dam that hardhats were first mandated for use by workers.

Was this sufficient to bring a flood of new people to Nevada?

Not quite. World War II was needed, to chase away the last vestige of the Great Depression and convince Americans, giving them a new belief in their future. The population
of Las Vegas tripled during the 1940s, while that of the state as a whole doubled. And
some of the most iconic establishments—those that came to define Sin City—were built
around this time.

At first, the colorful businesses and corrupt politicians seemed charming. Old-time
Nevadans soon regretted the change, however, because it seemed that people from very
different places (East Coasters in general) were taking over the state.

How significant were the atomic tests conducted in the Nevada desert?

In 1951, President Harry Truman approved atomic tests in Nevada, where the federal
government owned—then and now—nearly three-quarters of all the land. The popular
governor could do nothing to prevent the federal government from exercising control
over land that it owned. And in February 1951, the first atomic test was conducted.

Nevadans took the whole matter with great aplomb, even cheer. Many Las Vegas
parties ended at dawn, about the time the tests were conducted, and numerous people
drove out to enjoy better views. What they did not realize, of course, was the amount of
radiation to which they were exposed. The federal government continued to conduct

atomic tests into the mid-1960s, when they were finally brought to an end.

What is Area 51?

Area 51 is a U.S. Air Force facility located about eight miles northwest of Las Vegas that is believed to be the site where aircraft and weapons testing takes place. The airspace surrounding Area 51, located within the Nevada Test and Training Range, is restricted. The highly secretive nature of the location has led to speculation centered around unidentified flying objects (UFOs). A nearby remote road is dubbed the Extraterrestrial Highway.

What stretch of highway is known as the Loneliest Road in America?

The 409-mile mostly desolate stretch of U.S. 50, running from Fallon, Nevada, to the west and Delta, Utah, to the east, was dubbed the Loneliest Road in America in a *Life* magazine article in 1986. The three largest towns in between Fallon and Delta are in Nevada—Austin, Eureka, and Ely. In between, though, dining, lodging, and gas fill-up opportunities are sparse.

How did Nevada fare during the 1960s and 1970s?

This was the tail-end of the first era of Las Vegas's incredible rise. Performers such as Wayne Newton and Liberace made Las Vegas more noticeable to the rest of the nation through a number of highly publicized television specials. Female entertainers such as Raquel Welch and Mae West did likewise. There was a sense, however, that Vegas was trading on the careers of entertainers from an earlier time, and that fresh blood was needed.

How did Las Vegas ever get the money to build the enormous casinos and hotels that dominate The Strip today?

Only the insiders know and they aren't telling. But organized crime, and strong connections to organized crime in Mexico, definitely sent along plenty of cash. Las Vegas was already impressive by 1985; from then on, it grew from the marvelous to the phenomenal. When The Mirage Hotel and Casino was completed in 1993, it marked an entirely new era, one in which the fortunes made and lost tripled in size.

Is there anything to the marvelous movie *Casino*? Or is it largely a product of Oliver Stone's rich imagination?

The killings are far overdone, and the sinister characters, such as the one played by Joe Pesci, have no basis in reality. But in terms of the cold calculation and way in which the hapless tourist is fleeced of his or her dollars, this is very much in the Las Vegas tradition. Many Americans today shrug at the inequity between the "house" and the "bit player," saying that things have always been like this. They overlook the fact that never has so much money been made for so few at the expense of so many!

Las Vegas, Nevada, is the playground for people who love to gamble and visit the spectacular, themed hotels.

Millions of Americans had already come to Nevada—those numbers also tripled. Vegas became the subject of more television advertisements than any other American city, and yet one wondered whether it was really necessary to advertise at all. By 2000, Vegas was the internal destination for most American tourists, with London and Paris vying for the top spot internationally.

Did Vegas critics continue to point to the emptiness of it all—the sad spectacle of so many people trying to have fun with sex, booze, and gambling?

While many intellectuals often pooh-poohed the entire Las Vegas experience, declaring it a rip-off of more developed societies, many critics either gave up or were brushed aside. By 2010, Vegas was more popular than ever. A whole new generation of crooners and performers—none of them quite as successful as the 1950s and 1960s crowd—had taken over. Millions of visitors came to Vegas, certain that this was "their" night, their moment for pleasure and success.

What will Nevada look like a generation from now?

As with so many things, it's an up-or-down proposition, a roll of the dice. Either Nevada will become the most popular state in the nation, and Las Vegas will continue to be the pleasure capital, or the problems with water and clean air will sink the economy. As of 2015, residents of other states continue to move to Nevada, but the state has a high foreclosure rate and an increasing homeless population.

NEW HAMPSHIRE

Nickname: "The Granite State"
Capital: Concord
Statehood: June 21, 1788; 9th state

AT A GLANCE

What are the most important signs and symbols of the Granite State?

The "Old Man of the Mountain," a peculiar rock formation, was for a long time the best-known of all symbols of New Hampshire (before it came tumbling down in May 2003). The official state bird is the purple finch, and the purple lilac is the state flower. The white birch is the official state tree.

"Live Free or Die" is the official state motto.

How large, or small, is the Granite State?

New Hampshire is small, but it contains considerable variety of climate and topography. The short seacoast is very different from the mountainous north, for example. Comprised of 9,349 square miles (24,214 square kilometers), New Hampshire ranks forty-sixth among the fifty states in geographic size, and the population of 1,323,459 comes in at forty-second.

Is there any one place from which one can see the best that is New Hampshire?

Yes, and many thousands of people have done so. Mount Washington is daunting, even to the person with a well-equipped automobile, but this has not prevented many people from making the ascent. And no matter how long the journey, and how heart-pounding the drive can be, the summit is worth all the struggle. On a clear day, one can just make out the Atlantic Ocean.

How much variety can be found within the Granite State?

A great deal. New Hampshire has less than twenty miles of seacoast, but they include some truly beautiful beaches, and the seaside city of Portsmouth is one of the great undiscovered gems of all New England. Once the tourist gets away from that coast, however, he or she finds the flinty granite hills of rural New Hampshire, as well as many ski resorts and apple orchards. If one drives all the way to the Canadian border, he or she is rewarded with some of the most spectacular of all New England scenery.

Do New Hampshirites discuss the weather very much?

Of course. *Yankee Magazine*, the oldest of all surviving old-style magazines, is still published in New Hampshire, and the locals seldom tire of informing the newcomers about the variety that they've seen in winters of the past; those of 1978 and 1996 usually come at the top of the list. The working assumption, however, is that if one has chosen to come to the Granite State, he or she must be familiar with snowblowers and snowshoes, as well as skis.

Is the New Hampshire person culturally distinct, from, let's say, his or her neighbor in Massachusetts or Vermont?

Yes. In earlier times, New Hampshire had to struggle for an identity separate from the Bay State. In recent times the difference for those who live on the left, or east, bank of the Connecticut River and those on the right, or west, has become the more important differentiation. Of course there are some stereotypes involved, but it's generally safe to say that the moment one crosses the Connecticut River from Vermont into New Hampshire, he or she experiences a more conservative, as well as libertarian, area. "Live free or die!" is the New Hampshire state motto, and its citizens believe that government is best when it governs least. New Hampshire has no state income tax, and this is reflective of the beliefs of its residents.

Does Robert Frost, the great twentieth-century poet, belong to Vermont, New Hampshire, or Massachusetts?

Though he was born in California, Robert Frost came east at an early age, and over time he became identified with all three of these states. He gained academic prominence by teaching in Massachusetts—most notably at Amherst College—but he chose to live in upstate New Hampshire (when possible). Over time, he became equally identified with Vermont because the people of the Green Mountain State found his poetry celebrated their lifestyle.

EARLY HISTORY

For how long have Native Americans lived in what we call the Granite State?

For thousands of years. Relatively little of their material culture remains, so we have to evaluate their lives by the lifestyle of the Indians who lived in New Hampshire when the first white settlers and explorers arrived. To the best of our knowledge, the Indians were generally migratory, sometimes moving all the way to southern Connecticut in the winter and returning to New Hampshire each spring.

Who were the first white settlers of New Hampshire?

The very first, some of whose houses in Portsmouth still remain today, were Puritans from the Bay State. They arrived in the 1630s, and little differentiated them from Massachusetts, except that their form of Puritanism was even more severe. But between 1640 and 1660, the second generation of New Hampshire settlers arrived, and these tended to be Scots and Scots-Irish. They were not numerous, but they were filled with a truly granite-like spirit and heart.

By 1690, the Puritans and Scots-Irish had settled much of southern New Hampshire. This was the period of greatest testing, however, because the French and Indian Wars commenced in 1689. Several New Hampshire settlements were obliterated, and there were times when the colony was despaired of; New Hampshire persevered, however, and by 1700 it was evident that the colony would make it. One of the major reasons why New Hampshire would thrive was the quality of its trees.

When was Mount Washington first climbed?

To the best of our knowledge, Darby Field was the first white person to make the ascent (in 1642). He wrote a short description that matches almost perfectly the observations of the modern scientists who examine the mountain, both for its snow cover and for the speed of its winds. A follow-up to that first ascent did not occur for a long time, however, and not until the 1830s did New Hampshire people begin making regular ascents. Once they did, Mount Washington became an integral part of the tourist scene, and so it remains today.

What is one of the least-known of all New Hampshire colonial events?

Hannah Duston was a woman of great courage. In the late winter of 1697, a group of Indians on the warpath suddenly seized and captured Duston and took her from her Haver-

How important were American trees for the British Royal Navy?

Lacking the oak and pine of New Hampshire and Maine, it's quite possible that England never would have become the mistress of the seas. By 1650, England had cut down so many of its old-growth trees that its navy was in crisis. In this time, the British Royal Navy leaders declared that the biggest and broadest of all New England trees belonged to the navy alone; toward that end, the king's inspector marked these trees with a broad arrow, showing that they were reserved for the king.

hill, Massachusetts, home. About one-third of the way into New Hampshire, Duston learned that she and her fellow captives would be subjected to the gauntlet upon arriving in French Canada. Knowing she would not survive this cruel punishment, Duston persuaded two of her fellow captives to assist her. One night, she awoke them and declared they would kill all their Indian captors. While her wild-eyed associates looked on in fear, Duston started the work, and it appears that it was she who killed nearly all the ten Indians that night. Scalping the Indians, in order to prove what she'd done, Duston led her freed captives by canoe all the way home. She became a celebrity in Puritan Boston, and a statue to her stands today in Haverhill.

How important were the royal governors of the late colonial period?

Between about 1740 and 1770, New Hampshire became one of the most conservative of the original Thirteen Colonies. Some of this arose from the grassroots, but much was imposed by a set of governors who intended New Hampshire to become a model royal colony. Their efforts were successful right up to about the year 1770, but the five years that followed saw a reversal of the trend, and the people of New Hampshire were ready for independence when the Revolutionary War commenced.

Who is the most significant of all New Hampshire colonial heroes?

He is less known than in the past, but Robert Rogers (1731–1795) is the distant ancestor of the U.S. Special Forces. Born in northern Massachusetts, he crossed the border to New Hampshire at a young age and became a masterful frontiersman. When the French and Indian War (1754–1763) commenced, Rogers formed the Rangers, an irregular group of wilderness fighters to take on the French and their Indian allies.

Rogers' Rangers played a major role in winning the battles and skirmishes on Lake Champlain, and in 1759 he led them on a daring raid into French Canada. Rogers torched the Abenaki village of St. Francis and then brought his men back to Old Fort Number Four, on the east bank of the Connecticut River. Had he remained loyal to the American cause, Rogers might have been instrumental in the American Revolution. But he chose the British side, and this is another reason why he is not as well remembered as he should be.

How important was New Hampshire's role in the American Revolution?

The Granite State is seldom acknowledged for its contributions, in part because virtually none of the major political leaders, such as Sam Adams or John Hancock,

Robert Rogers commanded the famous Rogers' Rangers during the French and Indian War and went on to fight in the American Revolution.

I've heard the expression "the Hampshire Grants." What does it mean?

In the decade leading up to the American Revolution, both New Hampshire and New York laid claim to what is now Vermont (Vermont did not become a state until 1791). New Hampshire had the better claim, based on a previous royal land grant, and the "Hampshire Grants" was the unofficial name for the area until Ethan Allen and the Green Mountain Boys made everyone recognize that Vermont was independent.

came from New Hampshire. What the Granite State did have, however, was a large supply of earnest patriots, men and women eager to break from Great Britain. The best evidence of this comes from the Battle of Bennington, fought in the late summer of 1777.

Learning that the British, advancing south from Lake Champlain, sent a large detachment of Hessian soldiers to plunder the Vermont countryside, New Hampshire raised over a thousand men. Led by Colonel John Stark—from whose lips New Hampshire gets "Live free or die!"—the New Hampshire men crossed Vermont in a hurry to meet and defeat the Hessians. In the height of irony, so far as interstate relations go, the Battle of Bennington was fought in New York, near the Vermont-New York border and was won primarily by men from New Hampshire.

How did New Hampshire fare in the decades that followed political independence?

New Hampshire entered the Union on June 21, 1788, as the ninth state. The New Hampshire voters did not have a difficult time—they clearly believed in unification—but were aware that they would be one of the smaller states, without room to expand. It was during the three decades that followed the Revolution that New Hampshire's identity became muted. New Hampshirites never had any problem knowing who they were, but the rest of the nation—the newest states especially—hardly seemed to know that the Granite State existed. Two things conspired to keep New Hampshire relevant: a tough physical material, and the stentorian tones of a legislator on the national level.

What were the two materials that earned money for enterprising New Hampshire businessmen?

New Hampshire granite was in high demand throughout the nineteenth century, and it was used in the building of a variety of monuments, particularly in New York City, Washington, D.C., and Chicago.

Another New Hampshire product was much softer and less solid: ice. Starting in about 1830, New Hampshire ice was cut from ponds and lakes and brought by wagon all the way to Boston. Massachusetts entrepreneur Frederic Tudor mastered the art of keeping ice intact in warm areas (this was accomplished by packing the ice with sawdust).

New Hampshire ice was then shipped from the port of Boston, and some of it went halfway round the globe, to arrive in India, where British army officers developed the concept of "mixed" drinks, meaning beverages served with ice.

How important was Daniel Webster to the image—and the substance—of New Hampshire?

He was, and remains, the single most iconic political figure of New Hampshire history. Webster was born in Salisbury, New Hampshire, briefly lived in Boston, Massachusetts, after college, then moved back to New Hampshire, and then moved back yet again to Massachusetts. He served as a U.S. House representative from New Hampshire in 1813–1817 and from Massachusetts in 1823–1827, and he had two stints as a U.S. senator from Massachusetts: 1827–1841 and 1845–1850. As a senator, he gave numerous orations on all sorts of topics, but the most memorable ones dealt with the Union. In February 1830, Webster gave his "Second Reply to Hayne"—comments about South Carolina nullification in a debate with South Carolina senator Robert Hayne—which has never been equaled as a poetic expression of patriotic belief.

"Liberty *and* Union, one and inseparable." These are the concluding words to a political speech that resembles a sermon, and some of Webster's critics claimed that's just what he was: an old-fashioned New England minister, dressed up in the clothes of a politician. The people who heard him that day were persuaded, however, and two generations of schoolchildren repeated and recited his words. It's not too much to say that Webster influenced the outcome of the Civil War. Even though he died a decade before the first guns were fired, his spirit and patriotic expression lived on and persuaded many young Northerners to fight for the cause.

Webster also was the U.S. secretary of state in 1841–1843 under Presidents William Henry Harrison and John Tyler and in 1850–1852 under President Millard Fillmore.

Did New Hampshire accomplish anything in the Civil War?

On the individual level, the answer is yes. Thousands of New Hampshire men served and did so with honor. On the state level, the results were disappointing. New Hampshire did not produce any outstanding general or set of political leaders during the war. The Granite State certainly did its part, but it did not win kudos in the way that Maine, its eastern neighbor, did.

New Hampshire native Daniel Webster was famous for his skill as an orator. He served as a U.S. House representative, a U.S. senator, and a U.S. secretary of state.

Who was the best-known visual artist of nineteenth-century New Hampshire?

Augustus Saint-Gaudens is not as well-known as he should be. The son of a French emigrant, Saint-Gaudens became one of the finest sculptors of his day, and many of his cast models still exist at his homestead, in the town of Cornish along the east bank of the Connecticut River. New Hampshire had not accomplished great things in the Civil War, but Saint-Gaudens made the state an important place for Civil War buffs to visit. His work is in most of the major cities of the nation, but the best-known are two of President Abraham Lincoln in Chicago and a monument to Civil War admiral David Farragut in New York City.

What are some notable political facts about the capital city of Concord?

The New Hampshire State House in the capital city of Concord was first used by both houses of the state legislature in 1819. Both houses continue to meet in their original chambers—the only state who can make that claim.

One man who served in the State House as New Hampshire's Speaker of the House also went on to serve as president of the United States, the only New Hampshirite to be elected to that office. Pierce served from 1853 to 1857. The former president, who died in 1869, lived his final years in Concord, where he, his wife Jane, and his two sons are buried.

Concord also has some connections to the American space program; what are they?"

Concord is the site of the McAuliffe-Shepard Discovery Center. The museum honors two people: Concord resident McAuliffe, who was to be the first schoolteacher in space but who died in the explosion of the *Challenger* space shuttle in January 1986; and Derry native Alan Shepard, who was one of the original Mercury Seven astronauts, the first American to go into space, and the fifth person to walk on the moon.

When did New Hampshire become the center of the ski industry?

New Hampshirites have skied in unofficial ways for generations, but the industry itself began in the 1930s. A few clever inventors cooked up the idea of moving forward on parallel skis, and the first ski lift was established at Franconia Notch in 1935. The first twenty years or so were uneven, with only modest attendance, but from 1955 on, skiing became one of the central parts of New Hampshire's economy. Locals waited for "the season," anticipating the dollars that would come from out-of-state arrivals.

When did the differences between New Hampshire and Vermont really become apparent?

Until about 1930, the two states did not seem that different. For instance, they were both composed primarily of Yankees, and they both had emerging ski industries. And, as late as 1936, Vermont and New Hampshire still voted in tandem. Both voted against

Franklin Roosevelt in the banner year of 1936, when he swept most of the nation. There-fore, if one has to put a decade to it, the 1940s probably are the answer.

By the end of World War II, New Hampshire had become a bastion of old-fashioned Yankee conservatism; it was, in fact, the home of *Yankee Magazine*. Vermont, on the other hand, moved in a more liberal direction and has done so steadily ever since. The Connecticut River, which forms the boundary between the two states, has a number of fine bridges—including several covered ones—but the difference between the people and their attitudes are very clear. New Hampshire remains the land of "Live Free or Die," while Vermont has become the land of liberal experimentation.

How did New Hampshire become such a force in the selection of each U.S. president?

The tradition goes back to 1920, when New Hampshire was allowed to hold the first pri-mary in the nation, but during the long career of Franklin D. Roosevelt, primaries and caucuses were relatively unimportant, since everyone knew who the Democrats would nominate in the 1930s. It was during the presidency of Dwight D. Eisenhower (1953–1961) that New Hampshire began to play a pivotal role. The hotly contested nom-ination process—on the Democratic side—in 1960 had a lot to do with it.

In 1960, U.S. senator John F. Kennedy of Massachusetts announced he would enter as many primaries as possible. Until then, state caucuses, and the decisions of old-style polit-

Senator Bernie Sanders campaigns in New Hampshire in this 2015 photo. The state has been at the forefront of presidential campaigns since 1920.

ical bosses, had been instrumental in making or breaking candidates. Kennedy won almost every primary he entered, and this success lifted him to the Democratic nomination.

And how is it that the Granite State gets to cast the first votes in a presidential primary?

This, too, was decided back in 1920. Congress stipulated that the Granite State would have the honor of holding the first presidential primary. Little towns along the Canadian border vie with each other for the honor of rising early and casting the very first ballots in the nation. One can argue that early or late polling does not matter very much these days, because of the rapidity with which votes are tallied, but it still does present an interesting picture, with little New Hampshire voting first and huge California as one of the last states to vote.

Have there been any outstanding upsets or surprises in the New Hampshire primary over the years?

Harry S. Truman and Lyndon B. Johnson both entered the New Hampshire primary (in 1952 and 1968 respectively) in order to test the waters, to see whether they had a chance at another term. Both incumbent presidents performed poorly in the primary, and both quickly pulled out of the race. In more recent years, the really big surprise came in 1992, when Democrat Bill Clinton became the first person ever to lose the New Hampshire primary and still go on to secure the nomination of his party. Republican George W. Bush did the same in 2000.

The New Hampshire primary has plenty of critics. They contend that the Granite State is far too white and too rural to stand for the nation as a whole, and that some larger state would be a better choice. The Granite State still maintains its position as first in the nation, however.

Did any countercultural heroes come from New Hampshire?

One has to struggle to think even of one. New Hampshire has many writers, poets, and independent-minded thinkers, but the state has not produced any major rebels or "outsiders." Jack Kerouac, who helped launch the "Beat" generation, came from Lowell, Massachusetts, close to the New Hampshire border, but he is identified with neither of these New England states. New Hampshire does have one of the most serious, and admired, of all twentieth-century writers, however. Soon after the widespread fame through publication of *Catcher in the Rye*, J. D. Salinger retired to Cornish, New Hampshire, where he lived in almost total seclusion.

What was life in New Hampshire like at the turn of the twenty-first century?

If ever there has been a state that time seemed to forget, it is New Hampshire. Never as powerful or influential as its neighbors, and never as well-known as a vacationland as Maine, New Hampshire has nevertheless muddled through, one generation after another. Plenty of New Hamsphirites proudly proclaim that they would never choose to live anywhere else; their difficulty lies in persuading other people to join them.

Where will the Granite State be a generation from now?

Right about where it is today. New Hampshire prides itself on tradition rather than change, and its residents will, quite likely, continue to emphasize the former.

NEW JERSEY

Nickname: "The Garden State"
Capital: Trenton
Statehood: December 18, 1787; 3rd state

AT A GLANCE

What are the most important signs and symbols of the Garden State?

"Liberty and Prosperity" is the official state motto. The eastern goldfinch is the official state bird, and the purple violet is the state flower. The red oak is the state tree.

How large, or small, is New Jersey?

Comprised of only 7,812 square miles (20,233 square kilometers), New Jersey comes in at forty-sixth among the fifty states in geographic size. The population of 8,791,894, however, means that New Jersey is eleventh among the states in terms of population.

I can't help but think of the New Jersey Turnpike, one of the longest and least pleasant highway sections on the East Coast. How, then, can they call it the Garden State?

This is rather like judging Manhattan by 42nd Street, or by deciding that Chicago is unpleasant based on a section of the Lower South Side. New Jersey, in fact, has a beautiful coastline and many wooded areas inland. It's just that the traffic, which reflects the business of New Jersey commerce, runs right through the middle of the state, blocking the view.

291

Why does the Garden State suffer so when compared to its neighbors? For how long has Jersey been something akin to an insult?

Almost from its very beginnings. There's no really good reason for the defamation of the state's character. New Jersey has industrious people, a marvelous coastline, and some really fine inland areas. Almost from the colonial period, however, people have looked down on New Jersey, asserting that it is neither fish nor fowl, neither genteel nor couth.

Is New Jersey as low as it seems?

The Garden State is one of the lowest—in altitude—states in the nation. Sandy soil forms much of the Garden State, showing its connection to the nearby Atlantic Ocean. In the northwest corners of the state, there are some good-sized hills, however.

Do New Jerseyans discuss the weather very much?

Nine times out of ten, it has little relevance to their lives. New Jersey is known for its mild winters and fine summers, times when people wish to enjoy "The Boardwalk" of Atlantic City fame. Snowstorms seldom do very much to New Jersey. The one great, and sometimes terrible, exception, is formed by hurricanes, however, and in August and September, New Jerseyans tend to keep a close watch on the sky and a keen ear for the weather reports.

EARLY HISTORY

For how long have humans lived in what we now call the Garden State?

For perhaps 10,000 years. Many of the artifacts that might tell us about their lifeways lie under the western side of the Atlantic Ocean, and it's possible we will someday learn much more about these archaic ancestors. At present, all we can say is that when the first white Europeans showed up, they found New Jersey lightly populated but inhabited mostly by Indians of the same tribe. Their name for themselves was the Leni-Lenape; the whites often called them the Delaware Indians, after the state of that name.

Very little remains of the earliest inhabitants (we do not know their names, for example), but it's a good guess that the Leni-Lenape, the Indians who greeted the first European discoverers and settlers, are among their descendants. New Jersey was as pleasant a place to live then as it is today.

Who came first, the English or the Dutch?

Don't forget the Swedes, who briefly established a small area they called New Sweden, along the banks of the Delaware River. New Jersey, however, gained its real footing from English settlers who arrived in the 1670s. A majority of them were Quakers, members of the Society of Friends, and they brought a typically Quaker attitude to business and land transactions, meaning they were meticulous and precise.

This doesn't mean there were no conflicts with the local Indians, but New Jersey history shows few major wars or even skirmishes when compared with the majority of its neighbors. It's from those early Quaker settlers that New Jersey gains its name: it was to be the *new* Jersey, meaning the Channel island of Guernsey.

I sometimes hear of East and West Jersey as well as New Jersey. Are they all the same place?

Two colonies, rather than one, were established during the 1670s and 1680s. East Jersey was a brand-new place, reflecting the aims and desires of its Quaker leaders, while West Jersey was more of the frontier. This changed over time, however, as yet another Quaker group influenced West Jersey, right over the Delaware River in Pennsylvania.

For some time, New Jersey had two capitals and legislative assemblies, but this changed by about 1720, and from then forward the entire area was referred to as New Jersey. One reason New Jersey's neighbors often look down on the Garden State is because it took the colony so long to become fully established. By then, New York and Pennsylvania both had well-established reputations, and New Jersey was frequently thought of as an after-effect.

What kind of government prevailed in colonial New Jersey?

The colony was founded primarily by businessmen, and the colonial government took on a look that mirrored this fact. Most of the governors of New Jersey were conservative in that they favored economic growth over other interests. One of the strongest examples of New Jersey conservatism is that displayed by William Franklin (1731–1813), the son of Benjamin Franklin. Most of us are familiar with William Franklin from the fact that he assisted his father in the famous electricity experiments. Twenty-five years later, however, William Franklin was such a confirmed Loyalist that he spent some time in a Continental Army prison. Father and son parted ways over the American Revolution, and they never made up.

I've heard the expression "Cockpit of the Revolution" but don't know what it means. Can you enlighten me?

New Jersey was sometimes called the crossroads of the American colonies, because of the large number of people, horses, and wagons that crossed the area. Once the Revolution began, New Jersey was a strategic place, because it lay between Manhattan, the center of America's wealthiest merchants, and Philadelphia, where the Continental Congress held its meetings. As a result, New Jersey was involved in the Revolutionary War to an extraordinary degree.

Most know that George Washington crossed the Delaware to attack the Hessians at Trenton, but many don't realize that he had previously been pursued right across the Garden State. Washington subsequently won the Battle of Princeton against the British and then went into winter quarters at Morristown. If one totals up all the eight years

293

Washington spent in the effort to win America's independence, one will find that Washington and the Continental Army spent more time in the Garden State than any other.

How about the Battle of Monmouth? Is there anything to the story of Molly Pitcher and the buckets of water?

Many believe that the Battle of Monmouth, fought on June 28, 1778, took place on the hottest day of the Revolutionary War. Some observers claimed it was 98 degrees in the shade! That the men of both sides suffered in the severe heat is beyond question; perhaps eighty of them died from heat stroke. As to Molly Pitcher, we can neither confirm nor deny the wonderful story that she accompanied her husband in battle, and that when he fell, she took his place, firing one of the cannons several times. There is no special reason to disbelieve what we hear, however; quite a few American women participated in the Revolutionary War, though most of them were disguised as men.

What role did New Jersey play in the formation of the new government in 1787?

The New Jersey Plan, as articulated at the Constitutional Convention, was to provide security for the smaller states. By then, New Jersey people knew they would never be allowed to expand to the West. Pennsylvania lay smack in the way. But the New Jersey Plan did not win the acceptance of enough delegates. It was the so-called Connecticut Plan, or Connecticut Compromise, that forged a mixture of importance of states and size. The U.S. Senate is based entirely on statehood, with two senators for each state, while the U.S. House of Representatives is based on population. New Jersey voted swiftly to approve the new Constitution, however, and the Garden State was the third to enter the Union, in December 1787.

What unusual thing (for its time) happened for women in New Jersey?

Between 1788 and 1808, New Jersey women had the right to vote. It was not a powerful inclination on the part of the ruling men; rather, it emerged as happenstance, when the state constitution had not been written in a way that prevented female suffrage. Just how many New Jersey women voted in those years is not known, but in 1808 the constitution was changed, to prevent it from recurring.

What unusual scientific discovery was made in Haddonfield?

In 1858, William Foulke, a member of the Philadelphia Academy of Natural Sciences, and a group of diggers excavated the bones of a large prehistoric animal on the Haddonfield farm of John Estaugh Hopkins, who had found a few bones himself two decades earlier. Scientists determined that the skeleton was a dinosaur and the discovery was named Hadrosaurus *foulkii*.

What was life in New Jersey like during the antebellum years, those that led to the Civil War?

From a political point of view, life in New Jersey was ho-hum, with few major events. From an economic standpoint, the Garden State was one of the most dynamic places in the new nation. More railroads were built in New Jersey than in any of the original Thirteen States, other than Pennsylvania. Steamboats were invented for use on the Hudson River, but they soon spread to New Jersey, knitting together the industry and commerce of the Garden State. When the Civil War came, it found New Jersey one of the most prosperous states in the Union.

Was there any doubt New Jersey would fight with the Union?

Not a chance. The federal constitution had been signed in nearby Philadelphia, and there was no way the people of New Jersey would go back on the original agreement, the one that founded the nation. Over 200,000 New Jersey men served in the Civil War.

When did some of the unsavory aspects of New Jersey life begin to emerge?

This was during the two decades that followed the Civil War. New Jersey's very success led to issues of cronyism and corruption. The railroads, which made such a brilliant debut in the decades prior to the Civil War, saw some of the worst practices of overcharging in the decades that followed. Artists drew numerous cartoons of men with enormous bellies at the public trough. Though there were as many of these overfed businessmen in New York and Philadelphia, the label was attached to New Jersey, and it stuck. Then too, the very land and water of the Garden State was polluted in the three decades that followed the Civil War. Again, it was the very success of New Jersey that almost guaranteed it would have problems.

How important was Thomas Edison to the culture of the Garden State?

Edison was not a native. Born in Ohio in 1847, he did much of his early work in the Middle West. By 1870, he had come to the East Coast, however, and he soon established

A replica of Thomas Edison's laboratory that was in Menlo Park, New Jersey, can be seen at the Henry Ford Museum in Dearborn, Michigan.

the Menlo Park observatory near Newark. Edison became identified with New Jersey, and many of his inventions were first displayed, and used, there.

Edison made some of the first movies in the 1880s, and he filmed them in New Jersey. Over time, his name became associated with the Garden State, even though other states—notably Massachusetts and New York—lay claim to some of his inventions and breakthroughs.

How many presidents are associated with the Garden State?

President Grover Cleveland was born and died in New Jersey, but he made his name politically in New York, where he served as a sheriff, mayor of Buffalo, and governor. President Woodrow Wilson was a native of Virginia, but he moved to New Jersey, where he served as president of Princeton University and governor of the Garden State before winning the presidency in 1912. Wilson called his program the "New Freedom," and he based many of his policies on those he had employed while governor of the Garden State. Under Wilson, the federal government collected an income tax for the first time, and the federal government also assumed a greater responsibility for the well-being of the average citizen.

How did New Jersey fare during World War I and World War II?

Both world wars served as stimuli to the economy of the Garden State. Not only did New Jersey send over 300,000 men to the battlefields of the Second World War, but many thousands of others passed through New Jersey to federal training camps. The Garden State, too, profited from the many shipping connections along its coast, which sent men and materiel to the battlefronts. But if World War I and World War II can be seen as benefits to New Jersey, the same is not true of the Great Depression.

How bad was the Great Depression, so far as the average person of New Jersey was concerned?

It was the worst of times. Other states suffered, of course, but the Garden State's special emphasis on industry and commerce meant that many factories and plants closed (only the railroad companies continued to make money during the Depression). It was during the Great Depression that New Jersey lost some of its economic independence, as the state became more reliant on the economies of Manhattan and Philadelphia.

The Garden State rebounded nicely when the Great Depression ended (largely as a result of the beginning of the Second World War). People who had previously invested in railroads, steamboats, and the stock market now put their money in high-tech con-

The Atlantic City boardwalk is popular even on a rainy day.

> ## Are there as many Italians, and perhaps Sicilians, in New Jersey as *The Sopranos* seems to suggest?
>
> **B**eginning around 1890, Italians formed the largest of all immigrant groups to the Garden State, and their third-generation descendants can be found there today. By 1970, however, the state's population was beginning to diversify, and one hears many accents in New Jersey neighborhoods.

cerns, and for a time New Jersey was at the forefront of the new computer industry. New Jersey's more lasting economic success, however, came from the service industry (even today, New Jersey law prohibits pumping one's own gas!).

How important was Atlantic City, and the new casinos, to the growth of the Garden State?

New Jersey's population was plenty large already, but the legalization of casino gambling in 1977 made a very big difference. Until then, Atlantic City had been one of the truly charming resorts on the East Coast, a place of Ferris wheels, ferry rides, and the famous Boardwalk, which has been copied by many other cities. In the aftermath of that decision, New Jersey received more organized crime than ever before. Much of this information, naturally, is anecdotal, but there is no doubt that *The Sopranos*, one of the most popular of all cable television programs, was based at least in part on reality.

What else is Atlantic City known for?

The Miss America pageant has been held in Atlantic City since its debut in 1921. Entertainer Bert Parks was the long-time face of the pageant, as he hosted the program from 1955 to 1979. His singing of "There She Is, Miss America" as the winner was being crowned was an annual highlight.

How did New Jersey suddenly receive the spotlight of national attention on Halloween of 2012?

It was all the result of one enormous storm, known as Hurricane Sandy. New Jersey had dodged the bullet of so many hurricanes that its people were complacent when Sandy ripped up the East Coast in the autumn of 2012. Suddenly, Atlantic City and virtually all the beach communities to the north were in danger.

In the end, the Garden State did not suffer as badly as might have been the case. Loss in life was relatively low, but New Jersey took a big hit to the state's pocketbook and morale. Beachfront communities that had been deemed safe for decades were suddenly declared "at risk," and the state spent an enormous amount of money dredging local beaches and erecting both sea walls made of stone and beach defenses made of sand.

Hurricane Sandy, too, was one of the few occasions when New Jersey and New York State found common ground: the gigantic storm menaced people of both states.

What was life in New Jersey like in the years immediately following Hurricane Sandy?

Life returned to normal on the face of it, but the people of New Jersey felt a vulnerability that has seldom existed before.

NEW MEXICO

Nickname: "Land of Enchantment"
Capital: Albuquerque
Statehood: January 6, 1912; 47th state

AT A GLANCE

What are the most popular signs and symbols of the Land of Enchantment?

"It Grows as It Goes" is the official state motto. The roadrunner is the official state bird, and the yucca is the state flower. The piñon is the state tree.

How large, or small, is the Land of Enchantment?

Many of us underestimate New Mexico's physical size. Comprised of 121,590 square miles (314,917 square kilometers), New Mexico is fifth among the fifty states. The population of 2,085,287 places New Mexico at thirty-sixth among the states.

From a distance, we all get the impression New Mexico is unique. What does it look like close up?

The Land of Enchantment is about as different from the rest of the United States as a place possibly can be. Where New England has rocks and trees, New Mexico has canyons and mesas, and where the Midwest stretches on, one flat mile after another, most of New Mexico is at a high elevation. Perhaps most striking to the outsider, however, is the quality of the light.

The artist Georgia O'Keeffe spent many years in New Mexico; her belief was that once a person tasted, or experienced, the special quality of the sunlight, they would

301

come back for more. This certainly holds true for many Midwesterners who have moved to the Land of Enchantment over the past twenty years or so.

To what degree does nature make up the charms—and dangers—of life in New Mexico?

Some other states have the same amount of rugged space (Montana, for example), but almost none surpass New Mexico in that regard. Enormous canyons give way to flat land, which is at an elevation of 4,000 feet. Forests suddenly appear, as if by mirage. And when one looks for evidence of the oldest, most ancient, of all New Mexican people, he or she finds them in places like Chaco Canyon. New Mexicans realize that most East Coast Americans don't

Artist Georgia O'Keeffe drew upon the natural beauty of New Mexico for her inspiration.

know very much about them and their state, but they remain confident that once the ignorance is removed, all sorts of people will eagerly migrate there. Of course there is one major barrier: the limit imposed by the amount of water.

New Mexico is just about the driest place in the United States. Were it not for a number of dams—some dating to the early twentieth century—the Land of Enchantment would not be able to support one-tenth the number of people who reside there today.

Do New Mexicans talk about the weather very much?

Sure, but they do so with a shrug. New Mexicans have long since learned to get along with what Mother Nature provides: a fascinating mixture of abundant sunshine and intolerable dryness. The latter is a major reason why so many retirees head for New Mexico: the dry climate tends to clear up their allergies and asthma.

Winter can be surprisingly difficult. There isn't much snowfall, but the cold, especially in the northern mountains, can be intense.

Can the New Mexican be told apart from his or her Southwestern neighbors, such as the Texan and the Arizonan?

Definitely. The Texan tends to talk too much and expounds on the marvels of his or her state. The Arizonan is friendly but wants to know a lot about you (perhaps too much). Only the New Mexican gives that desert stare, which seems to look right through you. His or her visage appears to say that he or she has seen it all, and that you're no big exception to the rule.

Is alcohol a persistent difficulty in New Mexico?

It isn't so much the amount of alcohol consumed as the fact that so many people drink alone. Even one or two beers can take the edge off psychologically and render the person unfit for making those long automobile drives for which the state is famous. New Mexicans are libertarians on this subject, however; they believe an adult is an adult.

EARLY HISTORY

For how long have humans lived in what we now call the Land of Enchantment?

On and off for thousands of years. The people whose lives are the most apparent to us are known as the Anasazi, or Ancient Ones. They built the apartment-style adobe structures in Chaco Canyon and elsewhere. We have no record of their language, or how they completed those feats of engineering, but we believe a drought that lasted for around fifty years imperiled their civilization. By the year 1250, the Anasazi abandoned Chaco Canyon and other sites. Whether the Anasazi migrated elsewhere, or are the ancestors of most of the Indians in present-day New Mexico, is difficult to say.

Who were the first people of European descent to appear in New Mexico?

They were Spaniards, and the first ones came in 1539–1541. A Franciscan friar appears to have been the first; he returned to Mexico City, babbling about the cities of gold he'd seen. Whether this good brother was subjected to mirages, or whether the sun simply addled his brain has never been determined, but when Vásquez de Coronado led his men north, one year later, they found plenty of Indians and pueblos, but neither silver nor gold. Of all the European peoples that came to North America, Spaniards were the most gullible, and hopeful, where precious metals were concerned. They did find a great deal of silver in Old Mexico, but very little in the New.

Was it inevitable that the Spaniards and the Native Americans would conflict?

Yes. They came from utterly different religious and cultural backgrounds, and neither group was especially tolerant of difference. New Mexico was effectively brought under Spanish control at the end of the sixteenth century, and Santa Fe was established in 1608, meaning twelve years before the Pilgrims arrived at Plymouth Rock. This first Spanish conquest resulted in considerable bloodshed, especially when the Spaniards conquered Acoma, the town atop a mesa.

What Santa Fe building from 1610 still exists today?

The Palace of Governors, built in 1610, still stands today, at the north end of the plaza area in downtown Santa Fe. For years it was the seat of government for New Mexico when it was a Spanish colony. It is now the site of a history museum for Santa Fe and the nearby region.

What did the Spaniards do that infuriated the Native peoples to such a degree?

The well-intentioned Franciscan and Dominican friars upset the Indians by disrespecting their religion(s). The Indians were also disturbed by the way the Spaniards claimed so much of the land, acting as if they were the original inhabitants. In 1680, the natives—led by a medicine man named Pope—carried out a successful rebellion or revolt, one of the few of these that ever succeeded. The Spaniards were chased entirely out of New Mexico, and they lost about 300 of their people along the way.

Pope turned out not to be a great improvement, and the New Mexico Indians were not sad when the Spaniards returned in 1692. Pope was now dead, and Spain reclaimed the province of New Mexico, but this second phase of Spanish rule was different. The religious differences were put aside, and the land acquisitions took place in a slower manner. As a result, New Mexico did not grow very much in population for more than a century.

What did Americans know about New Mexico?

What they knew would fill a thimble. East Coast Americans tended to know a fair amount concerning Spanish Mexico, but the fact that there was a Spanish stronghold in North America was little-known. And had they known how small the Spanish numbers were, the Founding Fathers of the United States would have paid even less attention.

We keep speaking of Spaniards, but when I check other sources I more often find the name *Mexican*. When did this change come about?

Mexico carried out a long and bloody revolution, lasting from 1810 to 1821. Only at the latter date did the independent Republic of Mexico emerge. This change caused little effect to the people of New Mexico; they were so far from Mexico City that the administrators there seldom sent more than notices. But changes began to be revealed when the first American merchants made their way to Santa Fe.

Established in 1821, the Santa Fe Trail ran 1,200 miles from Independence, Missouri, to the heart of New Mexico. American merchants brought all manner of merchandise over the trail and returned with Mexican beads and blankets. This was not a way to become rich, but it was a diverting enterprise, and many Missouri merchants made the journey once a year. These trips allowed them to become more familiar with New Mexico, and when the United States-Mexican War commenced, there were plenty of trappers, traders, and guides to show the American soldiers the way.

A marker in New Mexico points out the location of the old Santa Fe Trail.

How difficult, or easy, was the American conquest of the Land of Enchantment?

The first part went very smoothly. Santa Fe yielded almost without a fight. A small group of New Mexicans fought on the rebound, however, and caused a number of casualties before they were defeated in 1847. By the end of that year all of New Mexico was in American hands, a fact confirmed by the Treaty of Guadalupe-Hidalgo in 1848.

Many, if not most, of the Americans who soldiered in New Mexico declared they had never seen anything so magnificent as its scenery. This is when some of the first watercolor paintings were executed, and when many East Coast Americans became aware of New Mexico for the first time.

Did New Mexico play any part in the American Civil War?

If Jefferson Davis and the Confederate Congress had their way, it would have been a much bigger role. Davis grandly established what he called the Territory of Arizona—encompassing New Mexico and Arizona—and sent some small detachments to win that area for the Confederacy. These Confederates came perilously close to success, but were then pushed back at Glorieta Pass early in 1862. From that month on, New Mexico was safe for the Union.

Would it have made any difference if the Confederates had won in New Mexico? Given that this was during the early stages of the war, it might have meant a longer struggle. The Confederates would have been disappointed by the land, however, which was not—at that time—ideal for the growing of cotton.

How did New Mexico fare in the final third of the nineteenth century?

New Mexico was never as wild or dangerous as Arizona, but it contained some desperados and gangs. Some banks were attacked and pilfered, and there were occasional fights between cattlemen and sheepherders (one of the most predictable of conflicts in the American West). The major concern, however, had to do with the Navajo Indians, who rose against the white settlers on several occasions. Kit Carson, the legendary Far Western traveler and guide, rounded up many Navajo in 1863 and marched them from New Mexico to Arizona.

What New Mexico territorial governor also had a literary flair?

Lew Wallace, who served as territorial governor of New Mexico in 1878–1881, also wrote the historical novel *Ben-Hur: A Tale of the Christ*. This book became a famous movie many years later, with Charlton Heston as its star. Wallace was also a Union general in the Civil War and he wrote other books, including a biography of President Benjamin Harrison.

What was life in New Mexico like at the turn of the twentieth century?

It was about as isolated as one could be. There were three main population groups: Anglo, Hispanic, and Native American. Though the three groups met on occasion, they did not mix; New Mexico was one of the most segregated parts of the nation.

Mineral wealth was discovered toward the end of the century, but this was not the kind that established great fortunes. Rather, the finds in silver and gold were just enough to float the New Mexico economy, to keep things on an even keel.

How was statehood achieved?

President Theodore Roosevelt showed more interest in the Southwest than most chief executives. In 1911 the Roosevelt Dam was completed. One year later, New Mexico became the forty-seventh state. The executive order was signed by President William Howard Taft.

NEW MEXICO
IN THE LIFE OF THE NATION

When did foreigners begin coming to New Mexico?

In the early twentieth century, quite a few people came from abroad. One was D. H. Lawrence, one of Victorian England's finest writers. Another was Georgia O'Keeffe, a native New Yorker who found herself drawn back to New Mexico, year after year.

Lawrence did not stay long, but he made some memorable utterances about New Mexico, calling it the most unforgettable landscape he'd ever seen. O'Keeffe outdid Lawrence by a long shot, executing one painting after another based on New Mexico scenes. She never tired of New Mexico and frequently painted the same location time and again.

When did the Pueblo Revival style commence?

As recently as 1890s most new houses in New Mexico were built in a style reminiscent of the Midwest, as many state residents sought to distance themselves from their Native American rooms. The University of New Mexico, founded in 1889, embarked on a building program in quite the opposite direction, seeking to utilize the best of the Pueblo building style of the sixteenth and seventeenth centuries. Before long, other towns in

---

How did one solitary artist have such an outsized impact on the perception of an entire state?

It helped that Georgia O'Keeffe had lots of contacts back in New York City and that her finest works quickly made their way into art museums. Even so, it is astonishing how many prints and reprints were made, and how her work popularized New Mexico for millions of Americans, many of whom never saw the Land of Enchantment.

the state were doing the same thing, and perhaps three-quarters of all housing built since 1950 has been in the Pueblo style.

Of course, there are anomalies. One is the so-called "earthship" building style pioneered just outside of Taos. These buildings employ all sorts of scrap, even plastic bottles, so that their builders can categorize them as true products of the region; they also employ passive solar heating, which New Mexico has in abundance. The most popular of these kind of homes are built by Michael Reynolds, of Taos, who claims they are the path of the future.

When did the population of New Mexico begin to rise?

As late as 1935, New Mexico seemed likely to remain the most remote and rural of all places in the Lower Forty-Eight. The advent of World War II changed the equation, however, and the building of the first atom bomb, in Los Alamos, was one of the major change agents.

The single biggest day in New Mexico history surely was July 23, 1945, when scientists detonated the world's first atomic explosion over the desert in northern New Mexico. One of the leaders of the project famously commented, "Now I am become Death, destroyer of worlds." J. Robert Oppenheimer was quoting from the Upanishads, but the sentiment seemed just as acute and profound in 1945.

Why is New Mexico included in so many conspiracy theories?

Let's begin by saying that some states are more susceptible than most. Because of its remoteness, and the sparseness of its population, New Mexico has always had more than its share of the mystical, and after 1947—the year of Roswell—the number of conspiracy theorists has more than quadrupled.

The basic facts are these. A New Mexico farmer reported seeing a strange object in his backyard, something that seemed "Martian" in origin. The U.S. Armed Forces denied any knowledge for years, but finally admitted that it had done some special tests in the area. The Roswell incident was the beginning of a long series of odd occurrences in New Mexico, many of them connected with the idea of extraterrestrial beings.

How do so many Americans have a decent ability to visualize the New Mexican countryside, even though they've never been?

Thanks to the Bonanza Creek Ranch, set in the southern part of the state. Since 1955, more than 130 movies have been filmed there, including *3:10 to Yuma* and *Cowboys & Aliens*. Numerous commercials are also filmed on this location, making it one of the most recognizable, even to people who've never departed the East Coast.

When did Navajo and Hopi blankets and rugs become the rage in other parts of the United States?

The 1950s seem to be the critical decade. Prior to then, there were plenty of people in New Mexico—white and Indian and Hispanic—who bought these items, but after 1955, Indian blankets and rugs became a status symbol in many parts of the nation, an indication that a person had "arrived" and that his or her artistic consciousness had "emerged."

This photo shows Navajo weaving a blanket in 1873. In the 1950s, this traditional, yet practical, art form became very popular throughout America.

How did New Mexico fare during the Youth Revolt of the 1960s?

New Mexicans are not, generally speaking, sentimental. They wrestle with a landscape so forbidding that they must keep their eye on the ball at all times. New Mexican schools and colleges were not hotbeds of youth rebellion, but many youth in other states looked to New Mexico and Arizona, declaring that the idealistic future would be achieved there. This belief had its culmination in the so-called "Harmonic Convergence" of August 1987, when many people expected a new era of consciousness to begin. It was not the wildly idealistic 1960s but the more practical 1980s that ushered in a new time in New Mexico, and it had more to do with the visions of retirees than the dreams of youth.

What was life in New Mexico like at the turn of the twenty-first century?

The Land of Enchantment was in good shape in nearly every respect except for water. New Mexicans have been conservationists for decades, using the little rainwater that comes their way, but the state has used more than its share of the water that comes from the dams along the Colorado River.

Even so, more people were moving to New Mexico than departing. The Land of Enchantment was more popular than ever.

What new kinds of housing emerged in New Mexico?

Earth shelters became quite popular in New Mexico around the turn of the twentieth century. Idealistic builders attempted to use local materials wherever possible, and they claimed that the price of their new shelters were comparable to traditional-style American homes.

Where will New Mexico be a generation from now?

One can, of course, be gloomy and predict that New Mexico will run out of water. One can also look with rose-colored glasses and say that the creative, purposeful New Mexicans will prevent that from happening. And perhaps one can declare that if a difficult place on the face of North America deserves to find an answer, it is New Mexico.

NEW YORK

Nickname: "The Empire State"
Capital: Albany
Statehood: July 26, 1788; 11th state

AT A GLANCE

What are the most popular signs and symbols of the Empire State?

"Ever upward" has been the official state motto since 1778. This happily coincides with the growth of Manhattan, which has since become home to some of the highest buildings in the world. The Empire State Building and Niagara Falls have long been staples in the popular mind. But in terms of natural identification, the bluebird is the state bird, and the rose is the state flower. The sugar maple is the state tree.

How large, or small, is the Empire State?

New York State comprises 49,105 square miles (127,181 square kilometers), making it thirtieth among the fifty states. The population of 19,651,127, as enumerated in the census of 2010, places it third among the states.

Is New York a city? A state? Or a state of mind?

All three. There's nothing like the Empire City, the Empire State, and their fascinating mixture of race, creed, and ethnicity.

Is there any one place where the tourist, or outsider, can go to see the best New York has to offer?

There are perhaps 500 places and scenes that would help do justice to New York, but the two that would accomplish the most are downtown Manhattan, particularly at sunset,   311 and Niagara Falls, especially at daybreak. Between them, midtown Manhattan and Niagara showcase the incredible diversity that is New York: a city, a state, a gathering of peoples, and a state of mind.

Of course this doesn't mean the people of New York are always harmonious. New York City taxi drivers are, perhaps, the nation's most aggressive. There's a lively competition between upstate and Manhattan, with the latter usually prevailing in economic terms, and the former doing better on the political level (it helps the upstate cause that the state capital is Albany, not Manhattan).

How many artists and writers have attempted to do justice to the beauty that exists in New York State?

It's almost impossible to count them all, or to make a complete list. One of the first that comes to mind is Washington Irving, whose stories of early New York and the Catskills put the area on the map, as far as European readers were concerned. James Fenimore Cooper followed him; his novels were so popular that they formed a whole new series, called the *Leatherstocking Tales*. The Brooklyn-born Walt Whitman wrote an amazing poem called "Song of Myself," but he also sang the praises of his home state. And a vast array of twentieth-century writers and songwriters followed these nineteenth-century greats. Perhaps the single most famous song having to do with the Empire City is Frank Sinatra's "New York, New York," in which he famously declares, "If I can make it there, I'll make it anywhere. It's up to you, New York, New York."

Is there any part of the Empire State that is not subject to major changes in weather?

New Yorkers have long been accustomed to severe temperature shifts, even in summer. A "Canadian High" can descend on the state, making the middle days of August much cooler, for example. But if there is one place in the state, in the nation even, where man makes his weather, it is New York City. All those people living in one compact area changes the temperature, which—usually—persuaded major winter storms to pass by rather than smack the city. Of course there is the occasional blizzard, and New Yorkers tend to talk about it for years to come, but this is the anomaly. In general, humans in Manhattan are better sheltered from changes in the weather than those anywhere else on the planet!

Are there any boring parts to the Empire State?

Just so long as one is willing to look at something with a fresh pair of eyes, the answer is no. From the eastern tip of Long Island, famous for bird migrations and New York City socialites, to the northern tip of the Adirondacks, from which one can see Montreal, and from Cohoes Falls, north of Albany, to Cooperstown and then Niagara, there is always something of interest.

Poets and writers have perhaps done the most to make New York well-known, but there is a whole school of painting devoted to Hudson River studies. The many paintings of Grandma Moses (who first took up the brush at the age of 65) have made the more rugged areas of eastern New York famous. Today, there are perhaps more photographs snapped each day in the Empire State than in any other part of the nation, with the possible exception of California.

Can any one person capture the sights, sounds, and accents of the Empire State?

It may have been possible in the time of Walt Whitman—just barely—but those days are long gone. Just in order to capture the sights, sounds, and accents of Manhattan would be the work of a lifetime, as most of the world's languages are spoken there. Once one realizes the impossibility of capturing the Empire City and the Empire State, he or she slows down and begins to enjoy the ride (as well as the view).

EARLY HISTORY

How many Native peoples lived in New York prior to the arrival of the first white settlers?

We aren't too sure about the precise numbers, but we're confident that the largest and most powerful of the Indians were the Five Nations of Iroquois, who, around 1711, became the Six Nations. Founded after a long and colorful power struggle, the Five Nations

Centuries-old stone houses (like this one in Hyde Park) that were built by early Dutch settlers in New York can still be found in some of the state's towns.

were centered at Onondaga (present-day Syracuse) while their tentacles spread to most corners of what is now the Empire State. The first white historians to study the Five Nations were persuaded that the League was a recent creation, having been established around 1570, but more recent evidence suggests that the Mohawk, Oneida, Onondaga, Cayuga, and Seneca were united as early as 1250!

Why don't the people of New York speak Dutch?

It was a real possibility this would happen. The Dutch came as early as 1626, and they reportedly purchased Manhattan from the local Indians for trade goods amounting to $24. Even if this is an exaggeration, there is no doubt the Dutch were expert merchant traders, and they seized upon the beaver trade as the means to make money.

The Dutch ruled New York and a narrow slice of land along the Hudson up to Albany for two generations. Legends developed about their craftiness and eccentricity, legends that Washington Irving later worked into his books. The home nation of Holland never gave enough backing to the colony, however, and English ships conquered it when they arrived in 1664. James, the Duke of York, who later became King James II, sent those ships, and his name was given to the town and colony.

How early did Manhattan become a place for various peoples, cultures, and faiths?

As early as the 1680s, an English governor complained that Manhattan was a virtual Babel, with all sorts of languages spoken and faiths practiced. This changed a bit during the early eighteenth century, and New York became stylishly English in the years leading up to the American Revolution. In the meantime, English merchants and sea captains made as much hay (figuratively speaking) as had the Dutch before them.

What role did New York play in the American Revolution?

A very large role, but New Yorkers are not always proud of it. Quite a few New Yorkers—city folk especially—favored the British cause and considered themselves faithful sub-

Who was America's first millionaire?

Born in Germany in 1763, John Jacob Astor arrived in New York City in 1783. Entering the fur trade, he made a fortune, and, eager to continue his winning ways, he was the first to send a fur trade expedition all the way to Oregon (Astoria, on the south side of the Columbia River, is named for him). Astor was more than a man of business, however. He set a precedent, an excellent one, of wealthy people contributing to philanthropic enterprises, and the family name of Astor has been associated with more charities and organizations than any other, save Vanderbilt and Rockefeller.

jects of King George III. This does not mean they exerted themselves very much on his behalf, but it led to Westchester County being one of the most divided areas of the entire nation during the Revolutionary War.

Following the British evacuation in November 1783, New Yorkers reclaimed their patriotic style, and the state was one of the first to join the Union. In fact, the *Federalist Papers*, penned by John Jay and Alexander Hamilton, were instrumental in swaying the minds of people in 1788, and they have been used in countless college classrooms ever since.

NEW YORK IN THE LIFE OF THE NATION

When did New York become the Empire State?

The expression was around as early as 1810, but it became reality in 1825, the year the Erie Canal was completed. Dug by poorly-paid laborers—many of them from Ireland—the Erie Canal connected Albany with Buffalo, and given that Albany was already connected with Manhattan, by means of the Hudson, this meant the Empire State was knit together, commercially speaking.

The advent of the steamboat made the commercial integration possible, and this was followed by the appearance of the railroad, which completed the task. By 1861, the year the Civil War began, New York was truly the Empire State, with more than a million people in greater Manhattan, and more land space and commercial activity than any other state.

What was New York State like in the antebellum years, just prior to the Civil War?

New York was one of the most exciting and dynamic of all the states, but New York City was—beyond a doubt—the most dynamic place in the entire nation. It was between 1820 and 1860 that Manhattan took strides to become the modern metropolis, the place that Americans either love or despise. The multiethnic and multinational characteristics emerged just prior to the Civil War, and the city saw more spirited debate than any other Northern city during the war.

Was New York City ever threatened during the Civil War?

Not in a military sense. But New York City's commerce was threatened for a time. New York merchants had to scramble to find alternative sources of cotton, for example. The adversity of the first and second year of the war changed by the third year, however, when it became evident that the Union would prevail. Stockholders who had previously waited on the sidelines now came in to invest. As a result, both the city and state were in fine shape economically when the war ended.

For many years in the nineteenth and early twentieth centuries, Ellis Island was the gateway to America through which over one million immigrants passed.

When did Manhattan and its boroughs become the vast, cosmopolitan place we know today?

The process began in the 1820s, when people speaking different languages began to arrive. A great leap forward happened in the late 1840s, when Irish and German immigrants arrived in great numbers. But the really big change took place in the 1880s and 1890s, when millions of immigrants from Eastern and Southern Europe came: they founded sections known as "Little Italy," "Little Russia," and so forth. By about 1890, Manhattan had irrevocably become the most recognizable and attractive of all American cities, the destination of choice for millions of people from abroad.

Who is the first Roosevelt to become thoroughly identified with the Empire State?

The Roosevelts were descendants of early Dutch settlers, and they succeeded early in their time in America. By the time Theodore Roosevelt became police commissioner of New York City, and then governor of the state, the Roosevelts were known as tough progressives, meaning that they cherished the past and were willing to make changes to preserve that which they saw as good.

Theodore Roosevelt went on to become vice president and then president (1901–1909) of the United States. In the White House, he demonstrated the same mixture of mental toughness and compassionate thinking.

What role did New York State play in World War I and World War II?

The two world wars made New York the hub of the East Coast commercially, socially, and militarily. *Millions* of men were mobilized and sent through New York, whether the

We all know that Ellis Island is where the majority of immigrants were processed (some, of course, were sent home). But what was the peak time for Ellis Island and migration to America?

In 1907, more than one million people passed through Ellis Island, on their way to a new life in America. Just how many of them made it, or succeeded in a financial sense, is unknown, but their mark is written directly on the heart of the nation and they helped make it what it is today.

Many newcomers remained in greater Manhattan, and quite a few of them never went anywhere else. A few moved to the New York countryside to settle. But on the whole, the options were two: stay in the great metropolis or move far inland, to places like Minnesota and Wisconsin, where work was plentiful.

Army camp at Plattsburgh or the Navy Yard at Brooklyn. New York City benefited hugely from both the world wars. Until 1914, London was the center of the English-speaking world, especially where banking and insurance were concerned; after 1918, New York took over that role.

The 1920s were especially good to the Empire State. Physical and material expansion were seen throughout New York, and the city became the center of publishing, theatre, dance, and many of the arts. The whole country gained status and stature during the 1920s, but New York was in the lead. And then came the devastating crash of October and November 1929.

What is meant by "Wall Street lays an egg"?

This was on the cover of many newspapers and magazines around the nation when the New York stock market collapsed in the autumn of 1929. Great profits were made in the 1920s, and suddenly the share prices of companies like General Electric, General Motors, and Radio Corporation of America came crashing down to earth. Many people, especially in the Empire State, came out of the year 1929 much poorer than they were at its start.

Who was the second member of the Roosevelt family to win high political office?

Franklin D. Roosevelt (FDR) was a fifth cousin of Theodore Roosevelt, and he moved, in succession, to occupy most of the same positions (they both were assistant secretary of the U.S. Navy, for example). In 1928, FDR won election as governor of New York. He neither expected nor welcomed the Great Depression, but, unlike quite a few other chief executives, he met it with urgency. FDR created a number of new state agencies and programs between 1929 and 1932, and when he went to the White House as the nation's thirty-second president in 1933, he had accomplished much through trial and error.

FDR was not universally popular, either in New York or the nation, but New Yorkers were proud of having "their man" in the White House. FDR's programs did not pull

It was under construction prior to the stock market crash, and nothing could persuade its backers to give up. In 1933, when the Great Depression was at its very worst, the Empire State Building opened, and it has been open nearly every day since.

At 103 stories and more than 1,250 feet, the Empire State Building was the tallest in the nation for many years. Even after it yielded this position in 1970 to the World Trade Center, also in New York City, the Empire State Building remained the most famous building in America. It helped, of course, that it was featured in so many films, including *King Kong*, which went to the screen in 1947.

the nation out of the Great Depression; rather, they gave both employers and workers some breathing space. And when World War II commenced in December 1941, New York—the city and the state—again became the proving ground for millions of young servicemen on their way overseas.

We all know that New York is the city that never sleeps. When did it become the center of the United Nations?

The United Nations was established, by charter, in San Francisco in the summer of 1945. Most people expected that it would find its permanent home in America. Even so, peo-

ple were amazed at the generosity of the Rockefeller family, who handed over a large section of extremely valuable Manhattan real estate so the gleaming blue building could be built. And ever since, Manhattan has been the center of world government, to the extent that this ideal has ever been realized.

What landmark cultural event took place in New York in 1969?

The Woodstock Music Festival took place in Bethel, New York—famously on Max Yasgur's dairy farm. Thirty-two acts performed over a span of four days. Some of the more famous acts included Joan Baez, the Grateful Dead, Creedance Clearwater Revival, Janis Joplin, the Who, the Jefferson Airplane, Crosby, Stills, Nash, and Young,

The headquarters for the United Nations is in New York City.

and Jimi Hendrix. Media coverage often referred to the combination of nudity, drugs, and rock-and-roll as a hippiefest. But there's no question that Woodstock was the most famous concert ever and a significant moment of the sixties generation.

When did the Empire State begin to slip, in the eyes of the nation and those of the world?

In terms of population, the slip commenced in the very decade of greatest success, the 1950s. New York had been the most populous state for almost a century, but it lost that position, first to California and then to Texas. This was by no means fatal, but it meant reduced clout on the national scale. And then came the great crisis of New York City.

In the first seven years of the 1970s, Greater Manhattan became increasingly dirty, poor, and even downright nasty. There were more muggings than ever before and a great deal of "white flight" from the city. The absolute low point came in July 1977, when the power plant at Consolidated Edison failed, leading to forty-eight hours of blackouts. Looting ensued, with thousands of people stealing from stores and quite a few gun and knife fights in the city. At almost the same time, New York City was poised to file for bankruptcy. If ever there was a moment when the great metropolitan experiment could have failed, this was it.

How did upstate New York respond to the crisis in New York City?

In 1977 and 1978, the attitude upstate toward New York City was one of neglect. Many members of the New York State assembly acted as if they didn't care whether the nation's signature city went into bankruptcy. Some upstate New Yorkers threatened to secede from the state if it did not let the great metropolis go. Fortunately, there were people who recognized the reality. New York City could not be divorced from New York State. The two belonged together.

Rebuilding Manhattan's finances took more than a decade, and there were moments (such as the Central Park mugging in the summer of 1988) when it seemed the city would again keel over. Instead, under the leadership of Mayors Ed Koch and David Dinkins, Manhattan began a revival that has lasted to the present day.

What made Mayor Ed Koch so unusual?

It was neither his policies nor his personal style, which could be rude on occasion. Rather, it was that he so clearly cared about the city and wanted it to succeed. New Yorkers had not seen a mayor like this since Fiorello La Guardia in the 1940s. Few of them loved Koch, but they said his heart was in the right place and that they would stick with him. This was a wise decision.

When was New York—the city and the state—back?

In July 1986, President Ronald Reagan attended ceremonies at the Statue of Liberty to commemorate the Fourth of July. A decade earlier, at the national Bicentennial, neither President Gerald Ford nor any other national dignitary had shown up. The Fourth of July festivities of 1986 showed that the city and state were back, even if they were not fully triumphant. And a decade later, in 1996, practically everyone agreed that New York—the Empire State and the Empire City—was back where it belonged, at the very top.

What architectural oddity sits in Oneida?

The world's smallest church, built in 1989, sits on pilings in the middle of a pond in Oneida, about halfway between Syracuse and Utica. Cross Island Chapel is 51 inches by 81 inches. Inside sits four chairs and a pulpit (but no altar). Two small stained glass windows adorn the structure. It is accessible only by boat (or by swimming there).

What did New York look like on the morning of September 11, 2001?

The city and state were at a high level of productivity and success. By sheer chance, September 11 was one of those truly cloudless days, in which the sun shines softly over Manhattan. All was well until 8:46 a.m. when an airplane, hijacked by terrorists, slammed into the North Tower of the Twin Towers of the World Trade Center, in Lower Manhattan. Seventeen minutes later, a second plane crashed into the South Tower.

Over the next hour, people watched in horror as the upper sections of the towers burned. They were completely stunned when the buildings practically melted and collapsed to the ground. Thousands of firefighters and rescue personnel, from the five boroughs and beyond, rushed to the scene, commencing an operation that lasted for days.

How well did the city and state come back from the attacks of September 11, 2001?

Many people, including New York City mayor Rudy Giuliani, exhibited bravery. Waves of support from around the nation and the world came quickly. Even so, it took a solid five years for the events of September 11 to fade from the mind of the general public, and for the people most intimately involved—firefighters, rescue personnel, and helpless bystanders—the chances are the memories will never dim. September 11 will, forever, be the day that marks their lives.

Mayor Rudy Giuliani became very popular for the way he handled the September 11, 2001, terrorist attack crisis in New York City.

How devastating was the attack of September 11 to the people of New York and the nation?

Had it been a cloudy day, or had there been anything with which to balance the horror, the impact might have been somewhat less. But the sheer, tantalizing beauty of the sunlight—September 11 was, perhaps, one of the ten best days of 2001, from a weather point of view—made matters much worse. Millions of viewers on television observed with horror as the scene of death and destruction so sharply contrasted with the natural scene of that day. Only one day in U.S. history—December 7, 1941—comes close to a parallel with September 11, and the big difference is that the Japanese attack on Pearl Harbor was not filmed and was not seen live.

Where was New York—the city and state—in the early 2010s?

Economically and financially, New York made a complete recovery from the terrorist attacks of September 11. Manhattan continued to be the tourist destination of the East Coast, the place everyone wanted to see. The United Nations continued to be the center of many tourist trips.

The division between upstate New York and greater Manhattan was smaller than before. The terrorist attacks did much to bring about solidarity between the farmers and artisans of upstate New York and their city cousins.

Where will the Empire State be a generation from now?

If past history is any guide, the Empire State will be on a roll. The great city that once seemed condemned to die a long lingering death turned out to be the American city of the twenty-first century. And, through it all, the people of the city and state continue to believe that they are number one, in sports, entertainment, and indeed, just about everything!

NORTH CAROLINA

Nickname: "The Tar Heel State"
Capital: Raleigh
Statehood: November 21, 1789; 12th state

AT A GLANCE

What are the most popular signs and symbols of the state?

"First in Flight," the theme on the North Carolina license plate, denotes the state's connection to Wilbur and Orville Wright and the beginning of aviation. "To Be Rather than to Seem" is the official state motto. On a natural level, however, the state is represented by the cardinal (state bird), the dogwood (state flower), and pine (state tree).

The nickname Tar Heel State comes from the eighteenth century, when the pine forests of North Carolina provided much of the tar, pitch, and turpentine needed for wooden ships. The first public use of the term comes from a Civil War battle.

How large, or small, is the Tar Heel State?

Comprised of 52,669 square miles (136,413 kilometers), North Carolina comes in at number twenty-eight of the fifty states. The Tar Heel state has 9,848,060 residents (as of the census of 2010), making it tenth among the states.

How much temperature variance can be seen in North Carolina?

The state has almost six months of summer, a beautiful spring, but also several months known simply as the rainy season. North Carolina is generally hot and sometimes muggy, but there are the occasional surprising exceptions to the rule. The highest temperature ever recorded was 109 degrees F, at Albemarle, on July 28, 1940, and the lowest was –29 degrees F, recorded at Mount Mitchell on January 30, 1966.

How does North Carolina manage to keep so "quiet" a reputation?

North Carolinians will tell you that there is an advantage to it, that it helps to keep a low profile. Perhaps, though, it is because the state has such flamboyant neighbors. Virginia, eldest of the Southern states, and South Carolina, queen of the Confederacy, have much more outsized reputations, and Tennessee, to the west, attracted fame because it was a frontier state. In each case, and in each comparison or competition, North Carolina has something to offer, but it is not outstanding in the fashion of its close neighbors.

Can anyone take in the whole of what North Carolina has to offer, visually speaking?

Of course. It might take a few months to do, however. The Tar Heel State contains great variety, from the Outer Banks on the coast to the Appalachian Mountains in the far west. In-between, one finds all sorts of mix and variety, from rolling hills to scrub and brush flatland. One thing is for certain: North Carolina is not boring.

Is the weather a topic of conversation in North Carolina?

Not to any significant degree. The locals shrug off most questions, as if to say that anyone who comes to their state should expect the extreme heat of high summer. In recent years, however, especially since about 1995, North Carolina has experienced stronger cold spells, as well, and when the ice or snow hits, North Carolinians tend to be unprepared.

Can the North Carolinian be distinguished from his or her South Carolina counterpart?

It depends on the age of the person. For men and women over the age of sixty, the difference is still strong, even profound. The North Carolinian tends to be even-keeled, while the South Carolinian is exuberant, even excessive. But for those folk under the age of fifty, the difference in style can hardly be noticed. It is as if modern culture, complete with the television and Internet, has wiped out some of the regional differences, even in this part of the American South.

How important was—and is—the Scottish presence in North Carolina?

In the early days of colonial settlement, North Carolina received more emigrants from Scotland than anywhere else, and it made all the difference in the world. These were both pure Scots and Scots-Irish, who were emigrants twice over, having been ejected first from their native land and then from Ireland. They brought a curiosity, especially where mechanical things are concerned, and a pioneer spirit that carried North Carolinians to Tennessee and beyond. Today, however, the Scottish presence is more muted, and given current population trends, there soon will be more persons claiming Hispanic than Scottish descent.

EARLY HISTORY

For how long have humans lived in what we call North Carolina?

For thousands of years. This does not mean we know—or can say—very much about the early peoples, however. They left very little in the way of material culture for us to examine. We can say a fair bit about the Indians who were in the Tar Heel State when the Europeans first arrived. Foremost among them were the Lumbee, who constitute one of the most numerous of all federally recognized tribes today.

North Carolina Indians lived by a combination of hunting and fishing, with farming coming in a very distant third. Though the illustration was made of Indians in northern Florida, John White's famous depiction of Indian villages can be applied to North Carolina as well; if the artist can be trusted, the Indians lived in neat, well-ordered villages, probably under leaders who were a combination of tribal chief and medicine man. These Indians met their first white people in the 1540s, when explorers from Hernando de Soto's expedition passed through, but there was little memory of this event. Not until the late sixteenth century did white-Indian contact really commence.

How important was Sir Walter Raleigh, and Queen Elizabeth for that matter, to the founding of North Carolina?

Queen Elizabeth and her counselors were envious of the Spanish success in Central America and the Caribbean. Sir Walter Raleigh, one of the most successful courtiers of

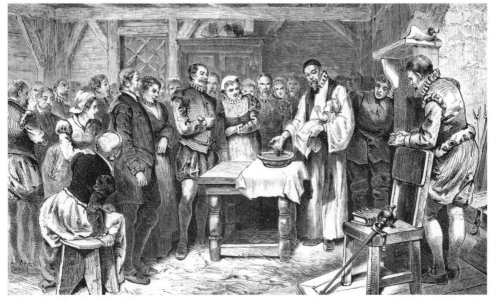

An 1876 lithography by William A. Crafts depicts the baptism of Virginia Dare—the first English colonist born in the New World—at Roanoke Colony in present-day North Carolina.

the day, organized a group of more than 100 settlers who sailed from England in 1587. They landed on the Outer Banks of North Carolina and established the first small settlement on Roanoke Island. The leader sailed back to England soon thereafter, and when he returned in 1590, all the settlers were gone. The only clue was a tree with the word CROATON carved upon it. The mystery of the Lost Colony continues to perplex historians today. The most likely answer is that the settlers went to live with the Lumbee Indians, but this has never been proven beyond a reasonable doubt.

How long did it take before the English came back to North Carolina?

Close to a century. Not until 1670 did King Charles II issue a land grant for a large colony named Carolina (North and South were not yet contemplated). The first settlers arrived at Charleston that year, and a few handfuls of others began landing on the Outer Banks and finding their way to the interior. Right from the beginning, there were marked differences between North and South.

The northern part of Carolina was rougher and more difficult to settle than the southern section. The northern part began to cultivate tobacco, while rice and, later, cotton were easier to grow in the south. As a result, the two sections began growing apart, and by 1704 there was a clear distinction between the two, with people speaking of "North" and "South" Carolina.

How did North Carolina develop during the late colonial period?

The colony was restricted to an area twenty miles from the coast for a long time, but when the Scottish Highlanders began arriving, in the wake of the failed Scottish revolt of 1745, the movement westward began with speed. The settlers found different types of soil in the interior, and some pushed all the way to the Great Smoky Mountains. Last to come were the Scots-Irish, who found most of the good, coastal land taken up; they became the foremost North Carolina pioneers out of necessity.

Colonial North Carolina never boomed like its southern counterpart, but there was a respectable population when the American Revolution began in 1775. Just a year before that event, a British postal inspector traveled much of the coast of the Southern colonies, and he concluded that North and South Carolina between them had the worst roads and taverns he had ever seen. One curiosity he noted was the "Half-Way House"

> ## Who was Flora MacDonald, and how did she figure in the story of not one but two popular revolts?
>
> **W**hen Bonnie Prince Charlie lost the Battle of Culloden to the British in 1745, sixteen-year-old Flora MacDonald guided him to safety. She brought him to the Isle of Skye and saw him get aboard a French privateer (this was the last that the Highlands ever saw of their bonny prince). Thirty years later, Flora MacDonald was living in North Carolina. Her husband, Allen MacDonald, was one of the principal king's supporters at the Battle of Moore's Creek Bridge. Not long after, the MacDonald couple sailed home to Scotland.

or "Boundary House," a public inn that had its anteroom in one colony and its back quarters in another.

How significant a role did North Carolina play in the American Revolution?

One can say that the North Carolinians jumped the gun, that the War of the Regulation of 1771 was one of the harbingers of that event. But North Carolina governor William Tryon crushed the Regulators, and when the Revolution commenced in earnest in 1775, quite a few North Carolinians were apprehensive about joining the patriot cause. This was most true of the Scottish Highlanders, who'd witnessed the defeat of their own revolt in 1745. As a result, the first major battle fought in North Carolina was between Scottish Highlanders who professed loyalty to King George III, and their neighbors, who espoused the patriot cause. The Battle of Moore's Creek Bridge was an outstanding victory for the patriots.

How did the American Revolution play out in North Carolina?

Between 1776 and 1780, the Tar Heel State was relatively free from pressure or big war events. In May 1780, the British captured Charleston, however, and from that moment forward, the North Carolina–South Carolina border was the scene of numerous battles and skirmishes. Time and again, the British cleared the rebels—as they called them—from South Carolina and crossed the border, only to experience a bad beating. And it was North Carolina forces that helped turn the Battle of Kings Mountain (1780) and the Battle of Cowpens (1781) in South Carolina into victories for the patriots. Even after that, however, the Continental Army continued to operate out of North Carolina, seeking to accomplish what the British had done, only to do so in reverse. And the final set of skirmishes ended with complete victory for the patriot cause.

NORTH CAROLINA
IN THE LIFE OF THE NATION

Was there ever a chance that North Carolina would expand to the west and take up the area currently known as Tennessee?

This was a real possibility, and many North Carolinians were willing to fight to turn it into reality. But the compromises and agreements that led to the writing of the U.S. Constitution, in 1787, contained significant clauses that required virtually all the states to give up their "western claims." As a result, North Carolina never had a chance to expand to the west. Plenty of its residents did so, however.

Was there any chance slavery would fade and die of its own in North Carolina?

Virtually all the major tobacco planters experienced declining yields in the nineteenth century, but the sheer weight of the investment—slaves sometimes sold for as much as $2,000—prevented most slaveholders from emancipating their people. As a result, slavery held steady in North Carolina till the Civil War began, and it was then too late for North Carolinians to change their culture or economy. North Carolina was not one of the Deep South states that jumped into the Confederacy right away; rather, the Tar Heel State joined the conflict after the attack on Fort Sumter in April 1861.

How did North Carolina fare in the Civil War?

The Civil War was one unrelenting disaster for North Carolina. The Union navy blockaded the coast right away, preventing Carolinians from exporting their goods. The Union army captured several coastal towns early on, and the Confederates never regained control. And the sheer number of men who were drained out of North Carolina, primarily to serve in Virginia, was simply staggering. To top off all the other setbacks, North Carolina was the final state to feel the heavy hand of General William T. Sherman's Union soldiers. The Tar Heel State was on the verge of complete ruin when the war ended, with General Joseph Johnston's surrender near Durham.

What was the beginning of the turnaround for North Carolina?

James Buchanan Duke, for whom the university is named, was the first entrepreneur to make a real go of rolling tobacco in the late nineteenth century. This type of tobacco production was perfect for the making of cigars and, later, cigarettes. Though it was founded on an old-style product, rolling tobacco was an innovation that led to new wealth generation in North Carolina.

What was life in North Carolina like at the turn of the twentieth century?

It was very slow. Of all the Southern states, North Carolina prided itself the most on a pleasant lifestyle, with a heavy dose of rural flavor. To be sure, there were some cities—

Raleigh, Durham, Charlotte, and Asheville—but even these tasted more of Down South easygoingness than urban bustle.

If there was a North Carolina style at this time, it was one of long afternoons. The one great exception to the rule came in an area that almost no one anticipated: the beginning of human flight.

Weren't the Wright Brothers natives of Ohio?

They were indeed, and the Buckeye State and the Tar Heel State have competed for their share of the glory ever since. Wilbur and Orville Wright were sons of a Protestant bishop, and though they had a quiet religiosity, flight entranced them more than spiritual matters. After many attempts, and quite a few discouraging setbacks, they succeeded in making the first true flight in the air. Orville piloted the little plane for about fifty-seven seconds, while Wilbur almost ran alongside. Theirs was a uniquely personal triumph, leading to great success for the brothers, but it also had the effect of changing the face of modern transportation. Seven years later, Wilbur Wright made the first circumnavigation of Manhattan by plane. The two million New Yorkers who watched that day knew, down deep, that the world had changed. Today there is a monument in Kill Devil Hills, on the Outer Banks, where the Wright Brothers enjoyed their first success.

How did the Tar Heel State fare during World War I and World War II?

Both wars ended up helping North Carolina. The U.S. Marine Corps conducted much of its training in the Tar Heel State, and the U.S. Army basic training at Fayetteville meant

Possibly the most famous event in invention history to occur in North Carolina was the flight of the first airplane created by Wilbur (left) and Orville Wright.

that many residents from other states spent time in North Carolina. North Carolina emerged from both world wars in better shape than it entered them.

Fort Bragg was built in 1918, and training began in 1921. Conceived as a school for World War I artillerymen, Fort Bragg—named for Confederate general Braxton Bragg—expanded between the two world wars and really hit its stride in 1942 when it became the home of the 82nd and 101st Airborne, divisions that played a leading role in American victories throughout World War II. As of 2000, it was home to 45,000 soldiers and 8,000 civilians, and it was one of the largest military bases in the entire world. In 2016, however, it was anticipated that about 16,000 soldiers would leave the base because of spending cuts in the military, a loss that would cost the local economy about 21,500 jobs.

What part did North Carolina and its residents play in the civil rights struggle?

Most white North Carolinians expressed surprise that any such struggle was necessary. The blacks of their state were doing just fine, they declared. African Americans felt quite

Duke University basketball is a favorite spectator sport for many North Carolinans, as well as the teams from North Carolina State University and the University of North Carolina at Chapel Hill.

When did the great basketball rivalry between the leading universities develop?

Duke University, the University of North Carolina at Chapel Hill, and North Carolina State University in Raleigh all had good-sized sports teams prior to the 1960s, but they all aimed in a new direction during that decade. Big-time basketball came to the Triangle, as the area between the three schools is named.

the opposite, and this was shown when four young college students conducted a sit-in at the lunch counter at a Woolworth's store in Greensboro, starting on February 1, 1960. The incident won national attention, and Woolworth's agreed to change its policy (up to that time, the store served blacks only at a stand-up counter).

How and when did Jesse Helms become one of the best-known of all U.S. senators?

Born in Monroe, North Carolina, in 1921, Jesse Helms entered the U.S. Senate in 1973 and soon became one of the most iconoclastic of U.S. senators. Well-liked on a personal level, he was often testy on policy matters, and he wished to spearhead a new, deeply conservative North Carolina approach to politics. He succeeded to such an extent that his presence can still be felt today, even though he died in 2008.

As chairman of the Senate Foreign Affairs committee, Helms unsuccessfully attempted to link U.S. foreign policy with moral behavior on the part of dictators around the globe. During his last years, Helms served as the gadfly of the Senate, reminding his colleagues of procedural matters many of them had forgotten. His deepest imprint on state and national politics came about as the result of his tempestuous reelection in 1984. He and his Democratic opponent, Governor Jim Hunt, continually outspent one another, raising the stakes. Though Helms won by a vote of 52–48 percent, the damage had been done. A U.S. Senate seat had always been highly prized, but it now became almost exclusively the perquisite of wealthy men and women.

What was life in North Carolina like at the beginning of the twenty-first century?

One still found pockets of rural isolation—and perhaps deep contentment—but life in North Carolina had fundamentally changed. The growing metropolises of Winston-Salem and Charlotte had joined the small cities of Raleigh, Durham, and Chapel Hill, and the state, while still rural in feel, had become easily accessible to people from all parts of the world. Part of the reason for this change was the creation of the Research Triangle, in the central-east part of the state, where the National Endowment for the Humanities hosted scholars and ran programs.

331

THE WORST

What was the single worst day in North Carolina history?

On an emotional level, it may well have been April 26, 1865, the day General Joseph E. Johnston surrendered all the men under his command to General William T. Sherman. But in terms of loss of life and property, the sharpest and meanest cut was when Hurricane Hugo slammed into North Carolina.

Where will the Tar Heel State be a generation from now?

The chances are that its population will continue to diversify and that Hispanics will form the majority by about the year 2050. North Carolina will never lose all of its rural heritage; there will be spots from which one can view the past. The temper and tone of the Tar Heel State will be increasingly urban and industrial, however, with a marked trend toward the high-tech industries.

NORTH DAKOTA

Nicknames: "Peace Garden State"; "Flickertail State"; "Roughrider State"
Capital: Bismarck
Statehood: November 2, 1889; 39th state

AT A GLANCE

What are the most popular signs and symbols of the Peace Garden State?

"Liberty and Union Now and Forever, One and Inseparable" is the official state motto (the words come from Daniel Webster's famous words to the U.S. Senate).

The western meadowlark is the official state bird, and the wild prairie rose is the state flower. The American elm is the official tree.

How large, or small, is North Dakota?

Comprising 70,698 square miles (183,107 square kilometers), North Dakota is nineteenth among the fifty states in geographic size. The population of 723,393, as enumerated in the 2010 census, reveals that North Dakota ranks forty-eighth among the states in terms of population.

What makes North Dakota so clearly different from most other states of the nation?

It's not easy to put one's finger directly on the answer, but weather and climate handle at least half of it. Unlike most of the other American states, the people of North Dakota live very much at the mercy of the elements.

The sheer openness of the sky, and the vastness of the land, can astonish, bewilder, and even terrify. One can say much the same for parts of Montana, but there, at least, the sight of the Rocky Mountains is consoling and provides context. In North Dakota, however, one sees, and senses, nearly endless undulating plains.

Are the residents of North Dakota conscious of their close proximity to Canada?

Not really. Canada and the United States are two of the friendliest nations in the world, but the people of these two republics do not meet and greet each other on the border. Canadians are dimly aware that North Dakota could have been theirs, and residents of North Dakota feel that the world ends at the International Boundary line. It's true that the International Peace Garden spans a short section of that border, and that there is an international golf course, half in the United States and the other half in Canada. Even so, one would be hard pressed to find a bleaker, or more lonely, spot than the U.S.-Canadian border in North Dakota.

If that is the case, then where do the people of North Dakota look for personal and national identity?

They look primarily to themselves. Both the Dakotas—North and South—are filled with people whose ancestors created their lives from scratch. They, therefore, are highly self-reliant and do not look outside for help (at least not in any of the normal sorts of emergencies). North and South Dakota both have significant ethnic variety, with many northern and western Europeans coming at the end of the nineteenth century. Though the Stars and Stripes fly boldly over the Dakotas, they do not enjoy 100 percent fidelity.

Was North Dakota ever part of the "Wild West"?

Only in the smallest way. The people who settled North Dakota were rugged but simple farmers who loved quiet ways and consistent patterns of behavior. There were a hand-

North Dakota was never really part of the "Wild West," but, instead, enjoyed peaceful years during much of the country's expansion West.

ful of North Dakota towns where one could see the "Wild West," but it's safer to refer to the state, as a whole, as the farthest extension of the "Middle West."

Has anyone ever captured the soft beauty of North Dakota in poetry or song?

Not to its full extent. Only with the advent of the airplane did North Dakota's exceptional natural beauty become apparent. He or she who flies over the Peace Garden State is treated to endless miles of fields of wheat, punctuated only by the occasional large farmhouse or farmer's silo. The Native Americans who were on this land first—and they were walkers, not horsemen—knew it as one of the quietest places of the North American continent. Of course, the January and February wind can cut a person to the bone, but that's why summer and autumn are so important—for laying in the supplies that allow one to endure the frigid winter.

EARLY HISTORY

For how long have humans lived in what we now call the Peace Garden State?

For something between 15,000 and 20,000 years. During most of that time, North Dakota was thinly populated with tribal groups who lived nomadic lives, moving south in the winter, and north each spring. When the first people of European descent arrived, they found the region populated by various Indian groups, including the Cheyenne and the Sioux, who are often divided into the Lakota and Dakota sections.

These Indian tribes lived by a mixture of hunting and farming. The appearance of the horse from Spanish Mexico revolutionized their lives in the early eighteenth century. Even so, quite a few of the Indians of North Dakota lived much as their ancestors did, at the time when the first people of European descent arrived.

What did those first explorers come in search of?

French fur trappers and traders were the first Europeans to reach this land, and they hurriedly crossed it on their way to see the Rocky Mountains. These French were primarily in search of beaver fur, which could be converted into hats and coats. The French—of whom Pierre La Vérendrye is the best-known—never made a deep imprint in what is now North Dakota. France was too busy developing its colonies in Canada and Louisiana.

The first tiny scattering of names from the Sioux language made their way back east in a generation or two, and by 1820 quite a few Americans had heard the words Lakota, Dakota, and Sioux, even if they could not place the peoples on a map.

Who were the first Europeans to actually settle in North Dakota?

Lord Selkirk brought a group of Scottish settlers over the border to what is now Pembina, in the northeastern part of the state, in 1811. This was a time when the British government was willing to contest ownership of the area with the United States, but the international boundary settlement of 1817 brought that to an end. Thereafter, it was primarily Anglo-Americans who arrived, and they, too, tended to be keen on the fur trade.

The tribal peoples of North Dakota were not alarmed at first. The arrival of large numbers of settlers in the 1830s and 1840s changed this, however, and the incidental spreading of disease—smallpox most especially—weakened these tribes to the point where they could not resist. Even so, settlement of the Dakotas—North and South— might have waited another generation if not for the advent of the Civil War.

When did Congress establish the Dakota Territory, and why was it so large?

The Dakota Territory was established in 1861, and both President Lincoln and the Congress wished to bring in as large an area as possible, in order to reject any potential Confederate claims to the region. Any Confederate ideas of reaching the Dakotas were, of course, short-lived, but it made sense to create as large a territory as possible. The original Dakota Territory therefore included all of present-day North and South Dakota and a large chunk of present-day Montana.

The northern part of the Dakota Territory was ignored in favor of the southern part for the first generation of life as a territory. The discovery of gold in the Black Hills brought thousands of prospectors, miners, and settlers, but most of them remained in what is now South Dakota. Not until 1880, or thereabouts, did immigrant populations head to North Dakota, and they found—much to their surprise—that the land there was undervalued. North Dakota proved superb for the growing of spring wheat, and farmers made some modest fortunes in the 1880s. Cattle ranching was the second most successful industry in North Dakota.

I've long been curious as to how North Dakota became the thirty-ninth state of the Union, and why South Dakota is labelled as number forty. Can you enlighten me?

During the late 1880s, there was intense pressure, from businessmen around the nation and from politicians in Washington, D.C., to bring in as many new states as possible. The U.S. Census of 1890 declared the American frontier officially "closed," and it was important to organize as many areas as could be accomplished in a short time.

On November 2, 1889, President Benjamin Harrison sat at his White House desk with two approved documents. One was for the admission of North Dakota; the other was for the entrance of South Dakota. Tradition has it that the president juggled and then shuffled the papers for some time before signing them, in order that no one would claim either state had been first. In the end, however, the record books assigned thirty-ninth place to North Dakota and fortieth to South Dakota based solely on alphabetical order.

NORTH DAKOTA
IN THE LIFE OF THE NATION

How did North Dakota fare in the first decade or so of statehood?

The state simply boomed. Not only people from other Midwestern states, but also East Coast Americans and quite a few Northern and Western European peoples made a beeline for the Peace Garden State. They'd heard of the excellent wheat crops to be harvested in North Dakota, and they came expecting to take up 160-acre sections of land under the Homestead Act.

What does "sodbuster" mean?

Sodbuster refers to the fact that there were not enough trees to build wooden houses; North Dakota settlers therefore cut sections of soil, or sod, and built houses from them. The result was that buildings were warm enough but did not contain the amenities many East Coast Americans had come to expect. For some time, "sodbuster" was used as a derogatory term.

How rapidly did the population grow?

In 1890 there were 190,000 people in North Dakota but the really amazing fact is that *43 percent* of them were foreign-born. That put North Dakota at number one in the nation for the percentage of foreign-born in its population. Many of these were recent emigrants from Europe who came straight to the Upper Midwest, immediately upon arriving in New York City or Philadelphia.

Homesteading in North Dakota hit its peak around 1906. In 1920, immigrants and their children made up 66.7 percent of the North Dakota population. Had this trend continued, North Dakota would surely have become the most ethnically diverse of all the fifty states. Big changes were on the way, however, and many of them were not pleasant ones.

Was there any "best" time to come to North Dakota?

If so, it was the very beginning of the twentieth century. Norwegians, Germans, Swiss, and others arrived, turning North Dakota into one of the most ethnically diverse states of the Union. The drought that commenced in 1911 proved catastrophic for many of these early settlers, however, and quite a few abandoned the state entirely.

Early North Dakota settlers were compelled to build their homes out of sod because trees were scarce.

337

It seems so unfair. Why do these states of the Upper Midwest get smacked by so many natural disasters and setbacks?

Most Dakotans—North and South—have long since turned to religion as the only means by which one can explain the difficulties they encounter. Outsiders often comment on the vigorous nature of religious ceremonies in the Dakotas, and the accompanying spirit with which people handle what might be unbearable conditions.

Outsiders (and one of the best commentaries comes in *Badlands*, by Melinda Camber Porter) marvel at how residents of North Dakota handle the long winter, short spring, and then the attendant long work hours of the growing season. Perhaps the best answer that can be offered is that many North and South Dakotans love their lonely landscape and feel that it brings out the best in them. One writer who eloquently testifies to that spirit is Kathleen Norris, author of *Dakota: A Spiritual Odyssey*.

Is there anything remaining of the Theodore Roosevelt spirit in North Dakota?

Roosevelt only lived in the Dakota Territory for three years, but some biographers believe that short span was the making of him (as a man and political leader). Following the death of his mother and first wife (in a span of thirty-six hours), Roosevelt left New York City's comforts for life on the frontier. The Theodore Roosevelt National Park, in the southwest corner of the state, is named in his honor.

Roosevelt later claimed that the years in North Dakota were his best and that they changed him from a relatively "soft" East Coast American into one who knew and understood the Midwest. There is little doubt that he enjoyed the cattle drives, the long days in the saddle, and even fighting the occasional flood. By the time he returned east, Roosevelt had become tougher and more resilient.

North Dakota seems like such a "he-man" area that I marvel it ever could have supported any socialist ideas. How did that come about?

It was the drought of 1911 that persuaded many North Dakotans to examine their state government from a fresh perspective. The drought hurt all the Midwestern states, but the Dakotas suffered the worst. Perhaps the abundance of Norwegians and Swedes in North Dakota persuaded the state to make a bold move. In 1916, the Progressive League (also known as the PL) won a majority in the state legislature. From the outset, the PL declared its goal to make the machinery of modern farming available to the average farmer, and to do so at the expense of the state. Within two years, North Dakota had the only state-owned bank in the nation and the first state-sponsored flour mill. Other changes would likely have occurred had the PL not been voted out in the next election.

How did North Dakotans respond to the beginning of World War I?

They were deeply divided. The settlers of German descent, who had arrived in the 1890s, were naturally against American participation in the First World War. Many recent arrivals from other Midwestern states were equally anxious to demonstrate their patriotism and loyalty. As a result, North Dakota was split to a greater degree than almost any other state in the Union. This did not prevent the Peace Garden State from turning out bumper crops of wheat for the war effort, however, and North Dakota emerged from World War I in a stronger economic condition.

Did the Great Depression hit North Dakota to a significant degree?

It hit North Dakota so hard that there were times when people despaired of the state. North Dakota's overall population dropped during the 1930s, as tens of thousands fled the state, most of them heading to the Far West. Many Dakotans who had opposed entry to the First World War called the Great Depression God's revenge on the state, and there were times when it seemed North Dakota would not survive. The Dust Bowl was not as extreme as in South Dakota, but it certainly piled one misery atop another.

North Dakota has long been known for unusual swings of temperature, but 1936 remains the year that holds most of the records. In early July, sections of North Dakota reported heat that exceeded 110 degrees F, while that winter the state saw some lows that approached 60 degrees below zero. Climate historians believe that the dry conditions that brought on the Dust Bowl also did their work in making the winters worse than usual.

Given all this disaster, how did North Dakota make its way up from the bottom?

World War II furnishes most of the answer. It's a truism that neither Franklin Roosevelt nor the New Deal ended the Great Depression; World War II accomplished that. This was especially true for North Dakota, which turned out bumper crops of agricultural surplus for the war effort.

MODERN-DAY NORTH DAKOTA

How did North Dakota fare in the decades that followed World War II?

The Peace Garden State seemed to be forgotten. A modest economic revival came in the 1950s and 1960s, but culturally the state seemed further from the mainstream than ever. The social and cultural upheavals of the 1960s, for example, seemed to bypass North Dakota entirely, and the popular perception was that North Dakota was good at the production of only certain foods, and just about nothing else.

Fortunately, some experts in agriculture and irrigation turned their attention to the Peace Garden State, and a series of dams were built. Garrison Dam, completed in 1960, was the largest, and the Garrison Diversion Project, which commenced later in that decade, had the effect of creating stable bodies of freshwater for consumption and for improving the irrigation systems of the state. Oil, too, was discovered near Tioga, and there was a serious oil boom, beginning around 1978. Quite a few people made modest fortunes, but the oil boom went bust in 1986, when worldwide oil prices suddenly dropped. There was another boom that began in 2006 when the Parshall Oil Field was discovered; that one, too, went bust in 2015 when gas prices fell due to OPEC refusing to cut production when there was a market glut.

What flower grows in abundance in North Dakota?

Even though Kansas is known as the Sunflower State, North Dakota actually produces a little more than half of the total sunflower crop in the United States. Sunflowers are used to produce oils and seed snacks. Because bees are needed for pollination of the sunflowers, North Dakota also ranks number one in the production of honey.

An oil rig in North Dakota during the recent boom. The state has experienced a couple periods of prosperity when oil fields were discovered, but they inevitably go bust again.

Is there any chance the North Dakota economy will find stability?

This question speaks to one of the enduring frustrations in the lives of North Dakotans. The state has lower crime, on average, than nearly all the others, and it has one of the highest rates of high school graduation in the nation. But North Dakota hasn't experienced a stable economy.

The 1970s were relatively good for North Dakota, but another downturn in farm fortunes commenced in the 1980s. This time, the fear was not that the state would lose population, but that it would lose practically all of its young people. Politically, too, North Dakota seemed to lose its way. It identified with neither of the major parties, and the major presidential candidates seldom, if ever, visited the Peace Garden State.

Where will the Peace Garden State be a generation from now?

The chances are that the people will be very much the same: hard-working folk who conscientiously go about their work. The deepest concern is that the state will be drained of its young people and that North Dakota will look like a late nineteenth-century state, which has somehow made it into the early twenty-first.

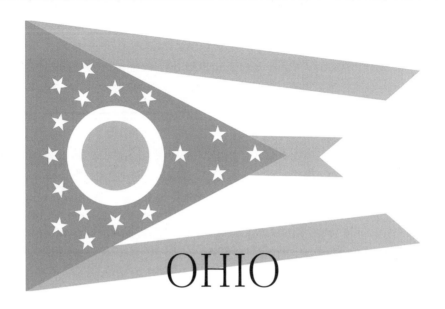

OHIO

Nickname: "The Buckeye State"
Capital: Columbus
Statehood: February 19, 1803; 17th state

AT A GLANCE

What are some of the most important signs and symbols of the Buckeye State?

"With God, All Things Are Possible" is the state motto. The state bird is the cardinal, and the scarlet carnation is the state flower. The official state tree is the buckeye.

How large, or small, is the Buckeye State?

Comprising 44,826 square miles (116,099 square kilometers), Ohio is thirty-fourth among the fifty states in geographic size. Its population of 11,570,808, as enumerated in the census of 2010, places it seventh in size in terms of population.

How did the Buckeye State ever become so important in American presidential politics?

It happened over time. Seven American presidents—Ulysses S. Grant, Rutherford B. Hayes, James A. Garfield, Benjamin Harrison, William McKinley, William Howard Taft, and Warren G. Harding—were born in Ohio; one other president—William Henry Harrison—was born elsewhere but made Ohio his home. Their presence and style were, for a long time, seen as the way to go. Then, too, Ohio is in the middle of the middle, meaning that it borders on the Mid-Atlantic states while being part of the Midwest.

Over time it became apparent that Ohio, while important to both parties, is absolutely vital to the hopes of any Republican presidential candidate; no Republican has ever taken the White House without capturing Ohio's electoral votes. Some candidates become thoroughly obsessed with the Buckeye State, learning about all its voting districts and precincts, but the winning formula isn't that hard to come by. Ohioans respond to common-sense measures and a balanced policy approach.

Are any parts of Ohio as wild and scenic as when John Chapman, better known as Johnny Appleseed, came that way in the early nineteenth century?

Very few. Ohio has nature preserves and significant stretches of farmland, but the unspoiled, virgin land that Johnny Appleseed saw has mostly disappeared. During its industrial heyday, Ohio made numerous compromises, and most of them were for the negative, so far as the natural environment was concerned.

Is there a distinctive Ohio culture?

There isn't. For the same reason that Ohio is a political swing state, meaning that it combines Mid-Atlantic with Midwest politics, the Buckeye State does not have a distinct cultural voice. This is the land of the Wright Brothers, other inventors, and politicians, but it does not speak with one voice, as does its neighbor Indiana.

EARLY HISTORY

For how long have humans lived in what we now call Ohio?

For thousands of years. We don't know when the first Native Americans arrived, but we suspect they delighted in the area because of its wonderful tree canopy and the rivers that head to the Ohio, then traverse to the Mississippi. Ohio was a well-kept secret, in that the first European colonists knew nothing about it. Perhaps it was René-Robert Cavelier de La Salle who first heard of Ohio, the mysterious land crowned by the beautiful river. Historians are uncertain, however, whether La Salle was the first European to see Ohio.

The Wyandot, Huron, Shawnee, and other tribes populated Ohio in the seventeenth century. These tribes occasionally fought each other, but their tribal battles were nothing compared to the storm that was on the way. In the late seventeenth century, the Five Nations of Iroquois (soon to become the Six) invaded Ohio from present-day New York State. The Five Nations were the most organized, and brutal, of all Indian groups in the Northeast, and they soon eliminated or pushed out virtually all their rivals. The Iroquois did not want Ohio for its land or waterways; it wanted to dominate the area's fur trade.

When did the different European groups begin to contest for the Ohio Country, as it then was called?

The French were first on the scene. By 1740, they were masters of most of the Great Lakes region, and in the decade that followed they went south to claim the Ohio Country. France built forts in the present-day Pennsylvania cities of Erie and Pittsburgh, but their claim on the area was fragile at best. In 1754, the young George Washington, a major in the Virginia militia, led a force north to contest control of the Ohio Country. In May 1754, Washington ambushed and defeated a small French force near Pittsburgh; this skirmish provided the pretext for England and France to clash in the French and Indian War (1754–1763).

A defeat at the Great Meadow followed Washington's wilderness victory. Defeated at Fort Necessity, he and his men were paroled, on their honor not to fight against France for the duration of the war. Casting that aside, Washington fought with British general Edward Braddock in 1755 and witnessed the appalling defeat at the Battle of the Monongahela. For the next two years, the French and their Indian allies had the run of the Ohio Country, pushing out the English settlers, and enjoying a remarkable run of success. All this came to an end in 1758, however, when British colonel John Forbes—assisted by Washington—captured Fort Duquesne and began building Fort Pitt, where Pittsburgh now stands.

How important was the Ohio Country to Pontiac's Rebellion (or Pontiac's War)?

The Ohio Country was the center of the action. Knowing that France was defeated, and that Britain was now the imperial master, Ojibway chief Pontiac masterminded a series of attacks on British-held forts, from the Great Lakes to the Ohio River. Nearly a dozen forts either were captured or overrun in a matter of weeks, but the two key places—

Ojibway chief Pontiac meets with a major of the British army in 1760 as depicted in this 1887 illustration preserved by the Ohio State Archaeological and Historical Society.

343

Fort Detroit and Fort Pitt—managed to hold out. Nearly all of the Ohio Country was in Indian hands that summer, but as long as those two fortified places remained, Pontiac could not claim victory. And when Fort Pitt and Fort Detroit were relieved, and the sieges broken, Pontiac made peace with the British.

Was there any fighting in Ohio during the Revolutionary War?

Yes, but it was not nearly as intense as in neighboring Indiana. The campaigns of George Rogers Clark, in 1778–1779, ensured that Indiana, and therefore Ohio, too, would come under the American umbrella when the war ended. And the Treaty of Paris confirmed this in 1783. The much larger question, and the one with long-lasting consequences, was how the brand-new Ohio Country—as it still was called—would be governed.

In 1785, following suggestions made by Thomas Jefferson, the Confederation Congress passed the Northwest Territory Act, which became known to the general public in 1787 as the Northwest Ordinance. Under its provisions, the Ohio Country, which then included all of Indiana, Michigan, and much of Illinois, would be sectioned off in a new style, one that shaped the future of the American Midwest. Unlike New England and the Mid-Atlantic states, which were settled in a haphazard manner, the Midwest areas were sectioned into areas of thirty-six square miles. Each township therefore had recognizable land boundaries, and there were far fewer controversies over land titles (of course, the relatively flat countryside of the Midwest made this possible).

How did Ohio become the seventeenth state?

As soon as the Northwest Ordinance became known, settlers began departing the Mid-Atlantic States and heading to Ohio, where there were vast tracts of unclaimed land. Marietta, settled by a group of Revolutionary War veterans, was the first real township; others rapidly followed. As a result, Ohio had the requisite number of settlers, or permanent residents, and on March 1, 1803, it entered the Union as the seventeenth star on the flag. This was a significant achievement for Ohio, and the young nation, which showed that it would not follow in the imperial footsteps of Britain, France, and Spain: each new state would be completely equal with all the others.

How much truth is there to the wonderful story of Johnny Appleseed?

John Chapman was a real person, born in Massachusetts in 1774. He went west at an early age and was persuaded that Ohio, with its natural beauty, was the fairest part of North America. Johnny Appleseed spent years distributing apple seeds throughout Ohio, both planting them himself and handing them to farmers. Less-known is that he was an ardent follower of the Swedish religious philosopher Emanuel Swedenborg and that he distributed religious pamphlets along with bags of apple seeds!

OHIO IN THE LIFE OF THE NATION

How important was Ohio in the War of 1812?

To the British opponents, Ohio was important not for its land but its waterways. Most important of all was Lake Erie. Toward that end, the British built a formidable fleet, intended to dominate the Great Lakes. In answer, the Americans sent Commandant Oliver Hazard Perry to Sandusky, where he painstakingly built a fleet, or squadron, of his own. On September 11, 1813, Perry fought the Battle of Lake Erie against the British at Put-in-Bay, on South Bass Island. The battle was hard fought, and late in the afternoon Perry transferred his flag from his sinking ship *Lawrence* to the *Niagara*. His determination won the day, however, and he soon penned one of the most famous dispatches from all of American military history: "We have met the enemy and they are ours." Perry had sunk or captured the entire British fleet.

How did Ohio fare in the years following the War of 1812?

The state thrived. Thousands of new settlers arrived each year, with 1816 (the infamous "Year without a Summer") seeing many come from New Hampshire and Vermont. Ohioans quickly showed the public spirit that has made them famous. They established some of the first newspapers in the Midwest, and Oberlin College became known as one of the most liberal and progressive of all Midwestern schools.

This painting by artist William Henry Powell hangs in the state capitol in Columbus. It depicts Oliver Hazard Perry leading U.S. ships to victory against the British on Lake Erie.

The Northwest Ordinance forbade slavery in Ohio and the new territories, but Ohioans became involved in the 1840s and 1850s. Many of them provided refuge to escaped black slaves from Kentucky, and Ohio became one of the most important conduits along the Underground Railroad, which brought African Americans to freedom. We, naturally, associate Harriet Beecher Stowe with Connecticut—the state of her birth—and with Maine, where she settled in midlife, but she spent some very important years in southern Ohio. Stowe interviewed escaped slaves, and these conversations helped form what became the most important American book of that era, *Uncle Tom's Cabin*.

Is there anything to the notion that Ohioans, and other Midwesterners, were quiet racists, who did not like blacks very much?

There is. Midwesterners on the whole, and Ohioans most especially, detested slavery, seeing it as un-Christian and as a backward form of economic development. This does not mean that they loved African Americans or wished them to settle in their midst. A real connection between the races took a long time in Ohio, just as in other parts of the nation.

What is noteworthy about Ohio's Oberlin College?

Oberlin College, located in Lorain County, just southwest of Cleveland, was the first college or university to admit African Americans and women. Oberlin was also heavily involved in the abolitionist movement during the Civil War era and was a stop along the Underground Railroad.

How important was the Civil War to the formation of Ohio's identity?

The people of Ohio already possessed a strong personal identity as early as 1840, but it took the Civil War to bring them together, in one of the tightest and strongest of all state identities. Almost as soon as the Civil War commenced, Ohio began fielding companies and brigades, and by its end the Buckeye State furnished nearly 350,000 men to the Union cause. Little towns that previously had been cordial but distant now became firmly united by their Civil War experience. It helped, too, that Ohio produced two of the most outstanding of all Northern military leaders: Ulysses S. Grant and William T. Sherman.

It was during the Civil War that Ohio forged its identity as the "middle of the middle," the strong center on which the Union was established. Ohioans today celebrate that tradition, in their politics most especially. It is a truism that a Republican presidential candidate must win Ohio to take the presidency. The electoral votes are important on their own, but it is the fact that Ohio acts like the nation in miniature, making the Buckeye State so important.

What was life in Ohio like in the last third of the nineteenth century (1866–1899)?

It was a very exciting time. Oil was discovered. Various companies established railroads that practically crisscrossed the state, making it one of the most developed and prosperous states at the time. And inventors such as Thomas Edison and Ransom Olds brought glory to the Buckeye State. Most important of all were the Wright Brothers, whose actions bore fruit in the first decade of the twentieth century.

Wilbur and Orville Wright are justly famous as the brothers who built and flew the first flying machine. The first human flight was achieved at Kitty Hawk, North Carolina, but the brothers had their permanent base in Dayton, and it was in Ohio that Orville accomplished the first true lasting flight (33 minutes in the air) in 1905. By 1910, the year that Wilbur Wright made a sensational airplane flight around Manhattan Island, Ohio was the center of the new airplane industry.

Was there any limit to what the men of Ohio could accomplish?

We cautiously employ the male gender here, because the women of Ohio were doing plenty of their own. In the public sphere, in engineering and technical accomplishment, however, Ohio was very much a "male" state, with men leading the way. And in the 1920s and 1930s, Ohio continued to produce many of the finest, most accomplished engineers and technicians. The designs of Ohioans led to the building of numerous great bridges and buildings across the nation. Of course, Ohio did not completely escape the gutting aspects of the Great Depression (1929–1940), but the Buckeye State suffered less than what was the national average.

How did Ohio—and West Virginia—become so identified with the aerospace industry?

Parts of southern Ohio and parts of West Virginia share a regional dialect that became, over time, the "voice of choice" of the airline industry. Even today, airline pilots deliver

a slow, calm, and methodical tone of voice when speaking to their passengers; this is because in tests the airlines found that this particular speech pattern was most soothing to passengers. Not only did the voice help, but Ohio and West Virginia provided many of the first test pilots for the U.S. Air Force. These men, who did their most important work in distant locations such as Nevada and New Mexico, were instrumental in pacing the way toward space flight.

What was the single proudest moment for the people of Ohio?

Beyond a doubt this came on July 20, 1969, when Neil Armstrong, a native of Wapakoneta, Ohio, slowly descended from the lunar module to step on the surface of

Ohioans are proud of their native son and astronaut, Neil Armstrong.

the Moon (he was the first human to achieve this). Armstrong was followed a short time later by New Jersey native Buzz Aldrin, but the old adage that everyone remembers the first—and few recall the second—applied here. Of the millions of television viewers on that day, the great majority remembered Armstrong. The Buckeye State, humble and normal as apple pie, had produced one of the true superstars of the twentieth century.

What other native Ohioan was a prominent astronaut?

John Glenn, born in Cambridge, Ohio, was a member of the original Mercury Seven group of astronauts in the early 1960s. In 1962, Glenn was the first American to orbit the Earth. From 1974 to 1999, he served as a U.S. senator from his home state. And while still a senator, at the age of seventy-seven, Glenn became the oldest person to go into space when he served as a payload specialist on a *Discovery* space shuttle mission in 1998. His primary role on the mission was to be the source of geriatric studies in space.

What was one of the worst moments for the people of Ohio?

It is the height of irony that one of the very worst times for the Buckeye State came just days after Neil Armstrong stepped on the lunar surface. The industrial city of Cleveland had long been known for its dirty water and pollution, but in August 1969, a section of the Cuyahoga River actually caught fire, and the action was photographed and shown on television. Nothing this bad—or unseemly—had ever been associated with Ohio before, and the people of the Buckeye State endured what was, for them, an uncommon amount of shame. On the positive side, the Cleveland fire led to the establishment of the Environmental Protection Agency, just a few years later.

How did Ohio fare in the 1970s and 1980s?

These were the worst of times, so far as Ohioans were concerned. First came the tragedy at Kent State University on May 4, 1970, when the National Guard shot and killed four students. Then came a decade and more of economic recession, as American industries reeled from the effect of new competition, coming primarily from Japan. By the mid-

Why is the Rock-and-Roll Hall of Fame in Ohio? California seems like a more natural choice.

Cleveland is often called the birthplace of rock-and-roll, because the first authenticated use of that term came from a Cleveland disc jockey in 1951. Beyond that, however, many of the great rock-and-roll performers come from humble places and end up in mansions in California later on. One of the most noticeable, and sometimes notorious, Ohio performers is Chrissie Hynde, lead singer for The Pretenders. Born in Akron in 1951, one of her first hits, "My City Was Gone," included the memorable lyrics, "Ay, oh, where did you go, Ohio?"

1980s, people referred to Ohio as the center of the so-called "Rust Belt," meaning a large area of the Midwest where decaying factories produced few products, and when millions of people were unemployed. One of the few bright spots at the time was the development of the Rock-and-Roll Hall of Fame, which stands today in Cleveland.

Where will Ohio be a generation from now?

Ohio has overcome many obstacles. The Rust Belt remains a reality, but the Buckeye State will, in all likelihood, find a way to develop new sources of wealth. If there is any permanent danger on the horizon, it is that Ohio's weather has not changed very much, and that when it has altered, it has mostly been for the colder. Like nearly all the Northern and Midwestern States, Ohio faces the loss of many of its most valuable residents to "cold flight," meaning that they move south and west to escape the tough winters.

OKLAHOMA

OKLAHOMA

Nickname: "The Sooner State"
Capital: Oklahoma City
Statehood: November 16, 1907; 46th state

AT A GLANCE

What are some of the most important signs and symbols of the Sooner State?

"Labor Conquers All Things" is the state motto. The scissor-tailed flycatcher is the state bird, and the mistletoe is the state flower. The redbud is the state tree.

Where did Oklahoma come by its nickname?

The Sooner State refers to the early conflict between "boomers" and "sooners." A boomer was a person who lined up near a state or county border, eager to charge across it to claim land, once the signal gun was fired, while a sooner was someone who staked out his claim in advance, either by evading the rules or because his position (land surveyor, for instance) allowed early entry. In time, "sooner" came to be known as someone who was energetic and ambitious.

How did Oklahoma get its rather strange shape?

One can, of course, ask much the same question about many of the states, but Oklahoma is a special case, thanks to the lateness of its settlement. Not until 1893 was the area opened to white settlers, and they came on in a spectacular rush, seizing land and moving rapidly to the west. Texas, meanwhile, had long since established its northern border, and the Oklahoma settlers therefore had to move around it, creating the Oklahoma Panhandle.

351

How large, or small, is the Sooner State?

Comprising 69,899 square miles (181,036 square kilometers), Oklahoma is twentieth among the fifty states in geographic size. The population of 3,850,586, as enumerated in the 2010 census, places Oklahoma at twenty-eighth among the states.

What makes the Sooner State different from its close neighbors?

No other state in the Union has so complicated and lengthy a story of settlement. First there were the Native Americans indigenous to the region; then came other Indians, who were sent (or exiled) West by the federal government. Both the Union and the Confederacy claimed Oklahoma, and when the Civil War ended, there was tragedy enough for all concerned. Even when one considers all these factors, there remains the overwhelming fact that Oklahoma was settled in land "rushes" by white settlers who lined up along boundaries, waited for the shotgun or cannon to sound, and then charged into the great openness. No other state has such a violent and aggressive beginning.

Is the land itself any different from that of its neighbors, in northern Texas and southern Colorado?

Oklahoma is quite different from its neighbors. The land sometimes looks the same as northern Texas, but as soon as one progresses from the eastern to middle section of Oklahoma, one realizes that this place is quite different. As one fine historian commented, Oklahoma is composed of the three great terrains that make up the Lower Forty-Eight: forest, meadow, and rough plain. One can also comment, however, on how truly different the wind in Oklahoma is; Texas, Arkansas, and Kansas all experience plenty of wind, but there is a different quality to that of Oklahoma. At times it is refreshing; at other times it can be deadly.

If there are so many topographical and weather difficulties, why did so many people move to Oklahoma in the 1890s?

Congress passed the Homestead Act, and for almost three decades would-be settlers found enough land in the upper and central Midwest. Not until 1889 did they come to Oklahoma, and they did so in spectacular land "rushes" that resulted in much of the state being settled in record time. The settlement speed did not lead to an easy or genteel way of life, however; something about Oklahoma—the land of oil derricks and cattle drives—conspired to make life there quite rough.

Most of us have heard those wonderful words of Rodgers and Hammerstein, "Oklahoma—where the wind comes sweeping down the plain!" Did the artists, and their admirers, realize how painful and sometimes deadly that wind can be?

They did not. American frontier men and women of the eighteenth and nineteenth centuries did not talk much about the endless labor and difficulties of the landscape they settled. Rather, they waxed over its natural beauty. And it is true that Oklahoma is a land of spectacular sunrises followed by even grander sunsets. One just has to be careful to get all the animals in before dark!

How strong is the Native American presence in Oklahoma?

The Sooner State has very few reservations; its many Indian residents live in communities much like their white counterparts. One can detect the Native American feel, however, especially in the central and western parts of the state. Oklahoma is known as a meeting ground for different Indian tribes, some of whom were as different—at the time of white settlement—as the various European nations from which the white settlers came.

Oklahoma is smack in the middle of Tornado Alley, where twisters are common.

Is the weather a subject of much conversation?

It is discussed almost endlessly. It is a rare Oklahoman who does not realize that he or she is subject to the laws of nature. Many jokes, or examples of gallows humor, developed in the early decades of white settlement. One of the most common runs as follows:

A team of horses is brought out on a day in later winter to break the ground. The first horse exerts itself too strongly, becomes overheated, and collapses from the strain. The farmer rushes to bring another horse to the situation, but by the time he arrives, the second horse has frozen to death.

Who is the best-known of all Oklahomans?

His name is not as well-known as it was half a century ago, but Will Rogers was—and remains—the quintessential Oklahoman. Born in 1879, he was half-Cherokee and half-white. He became America's best-known humorist and was quoted as saying he never met a man he didn't like (this kind of hearty brotherhood is often declared in the Sooner State). Rogers benefited from the appearance of radio in the 1920s, and his career was at an all-time high when he died in a plane crash in Alaska in 1935. As far as Oklahomans are concerned, he is their greatest contribution to the nation.

EARLY HISTORY

For how long have human beings wandered the plains of Oklahoma?

For thousands of years. We don't know precisely when those first Paleo-Indians showed up, or how they found food and water, but we suspect they had a rough time of it. The area was not heavily populated at any time of its early existence, but when the first white

353

explorers appeared, they found Plains Apache, Osage, Kiowa, and other Indians in the region. A noticeable difference was observed, right from the beginning, with the Plains Indians—Kiowa, Apache, and Comanche—living different lifestyles from those of the village-dwellers, the Caddo, Wichita, and Pawnee.

Who were the first people of European descent to see what is now Oklahoma?

Coronado's expedition traveled across at least part of the Sooner State in 1540–1541, and the Spaniards maintained a long claim to the region based on this fact. In reality, however, Oklahoma had very few white people till the 1820s, and even then they arrived only in small numbers. The major turning point, which led to real colonization, was the removal of the Five Civilized Tribes from the Southeast. The administration of President Andrew Jackson (who certainly was not a lover of Indians) promised that the Creek, Cherokee, Choctaw, Seminole, and Cherokee would possess the lands in present-day Oklahoma forever, just as long as they gave up their claim to lands in Georgia, Alabama, and Mississippi.

What followed was the "Trail of Tears," when roughly 4,000 Indians died en route to their new lands in what was then called Indian Territory. Small wonder then that the Indians who arrived in Oklahoma put down firm roots, intending to remain there for the rest of their days. The great misfortune of these early tribes is that they had become acculturated to some of the white people's ways, slavery in particular.

How separated, or segregated, was Indian Country in those territorial days?

The tribes lived lives that can truly be called separate. Though they were all victims of the great forced relocation from the Southeast, the Five Civilized Tribes did not always get on that well among themselves.

Is it true that the Indians of Oklahoma sided with the Confederate States of America?

Perhaps 80 percent of the Indians of Oklahoma—both longtime residents and new arrivals—sided with the Confederacy, partially because the Cherokee and Creek held slaves. Missouri native Albert Pike, one of the most intriguing characters from the entire Civil War era, negotiated alliances between the Confederacy and most of the Indian tribes, and many warriors proved powerful allies. General Stand Watie, a Cherokee, was the last person of general rank to surrender in the Civil War.

How bad was the aftermath of the Civil War?

So far as the Indians were concerned, it could not have been worse. They had no reason to trust the federal government, which had forced them to relocate in the 1830s. They had put their trust in the Confederate States of America, only to wind up on the losing side. And they knew that the federal government would not protect them for long against the encroachment of white settlers.

For its part, the federal government regarded most of the Oklahoma Indians as traitors, and it was hard to elicit any sympathy for them, even on the East Coast. The pressure from settlers who wished to open the Indian Territory became more intense with each passing decade, and on April 22, 1889, thousands of would-be landowners were lined up on the border between the area of white settlement and Choctaw country.

What was the scene like on that opening day?

To an Indian observer, it had to be heart-breaking. To the journalist—and there were many on the scene—it had to be fascinating. And to the Sooner, meaning the person who wished to stake a claim sooner than anyone else, it was, quite likely, the most exciting day of his life. The scene is aptly described in *Oklahoma: A Bicentennial History*:

> Every aspect and aspiration of American society was represented in the first run. The typical frontier family consisted of a big-boned, shaggy father with a determined wife and several small children. Their prairie schooner bulged with chickens, farm implements, furniture and mattresses, and the ubiquitous family dog…. Next to such a family might be a span of prancing bays with a fine carriage, all shiny wheels and polished brass, in the hands of a more dapper pioneer. One man rode an ox. A girl in a billowing pink dress sat astride a spirited thoroughbred. But four circus midgets riding a single horse toward destiny surely provoked the most comment. (*Oklahoma: A Bicentennial History*, p. 51.)

How did this enormous event transpire?

A gun sounded, then a cannon shot, and all along a fifty-mile section of the border, settlers surged forth. They came by wagon, by horseback, and some even ran most of the way. Each person, or family group, attempted to stake out a claim, and many went much farther that day than anticipated; some settlers were setting up posts fifty miles into the former Indian Territory that evening. The "Magic City of Guthrie" appeared that day, with over 10,000 people and 500 makeshift homes. There has never, in American history, been anything quite like the Land Rush of April 22, 1889.

Could anything have stopped these people? Or were they an irresistible force?

The reason the Oklahoma Land Rush has such a powerful appeal is that most of the people participating knew that this was it—fewer lands would be available for the future. The cameramen that caught images of the Sooners surging across the barrier, and into Indian Territory, were also keenly aware of the fact that the frontier was rapidly disappearing. But the short answer is that nothing—not even a Supreme Court injunction or a presidential order—could have stopped the Sooners of 1889.

How quickly did the Oklahoma Territory come to be?

In May 1890, the new territory was created, and for the next few years, federal maps showed two sections of what we now call the Sooner State: the Oklahoma Territory (presumably

The federal government opened up the Oklahoma Territory to anyone who could grab a claim and improve the land (mostly through farming). The result was the Land Rush that settled the state in record time.

for whites only) and a much-diminished Indian Territory. Even that small remnant was eliminated in 1907, however, when Oklahoma entered the Union as the forty-sixth state.

Did any of the Sooners express regret for what they'd done, or apologize to the Indians?

Not to our knowledge. America, in 1907, was a fascinating mixture of the refined and the rough and tumble, and many Americans—even those who were not involved—approved of the land rushes and subsequent statehood. There was a prevailing belief that the Indians had once been romantic figures, but that they were doomed to either adapt completely to the white people's ways or disappear.

OKLAHOMA IN THE LIFE
OF THE NATION

How and when did the petroleum industry emerge?

Most of the settlers who poured forth in the great land rush did not realize that oil lay beneath the soil. It did not take their children very long to realize this, however, and the first significant oil well was drilled at Bartlesville in the 1890s. From then on, the discoveries of oil proliferated, and it seemed at times as if the entire eastern part of the state would become one enormous well. Oklahoma has the only state house in the nation to have an oil well on its land!

Some of the most famous names of the American oil industry derive from those early days in Oklahoma. Frank Phillips founded Phillips Petroleum, which later turned into Conoco-Phillips. State revenues boomed during the first two decades of the twentieth century, but not much of the profit sank down to the level of the Native Americans. Their numbers increased in the 1920s, but so did their economic plight.

Is there any exception to the general rule that Native Americans never get their share of the wealth?

There are a handful, and one of them is found in Oklahoma. The Osage Indians were relative newcomers to Oklahoma, having been forced to relocate from their lands in Kansas after the Civil War. The Osage leased much of their land to eager oil men; the Osage also invested the money they received from the federal government for their Kansas lands. As a result, stories spread of the Osage being the "richest" group of people in the world. And there have been times, such as the mid-1920s and the late 1970s, when oil and natural gas revenues made the Osage very well off. But as is so often the case, material prosperity came and went, with long periods of relative poverty in-between. Many Osage families, too, assert that their material success is a mixed blessing, as they have been hounded by fortune hunters and scoundrels.

I always think of Texas and Louisiana as the top two states for oil production. Is that accurate?

In our times it is. But when the sensational Oklahoma oil discoveries occurred in the early twentieth century, the Sooner State was number one. Oil strikes led to the establishment of cities such as Cushing, Seminole, Okmulgee, and Oklahoma City, and the Sooner State produced 27 million barrels of oil by the end of 1906. (There are even oil wells on the grounds of the state capitol in Oklahoma City.) This made Oklahoma the top oil producer, and it retained that position until 1928, when Texas surpassed it.

How did Oklahoma fare during the world wars and the Great Depression?

World War I proved a gold mine to many Oklahomans. Petroleum was needed in ever-greater quantities, and the Sooner State sent many shipments, most of them by railroad. Oklahoma farmers were also in a strange mood. Many expressed socialist sympathies, and when Socialist candidate Eugene Debs polled 6 percent nationwide (1912), he received 16 percent of the votes in Oklahoma. This turned out to be only a flirtation with socialism, however, and Oklahoma profited from both World War I and World War II by selling oil at much higher prices than before.

In the immediate aftermath of the war, it became apparent that the nation needed a better road system, and by mutual agreement plans were laid for the creation of that most famous of all American highways: Route 66. Intended to connect Chicago and Los Angeles, Route 66 cut right across Oklahoma. Sections of it have been left untouched to this day: a one-lane section is called the Ribbon Road.

In its heyday, though, Route 66 was known as the Mother Road, the one that connected all others, and it brought eager Americans from the Midwest to southern California. A playful, joyous spirit pervaded the travelers of this route until the Great Depression struck in all its fury. From then on, Route 66 bore a sorrowful aspect, as thousands of "Okies" pulled up stakes and moved west.

How bad was the Dust Bowl of the mid-1930s?

It was so bad—for the people of Oklahoma—that most of those who suffered through it preferred not to discuss it. Years of drought culminated in enormous clouds of black dust descending on the Great Plains, and the dust and sand went everywhere: into peoples' eyes, as well as their curtains and couches. Oklahoma witnessed an exodus of many of its most hard-working residents during the 1930s. There was nothing the state or federal governments could do.

The Native Americans suffered terribly during the Dust Bowl as well, but rather few of them departed. Having been ejected from one part of the country by the federal government, they were not about to let something else—even a great natural disaster— push them out again.

What unusual event occurred in Boise City, Oklahoma, during World War II?

On July 5, 1943, pilots from Dalhart Army Air Base in Texas, flying a U.S. B-17 Flying Fortress Bomber, mistook the lights surrounding the courthouse square of Boise City for a target during target practice. Fortunately, it was early morning, so the town was quiet, and no one was hurt or killed. Some buildings were damaged or destroyed, although it could have been worse, since only practice bombs were used. Boise City was the only continental U.S. town to be bombed.

How did Oklahoma change in the post-World War II years?

The state did not exactly boom; there was an exodus of younger people during the 1940s and 1950s. But economic matters improved, and Oklahoma was on a more stable footing than in the past.

What was the single worst day of Oklahoma history?

Beyond any doubt this was April 19, 1995. A truck backed up near the Federal Building, as many trucks did in those days. This one was left unattended, however, and at 9:20 A.M. the area shook from the effect of a violent explosion. The Federal Building did not collapse entirely, but it was ruined beyond repair. Nearly 170 people—most of them inside—were killed instantly.

That the tragedy occurred on Patriots Day—celebrated as a state holiday in Massachusetts but not elsewhere—only made matters worse. It seemed as if the bombers—who were soon apprehended—intended to rock the very foundations of the federal government, and the aspirations of the various states that collectively made up the nation. Oklahoma is seldom in the national news, but in the spring of 1995 it was on the minds of most Americans.

One of the worst terrorist attacks in U.S. history, the bombing of the Federal Building in Oklahoma City, was perpetrated by a white American named Timothy McVeigh.

How well—or poorly—did Oklahoma City recover from the bombing?

The city had a hard time of it. The shock was immediate, but also long-lasting, and many residents of Oklahoma City have invisible scars from the event. Not until the new Federal Building was constructed did residents begin to hold their heads high once more. The memorial to the disaster became a hallmark of downtown Oklahoma City, with two gates calmly proclaiming the difference that two minutes can make. The east gate bears the numbers 9:01, meaning the minute prior to the blast, and the west gate displays 9:03, meaning the minute after. In that interval, the lives of many Oklahomans had changed.

The nation, too, was profoundly affected by the Oklahoma City bombing. New rules for the safety of federal and municipal buildings soon went into effect, and the general belief was that security was much improved. Only when the September 11, 2001, terrorist attacks took place did Americans fully realize that they lived in a new era, one in which the safety of the public could not be taken for granted.

What other kind of disasters have been visited upon the Sooner State?

Thanks to the velocity and changeability of the wind, tornadoes have long had a tremendous impact on Oklahoma. A series of them struck the state in 1999, and another group

359

visited in 2013. The Moore EF5 tornado hit that town on May 21, 2013, causing enormous damage, and killing more than twenty people. Storm chasers—as they are called—tend to spend much time in Oklahoma, believing that major tornadoes can be spotted more quickly there than in any other state (of course this does not mean that the tornadoes are any easier to manage).

What was life in Oklahoma like at the turn of the twenty-first century?

The state was in better economic shape than at many previous times. The natural gas industry was making record profits, and at least some of these were trickling down to the common folk. The Native Americans were generally two steps behind their white neighbors, in terms of finances and quality of life, however.

Nickname: "The Beaver State"
Capital: Salem
Statehood: February 14, 1859; 33rd state

AT A GLANCE

What are some of the most important signs and symbols of the Beaver State?

"She Flies with Her Own Wings" is now the state motto, but there was a time, earlier in the state's history, when it was simply "The Union." The latter testifies to the fact that Oregon entered the Union at a dangerous time in its history, just two years prior to the outbreak of the Civil War. The western meadowlark is the state bird, and the Oregon grape is the state flower. The Douglas fir is the official state tree.

What is unusual about Oregon's state flag?

It is the only state in the union to have two different designs on its flag. On one side is the state seal and the words "State of Oregon" and "1859" (the year Oregon became a state), and the other side shows an image of a beaver. This design debuted in 1925.

What is unique about Oregon?

That we ask the question immediately suggests we are not natives of the Beaver State: residents know the answer almost intuitively. Oregon is one of the most unusual states of the nation, formed both by its superb natural environment and the open-mindedness of its people. But if we take the question seriously, we find that Oregon is complete unto itself: few states of the Union are so self-reliant.

361

How large, or small, is Oregon?

Comprising 98,379 square miles (254,500 square kilometers), Oregon is ninth among the fifty states in geographic size. The population of 3,930,065, as enumerated in the census of 2010, places Oregon as twenty-seventh among the states.

I often hear that the Oregon coast is truly spectacular. Can you say more about it?

Oregon's coastline runs for 296 miles (476 kilometers), and the visitor is treated to some of the most remarkable sights to be found on the West Coast. Long sections of the Oregon coastline are deserted, with only the occasional lighthouse and state park. One finds more peace and tranquility on the Oregon coast than in any comparable section of American coastline, east or west. Maine, for example, is often compared to Oregon, but its coast is much busier.

Is there any one place from which one can view the best that is Oregon?

There are two. The first, and the best-known, is from downtown Portland. Even the most casual tourist looks up at Mount Hood—only forty miles away—with something akin to reverence. There are no fewer than 140 parks in Portland, and the city has better "lungs" (meaning more trees and shrubs) than almost any other major American city. The second and less-known spot is at Astoria, near the mouth of the Columbia River. As one crosses the Four Miles Bridge from Oregon to Washington—or vice-versa—he or she is

The Oregon coastline is known for its spectacular beauty.

treated to a truly spectacular scene, one rather like what Lewis and Clark beheld in the autumn of 1805.

Is there any end to the natural splendors of the Beaver State?

Not to any lover of the great outdoors. Oregon has its share of small cities and suburbs, where one can live the cosmopolitan life, but even the most determined of city-dwellers tend to be pulled to the wildness of the state. From the Columbia River Gorge to Astoria at the mouth of the Columbia, and from Cannon Beach on the Pacific to any number of inland lakes and streams, Oregon is close to paradise. Very likely it helps that many Oregonians are sixth-generation descendants of pioneers who came all the way from the Midwest; these are not the type of people to shrink from confrontation with the natural world.

Do Oregonians discuss the weather very much?

Not to any significant degree. Natives are completely inured to the one minor hardship that the area hands its residents: frequent drops of soft rain. What many outsiders don't understand is that Oregon is not subject to frequent downpours; its rains are of a gentle kind. On average, the Pacific Northwest receives less precipitation than the East Coast. Wintertime is another time of sportsman's delight in Oregon; residents are into skiing, snowshoeing, and, more recently, snowboarding.

Can the man or woman of Oregon be told apart, from his or her neighbors in southern Washington and northern California?

Absolutely. The Oregonian is immediately friendly—as is the northern Californian—but his or her conversation tends to be in one of two directions: politics or nature. Sometimes the two intertwine. The person of southern Washington State is more likely to discuss computers or brands of coffee.

EARLY HISTORY

For how long have humans lived in what we now call the Beaver State?

For thousands of years. When the first Paleo-Indians arrived, perhaps 11,000 years ago, they discovered something close to paradise in the Pacific Northwest. Hunting was fine, but fishing was superb, and the salmon became the closest thing to a staple for the Native Americans. We don't know if the Indians who greeted Lewis, Clark, and others were direct descendants of these first Indians, but their lifestyles and lifeways certainly didn't change very much (because they didn't need to).

Indians who lived along the banks of the Columbia River had an abundance of food to draw upon, and their populations swelled to a greater degree than most Indian tribes nationwide. The potlatch is most closely identified with Washington State, but it existed in Oregon as well. Under its provisions, the wealthiest man in the village spent an entire day giving away all his possessions, and his social status became larger based on the amount he gave away. This was only possible in a society where the population as a whole was doing rather well.

To what degree were the Indians disturbed by the arrival of Europeans on the coast?

To only a minor extent. Many inland Indians didn't even know that Spaniards appeared in the sixteenth century and that the Spanish monarchy lay claim to Oregon, based on their discoveries. It was otherwise, however, when the British arrived in the presence of the Hudson's Bay Company, and when Lewis, Clark, and the Corps of Discovery came down the Columbia River in canoes.

Lewis and Clark both possessed talent in ethnohistory, and they took care to document all they could about the tribes of northern Oregon and southern Washington State. From Lewis and Clark, we learned an immense number of individual and tribal names, and the picture that developed was of a truly varied group of peoples. Unfortunately, many years passed before any other whites of Lewis and Clark's talent appeared, and in that meantime, many of the Indians either died from disease (presumably brought by the white explorers) or moved away.

When did the first Americans land on the Oregon coast?

Captain Robert Gray named the Columbia River in 1788, and he returned in 1792 to become the first person to bring a ship over the Columbia Bar, which posed one of the great hazards to West Coast shipping. The Americans laid claim to the area just in time to joust with the British, who did the same based on the discoveries of Captain James Cook, and then the Hudson's Bay Company. Most of the time, the British and Americans got along reasonably well. Most of them were merchants, rather than settlers, and it made sense for them to cooperate, at least to some degree. John McLoughlin, the Quebec-born head of the North West Company, entertained many American travelers at Fort Vancouver, and even when the two nations were at odds, the peoples got along fairly well.

A statue of Lewis and Clark stands in Seaside, Oregon, to honor the explorers' achievement of reaching the Pacific Coast.

Today we call it Oregon but they called it the Oregon Country. Can you explain the difference?

The Beaver State is large, but the Oregon Country, as it was known, was truly enormous. On the maps of both the British and American governments, the Oregon Country ran from the northern tip of California all the way to southern Alaska. Both governments, and peoples, viewed the Oregon Country as a great prize, and it was possible they would go to war in order to secure it.

The first major conflict between the British and Americans was at Astoria, on the southern side of the Columbia River estuary. A group of Americans came overland from Missouri in 1812, but they sold the fort and fur trading post to the British just two years later. Oregon did not see a campaign during the War of 1812, but it was a lucky thing when the British and American governments agreed to join occupation of the area in 1818.

How did East Coast Americans, as well as those in the Midwest, become aware of the vast potential of Oregon?

It was due to a handful of persons, many of them missionaries. In 1834, Methodist missionary Jason Lee established a tiny settlement in the Willamette Valley. Two years later, Dr. Marcus Whitman and his wife Narcissa Prentiss Whitman arrived in present-day Walla Walla, having made the first trip over the Rocky Mountains by covered wagon. Tragically, the Cayuse Indians massacred the Whitmans in 1847, but the Whitmans' reports of the land—and its peoples—made journalists and promoters aware of Oregon. As a result, promotional brochures were written, and some daring East Coast Americans began making the long trip to Oregon.

The Oregon Trail became popularized during the 1840s, and perhaps 400,000 people made that long and difficult journey. Selling virtually all their possessions—either on the East Coast or in Missouri—these pioneers set out first across the Great Plains and then into the Rocky Mountains. Most of them did not suffer from Indian attacks. Nearly all of them experienced drenching rainstorms, high winds, intense heat of the Plains, and moderate cold in the mountains. The story of the Oregon Trail never goes out of style because it appeals to some of the best aspects of the American character: a gritty

What was the reward for these migrants when they reached the Willamette Valley?

Quite a few diaries and journals say the same thing. On a Tuesday, for example, the settler reached his destination. On a Wednesday, he made the simple notation, "To work." Work, for these settlers, did not mean an office or a cubicle; rather, it meant an endless number of chores and tasks, in order to erect housing, and to turn that housing into a home.

determination and a keen ability to improvise. Perhaps six months after departure, the emigrants came down on the west side of the Cascade Mountains. Many of them settled in the Willamette Valley.

When did the Indians of Oregon, and the Pacific Northwest, realize that these settlers had come to stay?

They realized it too late. In 1847, there were determined attacks by Cayuse Indians against the settlers of northern Oregon and southern Washington State. The Indians achieved surprise and killed a number of settlers. But the white settlers took prompt and severe revenge, and the Indians, whose lifeways were already disrupted, began to leave the Columbia River for the Oregon forests, mistakenly believing they would be safe from further white incursion.

OREGON IN THE LIFE OF THE NATION

What was meant by that marvelous expression "Fifty-four Forty or Fight"?

This was the rallying cry of the Democratic Party in 1844, the year it nominated James Knox Polk for the presidency. Polk, who had never been west of the Mississippi River, declared he would not compromise with Great Britain, that America must have all the land on the Pacific Coast to 54 degrees 40 minutes of north latitude. Had this happened, there would be no break between the Lower Forty-Eight and Alaska today!

Polk won the presidency and proved more reasonable: the Treaty of 1836 divided the United States from British Canada at the line of 49 degree north latitude. That still meant an enormous amount of new land, and Americans were not shy at grabbing up areas of Oregon and Washington State. By now, the sale of farm products had outpaced the fur trade as the number-one moneymaker in Oregon.

What role did Oregon play in the American Civil War (1861–1865)?

Almost none. Oregon was so far removed that its people felt little connection to the conflict. Oregon did attain statehood earlier than would otherwise have been the case, however, because President James Buchanan wanted as many new Northern states as possible. Oregon entered the Union as the thirty-third state in 1859.

An 1882 illustration of the Northern Pacific Railroad company office in Portland, Oregon. The arrival of train service in 1883 helped the state's economy immensely.

What made the biggest difference for the economy of Oregon, ships or trains?

One can argue for either, but Oregonians were accustomed to the presence of ships in the Columbia. The really big surprise was in 1883, when the Northern Pacific Railroad came all the way to Portland. From that year forward, the farm products of Oregon were shipped east in railroad cars, and life in Oregon became decidedly prosperous.

Vegetables were major moneymakers, but the people of Oregon also turned their attention to wheat, sheep, and cattle. And by the end of the nineteenth century, the Beaver State became known for the quality of its lumber, the Douglas fir most especially. Many Oregonians made good money floating immense amounts of lumber on the state's rivers, while others earned good money in the apple industry. Of course it would be too much to say that Oregon showed no signs of poverty, but at least four-fifths of the state's residents were doing reasonably well by 1900.

TWENTIETH-CENTURY POLITICS

When did Oregon become known as a state that practices innovative politics?

Today it is an axiom that Oregon is a liberal state, but a century ago it was called a progressive one, a reference to the Progressive Movement that took hold there. In 1902, Oregon pioneered the way with use of the initiative and the referendum, which allowed voters to put issues, even very controversial ones, on the ballot. Two years later, Oregon became the first state to legalize direct primary elections, and in 1903 a law allowed for the recall of public officials. Completing the round of Progressive reforms in 1912 was the enfranchisement of Oregon women.

Why the Beaver State was so receptive to political reforms is difficult to say, but once the momentum built, it proved nearly impossible to stop. This was not always a positive thing. In 1923, a new state law temporarily prevented aliens (primarily Asians) from owning land in Oregon. Generally speaking, however, Oregon's politics have consistently moved in the direction of greater freedom for the individual, as well as greater restrictions on business, requiring it to be a good neighbor.

How did Oregon fare during World War I and the Great Depression?

There was a strong labor union movement in Oregon, and many union members were initially against American entry to World War I. Jack Reed—still lionized as one of the legendary leaders of the liberal movement—was a native-born Oregonian who claimed big business—on Wall Street especially—was the reason the war started in the first place. But as the conflict went on, many Oregonians saw positive results. Portland especially benefited from the demand made on its naval yard and port facilities.

The Great Depression was a whole other matter. Many prominent American leftists today claim that their childhood—in Oregon during the Great Depression—was the best time of their lives, that they witnessed neighbor helping neighbor, and so forth. Some of this is undoubtedly true, but the Beaver State suffered during the Depression. The state saw many hobos riding the rails and plenty of people go unemployed.

How "good" was World War II to the state of Oregon?

From a personal perspective, the war brought some hardships and some painful losses. From an economic point of view, however, things could hardly have gone better. Oregon boomed throughout the Second World War, as it sent foodstuffs and raw materials to the Army and Navy. Many old-time Oregonians today claim that the Second World War was the very best of times for their state.

The postwar boom was just as strong, however. Migration to Oregon—which had languished for decades—picked up in the 1950s, as many U.S. servicemen, who'd seen the Pacific Northwest during the war, decided to relocate. As late as 1960, Oregon seemed like prime territory for the Republican Party, which claimed that the Pacific Northwest prosperity was the result of its policies.

When did Oregon make that sharp turn to the left that still characterizes its politics?

It was shortly after 1960. The Sixties were fertile times for liberal and progressive politics, and many Oregonians harkened back to the policies and politics of their grandparents (Jack Reed, for example, experienced a resurgence of popularity). Personal freedom was the number-one issue for many young Oregonians of the 1960s, and their children today pursue much the same agenda.

How did the Right to Die movement become so important in the political life of Oregon?

Oregonians will, to be sure, retort that it's not a political issue, but a personal one. To the majority of folk in the Beaver State, the right to choose one's death and to die with dignity is one of the most important issues of the early twenty-first century. Oregon was the first state to legalize euthanasia.

TWENTY–FIRST CENTURY OREGON

When did the backpacking craze begin?

For some Oregonians, backpacking reminds them of what their great-great-grandparents did while crossing the Oregon Trail. For others, wandering in the woods is the highest expression of personal freedom. And for still others, the woods are the ultimate refuge from the pressures of modern society. Put all these together, and one has the recipe for a movement that seems to have taken over the Beaver State. Oregonians are not averse to couches or television sets, but they believe in taking long breaks from both.

The chain stores of Portland, Salem, and Eugene cater to outdoor experience: it's no coincidence that Eddie Bauer flourishes in the Pacific Northwest. At the same time, the people of Oregon seldom go without their coffee. Like their neighbors in Washington State, they're nuts about all sorts of coffee flavors.

What was life in Oregon like at the turn of the twenty-first century?

Most Oregonians would quickly reply that the state was the best it had ever been. A century and a half of statehood was important, but a century of progressive politics had made Oregon into one of the signature states of the nation. To be sure, though, there was some concern that the state had grown too insular, and that it was difficult for its political leaders to converse with their counterparts in other states.

Where will the Beaver State be a generation from now?

In terms of its natural environment, Oregon will be very much what it is today: one of the most outdoor of all the fifty states, with a population that delights in all sorts of outdoor activities. In terms of its politics, Oregon is typically Democratic and leftist-leaning, but this is not a certainty for the future. The state could turn in a strong libertarian direction.

PENNSYLVANIA

Nickname: "The Keystone State"
Capital: Harrisburg
Statehood: December 12, 1787; 2nd state

AT A GLANCE

Where does Pennsylvania get its nickname?

They Keystone State earned its moniker during the struggle to establish the nation. The Constitutional Convention of 1787 was held in Philadelphia and the Constitution was written, but it was by no means certain that the necessary three-fifths of the thirteen states would approve the document. In letters between Alexander Hamilton and James Madison, Pennsylvania was referred to as the Keystone State, meaning the one where the Constitution either would be approved or where it would perish. The nickname stuck. Twenty-first century politicians know that Pennsylvania is one of the keys to winning a national election.

What are some of the most important signs and symbols of the Keystone State?

"Virtue, Liberty, and Independence" became the official state motto in 1875. It was important to have Philadelphia, and the state, ready for the big celebration to commemorate the Centennial of 1876, and Pennsylvania has kept this as its motto ever since. The ruffled grouse is the state bird, and the mountain laurel is the state flower. The hemlock is the official state tree.

How large, or small, is Pennsylvania?

Comprising 46,054 square miles (119,280 square kilometers), Pennsylvania is thirty-third among the fifty states in geographic size. It seems larger than that, however, because the state acts as a bridge between the coastal lowlands and the Allegheny and Appalachian Mountains. The population of 12,773,801, as enumerated in the census of 2010, means that Pennsylvania is sixth among the states in terms of population.

What is the best place to see Pennsylvania and its people at work?

There are actually two such places. The first is downtown Philadelphia, close to the waterfront. This is one of the most historic places in the entire nation, and it fully lives up to all the advertising. The second is downtown Pittsburgh, which once was the industrial and commercial center of the Northeast. The two cities display marked contrasts, with Philadelphia generally showing more wealth. Though Pittsburgh does not thrive today in the way Philadelphia does, between them these two cities showcase the best that Pennsylvania has to offer.

Is there more to Pennsylvania than its two biggest cities?

To be sure! Geographers sometimes describe the state as two urban centers with a whole lot of Appalachia thrown in-between, but even this does not convey the whole truth. Pennsylvania also has thousands of acres of rolling farmland, places where the Amish and Mennonites have flourished. Pennsylvania is also the only one of the Mid-Atlantic states that stretches significantly to the west; its border with Ohio is the transition point between the Mid-Atlantic and the Midwest.

What happens every year in the small town of Punxsutawney?

Legend has it that every year on February 2, Punxsutawney Phil, a groundhog, emerges from his hole to look for his shadow. If he sees it, then there will be six more weeks of winter weather; if he doesn't see it, it's a sign of spring. As a result, February 2 is known as Groundhog Day. The practice seems to have a German origin.

Is the weather in Pennsylvania monotonous?

Not really, but it is true that the Keystone State usually enjoys predictable weather. Summers are quite warm, especially in Philadelphia and its suburbs, while winters can be surprisingly severe.

What makes a Pennsylvanian different from a Marylander or an Ohioan?

Pennsylvania culture is an intriguing mixture of the practical and the humane, a no-nonsense business approach mixed with philanthropy. In this, Pennsylvania echoes the life and incredible career of its favorite son, Benjamin Franklin. During his long lifetime (1706–1790), Franklin was keenly interested in material advancement, but he also was interested in his fellow man (he seldom spoke of women). Franklin's influence is still felt today, but so is that of Andrew Carnegie, another self-made man who believed in giving away as much as he could.

EARLY HISTORY

For how long have humans lived in what we now call the Keystone State?

For perhaps 10,000 years. We know very little about the first comers, or their lifeways, and can only speak to the Indians who lived in the area when the first European explorers and settlers arrived. The Leni-Lenape, often called the Delaware, lived along the coast, and inland were the Susquehanna. Both these groups felt ever-increasing pressure from the Five Nations of Iroquois, who were eager to come south and dominate the region.

Who were the Quakers?

Known as the Society of Friends, the Quakers were founded in England in the seventeenth century. In truth, however, they belong to no particular nation, being one of the most free-thinking set of people ever seen in the Western world.

The Quakers were centuries ahead of their time, believing in the equality of men and women, of black and white, and of all social and economic groups. They were also quite skillful at business matters, and many of them eventually became successful, even wealthy, merchants. The Quakers were persecuted in England, and many of them looked to New World emigration as the answer. For this they needed Sir William Penn, the most famous Quaker of his time.

How important is William Penn to the founding of Pennsylvania?

He's as big to the people of Pennsylvania as Captain John Smith is to those of Virginia. He's the founding father, the person who set the colonial pattern.

Penn's father was an English admiral. King Charles II owed a large debt of money to the Penn family, and, rather than pay it outright, he asked William Penn what he could do. Penn asked for a land grant in America, and for the right to settle Quakers there. Charles agreed, and the resulting land grant was one of the largest ever seen, so large that it conflicted with Lord Baltimore's patent for the colony of Maryland. In 1682, Penn came to his brand-new colony with the first settlers. He helped lay out the streets of Philadelphia, but soon he had to return to England to defend his land grant (this also established a pattern that was repeated several times).

William Penn was a Quaker and the founder of Pennsylvania (the state's name means "Penn's Woods").

373

How much "better" were the Quakers as colonists and neighbors?

The term "environmentalist" had not yet been coined, but some of the early Quakers fit the bill. They were much more conscious of the scarcity of natural resources than their neighbors. The Quakers also drew up fair and honest land treaties with the Native Americans; one of the most famous images of William Penn is of him negotiating with the Indians under the Great Treaty Elm. The second generation of Quakers were not as magnanimous, however, and Penn's grandson negotiated the infamous "Walking Purchase" in 1743. He hired a professional athlete to *run* what was intended to be the length of ground a man could *walk* in one day. As a result of the Indians losing out on a larger-than-expected piece of land in what they viewed as a swindle, they became disenchanted by the Quakers, but by then it was too late. The eastern half of Pennsylvania was already in their hands.

When did Benjamin Franklin come to Philadelphia, and how did he rise so quickly?

Born in Boston in 1706, Franklin seemed destined to lead the life of a latter-day Puritan. But, after suffering numerous beatings from his elder brother James—who owned a print shop—Franklin moved to Philadelphia in 1723, and he never looked back. Within a decade, he was one of Philadelphia's leading citizens, and a decade after that he was ready to retire from material concerns and devote himself to the betterment of mankind. Very few people—American or otherwise—have been so fortunate or have devoted themselves so wholeheartedly.

What was Philadelphia like on the eve of the American Revolution?

In 1774, there were more than 20,000 people in Philadelphia, and they were an interesting mixture of English, Scots, Irish, and Germans, as well as divided between merchant and working class. Philadelphia had few truly rich people in 1774, but this would change, and "old wealth" would become one of the hallmarks of the Philadelphia experience.

Much of our knowledge of early Philadelphia comes from the many newspapers of that time, and we know that the advertisements were filled with descriptions of runaway servants and slaves. Indentured servants formed an important part of the Pennsylvania economy, and masters had a clear interest in having their servants returned. The American Revolution provided an escape opportunity for many of these servants, however, and it is likely that rather few of them ever returned to a state of servitude.

What were the meetings of the Continental Congress like?

The First Continental Congress met in the autumn of 1774, and the Second Continental Congress arrived in the spring of 1775. Even when we allow for some exaggeration and puffed-up patriotism, it is likely that very few legislative bodies—since Roman times at least—contained so much talent as these congresses. Almost every one of the legislators had practical as well as theoretical skills, and nearly all of them made a living in one fashion or another. Some of these men were truly multitalented, while others were men of tunnel vision, who kept at the same trade or craft until they got it right.

As almost the entire world knows, the Second Continental Congress approved the Declaration of Independence in July 1776. The Congress had to remain in session for another five years, however, before the Revolutionary War was won, and during that time its members faced many crises. Some of these were monetary, as when it was impossible to pay the soldiers, and others were more direct, as when the British captured Philadelphia in the autumn of 1777 (the Congress relocated to York, Pennsylvania). This was not the sum total of what Philadelphia gave the nation, however.

Was there any chance that the Constitutional Convention would meet in some other place?

Delegates briefly considered Annapolis, Maryland, but it was nearly inevitable that the Constitutional Convention of 1788 would meet in Philadelphia. Many of the men had been in the Second Continental Congress, and they were familiar with the city and its people. Between May and September 1787, the delegates thrashed out what became the Constitution of the United States. Signed by thirty-nine men on September 17, 1787, the document was then submitted to the states, and in 1788 it became the law of the land.

PENNSYLVANIA IN THE LIFE OF THE NATION

Which presidents lived in Philadelphia when it was the temporary capital?

While Washington, D.C., was being readied as the permanent capital of the United States, Philadelphia served as the temporary capital. The first two U.S. presidents, George Washington and John Adams, lived in the President's House on Market Street. Washington lived there for both his terms, while Adams lived there until November 1, 1800, at which time he moved into the White House (though it wasn't yet called that) for the final four and a half months of his only term in office.

How did Pennsylvania fare in the decades that followed the establishment of the nation?

For several decades Pennsylvania, and Philadelphia especially, formed the central part of the American economy. Not only did the rich Pennsylvania soil provide many crops, but the inventiveness of the locals meant that Pennsylvania became a land of inventors, designers, and specialty carpenters. Then, too, the first Bank of the United States was chartered in Philadelphia.

Manhattan surpassed Philadelphia in population by 1820, but Pennsylvania had an ace up its sleeve. Pittsburgh was already coming along nicely, when the oil and coal industries emerged to make it one of the wealthiest places in the United States. Pennsylvania had the nation's first oil well, in 1859, and the famous Standard Oil Company was organized in the 1870s, By then, railroads crisscrossed Pennsylvania, making it truly the "keystone" state.

How important was the Civil War in the making of Pennsylvania's identity?

Nearly all the Northern states had a surge of pride as the Civil War was won, but Pennsylvania felt this with special keenness. The Keystone State was the center of the campaign that culminated in the three-day Battle of Gettysburg (July 1–3, 1863). Pennsylvania native George Meade led the victorious Army of the Potomac.

When did Pennsylvania become a titan of heavy industry?

During the last third of the nineteenth century. People saw it coming, but even so, the size and strength of the Pennsylvania economy astonished them. Railroad cars carried coal; oil was spurting from the ground; forests were cut down; and Pennsylvania, at times, resembled one enormous work depot. Fortunes were made simultaneously, and unlike many other rushes, this one brought quite a few people to the top. Many of the fortunes made in the 1880s and 1890s still exist today.

How did the working class folk make their way through during those years?

Most of our reports are anecdotal, and the majority of them suggest that life was very hard. One anonymous miner had this put on his tombstone:

The Battle of Gettysburg in Pennsylvania is possibly the most famous battle of the American Civil War.

Forty years I worked with pick and drill
Down in the mines against my will
The Coal King's slave, but now it's passed
Thanks be to God I am free at last.

What was life in Pennsylvania like at the beginning of the twentieth century?

For perhaps 20 percent of the population, life could not have been better. They lived in the most modern and up-to-date homes and were kept warm in the winter by coal, which still sold for low prices. For perhaps another 30 percent of the Pennsylvania population, things weren't too bad. But for the bottom half of Pennsylvania society, life was grim. Not only did they labor long hours (and were told by the bosses to feel good about the fact they had jobs), but the air quality in the cities was bad.

When did Pennsylvania's economy take a downturn?

Up to about the year 1920, Pennsylvania continued to thrive on a combination of the oil and coal industries. After that year, however, Pennsylvania suffered from a reduced demand for coal, nationwide; at the same time, the new oil-rich states of Oklahoma and Texas deprived Pennsylvania of its former leadership in the oil industry. As a result, Pennsylvania was hard-hit during the 1920s, and when the Great Depression arrived, it could hardly have been at a worse time.

How did Pennsylvania fare during the First and Second World Wars?

World War I played an important role in the lives of many young men, but the really big event took place after the war was over. The Spanish Influenza hit Philadelphia perhaps the hardest. Thousands of Pennsylvanians died, but the single worst toll was when 800 people died in Philadelphia hospitals in one day.

World War II, on the other hand, proved a real boon to Pennsylvania's economy. The giant steelyards and shipyards of eastern Pennsylvania produced vast amounts of materiel for the war effort, and it seemed, for a time, that the good days of Pennsylvania's early economy had returned.

How important was the movie *Rocky* to the identity of Pennsylvanians?

When *Rocky* arrived in U.S. theatres in 1977, most critics anticipated a moderate turnout. Instead, millions of Americans flocked to the film, which pitted a Philadelphia underdog, played by Sylvester Stallone, against an incredibly successful African American champion, portrayed by Carl Weathers. *Rocky* was a box-office smash, and it led to six sequels.

One of the most iconic images of the movie—one that long remained in American culture—was of Stallone taking an aggressive early-morning jog. Running past the low-rise tenements of the row district, "Rocky" saw former pals and buddies who were *not* embarked on an incredible fitness program. Going past them, he reached the more fashionable part of the city, and jogged up the steps of the Philadelphia Museum of Art, raising his arms and pumping his fists in a gesture of triumph. As an example of a human beating the odds, it was unforgettable.

When did Philadelphia make a comeback?

The Bicentennial of 1976 was good for the city and the state as a whole, but prosperity did not return until the early 1990s. Even then, it was a bifurcated kind of prosperity, with many urbanites and suburbanites doing well, and many rural Pennsylvanians griping about the result.

What was life in Pennsylvania like at the turn of the twenty-first century?

A profound and rather awful feeling prevailed, the idea that the Keystone State was about to enter another of its vicious

Even though the character "Rocky" Balboa is a fictional boxer, he is so famous in Philadelphia that there is a statue of him in front of the Philadelphia Museum of Art.

cycles of bust. Something happened to transform this, however, and it was from a most unexpected source. The Keystone State had long since exhausted its major sources of petroleum, but its reserves of natural gas had scarcely been touched. And when a new process—hydraulic fracturing, better known as "fracking"—appeared, many Pennsylvanians suddenly saw a new avenue to prosperity and success.

What will the Keystone State look like a generation from now?

One thing's for sure: Pennsylvania will not lose its population to the South or Southwest. Many Pennsylvanians frankly admit that they could not conceive of living in any other state, and that they'll make it at home or they won't make it at all. One of the big unresolved questions is whether hydraulic fracturing can be done in ways that keep humans—and waterways—safe. If this is accomplished, the chances are that the Keystone State will do well throughout the twenty-first century.

RHODE ISLAND

Nickname: "The Ocean State"; "Little Rhody"
Capital: Providence
Statehood: May 29, 1790; 13th state

AT A GLANCE

What are some of the most important of the state's signs and symbols?

"Hope," the official state motto, was adopted in the seventeenth century, directly after the colony received a new, more liberal, charter from England. The sign of the state has almost always been an anchor, signifying Rhode Island's close connection to the sea. The Rhode Island red is the state bird, and the violet is the state flower. The red maple is the official state tree.

How large, or small, is the Ocean State?

Comprising 1,545 square miles (4,002 kilometers), Rhode Island is fiftieth among the fifty states, dead last. The population of 1,051,511, as enumerated in the census of 2010, reveals that Rhode Island is forty-third among the states.

How does so small a state manage to remain relevant in a time when "bigness" is so celebrated?

Rhode Islanders don't worry about this very much. They've been the smallest of all American political units since the very beginning, and it never seems to hinder them. Through the good times (the eighteenth century), the bad times (the mid-twentieth) and all manner in-between, Rhode Island has been what it is: a gem of a state set by the majestic ocean.

Is there more to Rhode Island than stunning mansions?

Yes indeed. The mansions came later, as a result of the wealth that came to the Ocean State. Long before the Astors and Vanderbilts erected their mansions, most of them in Newport, the people of Rhode Island were making money from any number of enterprises. Then, too, where nature is concerned, Rhode Island is also blessed.

The ocean and Narragansett Bay dominate, to be sure, but there are inland stretches to the state and more square miles of forest than one would expect. Ever since Roger Williams came in the 1630s, Rhode Island has been known for physical beauty, as well as economic success.

Do Rhode Islanders talk about the weather very much?

Not like the rest of us do. For about fifty weeks out of the year, the Rhode Island weather is marvelously predictable: damp and cold during the winter, amazing in spring, and a series of delights in summer. It's only during two to three weeks of the year, during the height of hurricane season, that Rhode Islanders wake up and pay attention.

Many hurricanes have lashed the Ocean State, but it generally escapes the worst, because of the way the storms "bounce" off the northern tip of Long Island. On the rare occasions when this does not happen, Rhode Island is right in the path of a hurricane, any one of which can wreak great devastation (see Rhode Island's worst day).

Can the Rhode Islander be told apart from his or her Connecticut and Massachusetts neighbors?

Yes. There's an earnest quality in the conversation that stands out from the laconic Boston style of speech. Just as important, the Rhode Islander is much more likely to be Roman Catholic than his or her Connecticut counterpart. And in conversation, the Rhode Islander tends to be more engaging, seeking to draw out his or her newfound friend.

EARLY HISTORY

For how long have humans lived in what we now call the Ocean State?

For thousands of years. How they made their living is anyone's guess, but the chances are they spent more time on fishing than hunting. When the first people of European descent arrived in the seventeenth century, they found a number of tribes in Rhode Island, with the Narragansett being the most dominant.

What the Indians thought of those first white settlers will always remain a mystery, but they soon discovered that the European peoples had very different ideas about what constitutes land ownership. And, given that Rhode Island has so little land, this led to a series of conflicts. What is most remarkable is not that there were settler-Indian wars, but that there were fewer than we might expect. Part of the credit for this rightly belongs to Roger Williams, the founder of the colony that became the Ocean State.

This 1886 engraving, based on a painting by C. R. Grant, shows Roger Williams returning to Providence in 1644 after obtaining a charter from England (the first step toward being an official colony).

How important is Roger Williams to the self-concept of the people of Rhode Island today?

It's hard to overstate his significance. Once one departs New England, Williams is little known, but in Rhode Island, he's the original founding father, and many consider him just as important—and noble—as George Washington. Williams was a Puritan minister who first arrived in Salem, Massachusetts, later infamous for its witch trials. Finding the Bay colony stifling in terms of religious orthodoxy, Williams moved to what is now the city of Providence, where he spent his first winter with the Indians. He later compiled a book on Indian grammar and is one of the most appealing of all English leaders where Indian–white relations are concerned.

Down deep, Williams may have remained a Puritan, but his religious ideas tended to the unorthodox, and many American Baptists now consider him their colonial founding father. In truth, Williams was more interested in freedom of religion than the spread of any particular faith. Rhode Island was the only colony that allowed freedom to all Christian faiths, and it also became the site of the first Jewish synagogue in North America.

Were the English first on the scene?

A handful of Dutch explorers sailed by Rhode Island, but the only one who is remembered today is Adriaen Block, for whom Block Island is named. Just twelve miles off shore, Block Island sometimes seems like its own tiny colony. It's a favorite destination for summer tourists.

381

What did Rhode Island look like in the middle of the colonial period?

The boundaries of Massachusetts and Connecticut already thwarted Rhode Island's landward expansion, and its people were already turning toward the sea. Newport and Providence both were coastal communities, with large populations, and Rhode Island was prospering through the trade in sugar, molasses, beer, and, of course, slaves.

Given that many Quakers—members of the Society of Friends—moved to Rhode Island, it seems surprising that the Ocean State would make such profits from the trade in human beings; Quakers were among the first Americans to protest the "peculiar institution." But sea captains of Providence and Newport were keen to gain money from almost any type of enterprise, and this led to a conflict between a pair of brothers, whose names are enshrined in Brown University.

How different were the Brown brothers?

John and Nicholas Brown were actually a fair bit alike. Quaker brothers, they grew up in Rhode Island and moved rather quickly from sea captains to prosperous merchants. Over time, John became a pioneer abolitionist, first questioning and then denouncing the trade in human beings. Nicholas, on the other hand, made a lot of money in the slave trade and did not question the hand that fed him. Both Brown brothers became quite wealthy, and some of their family money went to the founding of Brown University in Providence, one of the most renowned institutes of higher learning in America today.

How did Rhode Islanders feel about the coming of the American Revolution?

They were keenly in favor. One might expect that Rhode Islanders would fear the British Royal Navy, which could sail right into Narragansett Bay, but very few Loyalists lived in Rhode Island (and those who did live there did not want their identities known). Three years prior to the Battles of Lexington and Concord, men from Providence rowed out into the bay to capture and then burn a British revenue ship. The HMS *Gaspee* was the first significant loss to the British navy while patrolling the American coast, and King George III was rightly outraged. The trouble was that the king's attorneys and supporters could not find anyone in Providence willing to testify about the matter, or to identify any of the men involved.

How did Rhode Island fare during the Revolutionary War?

The Ocean State generally came off rather well. The British occupied Newport for two years, but when Americans and their French allies came to besiege the town, both a hurricane and difficult communications between the allies thwarted their plans. The British pulled out in 1779, however, and the French, led by General Rochambeau, came to Newport a year later. These men later marched all the way to Virginia to take part in the glorious campaign that culminated with the British surrender at Yorktown.

Rhode Island came out of the Revolution in rather good shape, and its skippers and sailors continued their tradition as among the best in North America. One thing Rhode

Islanders were not keen about was the new Constitution. Written in 1787, the document was submitted to the original thirteen states for approval. Rhode Island was the last state to come to the table, and it seems clear that most of its residents preferred a loose league of states to a compact new form of federal government.

What was Rhode Island's role in the early decades of the young republic?

Rhode Island shipping captains absorbed a big blow in 1808, when Congress forbade the bringing in of any more African slaves. While a slave trade still existed in the Southern states, no one could legally bring in any more human cargoes. Rhode Islanders, therefore, embarked on new areas of commerce, with a noticeable trend toward the transportation of luxury goods. Porcelain from China, ivory from Africa, and a new type of British ceramics all became part of the carrying trade for ships from Rhode Island.

Rhode Islanders displayed a surprising conservatism in one area, however. They liked the colonial charter that King Charles II gave them so well that they did not abandon it or write a new state constitution until 1843. The so-called Dorr Rebellion (in which no blood was shed) was necessary to propel Rhode Islanders in this new direction.

How did Rhode Island do during the American Civil War?

Of all the New England states, Rhode Island has the least to say about its Civil War years; one does not find the proliferation of Civil War monuments as in the state of Maine, for example. Rhode Island was one of the least-affected of all the Northern states. The Union navy controlled most of the seas, and the Rhode Island trade flourished much as in the past. If it were not for the presence of Ambrose Burnside, one hardly would know that there was a Civil War!

Born in Indiana, Burnside went to West Point, and was commissioned in the U.S. Army. He moved to Rhode Island in 1853. During the Civil War, Burnside rose to lieutenant-general, and he was briefly commander of the Army of the Potomac. Most historians believe this to be a sad case of being promoted to one's level of incompetence. Burnside was an excellent officer, one who cared about his men, but he was only a mediocre corps commander and should never have been considered for a top post. This became evident at the disastrous Battle of Fredericksburg, one of the worst losses suffered by the Union.

ENTER THE MILLIONAIRES

How did life in Rhode Island change in the decades following the Civil War?

The rich and famous, New Yorkers especially, began to summer in Newport. There had previously been some small cottages there that were much-admired; between 1860 and 1890, these were turned into immense mansions that the wealthy delighted in calling "cottages." The Vanderbilts, Astors, Whitneys, and Rockefellers all came to Newport,

383

Newport, Rhode Island, became the second home for many of New York's high society members, such as the Astors and Rockefellers.

which became the center of New York society during the summer and autumn (each fall, the staffs carefully packed everything for transfer back to Manhattan.

The parties held on the lawns of these mansions really had to be seen to be believed. Caroline Astor, who required that family, friends, and staff refer to her as "the Mrs. Astor," was the acknowledged queen of the social season till she "retired" in 1906. Almost anyone who takes the tour of the mansions, the Breakers most especially, asks the same question, "How on earth did they not go bankrupt, spending at such a rate?" And the answer is quite simple: there was no federal income tax until 1913. This means that the enormous profits the leading families earned from railroads, oil, and later from the management of utility companies remained in the same pockets for a very long time.

Was there ever any antagonism between the super-rich of Newport and the common folk who worked in the factories?

There may well have been on a deep level. In superficial contacts, however, the common folk seemed to like, or at least to tolerate, the super-rich, because they knew that these wealthy New Yorkers brought money with them. Rhode Island was almost recession-proof during the late nineteenth century, and even the Great Depression of 1929–1941 did not hurt the state as badly as its neighbors.

When did sailing become an outer expression of who was the wealthiest, as well as fittest?

The two went hand-in-hand, so far as the wealthy Rhode Island families were concerned. Any family of worth had to possess a sailboat, no matter how small; and any leading family had to own a yacht. Numerous fine paintings—many of them in Rhode Island and Connecticut museums today—celebrate the way of life of the super-rich, who basked in the sunshine on their wooden-hulled ships in Narragansett Bay, while hired hands worked the sails. To the super-rich, there was no contradiction in this; they believed they had earned their money and could afford to let other people do the work.

Did this incredible lifestyle ever end?

In some ways it never did. The luxurious style of life continued, with different social groups occupying the mansions and moving the ships. However, rather few fashionable New Yorkers go to Rhode Island these days. The Hamptons, at the outer expanse of Long Island, eventually replaced Newport as the place of choice. And quite a few families did finally run into high expenses, both from the new federal income tax and from high heating bills for their mansions. Most of the great estates are now held in trust, and quite a few are open to the public during the summer months. New money came to Newport in the 1980s, and one finds almost as many Arab oil sheikhs, aboard incredible pleasure yachts, as old-fashioned Yankee aristocrats.

What was life for the common Rhode Islander like during this time of great munificence?

In approximately 1905, Rhode Island hit its peak as the number-one manufacturing state in the nation, on a pound-for-pound basis. Of course the Ocean State could not turn out as much steel as Pennsylvania, and it had no oil to speak of, but all sorts of manufacturing concerns relocated to Rhode Island, and for a time Providence was a real workshop in the industrial Northeast. Much of the silverware used in North America was made in Rhode Island, as were many specialty items. While the workshop hours were long and often tedious, Rhode Islanders made rather decent money, and not many complaints were heard.

What was the single worst event in Rhode Island history?

Beyond any doubt this was September 21–22, 1938, when the worst hurricane of the century slammed right into the Ocean State. This enormous storm took its time coming up from the Caribbean, and Rhode Islanders, as well as their Connecticut neighbors, had plenty of warning. What no one anticipated was the sheer force of the storm, however.

All the New England states suffered to some degree, in part because this hurricane drifted over land, eventually reaching southern Canada. Rhode Island took the worst hit, however. Between 200 and 300 people lost their lives, and whole sections of the coast looked like a war zone for the next year or so. A storm surge hit Providence. There was some doubt, in the hurricane's aftermath, whether Rhode Island would ever be the same again.

How did Rhode Island fare in the decades that followed the Hurricane of '38?

Reasonably well, because the U.S. Navy located its submarine task force in Newport for much of that time. Naval traffic brought tourist, as well as sailor, dollars, and Newport also embarked on a restoration program in order to save its colonial houses (the state has more of these than any other). The completion of the Claiborne Pell Bridge, stretching from Jamestown Island to Newport, greatly assisted Rhode Island in 1965. This bridge made the state a more effective and compact economic unit.

The U.S. Navy pulled out its destroyers in the 1970s, but by then the economic comeback was substantially complete. Newport was the destination of choice for many New England tourists, and even Providence saw an increase in the number of factories and factory workers.

What is significant about St. Mary's Catholic Church in Newport?

St. Mary's parish was founded in 1828, making it the state's oldest Roman Catholic church. The current building opened on June 14, 1849. During the Civil War, the U.S. Naval Academy temporarily relocated from Annapolis, Maryland, to Newport, with St. Mary's serving as the academy's chapel. On September 12, 1953, U.S. senator John F. Kennedy of Massachusetts married Jacqueline Bouvier at St. Mary's; while Kennedy was president, the presidential couple often spent weekends in Newport and attended mass at St. Mary's.

What other interesting building is in Newport?

The White Horse Tavern, built in 1673, still exists as a tavern in Newport. According to the tavern, "the White Horse was a regular haunt for Colonists, British soldiers, Hessian mercenaries, pirates, sailors, founding fathers and all manner of early American folk." Restored in 1957, the White Horse is still serving customers in the twenty-first century—the oldest operating tavern in the United States.

How important did tourism become in the life of Rhode Islanders?

Until the 1980s, Rhode Islanders thought of tourism primarily in terms of big benefactors with deep pockets: millionaires and billionaires who came to spend their money. After about 1985, however, Rhode Island actually experienced more success with small-time travelers with light pockets: those who wanted to spend time on the state's many beaches, for example.

What was life in Rhode Island like around the turn of the twentieth century?

Rhode Island kept a low profile and was pleased to do so. The state rode out the big financial panic of 2000–2001 better than its neighbors, and all sorts of new money continued to flock to the Ocean State.

What will life in Rhode Island be like a generation from now?

One should bet on the Ocean State. Its people have shown a remarkable tendency to survive, and thrive, even in difficult times. The greatest resource of Rhode Island is its alert, industrious, and fairly humorous population of slightly more than 1 million. Rhode Islanders know what it takes to make it in the twenty-first century.

SOUTH CAROLINA

Nickname: "The Palmetto State"
Capital: Columbia
Statehood: May 23, 1788; 8th state

AT A GLANCE

What are some of the most important signs and symbols of the Palmetto State?

"Prepared in Mind and Resources" does not sound very inspiring, but it derives from South Carolina's readiness to fight the British in June 1776. There is also a second motto: "While I Breathe, I Hope." The Palmetto State also derives its nickname from the "fort of palmetto logs" that defied the British that month, denying them access to Charleston Harbor. The Carolina wren is the state bird, and the yellow jessamine is the state flower. The palmetto is the official state tree.

How large, or small, is the Palmetto State?

Comprising 32,020 square miles (82,932 square kilometers), South Carolina is fortieth among the fifty states in geographic size. The population of 4,774,839, as enumerated in the census of 2010, reveals that South Carolina is twenty-fourth among the states in terms of population.

Has South Carolina ever gotten over the fact that it was the leader of a losing cause?

Of course! South Carolinians today are proud of the fact that they stood for states' rights in 1861, but they are very mindful that this stance led them to disaster. Virtually no other Confederate state suffered more during the four years of combat. Today, South

Members of the 169th Fighter Wing, South Carolina Air National Guard, attend a class to qualify for M4 carbine operation in this 2013 photo. South Carolinians are proud of their strong support and presence of America's military.

Carolinians are much quicker to discuss how they have contributed to the national military in the twentieth and twenty-first centuries. The Palmetto State is a favored place for military retirees.

Does South Carolina possess much natural variety?

Quite a lot. Little of it is in the realm of the spectacular, but the Palmetto State has many miles of beaches, long stretches of white pine forest, and hilly sections in the interior. Much of it is taking on a Northern and suburban look these days, but as recently as 1950, South Carolina looked very much as it had a century earlier.

Do South Carolinians talk very much about the weather?

There is little reason to do so until hurricane season arrives, and when it does, the weather can block out conversations about anything else. South Carolinians are well-accustomed to the heat and humidity, but the idea of a hurricane coming to visit is their worst nightmare. Almost every store along the Carolina coast is well stocked with the ply board, nets, and nails necessary to board up buildings and boats, and the moment a hurricane warning is issued, people jump right into action.

Is South Carolina as distinctively Southern as it used to be?

For about 80 percent of the state's residents, the past is as important as ever. They know that they are Southern, and that they once fought the federal government in what they often call the War of Northern Aggression. But there are the other 20 percent, relative newcomers, to whom the events of 1861–1865 mean relatively little. South Carolina has a growing Hispanic population, and they are much more interested in where the state is going than where it has been.

Is there any one place from which one can see the best South Carolina has to offer?

If one desires companionship and activity, Myrtle Beach is probably the best answer. But for the person who desires a look at Southern culture at its best, the answer most likely is Middleton Place, the restored plantation in Charleston that has been cultivated so carefully that there is a flower in bloom every day of the year.

EARLY HISTORY

For how long have humans lived in what we now call South Carolina?

For thousands of years. The earliest Indian inhabitants lived by a combination of hunting, fishing, and light farming, and the indications are that they did quite well. South Carolina saw its first white intruders in 1540, when a group of Hernando de Soto's Spaniards came through. The record suggests that women ruled some of the South Carolina tribal groups, an anomaly in Native North America. Nearly a century and a half passed before these Indians saw other white peoples, and when they arrived, they came from the sea and spoke English rather than Spanish.

Why did it take so long for England to plant its first settlers in the Carolinas?

There seemed to be little need. Virginia was doing well, and the Virginia settlers wished for a buffer zone between them and the Spaniards in Florida. It was King Charles II, best-known as England's Merry Monarch, who took the first step toward colonizing the Carolinas. In 1669, he made a major land grant to seven of his top nobles, gifting them with all of what are now North and South Carolina. The colony was originally called

Did the Carolinians sometimes enslave Native Americans?

They did indeed, and for a time the two slave trades—one concerned with black Africans and the other with American natives—ran hand-in-hand. African slavery won out, however, because the Carolina planters, like the Spaniards in the Caribbean, discovered that black Africans would hold up and hold out against almost any hardship. Many Native Americans, by contrast, would give up and stop eating, preferring a slow suicide to life spent in slavery.

Carolina, in honor of the king, and was not separated into its northern and southern parts until 1702.

In the early days of colonization, most of the settlers came from Barbados, rather than Old England. They were English, to be sure, but the one or two generations they spent in the Caribbean proved decisive. These early settlers brought with them definite ideas about crops, plantations, and the value and even virtue of slavery. Africans were, by then, the slaves of choice, and it was therefore almost inevitable that South Carolina would become one of the strongholds for what Southerners sometimes call the "peculiar institution."

What were the major crops of Carolina during the colonial era?

The first planters attempted to plant tobacco but found it unsuccessful, and they soon turned to rice, cotton, and indigo (the last of these is used to make dye). Some of the most successful rice plantations in the Western world were established in South Carolina during the eighteenth century. And along with the profits came the belief that the South Carolina system—based on slavery—was the best to be found.

The major plantations—complete with massive manor houses in the Georgian style—did not come until the late eighteenth century, but the economic system was fully in place by 1750. Charles Town—the name was changed to Charleston during the

A tobacco barn, c. 1933, is a remnant from the history of tobacco farming in South Carolina that was a vital part of the state's economy for generations.

Revolutionary War—was the seat of government and elegant society, while the various plantations, connected by rivers and streams, were the source of the colony's wealth.

What was the Stono Rebellion?

Learning that Spanish Florida accepted black runaways, a large group of African American slaves revolted in 1739. They began marching to Florida but were attacked and massacred near the Stono River. This was one of the most dangerous of all the slave rebellions in the Southern states, and it led to newly written law codes, all of which conspired to make it impossible for slaves to read, write, or rise above their circumstances.

Do we know very much about the condition of life along the coast of South Carolina in the years prior to the American Revolution?

One of our best sources comes from a British postal inspector who made a tour of many of the colonies in 1773–1774. Hugh Finlay usually restricted his comments to the condition of the various post offices (he found a number of cases of corruption), but after traversing the coast of much of South Carolina, he wrote that the roads—if one chose to call them such—were shockingly bad and that the inhabitants seemed malnourished. On a lighter note, Finlay described the so-called Boundary House between North and South Carolina: the northern half of the inn lay in North Carolina and the southern part in South Carolina.

What role did South Carolina play in the politics of the American Revolution?

A medium-sized one. Many of the Carolina planters were not enthusiastic about the professed goals of the Revolution, which they suspected might one day lead to emancipation of the slaves. But several leading families of South Carolina, notably the Pinckneys, provided leaders in the First and Second Continental congresses. Much the same happened during the debates leading to the establishment of the Constitution. South Carolina as a whole was not eager to embrace the movement, but enough of its leading families got behind it to ensure success.

What about South Carolina's military presence in the Revolutionary War?

That was a whole different story. It was one thing to protest British taxes and import duties; it was another to feel the brunt of a British invasion. In 1776, Charleston held out against a British naval assault; the palmetto logs of Fort Moultrie, on Sullivan's Island, resisted the British cannonballs so successfully that South Carolina gained its nickname. This was only the prelude to a much-larger action, however.

In 1780, the British arrived in force and captured Charleston after a lengthy siege. The British then fanned out into the countryside, capturing towns, villages, and plantations; it seemed as if the fairest part of the South would return to British rule. But enough Carolinians resisted to make life difficult for the British, and they proceeded to make matters worse through their brutal methods. Colonel Banastre Tarleton became justifiably known as the worst of all British commanders (he sometimes killed men who attempted to surrender) and South Carolina found a new hero in Francis Marion. Best-known as the "Swamp Fox," Marion made life for the British miserable through his hit-and-run attacks. The hero of *The Patriot*, the 2000 film starring Mel Gibson, is loosely based on Marion's story.

SOUTH CAROLINA IN THE LIFE OF THE NATION

What was life in South Carolina like in the decades that followed the winning of national independence?

For the upper class, things could not have been better. Cotton increased in value almost every year, and South Carolina had enough slaves to keep things humming. For the typical black slave, things got worse in the first half of the nineteenth century. The slave codes (or laws) were written so severely as to restrict or restrain any attempt for a person to gain freedom. South Carolina was equaled only by Louisiana in terms of the severity of its slavery laws.

What was the Nullification Crisis?

In 1832, South Carolina held a special legislative session and proceeded to "nullify" or render null and void the federal law on tariffs. South Carolinians believed this was justified, because the tariff laws so clearly worked against them and in favor of Northern manufacturing states. Carolinians hoped and prayed that President Andrew Jackson would side with them; after all, he was a native, having been born in the Waxhaws, on the boundary with North Carolina. But Jackson proved a firm, even strict, Unionist. He denounced the nullification proceedings and threatened to use the U.S. army to invade South Carolina. The Palmetto State backed down, but the nullification controversy was a harbinger of the Civil War, which, not so coincidentally, began in the same state, twenty-nine years later.

How important was John C. Calhoun to the image of early South Carolina?

His name is seldom invoked today, in part because the few photographs that exist show a hard, unsmiling face, but Calhoun was practically the founding father of nineteenth-century South Carolina. Born in Abbeville District in 1782, Calhoun had some liberal qualities while he was young, but by the age of forty he became dead-set in the defense of the peculiar institution of slavery and was its number-one apologist. Calhoun developed the idea that the North was envious of the South and would do just about anything to destroy its economic system. Calhoun died in Washington, D.C., in 1850, just days after his last speech was read aloud to the U.S. Senate (he was too ill to deliver it). In this speech, Calhoun practically laid out the path to secession.

Who were the "Fire-Eaters"?

This name was given to a particular type of Southern politician, the majority of whom lived in South Carolina. The Fire-Eater promised to do what the circus entertainer did—to put the incendiary thing in his throat and yet emerge unharmed. In this case, the incendiary would be the dangerous trick of secession—departing the Union.

Why did the Civil War start in South Carolina, rather than, say, New Orleans?

Charleston and New Orleans were both hotbeds of secession fever, but Charleston won out thanks to its position on the eastern seaboard. The election of Abraham Lincoln in 1860 proved to be the final straw. On December 20, 1860, amid much fanfare and rejoicing, South Carolina formally seceded from the Union, taking its place among the nations of the world (as the secession document expressed it). Six other states soon followed South Carolina's example, and at the beginning of April 1861, there were seven states in the brand-new Confederacy.

The people of Charleston were as eager for war to commence as the Bostonians had been for the Revolutionary War, three generations earlier. Some half-hearted attempts at negotiation ended in failure, and early in the morning of April 12, 1861, the various Confederate batteries opened fire on Fort Sumter, in Charleston Harbor. One day's bombardment was sufficient to reduce Fort Sumter, and Carolinians claimed the honor of being the first to secede and the first to defeat the North in armed combat.

How could something that started so well ever go so wrong?

That is the question South Carolinians asked for generations after the war ended. In April 1861, all looked well, and South Carolina expected to dominate the new Confederacy. It would become the capital, the center of the new nation, many believed. Instead, war, destruction, and eventually ruin came to the Palmetto State.

How bad was the death, destruction, and mayhem?

Of all the fifty states in the Union, South Carolina has known the worst where warfare is concerned. World War II hardly touched American soil, but the Civil War came to the South, and South Carolina suffered the most of all.

The Union came to besiege Charleston in 1863, and two long years of fighting ended in the capture of the capital. Memorable moments, as when the all-black Massachusetts 54th Regiment attacked Battery Wagner, are not as fondly remembered in South Carolina as in the North. When the war finally ended in April 1865, much of the Carolina coast was in ruins. The economy was wrecked; the slaves were emancipated, and many

At the end of the Civil War, Charleston lay in ruins. The city paid a heavy price for being at the center of Confederate support.

white South Carolinians openly wondered if they would ever emerge from the nightmare brought by the Civil War (as well as by their own actions, in April 1861).

What was life in South Carolina like in the decades that followed the Civil War?

For black South Carolinians, there was a ray of hope, the idea that they might indeed be treated as citizens and equals. This hope was dashed a decade later, when federal troops were withdrawn, and Southern states—including South Carolina—began to write new legal codes to disenfranchise the blacks. But life for the typical white South Carolinian was not good either. Cotton still existed as a money producer, but many people, white and black alike, worked as sharecroppers, never really tasting the fruits of their labor.

Poverty in the rural areas was endemic, and public health perhaps reached its lowest point around 1900. From that point on, things began to improve, albeit in very long and slow stages. Two things that South Carolina had never anticipated came to its rescue: manufacturing and tourism.

How did South Carolina become one of the magnets for Northern industries?

Some people call it the South Carolina revenge. Others point to the economic factors. But even when all the calculations are made, it is astonishing the degree to which South Carolina took a page from the North and used it to its advantage.

Heating costs played an important role. The more that the price of heating oil rose, the more eager Northern manufacturers were to relocate to the Southern states, where air conditioning, while significant, was not as large an expense. North and South Carolina both became the states of choice, as numerous manufacturing concerns picked up and moved entire plants to the South.

How and when did tourism become so important a factor in South Carolina's economy?

Until about 1900, South Carolina was considered a backwater, and no place for a Northern person to go. This changed as Myrtle Beach rose to become one of the most fashionable and desirable of all places on the East Coast.

One could see Myrtle Beach's potential as early as 1900, but it was the dredging of nearby swamps, and the building of tourist places, golf courses especially, that really brought the tourists.

When did the change come about?

In 1901, a railway was constructed so that lumber products from the coast could be brought inland. This led to the construction of the Seaside Inn, which cost $2 a day, including meals. The war years (1914–1918 and 1941–1945) did not see much development, but the 1950s brought many tourists from the North. The so-called Great Strand now covers nearly sixty miles of the South Carolina coast, and it contains more golf courses, swimming pools, and beach resorts than any other comparable section of the South except Virginia Beach.

When did filmmaking become a significant business for South Carolina?

Thanks to its history—and numerous sponsors—the Palmetto State has been involved in the filmmaking business almost since its beginning. The real golden age for South Carolina films began in the 1980s, however, with *The Big Chill* (1983); *The Prince of Tides* (1991), *The Patriot* (2000), and *Cold Mountain* (2003) followed. South Carolina has consistently provided an excellent venue for filmmakers, and the chances are good that this will continue.

What was life in South Carolina like at the turn of the twenty-first century?

The Palmetto State had shed much, if not all, of its Confederate past, and its people seemed primed to become a model of a former Confederate state that now embraced the Yankee path to successful commerce and industry. There was a disturbing tendency to hang on to some last vestiges of the Confederate past, however; this was shown when the Confederate flag continued to be flown at the State House, in Columbia.

Where will the Palmetto State be a generation from now?

The optimist naturally claims that South Carolina will prosper, that the Palmetto State will continue on its current direction. The pessimist acknowledges all the progress that has been made but notes the state's continued vulnerability to major hurricanes, fifteen of which made direct hits on South Carolina between 1900 and 2004. If the past serves as a useful guide, the Palmetto State will weather the hurricanes when they appear. It helps that many of the state's wealthiest residents live near the coast, right in the hurricanes' path. They have proven quite willing to dig deep into their pockets in order to rebuild.

SOUTH DAKOTA

Nickname: "The Mount Rushmore State"
Capital: Pierre
Statehood: November 2, 1889; 40th state

AT A GLANCE

What are some important symbols of South Dakota?

"Under God, the people rule" is the state motto, and it also goes by the unofficial nicknames of "The Coyote State" and "The Sunshine State." Among its state symbols are the red-necked pheasant, the coyote, the honeybee, the American pasque flower, the walleye (state fish), and the Fairburn agate (state gem). Residents can belt out "Hail, South Dakota!" as the state song.

How big is South Dakota?

The state is 77,116 square miles (199,729 square kilometers) in area, making it the seventeenth largest in size. According to a 2015 estimate, the population of the state is 858,469, ranking it forty-sixth in the nation (not counting territories and Washington, D.C.)

What makes South Dakota so different from other parts of the Upper Midwest?

South Dakota borders on Iowa to the south and it looks across at Minnesota. In both cases, there are similarities, but everything about South Dakota is bigger: the sky, the plains, and of course the Black Hills, which have no parallel in North America. Along with the natural beauty, there's a brooding quality to South Dakota, inspired by two major events. First was the succession of Indian wars that left a deep scar on the people of both sides—Indian and white—and second was the terrible drought of the mid-1930s that saw many people leave the state. Of course the newcomer doesn't realize all this right away: his first perception is of the beauty of the landscape and the big empty places.

Do South Dakotans discuss the weather very much?

Some do, some don't. South Dakota receives some of the most piercing cold seen in North America, and the summers can be much hotter out of the plains than anyone anticipates. The weather can change, in South Dakota, so rapidly, that one must always keep one's face to the wind. Even the most pleasant day in August can see a sudden hailstorm, and the winter snows are legendary. This is a landscape where humans get by only with extreme exertions. One thing South Dakotans are spared is the tornadoes that strike 400 miles to the south, in Kansas. The cool air that comes down from Canada dispels most tornadoes.

Was there ever a time when the Dakotas—North and South—were more part of the national mainstream?

Only for a few brief years. In the mid-1870s, a spectacular gold rush was aimed at the western part of what is now South Dakota. And around the turn of the century, many emigrants from European nations headed straight to what is now North Dakota. But these are the rare exceptions. Most of the time, the Dakotas seem almost otherworldly.

EARLY HISTORY

How many Indian peoples lived in what we now call the Mount Rushmore State?

Four major tribes were in the region when the first white people showed up. The Cheyenne, Sioux (composed of Lakota and Dakota), the Arikara, and Assiniboine are the major tribes that were present when Lewis and Clark and the Corps of Discovery appeared in 1804.

The Indians of present-day South Dakota were primarily sedentary—meaning that they stayed in one place—until the appearance of the European horse around 1720. From that point forward, the Indian peoples became increasingly mobile and more successful in their buffalo hunts. They could not know that this golden age would be brief, because of the arrival of the white peoples.

What was life in South Dakota like when Lewis and Clark arrived?

In November 1804, Meriwether Lewis, William Clark, and the forty-odd members of the
Corps of Discovery settled into winter quarters, just a few miles from the major village

of the Mandan Indians. From Lewis and Clark's journals, we learn of the difficulties of that winter, when the mercury fell to 40 degrees below zero on a number of occasions. None of the members of the Corps of Discovery had even seen such sustained cold, but none of them died that winter. When spring came, Lewis, Clark and their men headed out, with one important addition. The Shoshone girl Sacajawea, who had been a captive of the Mandan for several years, went with them.

Was the winter Lewis and Clark experienced in 1804–1805 typical of life on the Northern Great Plains?

It was. There have been some mild Dakota winters over time, but a really fierce Dakota winter is something to behold. One positive is that one doesn't have to shovel as much as on the East Coast, because the winds are so fierce that they move the snow away from the houses!

When was the next major arrival of white people?

Fur traders began coming up the Missouri River at about the time of Lewis and Clark, but these newcomers had to adjust to the Indian way of life, rather than the other way around. It was when the steamboat *Yellowstone* made its way up the Missouri in 1831 that the lives of the Dakota Indians began to change. One of the first, and worst, of all the changes was the introduction of smallpox, which practically wiped out a number of tribes between 1833 and 1835.

The first Anglo-American forts appeared in the 1850s, and in 1861 Congress announced the creation of the new Dakota Territory, which encompassed all of present-day North Dakota, South Dakota, and large swathes of what now are Montana and Nebraska. The commencement of the Civil War hastened this move, but the Dakota Territory played no part in that conflict. Its few thousands of settlers were much more concerned with Indian conflicts, and Red Cloud's War, which raged in the middle part of the decade, was one of the few times when a Native American foe got the better of the whites.

Did Anglo-Americans realize just how different South Dakota was from the rest of the nation?

The Black Hills, in the western part of what is now South Dakota, were the most striking and obvious example of the differences: no other type of landscape in North America parallels them. And it is doubly ironic that the Black Hills are where many of the early settlers wanted to go, because they were sacred to several of the Indian tribes. The Holy Mountain of the Cheyenne Nation, for example, is very close to where gold was first discovered in 1874. The resulting gold rush in 1876 saw the Black Hills crawling with prospectors.

What South Dakota town became famous as a result of the gold rush?

Deadwood surfaced following the discovery of gold in South Dakota in the early 1870s. It quickly became known for its gambling, prostitution, and lawlessness. The most famous resident—though he was only in Deadwood for a few weeks—was Wild Bill Hickok. He fought in the Civil War but was mostly known for his involvement in many shootouts. On August 2, 1876, Hickok was playing poker at Nuttal and Mann's Saloon in Deadwood; normally he sat with his back against the wall, but not on this particular day. Jack McCall entered the bar from behind and shot Hickok in the head. The hand Hickok was holding—two aces and two eights—came to be known as the "Dead Man's Hand." Hickok and fellow Deadwood acquaintance Calamity Jane are buried in Deadwood's Mount Moriah Cemetery.

Deadwood proceeded to go through ups and downs. Mining and electricity interests helped make Deadwood prosperous through the end of the nineteenth century. Fires in 1879, 1959, and 1987 hurt the town. Gambling became legal in 1989 and Deadwood's fortunes have improved.

Was gold the only incentive that pulled people from the East Coast to move to Dakota Territory?

It was the primary incentive. Some prospectors realized that the area had other resources, however, and small numbers of farmers arrived to plant and harvest wheat. The Homestead Act allowed ambitious settlers to gain title to 160 acres of land, so long as they settled them for five years. This brought many people, and in 1889 President Benjamin Harrison signed proclamations for the establishment of two new states. North Dakota came in as the thirty-ninth, and South Dakota entered as the fortieth.

SOUTH DAKOTA IN THE LIFE OF THE NATION

Were the Indian troubles—as the settlers called them—finally over?

Not quite. In 1890, numerous tribes of the Northern Great Plains experienced a religious revival. Known as the Ghost Dance, this revival promised that the Great Spirit would eject the whites. Few Indians actually took up arms, but the state government—and then the federal—became alarmed by the possibility. The last terrible battle, or massacre, was at Wounded Knee, South Dakota, where more than 200 Indians were killed. That was the end of the Indian conflicts.

Where did the new settlers come from?

They came from all over the United States, and perhaps 20 percent of them came from Western Europe. North and South Dakota were the last areas to benefit from the Homestead Act, and thousands of people arrived each year. South Dakota experienced one perpetual boom through the 1890s, but it came to a sudden halt with a drought that began

In 1913 Lakota Indians and U.S. troops staged a reenactment of the 1890 Battle of Wounded Knee, as shown in this photo.

in 1901. This inaugurated a pattern that lasted through much of the twentieth century, with boom and bust cycles in the economy of the state.

How did South Dakota fare during World War I?

The war proved a definite boon for the economy. South Dakota produced record amounts of wheat, corn, and potatoes for the U.S. Army. This is also when a number of young men from South Dakota had their first experience of the outside world. But a second drought hit the region, beginning in 1917, and many homesteaders—or sodbusters, as they were called—gave up the fight, returning to the East Coast.

MOUNT RUSHMORE

How did Mount Rushmore come to be?

The early twentieth century was a time when great, and even good, sculptors had a field day. Many American cities wanted to commemorate their heroes from the nineteenth century, and men like Augustus Saint-Gaudens and Daniel Chester French did extremely well creating sculptures for public gardens and parks in places like Chicago and New York City. A small number of these sculptors were ambitious to do something different, to produce great works of art in rural areas. One of these men was Gutzon Borglum.

Born in the Idaho Territory in 1867, Borglum was an accomplished sculptor who made his name working on Stone Mountain, just outside of Atlanta. He was a member   403

One of the most famous landmarks in America, Mount Rushmore portrays (left to right) Presidents George Washington, Thomas Jefferson, Theodore Roosevelt, and Abraham Lincoln.

of the team that labored to create the likenesses of Robert E. Lee, Jefferson Davis, and Stonewall Jackson, but when he came to South Dakota, Borglum was eager to commemorate the heroes of the Union, not the Confederacy. He selected a mountain in southwest South Dakota and went to work.

How did Borglum decide on the four presidents to be carved, and how long did the work take?

Borglum was convinced that the greatest of the presidents were Washington, Jefferson, Lincoln, and Theodore Roosevelt (he began carving the mountain before *Franklin* Roosevelt was even elected). Borglum hired large teams of men who did most of the actual carving, while he stood below, directing their efforts. To say this was a monumental effort is an understatement. The heads of the four presidents were huge, and even Roosevelt's eyeglasses are twelve feet high.

As his work neared completion, Borglum began a series of tours to persuade notable Americans to come visit the mountain. He died in 1941, the same year that Mount Rushmore was finished. Since then, tens of millions of people have viewed the monument, one of the great outdoor masterpieces of art in the United States, or, indeed, the world.

Who was Borglum's successor?

Korczak Ziolkowski was one of the workers on Gutzon Borglum's team, and soon after Mount Rushmore was completed, Ziolkowski announced his intention to do something similar in honor of the Native Americans. After long conversations with Sioux and

Cheyenne leaders, Ziolkowski decided to build a magnificent monument in honor of Crazy Horse, one of the leaders of the Indians who fought Lieutenant Colonel George A. Custer in 1876.

Starting to work on a mountain about twenty-six miles from Mount Rushmore, Ziolkowski went to work with a will. He died in 1980, but his large family carried on his work. As of 2016, the Crazy Horse Monument is still not finished, but it is much larger even than Mount Rushmore.

SOUTH DAKOTA AND THE INDIAN NATIONS

Why is it that almost every time I hear of a major disturbance on an Indian reservation, it turns out to have something to do with South Dakota?

Most observers believe that the Indians of present-day South Dakota may have suffered more—over the last century and a half—than almost any others. First came the rush of settlement, then the last Indian wars, and for a time many Native American children were taken from their families and sent to the East Coast, to learn the ways of the white people.

The Indians of South Dakota live on a number of reservations, the largest of which is Pine Ridge, in the southwestern part of the state. Living there, within seventy-five miles of Mount Rushmore, they are particularly conscious of how the Anglo-American civilization trampled them, in its incredible haste to take over the entire North American continent. Perhaps we should not be surprised to hear that so many disturbances take place in South Dakota.

What happened at Pine Ridge in 1971?

The activist group American Indian Movement (AIM) had searched for some time to find a proper avenue to reach the American public. It had already held protests in New York

How many films have been made in South Dakota?

It would make a very long list, because there is something special about the afternoon light that bathes much of the state. Of all those having to do with Native American themes, *Dances with Wolves* and *Thunderheart* stand at the top of the list. In the former, a U.S. Army officer is charmed and seduced by the free life of the Sioux Indians he meets; in the latter, an FBI agent struggles with issues of his own identity (he is half Indian). For the many millions of Americans who have not seen South Dakota, watching these films is almost as good as being there.

and San Francisco, but it made sense to utilize the Black Hills of South Dakota to make a strong symbolic stand.

AIM members took over Wounded Knee, the section of the reservation that had seen the end of the Plains Indian Wars. For roughly seventy days, they held the area, arousing intense feelings on the part of many white Americans (many sympathized strongly, while numerous others were incensed). When the "siege" finally ended, there was one person dead and several hundred arrested. AIM intended for the event to kick off a series of Native American protests around the nation.

What discovery was made in Hot Springs, South Dakota, in 1974

In 1974, construction crews were preparing an area for new housing in Hot Springs, located in the far southwestern part of the state. A worker found some bones, excavation followed, and the discovery of mammoth bones was made. The bones have been left the way they were found and are part of a museum and excavation site known as Mammoth Site of Hot Springs. One theory has it that 26,000 years ago, a cavern collapsed and young mammoths fell into a sixty-five foot hole, unable to escape.

Which South Dakotan was on the losing end of the biggest presidential landslide in history at the time?

U.S. senator George McGovern, a native of Avon, was the Democratic presidential nominee in 1972. At the time, he had been in the Senate since 1963. His task: taking on incumbent Republican president Richard Nixon. McGovern could garner only seventeen electoral votes: fourteen from Massachusetts and three from the District of Columbia; Nixon won 520 votes (and over 60 percent of the popular vote). Nixon soon thereafter became embroiled in the Watergate scandal and resigned in 1974; McGovern continued to serve in the Senate until 1981. The 1984 presidential election, in which Ronald Reagan defeated Walter Mondale, surpassed the Nixon-McGovern results in the "lopsided victories" category.

THE LOUDEST EVENT

What is the single loudest event that takes place in South Dakota, a land known for its brooding quietness?

Located almost due north of Mount Rushmore, Sturgis is a quiet Midwestern town most of the year. But when the annual biker rendezvous takes place for a few days each year, Sturgis becomes nearly the loudest place in all of North America.

First held in 1938, the Sturgis motorcycle event takes place the first full week of August. Perhaps 20,000 Harleys and other brands of motorcycles converge on Sturgis, generating an unprecedented amount of noise. For most of the motorcyclists, the event is the highlight of their year, a demonstration of personal freedom, but for many Native Americans, Sturgis threatens the peacefulness of Butte, one of the holy mountains of the Sioux and Cheyenne. In recent years, there has been an unwritten rule that motorcyclists do not attempt to climb, or zoom up, the holy mountain.

Where will the Mount Rushmore State be a generation from now?

The chances are that the current trends will continue. South Dakota will remain one the smaller, less-inhabited states of the nation, but it will continue to be a place that generates controversy, much of it heated.

TENNESSEE

Nickname: "The Volunteer State"
Capital: Nashville
Statehood: June 1, 1796; 16th state

AT A GLANCE

What are the major signs and symbols of the Volunteer State?

"Agriculture and Commerce" is the official state motto, adopted in 1987. For some states, this might sound rather routine, but Tennessee has altered its identity significantly in recent decades. Once known as the land of tobacco and moonshine, Tennessee now aggressively markets itself and its products to the rest of the nation.

The mockingbird is the state bird, and the iris is the state flower. The tulip poplar is the official state tree.

How large, or small, is the Volunteer State?

Comprising 42,114 square miles (67,776 kilometers), Tennessee is thirty-fourth among the fifty states in geographic size. The population of 6,495,978, as enumerated in the census of 2010, reveals that Tennessee is seventeenth among the states in terms of population.

Is there any one spot, or place, from which the tourist can view the best that is Tennessee?

Tennesseans love their mountains and rivers so passionately that many individuals will select different places as the "one best spot," but for the outsider the choice is clear: Lookout Mountain, near the southeast border of the state. Lookout Mountain forms

409

part of the end of the Appalachian mountain chain, and it looks down on a scene that is truly sublime. The Tennessee River makes an abrupt turn here, and the mist rising from nearby mountains allows for a truly amazing sight. Of course there are days, and times, when Lookout Mountain is itself shrouded by clouds or mist; it was on one such occasion that the "Battle Above the Clouds" was fought in 1863.

Just how seriously do the people of Tennessee take their natural surroundings?

The typical Tennessean—and of course it is difficult to find this precise person—is proud of his or her family, country, and state, usually in that order. He or she is most impressed by natural beauty and cannot understand why anyone would ever move away from a place like Tennessee.

To be sure, there are newcomers and outsiders as well, but they, too, often fall under the spell of the natural surroundings. Everyone knows that Tennessee has many mountains and valleys; less known is that it has more miles of natural waterways than any other state except Alaska.

Do Tennesseans discuss the weather very much?

No. Six months of the year are downright hot; four are muggy, rainy, or a combination of the two; and two are chilly. There have been the rare occasions when Tennessee became very cold, as in the winter of 1917, but these are exceptions.

The warmest temperature ever recorded was 113 degrees F at Perryville on July 29, 1930. The coldest—and this comes as something of a shock—was –32 degrees F at Mountain City on December 30, 1917.

Can Tennesseans be told apart from their neighbors in northern Georgia or southern Kentucky?

Beyond a doubt. Tennesseans are more talkative than Georgians and less expressive than Kentuckians. They do not feel the need to talk up the many wonders of their state: they leave these for outsiders to discover for themselves. Tennesseans find common cause with some of the rural folk of Georgia, but they are bemused, and sometimes irritated, by all the attention paid to the great metropolis of Atlanta. Don't people know that the Southern life is the rural life?

EARLY HISTORY

For how long have humans lived in what we now call the Volunteer State?

For thousands of years. There are not as many mounds in Tennessee as in Mississippi, for example, but there's plenty of evidence that people lived here and that they had rather successful cultures.

By the time the first white explorers arrived, Tennessee was shared by the Creek, Cherokee, and Chickasaw. These tribes were relatively friendly with one another, but if there was a major conflict, there was no doubt that tribal loyalty trumped all others.

Who were the first Europeans to pass through?

Hernando de Soto's Spaniards passed through parts of Tennessee, but they did not stay very long. Subsequent Spaniards skirted the state, and the yellow flag of Spain never flew over the region. René-Robert Cavelier de La Salle, the great French explorer of the Mississippi River, passed by Tennessee, but he never saw any of its interior, and France, likewise, did not make any progress in what could have been an attempt at settlement. Even England, however, did not make much headway at first. Tennessee was just far enough inland, and just on the other side of the Appalachian Mountains, making it difficult for the Europeans to colonize or settle.

Therefore, it was left to the Anglo-Americans who were involved in fighting for their independence from England to become the first settlers of Tennessee. They entered the area in the 1770s, but not until the early 1790s did they develop a good-sized population. In-between those dates, the mountain men of Tennessee became famous for their quickness to the draw and eagerness to solve what should have been political matters with the draw of a gun. In many ways, Tennessee was the first Wild West.

How important was Andrew Jackson to the making of Tennessee?

He is so important, even today, that one cannot really draw a parallel. One can mention that Abraham Lincoln was important to the self-concept of the people of Illinois, but by the time he moved there, in his early twenties, Illinois was in the process of becoming settled. When Andrew Jackson arrived in Tennessee, it was the true frontier, and he was one of a trickle of daring individuals willing to leave the relative safety of the East Coast for the wilder, more rugged life in the mountains.

Leaving his native South Carolina, Jackson arrived in Tennessee in 1788. He rose to become a land speculator, a leader of the local militia, and a judge, but it was as a military man that he acquired the most fame. Jackson led the Tennessee militia to victory over the Creek Indians at the Battle of Horseshoe Bend in 1814, and one year later, he led Southeast frontiers-

Andrew Jackson, who went on to become the seventh president of the United States, was a military hero in Tennessee.

411

Was the young Andrew Jackson a duelist? And if so, was that typical of Tennessee?

Actually he remained a duelist till he was well into middle age. Jackson fought an impromptu duel in downtown Nashville in 1813; he wounded Thomas Hart Benton, with whom he later collaborated in national politics. Jackson was a hot-tempered Irish American, and he was one of the foremost examples of the Tennessee tendency to shoot first and ask questions afterwards.

men to victory over the British at the Battle of New Orleans. Given his military success and popularity, it is not surprising that Jackson became the seventh president of the United States, serving from 1829 to 1837.

Why is Tennessee known as the Volunteer State?

Volunteer soldiers serving under General Andrew Jackson's command in the Battle of New Orleans during the War of 1812 displayed courage and bravery, leading to the state being known as the Volunteer State.

What was the most important natural event in recent Tennessee history?

Some might point to the numerous twisters that pass through, and others might say that the ice storm of 2009 was one of the largest events, but the one that affected the landscape more than any other was the New Madrid Earthquake of 1811. Centered in New Madrid, Missouri, the quake was so powerful that the Mississippi turned and ran in the opposite direction for several days. A huge amount of water overflow from the Mississippi created Reelfoot Lake, in extreme southwestern Tennessee, a visible effect of one of the largest of all natural events in recorded history.

Where was the Natchez Trace, and how did it become so important to the future of Tennessee?

The Trace runs 444 miles from Mississippi to Nashville. It follows what was once an Indian trail that ran through the lands of the Mound Builder peoples. The Trace was developed in the mid-nineteenth century, and many legends and curiosities—including ghosts and haunted areas—have sprung up around it. Today the Trace remains a single-lane highway, enabling the visitor to slow down and enjoy the scenery.

How important is Davy Crockett to the image of the Tennessean?

Crockett stands just one step behind Andrew Jackson (the two knew each other) as the number one hero of the state of Tennessee. Born near Limestone in 1786, Crockett established his reputation both as a frontier warrior (he was at the Battle of Horseshoe

Bend) and as a bear hunter (he claimed to have killed over 400 in total). Beyond this, however, Crockett was a genuine wit, and one wonders how famous he might have become had radio or television arrived during his lifetime.

Crockett served Tennessee in the U.S. House of Representatives, where he popularized the coonskin cap and plain speaking. His best-loved expression was "Just be sure you're right—then go straight ahead." He might have gone on to even greater success, but in 1836 he went to Texas, just in time to participate at the Siege of the Alamo. We don't know who was the last American, or Texan, standing, but many of the popular images focus on Crockett, showing him wielding his rifle and knife to the very last.

How did Tennessee fare in the antebellum years, those leading up to the Civil War?

Tennessee never really thrived like some of its Deep South neighbors. The state had plenty of good soil—and tobacco earned money for many planters—but the quintessential Southern society, complete with plantation owners and numerous black slaves, never took hold in the Volunteer State. As a result, when the crisis came in 1861, Tennesseans were by no means certain they wished to depart the Union.

Today we usually look at the Volunteer State as split in three parts: the eastern, central, and western. But in 1861 the state was composed of ardent Confederates in the southern part, ardent Unionists in the northern, and quite a few people of lukewarm persuasion in-between. Secessionist fervor was not strong enough to take the state out of the Union until the first guns were fired at Fort Sumter; that, and President Lincoln's subsequent call for volunteers, was enough to bring about a vote in favor of secession.

How did Tennessee fare during the Civil War?

Terribly. Like Kentucky, Tennessee was right on the edge between North and South, and its people actually suffered ravages from the armies of both sides. Then, too, Tennesseans often fought each other in major battles, such as Shiloh and Stones River. Thousands of Tennesseans were killed, many other thousands were wounded, and the farmlands of the state were subjected to continued expropriation.

One of the most important battles fought in the Volunteer State was at Lookout Mountain, overlooking the vital railroad center at Chattanooga. The Army of the Cumberland ejected Braxton Bragg's Confederates in November 1863, and many claim that the Confederates did not stop running till they reached the border with Georgia. When the war ended, a year and a half later, Tennessee's economy and, to some extent its society as well, lay in ruins.

How did Tennessee eventually pull itself off the floor (where the Civil War had put it)?

The tobacco industry came back fairly rapidly, but with a new labor system. Tennesseans were among the first to use sharecropping, which clearly benefited the owner of the   413 land much more than the tenant farmer. It can be argued, however, that Tennessee had no choice, that this was the only means by which to engineer a comeback.

Moonshine was another means by which Tennesseans made money, or at least did better in the barter economy. Numerous Irish and Scots-Irish lived in the mountains of Tennessee, and they proved adept at pioneering new types of liquor (Jack Daniels being a prime example).

What is unique about one of Tennessee's most famous citizens?

Andrew Johnson was born in North Carolina in 1808 and lived there until he moved briefly to South Carolina in his teens. In 1826 he moved to Greeneville, Tennessee, where he started his long political career. Johnson is unique in that he served at every level of government: Greeneville alderman, Greeneville mayor, state representative, state senator, U.S. congressman, state governor, U.S. senator, state military governor, vice president, and president. Johnson's term as president ended in 1869; six years later, he was again elected U.S. senator, representing Tennessee, one of the few ex-presidents to continue in politics after the presidency. However, he served not quite six months when he died of a stroke on July 30, 1875.

What was the single worst event in Tennessee history?

In the summer of 1878, Memphis and its outlying areas were hit by a cholera epidemic, by far the worst in the history of the Volunteer State. Several thousand people died that summer, and there was no bright spot because no one developed a plan for handling future outbreaks. Tennessee lagged behind many of its neighboring states in terms of public health well into the twentieth century.

When did the Tennessee rifleman suddenly reemerge into the national consciousness?

Born in a two-room log cabin near Pall Mall, Tennessee, in 1887, Alvin York was just a typical Tennessean, albeit with some special skills at hunting. He attempted to be a conscientious objector in World War I, but his case was denied, and York was sent to France to serve in the last campaigns of the Great War. During the Meuse-Argonne Offensive of the autumn of 1918, York performed something so unusual, so truly spectacular, that many people have openly wondered if it were even possible. In one single day—October

27—he killed nearly twenty-five Germans and brought more than one hundred of them in as prisoners. The difficulty with fully authenticating the story is that York did not regard himself as a hero, so he was unwilling to give the types of interviews that today would be considered the norm. That he performed most of the heroic deeds is accepted; that the Germans he captured were war-weary and ready to capitulate also seems to be part of the formula. But in the months and years that followed, York became a very special case, a modern example of the sterling qualities of the American frontiersman.

What is the TVA, and why is it both so important and so controversial?

When Franklin Roosevelt came to the White House in 1933, he initiated a series of public programs known collectively as the New Deal. One of the cornerstones of his work was creation of the Tennessee Valley Authority (TVA), passed by both houses of Congress in 1933. FDR wanted to expand the amount of electricity available to people in greater Tennessee, as well as parts of Kentucky, Alabama, and Mississippi. The best way to do this, he declared, was to harness the great power of Tennessee's many rivers, including the one of that name. Toward that end, many engineers, technicians, and government officials went to Tennessee and, generally speaking, found themselves unwelcomed.

To be sure there were Tennesseans who liked the idea of electricity for all, but the devil of the plan lay in its particulars. Many elderly people were slowly coerced into selling their homes to the TVA, and when all else failed, the government agency could expropriate the land. Many nasty scenes followed, with some evictions and hard feelings all around. Not even the end of the Great Depression removed all the negative attention, and the TVA—still around today—has had more than its share of controversies over the decades.

Is there any way in which the TVA can be called an outstanding success?

Yes, indeed. Had the TVA *not* been established and performed its work, there would today be millions of people in Tennessee either without electric power or with only minimal access (this has become even more important, because of the widespread use of computers and the Internet). When the TVA was established, the entire 40,910 square miles of the area used only 16,000 kilowatt hours per year. Today this same area uses more than 165 billion kilowatt hours. To be sure, all the rivers that have been damned cannot account for that difference; today, the TVA gains only 10 percent of its electricity from water sources.

What was the Scopes Trial, and why is it so important in the story of Tennessee?

In 1925, a young high school teacher in Dayton was charged with having taught the theory of evolution to his students (he had). John Scopes was not a crusader, but his case brought the attention of others who were. Famed defense attorney Clarence Darrow came to Dayton to offer his services; likewise, Midwestern crusader William Jennings Bryan lent his hand to the prosecution. At stake was whether a choice would be offered, or if the students of Tennessee schools would only be taught the story of creation as described in the Bible.

The trial was sensational, not least because of the intense heat of the summer of 1925. The judge took the proceedings from the courthouse to the lawn before the climactic event, when Bryan agreed to take the stand as an expert witness, on the subject of biblical creation. Darrow made Bryan twist and squirm during the two-hour cross-examination, at the end of which nearly all fair-minded persons agreed that Darrow had the better of the confrontation. In the end, the trial, sometimes called the Scopes Monkey Trial, came to a successful end for the prosecution. Scopes was found guilty and fined. Evolution was not taught in Tennessee schools until the late 1960s. But for most people who watched, and for others who read about the event, it seemed that a corner had in fact been turned, that a majority of Americans were willing to hear about evolution as well as the Bible.

John Scopes was a teacher from Dayton, Tennessee, who was found guilty of teaching evolution to his students in 1925.

When did country music become so important a part of the cultural life of Tennessee?

Music has been important to Tennesseans from the very beginning; their Scots-Irish ancestors were the best fiddlers on the East Coast even before they moved into the mountains. But organized music, as in the Grand Ole Opry, had its beginnings in the 1920s. Recording technology had come far enough that young talents, whose voices and instrumentality used to be confined to a twenty-square mile area, suddenly became known to thousands, and then hundreds of thousands, of listeners.

Radio was the breakthrough component that allowed the music of the Tennessee mountains and the Kentucky bluegrass to reach the rest of the nation. In the early days of country music, there were a great number of talents, and only a limited amount of air time. Radio listeners therefore paid deeper attention to the few stars who emerged, and country music built its way to a grand future.

When did country music become a big business?

Some critics would claim that it was one even before 1980, but from that date forward, the country music scene has increasingly been led by only a handful of true superstars, crowding out the other talents, many of whom are only just a few steps behind, in terms of musical ability. Nashville has produced many of the best-loved of all country singers. Johnny Cash did not come from Tennessee—Arkansas was his home state—but he did a lot to make Nashville famous. So did Dolly Parton. Born near Sevierville in 1946, she was the fourth of twelve children, and she grew up in a mixture of poverty and home-spun happiness. Those who remember Dolly from her youth claim she never showed any doubt she would rise above her early circumstances and become a major star.

What national tragedy occurred in Memphis in 1968?

Civil rights leader Martin Luther King Jr. was in Memphis to support striking African American sanitation workers when he was shot to death on the balcony of the Lorraine Motel on the evening of April 4, 1968. A memorial service was held the next day in Memphis; two days later, two funerals were held in Atlanta—a private ceremony at Ebenezer Baptist Church, where King and his father were pastors, and a public ceremony at Morehouse College.

How important does Elvis Presley remain to the culture, as well as tourism, of Tennessee?

Elvis hailed from Mississippi, but his last years were spent at Graceland, his mansion in Memphis. When "the King of Rock and Roll" died suddenly in 1977, there was a major outpouring of grief, but few people suspected his former home would become a virtual shrine to the man and his times. Millions of tourists come to Graceland every year, making Elvis the single most-adored of all American singers.

What was the turning point for modern Tennessee?

There was a gritty, sometimes grimy, look to Tennessee in the 1970s; it looked as if the twentieth century had passed the state by. This changed in a hurry when it was an-

Graceland in Memphis was Elvis Presley's home for the last years of his life. Today it is a hugely popular tourist attraction.

nounced that Knoxville would host the World's Fair of 1982. Eleven million people came to Knoxville, which dressed itself up for the occasion.

The theme was "Energy Turns the World," and all sorts of futuristic gadgets were displayed, many of them influenced, poetically at least, by the recent phenomenal success of the film *Star Wars*. It is astonishing how many of those gadgets eventually did find their way into normal American life.

What was life in Tennessee like at the turn of the twentieth century?

It was a mixture of the old and the new, the Confederate and the Unionist, and the rural and city scene. Tennessee has long embraced differences, and the state shows no alteration in that pattern.

What does the future hold for Tennessee?

Some mean-spirited critics claim that the Volunteer State has seen its best days, while admirers say that the best is yet to come. Given the importance of the rural life to the people of Tennessee, it seems likely that many of the new leaders will come from country folk, whether in politics or music, and that the ever-increasing urban areas will be the scene where their talents are showcased.

TEXAS

Nickname: "The Lone Star State"
Capital: Austin
Statehood: December 29, 1845; 28th state

AT A GLANCE

What are some of the major signs and symbols of the Lone Star State?

"Friendship," the official state motto, harkens to the fact that *Tejas*—a Native American word—means "friend." The mockingbird is the state bird, and the bluebonnet is the state flower. The pecan is the official state tree.

Is there anything small about the state of Texas?

Not if you ask its residents. They are accustomed to being number one and the largest in almost everything. Even when Alaska surpassed Texas as the largest state in the Union, Texans mostly shrugged. That land was only good for polar bears, they said.

It's been this way since the beginning of Texas history. The land was bigger than anything previously seen, and the people took on both an outsized ego and an oversized approach to all their projects. Texas, therefore, doesn't just have oil wells, it has the "oil business." Texans don't just play football; they make it the center of their week (Friday evenings are pretty much reserved for that purpose). And when the space industry came to Texas in the 1950s, this became another reason to celebrate the size and power of the Lone Star State. Of course, the earliest Texans had to do some building along the way, to make everything turn out so spectacularly.

How big is the Lone Star State?

Comprising 268,820 square miles (696,200 square kilometers), Texas is second among the fifty states: only Alaska is larger. Texas is roughly the size of France, and the two can be compared in other ways. Both have gregarious, expansive people, and both contain far more natural variety than one perceives at first glance. Texas's population of 25,145,561, as enumerated in the census of 2010, means that the Lone Star State is also number two in terms of population, surpassed only by California.

Is Texas one long row of flat plains?

It is far more than that. While most of Texas is indeed flat and hot, there are surprising riverbed canyons and all sorts of variety in the landscape. Often overlooked are the hundreds of miles of coastline, making Texas one of the most coastal of all states. It's true that Texas views sometimes start to look the same, and that the state lacks the mountains of its neighbor, New Mexico. Very few people would call Texas boring, however.

Do the people of Texas discuss the weather very much?

Not like they used to. Prior to the advent of air conditioning, the weather was perhaps the number-one topic of conversation throughout Texas, and even today the state regularly breaks previous records for heat and humidity. But modern conveniences have made a very big difference.

Is there anything resembling J. R. and the Ewing family in Texas culture?

Dallas, which ran on CBS between 1977 and 1989 and on TNT between 2012 and 2014, was one of the most successful programs in television history. Millions of Americans, even today, can instantly identify the music that came on when the camera focused on Southfork Ranch, the Ewing mansion outside of Dallas. The program took a stereotype—the aggressive Texas oil man—and turned it into a caricature, displaying J. R. as a maniacal despot and most of the rest of the family as his hapless fools.

There was no actual Ewing family that played a major role in the development of the oil industry. But there was—and is—the King family that established the King Ranch around 1853. The clan's founder hailed from upstate New York, and in a relatively short time he became the owner of 50,000 head of cattle and a ranch that was bigger than the state of Rhode Island.

EARLY HISTORY

For how long have humans lived in what we call the Lone Star State?

For thousands of years. There were no mound builders in Texas, and the population may have been rather thin, but there have been people in the region for a very long time.

When the first white explorers and settlers arrived, they found Texas populated by at least four tribes and a scattering of smaller subdivisions.

Who were the first Europeans to see Texas and live to tell the tale?

Álvar Núñez Cabeza de Vaca

There may be some others we don't know about but Álvar Núñez Cabeza de Vaca, a Moor among a group of exploring Spaniards, was the first to leave a good record. In 1534, Cabeza de Vaca was shipwrecked off the coast of Texas. He and his fellow explorers made desperate attempts to return to Mexico City but went in the wrong direction and spent years wandering the plains of Texas and the high altitude country of New Mexico. Cabeza de Vaca finally made it to Mexico City in 1547, where he related his story to Franciscan friars. Most of what he reported has been verified.

Rather few Spaniards followed Cabeza de Vaca's footsteps. They had their hands full settling Mexico and did not, as yet, see much importance in the land called Texas. It took an incursion by French explorers to wake up the Spaniards.

How did a fur-seeking Frenchman ever wind up on the plains of Texas?

It's one of the saddest of the early explorer stories. René-Robert Cavelier de La Salle, is, of course, the daring Frenchman who canoed all the way down the Mississippi River to the Gulf in 1682, and who then claimed all the land for King Louis XIV of France. Returning to the fatherland, La Salle persuaded Louis XIV to fund a settlement on the lower Mississippi River. Just about everything that could go wrong did so.

Lightning storms struck the fleet. Tools were mislaid. Worst, by far, is that the pilots overshot the mouth of the Mississippi River. Believing he was 300 miles further east than was really the case, La Salle kept on sailing, till he landed on the coast of Texas (the wreck of one of his ships has been excavated). After building Fort Saint Louis, La Salle watched the last of his ships head home for France. Months later, completely out of supplies, he made a desperate attempt to reach Canada by walking overland. He was not as lucky as Cabeza de Vaca. Shot and killed by one of his own men, La Salle died a lonely death in the Texas desert (the precise spot has never been identified).

What did Spain do in response to the La Salle expedition?

Spain was jolted out of its lethargy. Over the next decade, at least five major expeditions—both by ship and on land—were sent from Mexico City. The Spaniards wished to eradicate La Salle's tiny settlement; they found it already destroyed by the local Indians. These exploratory journeys started a new burst of Spanish interest in Texas, and a number of missions, planted in order to convert the Indians, grew during the early eighteenth century. Had Spain been stronger, she might well have made a new empire in Texas; as it was, she was only able to hang on to little sections of the vast area.

When did Anglo-Americans first become aware of Texas?

We don't know the precise date, or the first time that Texas was mentioned in an American newspaper, but we are certain that the remote area inspired interest and speculation, right from the beginning. Early in the nineteenth century, small groups of Americans departed New Orleans on their way to Texas. Some of them attempted to stir up trouble for the local Spanish authorities, and "gringo" became a byword for troublemaker.

Spain, meanwhile, lost its imperial group. Mexico overthrew Spanish rule in a decade-long revolution, and the new Mexican republic was established in 1823. By then, Americans were looking with even greater longing at Texas, and a handful of land grants had been issued. One of the largest of these went to Moses Austin (who hailed from Connecticut). He died just before leaving, and leadership of the small colony of Americans passed to his son, Stephen Austin.

So the first Americans in Texas were not lawbreakers or desperadoes?

They were not. The first Americans to move to Texas had to swear loyalty to the Republic of Mexico and membership to the Roman Catholic Church. They do not seem to have taken either oath terribly seriously, but they were content to leave well enough alone, until the government in Mexico City applied pressure on them.

Mexico outlawed slavery in 1830, and this applied to a considerable number of Americans who had brought their slaves to Texas. A series of negotiations followed, with the Americans in Texas refusing to go along with the federal government in Mexico City. This was not the only reason the Texas Revolution began in 1835, but it was a factor.

THE LONE STAR REPUBLIC

Is "The Alamo" as important as we usually hear?

Beyond any doubt. In March 1836, Mexican general Antonio López de Santa Anna arrived at The Alamo, in present-day San Antonio, with 6,000 well-armed and well-trained soldiers. The Alamo was defended by about 185 men, many of them Texans, but with a sprinkling of men from elsewhere, including Jim Bowie and Davy Crockett. The Americans refused to surrender, and after a week-long siege, the Mexicans stormed and took the place, at a cost of about 1,500 casualties. "Remember the Alamo" immediately became the rallying cry of the Texas revolutionaries.

The Alamo in San Antonio is a well-preserved historical site and popular tourist attraction, as well as a rallying cry for Texas pride.

What we often forget is that "Remember Goliad!" was equally important. Weeks after capturing the Alamo, Santa Anna captured roughly 300 Americans at the Battle of Goliad. In the aftermath of the battle, Santa Anna decided he did not wish to feed all his prisoners, so he had them shot in the back. The massacre at Goliad was just as important as the loss at The Alamo in inspiring Texan Americans to fight.

When did Texas finally win its independence?

In May 1836, just two months after the Battle of The Alamo, Texas leader Sam Houston surprised and completely defeated the Mexicans at the Battle of San Jacinto (a towering granite monument marks the spot today). The captured Santa Anna signed a treaty under which Texas gained its independence. Not surprisingly, the government in Mexico City declared that it was signed under duress and refused to honor the agreement, but Texas had accomplished its beginning as an independent nation.

Many Texans wished to enter the Union right away, but the U.S. Congress was deeply divided over the issue of slavery. To bring in Texas in 1836 seemed as if Congress were intending to advance the cause of the "slave interest." For nine years, therefore, Texas was an independent nation, with its own president, vice president, and legislature. Houston served as one of the most important of the early leaders.

TEXAS IN THE LIFE OF THE NATION

When did Texas finally enter the Union, and what kind of issues did that raise?

President John Tyler set things in motion, but it was during the presidency of James K. Polk that Texas finally entered the Union as the twenty-eighth state. Almost immediately,

Mexico declared that Texas still belonged to it, and part of the U.S. Army was sent to defend the Texas border. To make matters even worse, Texas claimed the Rio Grande as its southern extent, while even the moderate factions in Mexico City demanded it be set at the Nueces River.

The Mexican War began in the spring of 1846. That the United States would prevail was never in doubt. Texans played a big part in driving into northern Mexico and conquering a large area of land (all of which was returned under the eventual peace treaty). Perhaps most important, from the American point of view, is that so many New Englanders and Midwesterners saw Texas during the war. Many of these Northerners became entranced with the Lone Star State, and quite a few eventually moved there.

How did Texas fare in the years just before the Civil War?

The Lone Star State boomed. The population reached a quarter of a million, as people from all over the United States headed to Texas to gain large sections of land. Cattle formed the number-one source of wealth, but cotton came on strong.

Was there any chance Texas would stay out of the Civil War?

The Lone Star State would have done itself a great favor by doing so. But in the winter of 1861, as they watched other Southern states drop out of the Union, Texans began a drumbeat that led to their ordinance of secession, which passed the legislature on March 1. Old Sam Houston, then the governor, tried to talk his fellow Texans out of it. He told them that they were mistaken in thinking that Northern and Eastern men were weak; the Northerners were slow to anger, but once it built, they would fall on the Confederacy with the power of an avalanche. Houston's words were ignored.

How did Texas fare in the Civil War itself?

Very badly. Texas was one of the original seven Confederate states; the legislature chose to depart the Union in March 1861. Governor Sam Houston was deposed, after he warned his fellow Texans not to underestimate the fighting power of the North.

The Civil War was one long, unrelieved agony for the Lone Star State. Many of its finest young men went off to serve in Virginia and never returned (Houston's son died at the Siege of Vicksburg, for example). Thousands of cattle either were lost, or were driven off by bandits. It's not too much to say that the Lone Star State was on its knees when the war ended in 1865. Even then, some holdouts decided they could not live under the Stars and Stripes. A few thousand of them went south to Mexico to offer their services to Emperor Maximilian. Having been an important part of one losing cause, they now embraced another!

How and when did the Texas economy recover?

The emancipation of the black slaves hit the Texas economy hard. Cotton became less profitable in the years that followed. Cattle, however, became a mainstay. The Texan had

> ## Is it from this period that Texans got their image as men with six-shooters?
>
> It is. The mid-to-late nineteenth century saw the rise of a special type of Westerner, the Texan armed with rifle and six-shooter. Quite a few of these fast-shooting Texans were on the right side of the law—such as the Texas Rangers—but many were not!

already shown himself an excellent Indian-fighter and tracker; he now began to excel as a cowboy. In the height of irony, some of the most successful of these new cowboys were recently emancipated African Americans, some of whom pioneered the cattle trails from the plains of Texas to central Kansas.

In and of itself, the cattle industry was not sufficient to bring the state's economy all the way back, and Texans began to diversify. The seaside city of Galveston, laid out in the 1870s, became a model for the new Texas, industry and commerce existing side-by-side. In the boom years of the 1890s, Galveston was the exemplar of the new Texas. And then disaster struck.

What was the single worst day of Texas history?

On September 8, 1900, the very year that the Texas oil industry was making its first steps, an enormous hurricane barreled down on the city of Galveston. Roughly 8,000 people lost their lives, as the sea water crashed over all the primitive defenses (the locals had none of the foreknowledge that we today have come to expect). Galveston lay in ruins, and the Lone Star State had lost the best example of its new success.

Texans have faced many difficulties and danger, from flash floods to tornadoes, but the hurricane of 1900 represented the single greatest loss of life and property that they have ever witnessed. It seemed for a time that Galveston would be abandoned. The site was so good, however, that Galveston was rebuilt, with a brand-new sea wall. To date, the sea wall has done its work, and Galveston has not been ravaged again.

When did Texas become known as the land of big oil?

In 1901, the first good-sized oil well was discovered at "Spindletop" near Beaumont, Texas. That first well gushed for nine days before it was capped. During that time, Texans became aware of the precious resource that lay beneath their feet.

Pennsylvania had, till then, been the center of the oil industry, and many technicians migrated from the Keystone State to Texas. Big production began in the 1920s. Oil men from Texas then branched out to other parts of the country, and even the world. Quite a few of the men who pioneered the Saudi Arabian oil industry in the 1930s and 1940s came from the Lone Star State.

425

How large a role did Texas play in World War I and World War II?

Texas mobilized for World War I, but the East Coast states had the jump on the Lone Star State, simply by virtue of their location. World War II was a whole different ballgame though, with Texas supplying hundreds of thousands of young men for the Armed Forces, and with the state seeing a huge increase in its trucking, hauling, and shipping capacities.

The years immediately following World War II saw the Lone Star State boom. One reason it did so well in the U.S. Congress, obtaining pork-barrel projects, is that Lyndon B. Johnson was the leader of its delegation. Born in Stonewall in 1908, LBJ—as he was best-known—was a U.S. House representative from 1937 to 1949 and a U.S. senator from 1949 to 1961, serving as majority leader from 1955 to 1961. In 1960, he made an unsuccessful attempt at the Democratic presidential nomination, but became the vice presidential running mate of John F. Kennedy. The pair won the election in the fall.

What was the most fateful day in Texas history?

While the Galveston hurricane of 1900 was the worst natural event to occur in Texas, Dallas and Texas history remain fixated on another disaster: the assassination of President John F. Kennedy. On the morning of November 22, 1963, President Kennedy, Vice President Johnson, and Texas governor John Connolly met at the airport to commence a motorcade through the streets of Dallas. Ugly rumors about Dallas's hostility to the president had circulated, but on that day, first lady Nellie Connolly pointed to the cheers, and declared, "Mr. President, you can't say Dallas doesn't love you." Just moments later, shots rang out.

President Lyndon Johnson takes the oath of office after John F. Kennedy's assassination in 1963 (at right is Kennedy's widow, Jacqueline Kennedy).

Governor Connolly was injured, but the president was killed. Vice President Johnson was speedily sworn in as the nation's thirty-sixth president, and *Air Force One* returned to Washington, D.C.

How good was LBJ to his home state?

Because he had been known as one of the kings of pork-barrel legislation in Congress, President Johnson did not engage in much while in the Oval Office. He did bring much publicity to Texas, however. Just weeks after the assassination, he hosted his first state dinner, and did so at the Circle Bar Ranch, the 43,000-acre estate he'd purchased from his aunt many years earlier. This state dinner was held outside, under tents, and it specialized in Texas-style barbecue. It was a first for the nation.

How did Texas fare during the lean years, so far as oil production was concerned?

Texans have long since become accustomed to boom and bust; even so, the decline in international oil prices during the late 1980s caught them off-guard. Not for a decade did prices recover, and by then Texans were as keen on natural gas as oil.

What is the American "town" identified solely with disaster and its prevention?

Established in 1998, the self-described "mock community" of Disaster City, located in College Station, Texas, concerns itself with one type of job: training for disaster. Fire crews train here, as do specialists in putting out fires on oil rigs. Disaster City has more than proved its worth.

When did the Bush family become so identified with Texas and its politics?

George H. W. Bush (1923–) was the first scion of a Connecticut family to move to Texas. He used the state as a springboard to the U.S. House of Representatives, various high-level political jobs, the vice presidency, and finally the presidency in 1989. His son, George W. Bush, was much more of a native Texan. Even though he went to prep school and college on the East Coast, the younger Bush seemed much more authentically Southern than his father. George W. Bush won the Texas gubernatorial race in 1994, and then—to the surprise of many—became the Republican presidential nominee six years later. He won the elections of 2000 and 2004.

What did the people of Texas think of LBJ?

It was remarkably similar. To non-Texans, LBJ seemed like the epitome of Texan arrogance, spending money like water, and living high on the hog. To his fellow Texans, it seemed that LBJ did not go far *enough*, as if the Washington, D.C., establishment had co-opted him. Johnson was, therefore, not well-loved either in the nation or his home state.

What was life in Texas like around the year 2010?

The state was much more ethnically divided in the past, with Hispanics nearly surging to form the majority of the population. Plenty of Texas towns were divided between their respective Anglo and Hispanic communities. At the same time, however, Texas seemed to form the single best hope of the nation for ethnic integration.

Where will the Lone Star State be a generation from now?

As of 2016, Texas is the second most populous state, and it will most likely remain in that position (it's difficult to see how it could catch up to California). The ethnic composition of Texas will continue to move in favor of Hispanics. As long as oil and natural gas remain in high demand, the Texas economy will continue to hum along.

SPORTS/ATHLETICS

How important is football in the Lone Star State?

It's about as big as baseball, football, and hockey are in most other states, combined. Texas weather seems tailor-made to the production of excellent football players and

Football is huge in Texas, almost as huge as the state itself. Whether it's pro ball (the Dallas Cowboys skirmish with the Houston Texans in this 2010 photo), college, or high school, it's all good in the Lone Star State.

teams. Friday nights are pretty much reserved for high-school football: one doesn't make other plans on Fridays in the fall.

How did the Dallas Cowboys become "America's Team"?

There were plenty of rivals, other teams that would love to have claimed that distinction. But the Cowboys became number one in public relations during the late 1970s, when Roger Staubach was their outstanding quarterback. Huge amounts of money were subsequently spent both on a new stadium and on the famous Dallas Cowboy Cheerleaders, who are often featured on cable television. The result was that Dallas became the best-known and most recognizable of all NFL teams.

UTAH

Nickname: "The Beehive State"
Capital: Salt Lake City
Statehood: January 4, 1896; 45th state

AT A GLANCE

What makes the Beehive State so dramatically different from the other states of the Union? Sometimes when I'm in Utah, it feels as if I'm actually in a different nation.

The two-part answer can be phrased swiftly: geography and religion. But to go deeper, one must examine both the natural conditions of the state and the remarkable religious impulse that gave it birth. There is no other state like Utah, no other where the hand of nature and the works of man have created so distinct a place.

What are some important symbols of Utah?

"Industry" is the extremely simple motto of the state and pretty much captures the attitude of its people. Among its state symbols are the Rocky Mountain elk, the sego lily, the quaking aspen, and, for the state bird, the interesting choice of California seagull.

Do the people of Utah talk about the weather?

Not to any great extent. On seven days out of ten, Utah is favored by early sunrises, cloudless days, and magnificent sunsets. Utah does experience the occasional tornado, as well as some flash floods, but the single greatest danger is almost certainly that posed by forest fires. Winter brings some cold days and snow, but it seldom prevents people from enjoying a combination of outdoor sports that puts their East Coast contemporaries to shame.

How big is Utah?

One of the large western states, Utah has an area of 84,897 square miles (219,882 square kilometers), which makes it the thirteenth-largest state in the Union. There are 2,995,919 residents in Utah, per recent estimates, which ranks it thirty-first in the nation.

Can the Mormon man or woman be readily detected?

Yes, and most of the time the noted differences reflect to the advantage of the Mormon. He or she is unfailingly friendly and helpful to strangers. The Mormons have built some of the most close-knit communities in North America.

EARLY HISTORY

For how long have humans lived in what we call the Beehive State?

They've been here for thousands of years, but they never existed in any great number until the last two centuries. The earliest Paleo-Indians probably admired Utah for the same reasons we do, but they found it exceedingly difficult to eke out a living. The area's population remained low, therefore, until the first descendants of Europeans arrived, and it must be said that they formed one of the strangest of all contingents of pioneers.

Who were the Native Americans of what we now call Utah?

The Ute Indians—for whom the state is named—were one of about a half-dozen tribes that wandered this landscape. Utah forms a big part of what sociologists call the "Empty Quarter," the section of the nation that has the fewest inhabitants. The reason is simple: the lack of water.

Very likely there were only about 30,000 Indians in all of Utah. They were among the last Indians—anywhere in the entire United States—to become aware of the white people and their settlement patterns. This is because the Oregon Trail did not carve through Utah, and because many of the migrants to California, especially during the Gold Rush of 1848, went by sea. If not for the Mormon Church, and the need of its people to find a new home, Utah might have remained relatively unsettled for another half century.

Who were the first white people to arrive in Utah?

Legendary explorer Jim Bridger was quite likely the first white person to see the Great Salt Lake, sometime in 1824. Others followed him, including the highly individualistic Jedediah Strong Smith and federal explorer John C. Frémont. All of these early visitors expressed admiration for the area, but none of them believed it was feasible to start a settlement in the region, due to its dryness and isolation.

What brought the Mormons to Utah?

Formed by Joseph Smith in the 1830s, the Mormons call themselves the Church of Jesus Christ of Latter-day Saints. Their beliefs are not readily understandable to many outsiders. From their earliest days, the Mormons demonstrated qualities of personal responsibility, loyalty to family, and thrift that distinguished them from their neighbors. Perhaps they are best remembered for their belief in polygamy, the marriage of one man or woman to multiple members of the opposite sex. (It is claimed that Brigham Young had more than twenty wives). Polygamy, plus the differences between Mormonism and other Christian faiths, led to the persecution of Mormons in Ohio, Missouri, and Illinois. Kicked out of all these areas—and following the assassination of Smith in 1844—the Mormons decided to get as far away from other white Americans as possible. In 1846–1847, the new leader, Brigham Young, led a remarkable group of pioneers nearly

Joseph Smith, founder of the Mormon Church.

2,000 miles, through the Great Plains and over the Rockies. Tradition has it that he was the first to sight the Great Salt Lake, and that he raised his hand and declared, "This is the place" (a state park honors the memory of that moment).

How did the Mormons fare in the first decade of their settlement of Utah?

They colonized the Great Salt Lake region in record time, and this remains the most thickly settled part of the state today. The Mormons had great ambitions, however, and they originally named the area the State of Deseret (which means "honey bee" in Mormon). The more the Mormons explored and colonized to the south, the more they came into conflict with non-Mormon settlers on their way to California. These encounters led to some brush fights and the savage massacre of approximately 200 emigrants in 1857. Learning of this, President James Buchanan sent federal troops to restore order in the region. He removed Brigham Young as territorial governor. The so-called Mormon War lasted for less than a year, but the federal troops remained for three. By the time they departed, the majority of Mormons were reconciled to the painful fact that they had escaped their former neighbors in the Midwest but were still under the rule of the Stars and Stripes.

Is Utah still dominated by the Church of Jesus Christ of Latter-day Saints (the Mormon Church)?

Not to the degree it was, say, fifty years ago. The Mormons remain the single most dynamic presence in the Beehive State, however, and almost any fair-minded visitor will conclude that they are among the most productive, industrious, and creative of all the nation's inhabitants.

433

Utah differentiates itself from its neighbors (such as Nevada and Idaho) through its friendliness; few states take in the outsider as readily as the people of the Beehive State. The assumption, upon the first meeting, is that the outsider is a good and useful person, and that he or she can be trusted.

What was the original capital of the Utah Territory?

The small town of Fillmore, named after U.S. president Millard Fillmore, was the capital of the territory from 1851 to 1856. The legislature moved the capital north to the larger Salt Lake City, and the capital remained there when Utah became a state in 1896. The original Utah Territorial Statehouse still stands in Fillmore today and is used as a museum.

Did Utah play any role in the American Civil War?

Virtually none. President Buchanan wished to humble the Mormons, and he succeeded to at least the half-way point, but President Abraham Lincoln only cared that the Mormons reject any advances made by the Confederates. Other than this, he was willing to leave well enough alone. It was during the 1880s, however, that the federal government began enforcing its laws against polygamy, and nearly 1,000 Mormons were fined and imprisoned. Even the new leaders of the Mormon Church (Brigham Young was now deceased) urged the faithful to abandon the practice. In 1895, Utah submitted a new state constitution to the U.S. Congress. The document—which renounced the practice of polygamy and made plain that Utah was not a theocracy—was accepted, and Utah attained statehood on January 4, 1896.

What was the single most dramatic moment in the history of Utah?

The entire nation claims the glory, but Utah was the place where the Central Pacific and Western Pacific railroads linked up on May 10, 1869, completing the establishment of the first transcontinental railroad. The driving of the so-called "Golden Spike" took place in the little town of Promontory, just to the east of the Great Salt Lake.

What was life in Utah like at the beginning of the twentieth century?

Most of the conflicts between the Mormons and the federal government were at an end; the same cannot be said for issues between Mormons and gentiles in Utah. There were

A photo of the Central Pacific and Western Pacific railroad teams meeting at Promontory, Utah, linking the country together with the first transcontinental railroad.

frequent brush fights between the two groups, with neither side prevailing. On a happier note, the economy of Utah chugged along merrily at this time. The irrigation systems the Mormons had created accomplished marvelous things in the desert, and the per capita income of most Utah residents was well above the national average.

When did Utah become such a haven for government agencies and installations?

This happened between World War I and World War II. As better railroad systems ran across Utah, the federal government realized this would be a great place for the storage of top-secret programs. Not all of them are known to the general public, even today, but the U.S. government continues to see Utah as one of the "solution" areas to its problems of space.

Today, the federal government owns about 65 percent of all the land in Utah, and the state government owns another 7 percent. Still another 4 percent is reserved for Indian use. This means that the great majority of the population lives in a narrow settlement area, between Ogden and Provo.

How did Utah fare during the two world wars?

In both cases, the conflict overseas proved a spur, even a boon, to the Utah economy. The state was still a major agricultural exporter as late as 1950, but the first new industries

435

contributed as well. As a result, Utah came out of both world wars in better shape than when the nation entered.

When did the Bonneville Salt Flats become so important to the world of auto racing?

The first races were run in the 1930s, but it was the 1950s that saw the explosion of the sport. No racer—whether from the East or West Coast—could possibly dream up a better location than the Salt Flats. Terrific visibility, amazing dryness, and wonderful flat drives make for terrific auto racing. Some of the cars recently used at the Salt Flats have exceeded 600 miles per hour.

When was the Mormon Tabernacle built, and how did its choir become so world-famous?

This is yet another example of Mormon ingenuity. Within two decades of first arriving in Utah, the Mormons completed the tabernacle, which is off-limits to non-believers. The tabernacle has the world's largest organ, with nearly 12,000 pipes, and the Mormon Tabernacle Choir, composed of 360 members, is one of the best in the world. The simple answer is that the Mormons are imitators, building off the best that other cultural and religious groups have accomplished, but that they perform almost everything with a special flair. Very likely it helps that Mormons have been trained, from their earliest days, to be team players, who work for the good of the religious whole, rather than concentrating on individual accomplishment.

How successful were the Olympic Winter Games of 2002?

There was some concern that the Salt Lake City region would not be able to pull it off, economically, but the fears proved groundless. The 2002 Games were a smashing success; they highlighted the many charms of the Beehive State. Former Massachusetts governor and future Republican presidential nominee Mitt Romney was lauded for his success as the CEO of the Salt Lake Organizing Committee. Members of the 1980 gold-medal-winning U.S. hockey team had the honor of lighting the Olympic cauldron.

What was life in Utah like at the turn of the twenty-first century?

The Mormon Church was, if anything, bigger and more prominent than before. Millions of Americans—many of whom had never seen the Beehive State—were now aware

Why is there an affinity for "z's" with the names of Utah sports teams?

Teams just seemed to like to have fun with the "z" (and, more often, "zz"). A list of the teams (both major and minor leagues and both active and inactive): Utah Jazz, Salt Lake Buzz, Utah Grizzlies, Utah Starzz, Utah Catzz, Utah Freezz, Utah Blitzz, St. George Pioneerzz, Orem Owlz, and Utah Blaze.

of the Mormons because of their missionizing activities. And if the Mormons were gaining acceptance in the United States, they were skyrocketing in their success in foreign lands: virtually all young Mormons embarked on a two-year missionizing tour.

The Beehive State continued to present a bifurcated appearance, with religion dominating among the common folk, and quiet, even secret federal government agencies doing much work behind the scenes. The natural scene continued to be extremely important, however, drawing millions of tourists each year.

VERMONT

Nickname: "The Green Mountain State"
Capital: Montpelier
Statehood: March 4, 1791; 14th state

AT A GLANCE

What are the most important signs and symbols of the Green Mountain State?

"Freedom and Unity" is the official state motto, but the symbol of the state is the magnificent Green Mountains, which run up the western part, forming a spine to the geography of the whole. The hermit thrush is the official state bird, and the red clover is the state flower. The sugar maple—sign of the state's maple sugar industry—is the official state tree.

How large, or small, is the Green Mountain State?

Comprising 9,617 square miles (24,908 square kilometers), Vermont is forty-fifth among the states in geographic size. The population of 625,741, as enumerated in the census of 2010, reveals that Vermont is fiftieth among the states in terms of population. Numbers do not tell the entire story, however. To the tourist driving through, Vermont seems large. This is both because of the mountains and the relatively small population: there seems to be more open space than in most other states east of the Mississippi.

Why do Vermonters tend to stay Vermonters?

This is one of the great questions having to do with the Green Mountain State. Its people endure frigid winters, and its young people experience lower economic prospects than in many other states. Spring and summer are tantalizingly short, and autumn, in all its glory, leads only to the challenge of another winter. And yet they remain.

Young Vermonters often leave for a year or two, even three or four, but they usually return. Time spent in Boston or New York generally persuades them of the incredible charm of their native state, where mud season is long but the country air is priceless.

For how long has Vermont been one of the most pristine of states?

Pretty much for its whole existence. Vermont never had any big-scale industry other than logging, and the skies were clear and blue throughout the nineteenth and twentieth centuries. Unlike its neighbor, New York, Vermont has never had to perform a major clean-up to remedy the ills of the past. But the present state of absolute loveliness is largely a product of legislation enacted in the 1960s and 1970s.

Realizing they had something special, Vermonters passed a series of laws making it difficult for outside industries to move in, and protecting the clean air and water of the Green Mountain State. Very few billboards are seen along Vermont's highways, part of the plan to reduce human presence.

Is there any one place where a person can view Vermont at its finest?

Many places exist where a person can see a lot, but the single best view is generally from the west side of Lake Champlain, toward the end of a long, cloudless summer day. Standing near the dock in Burlington, for example, the tourist can make out the Green Mountains to the right, the Adirondack Mountains of New York to the left, and the big shiny blue water of Lake Champlain in-between. As the sun slowly disappears over the Adirondacks, the tourist is struck by the extent of the natural beauty, and he or she begins to see why Vermonters tend to remain Vermonters.

Is there such a thing as a typical Vermonter?

The type has been altered by the appearance of many exurbanites since around 1970, but it still exists. The typical Vermonter is male, in his forties, and is the father of three children. He is strong, rugged, and thoroughly dependable. Rather than the vanities of urban or suburban life, he is pleased to dress in overalls and go about the business of working the farm, which, in many cases, has been in the family more than three generations.

Vermonters tend to be laconic, meaning they don't speak as much as other people do. The most famous case of this was Calvin Coolidge, a native of Plymouth Notch,

President Calvin Coolidge, a native of Plymouth Notch, epitomized the stereotype of the tight-lipped Vermonter.

who became the nation's thirtieth president in 1923. Coolidge was so tight-lipped that when a gregarious woman sat next to him at a dinner party and remarked that she'd made a bet she could get more than two words out of him, Coolidge gave a thin smile and replied, "You lose."

EARLY HISTORY

Who were the first inhabitants of what we call Vermont?

The Abenaki, whose name translates to "Dawnland People" are the ones we know the most about. They lived in the northern parts of what are now Maine, New Hampshire, and Vermont. The Abenaki were proud of being the first people to see the dawn of each day; this is especially true of those who lived on the coast of Maine.

When the first white peoples showed up, early in the seventeenth century, the Abenaki took a long look and decided that the French-Canadians presented less of a threat than the Anglo-Americans to the south. Over the next 150 years, the Abenaki were the staunchest allies of the French, and they often went south to attack English settlements in the French and Indian Wars, which raged, off and on, between 1680 and 1760.

When did the first permanent settlements appear?

The French-Canadians came south to establish a few settlements in the Champlain Valley, but it was the Anglo-Americans, coming from Massachusetts and New Hampshire, who really settled the land. As soon as the final French and Indian War ended in 1760, white settlers came to Brattleboro and Dummerston in the state's southeast corner, and they went from there to populate many, but not all, of the state's numerous hillsides and river valleys.

Vermont was not one of the original thirteen colonies. Rather, it was a contested area, with both New Hampshire and New York claiming what they called the "Hampshire Grants." The start of the American Revolution was a good thing for Vermont, because it staved off what might have been a really ugly contest between New York and New

Who are the two most influential of all Vermont farm boys?

Many candidates could be selected, but the two who had the largest effect were Joseph Smith (1800–1844) and Brigham Young. Both grew up on hardscrabble farms in central Vermont, and both became leaders of the Church of Jesus Christ of Latter-day Saints, better known as the Mormon Church. Their activities and careers took them far from Vermont, but the two leaders are remembered as Vermont farm boys who made good.

Hampshire. And when the Revolutionary War ended, Vermont called itself an independent republic for nine years. Not until 1791 did it join the Union, as the fourteenth state.

Did Vermont play any role in the chest-thumping that led to the Civil War?

No. It just wasn't the style of the Green Mountain State back then (it still isn't today). Once the war began, however, Vermont sent many of its finest young men to fight. No major Civil War leader emerged from Vermont, perhaps because so many Vermonters were farm boys, eager to get home and plant the next crop. Vermont is known, however, for being the only Northern state to be invaded from the north. This happened in 1864 when a group of Confederates snuck in from Canada and briefly occupied the town of Saint Albans.

Did Vermont have any outstanding statesmen of the late nineteenth century?

Justin Morrill, who served in the U.S. House of Representatives, presented the novel idea of establishing land-grant colleges, where the science of farming could be taught. The Morrill Land Act of 1864 accomplished this, and the University of Vermont, in Burlington, was one of the first to be founded.

What was Vermont best-known for during the late nineteenth century?

Time seemed to have passed the Green Mountain State by, and this did not concern its residents very much, as they cherished their place as one of the slow-growth parts of the nation. What they did point to with pride was the state's success in logging and the cutting of marble; many major national monuments have been carved with stone from Vermont.

The logging industry fell on hard times during the 1920s, and things got even worse during the Great Depression. Looking for new products to market, Vermonters began to produce maple sugar in greater amounts than before and ship it over long distances.

Who was the single most famous outsider to spend a short, but exciting, time in Vermont?

Beyond a doubt this was Rudyard Kipling. The poet of the British Empire, he was born in India but grew up in England and spent much of his life on the road. He and his wife settled in Brattleboro at the time of their marriage, and they built a fine-looking Victorian mansion on the outskirts of town. A few years later, Kipling had a much-publicized fistfight with his brother-in-law, and the Kiplings moved to England, never to return. During his time in Vermont, he wrote *The Jungle Book II*, and *Captains Courageous*.

What is the story of Calvin Coolidge being sworn into office?

On an August night in 1923, Vice President Calvin Coolidge and his wife Grace were at his father's home in Plymouth Notch, Vermont. Coolidge was awakened after a telegram arrived, declaring that President Warren G. Harding had died of a heart attack in San Francisco. Coolidge and his wife dressed and went downstairs, where his father, John Coolidge, a notary public, administered the presidential oath of office to his son. The ceremony was conducted under the light emanating from a kerosene lantern. Though it's not impossible, it's safe to say that it's very unlikely this event will ever be replicated.

Our image of the Vermonter working hard alongside his or her sugar maple tree essentially dates from the 1920s. But the other big "new" thing was skiing.

Why did it take so long for skiing to take off (figuratively speaking)?

The Green Mountains have been there for thousands of years, and the people have been present for more than two centuries, but it was not until the 1930s that skiing even had a tiny following. Vermont, New Hampshire, and upstate New York were the leaders, with the first ski lift and ski resort coming in the 1930s, but it was the advent of new and improved skis in the 1950s that really made the difference.

Then, too, the opening of new roads, with faster automobiles, allowed people from Connecticut and even New York to reach Vermont for a weekend of skiing. It's safe to say that if the outsiders had not come, skiing would have formed a small part of life in Vermont and that it never would have created a whole new industry.

Did the advent of the ski industry coincide with a change in Vermont's political landscape?

No one would say there was a one-to-one correlation, but it's a good bet that many of the newcomers—whether they came for a weekend or every weekend of the year—tended to be liberal Democrats. Vermont had a long tradition of being one of the most conservative of the Eastern states, and this changed in the 1960s.

How important was the University of Vermont in this political transition?

The University of Vermont, on the top of the hill that makes up Burlington, has long been one of the nation's finest. John Dewey, the father of the progressive movement in American thought, taught here for many years. But the 1960s saw a big change at UVM, with the professors more liberal and the students more activist. Rather than join in demonstrations, students tended to join the Peace Corps or other international agencies instead. By about 1980, the transition from conservative to liberal Vermont had been accomplished, even though plenty of backcountry farmers complained bitterly about the noise of the liberals in Montpelier (the state capital).

When did Vermont and New Hampshire become like "ships in the night," meaning that their politics and culture diverged?

As late as 1936, the year Vermont and New Hampshire both bucked the national trend and voted against Franklin D. Roosevelt, the Green Mountain State and the Granite State seemed in tandem. The 1940s was the crucial decade in which they diverged. Since about 1945, Vermont has been increasingly liberal-progressive, while New Hampshire has emerged as a bastion of rock-ribbed conservatism. The two states gaze at each other, across the Connecticut River, but they are not close culturally, economically, or politically.

How important was Norman Rockwell to the image of twentieth-century Vermont?

Rockwell was not a native of the Green Mountain State, but over time he became perhaps its most skilled propagandist, through the power of his paintbrush. Rockwell painted scenes that could have belonged to many parts of the United States in the 1920s, 1930s, and 1940s, but most critics believed—correctly—that he based many of his subjects on people he knew in Vermont. There is something about the gossipy but good-hearted neighbors, seen in paintings like the one that shows a team of telephone tag, that simply echoes of Vermont.

When did the hills become alive with the sound of music?

In 1965, Americans flocked to the newly released *The Sound of Music*, starring Julie Andrews and Christopher Plummer. Featuring an irresistible soundtrack, the film shows the struggles of an Austrian nobleman, with nine children, and the housekeeper who becomes his wife. Millions of moviegoers in 1965, and countless others who've since seen it on TV, simply delighted in the charming story of the Von Trapp family, who fled their beloved Austria for America. The hills refer, of course, to the mountains of Austria, famous for their skiing, but they could refer equally well to those of Vermont, because that is where the Von Trapp family relocated.

The Von Trapps were neither as good-looking nor as charismatic as portrayed in the 1965 film, but they did come to Vermont, where they founded the Ski Lodge at Stowe. Over many years, many guests at the lodge heard stories of the family's escape from Austria, and their Vermont lodge

Artist Norman Rockwell's paintings were often seen as exemplifying the life and beauty of Vermont.

resembled their homeland. A fire in 1980 destroyed the original lodge, but a new one re-placed it. The Von Trapp family still owes the complex.

When did those same hills come alive with the sight of enormous puppets?

Bread and Puppet Theater was founded in Vermont in the early 1970s. From the begin-ning, the organization intended to have an outsized impact on public opinion, and its puppet makers therefore built some of the largest ever seen. We tend to think of pup-pets as hand-held, but some of these were twenty or thirty feet high. Most of the pup-pets made in the 1970s focused on the environment and the caustic approach to it by corporations. "The Boss," an especially effective puppet, showed an oblivious American businessman, puffing on his cigar.

Bread and Puppet started small, but in the 1990s it became an enormous event, with perhaps 100,000 people attending a three-day weekend, usually in August. The fes-tivities, held in Glover, Vermont, in the Northeast Kingdom, have become a favorite with today's counterculture.

How did ice cream become so associated with a green lifestyle and the state of Vermont?

Two native New Yorkers, Ben Cohen and Jerry Greenfield, founded Ben & Jerry's in downtown Burlington in the summer of 1978; their migration to Burlington echoed the theme of many first-generation Vermonters of that time. Originally, there was noth-ing unique about Ben & Jerry's Ice Cream; it was the number of flavors, usually associ-ated with countercultural heroes, that made the stuff famous. Cherry Garcia, for example, is named after Jerry Garcia of the Grateful Dead. Many observers believed Ben & Jerry's to be a fad that would fade, but the opposite happened. Since about the year 2000, a whole new generation of young Americans have grown up on Ben and Jerry's Ice Cream, and they show no signs of defecting to another brand.

What was life in Vermont like at the turn of the twenty-first century?

It was remarkably similar to what it had been a half-century earlier. Route 89 did carry motorists from White River Junction to Burlington with greater speed than in the past, but the scenes they witnessed were nearly identical to those of 1950: long sections of farms, with great numbers of Jersey cows, the occasional twisting river or stream, and then, about two-thirds of the way to the destination, the amazing sight of the Champlain Valley below and

Jerry Greenfield (left) and Ben Cohen, the founders of Ben & Jerry's Ice Cream, which is headquartered in South Burlington, Vermont.

445

the Green Mountains above. Vermont and its people were little-changed, but there was one area where the state really needed improvement. For all its wonderful scenery, Vermont has become particularly vulnerable to air pollution, and several public-interest groups promptly responded to the challenge.

POLITICS

How did Vermont, with its strong rural traditions that emphasize the traditional family, become the first state in the nation to recognize civil unions?

In 2000, the Vermont legislature became the first in the United States to recognize civil unions between persons of the same sex. At the time, it seemed like a truly revolutionary move, and many people marveled that Vermont, instead of California or New York, led the way. As it turns out, Vermont was but a few years ahead of the nation as a whole, and in 2015, the U.S. Supreme Court recognized the legality of same-sex marriage.

Is it possible Vermont will ever again send a person to the Oval Office?

Vermonters remember that Chester A. Arthur, born near the Quebec border, and Calvin Coolidge, who hailed from Plymouth Notch, both became presidents. More recently, Democrat Howard Dean made an inspired, but ill-timed run for the Democratic nomination in 2004. Politicians from other and large states often scoff at Vermont, saying it is far too small ever to establish a base for a national candidacy. In the spring of 2015, however, Senator Bernie Sanders heeded the call of many of his constituents and announced his candidacy for the Democratic nomination.

Sanders was yet another newcomer, having arrived in Burlington in the 1960s. He ran for and became that city's Socialist mayor in 1981, and then became the only Vermont member of the U.S. House of Representatives in 1991. Moving from there to the U.S. Senate in 2007, Sanders became known for his iconoclastic style. Devoted to veterans and military families, and a strong advocate of same-sex marriage, Sanders was not a typical Democrat or even Independent. In the best of Vermont traditions, he was a real maverick.

446

What is the controversy surrounding the birthplace of President Chester A. Arthur?

It has long been claimed that Chester Arthur, twenty-first president of the United States, was born in Fairfield, Vermont, about fifteen miles south of the Canadian border. But some believe he was actually born in Bedford, Quebec. Arthur's father, William, was born in Ireland and didn't become a naturalized American citizen until 1843, fifteen years after Chester was born. Arthur's mother, Malvina, was a U.S. citizen, but her family had emigrated to Canada, near the Vermont-Quebec border. Frequently visiting Malvina's family nearby, some believe Chester may have been born during one of these visits. In those days, if an American baby was born on foreign soil, U.S. citizenship would pass to him or her if the father was also a U.S. citizen; but William was not. This would have made Chester a Canadian citizen.

The opposing Democratic Party hired a lawyer to look into the situation, but by the time his contention that Arthur was Canadian made it into book form, Arthur's term was nearly over and no further action took place. Arthur, who became president following the assassination of James A. Garfield, made only a mild, and unsuccessful, attempt at seeking the nomination in 1884, and, in fact, died only a year and a half after he left office.

VIRGINIA

Nickname: "The Old Dominion"
Capital: Richmond
Statehood: June 25, 1788; 10th state

AT A GLANCE

What are the most popular signs and symbols of the Old Dominion?

"Thus Always to Tyrants," the official state motto, dates to Revolutionary times. The American dogwood is the official state flower, and the cardinal is the state bird. The American dogwood is the state tree.

How large, or small, is the Old Dominion?

Comprising 42,775 square miles (110,787 square kilometers), Virginia is thirty-fifth among the fifty states in terms of geographic size. The population of 8,260,405, as enumerated in 2010, shows that Virginia is twelfth among the states in terms of population.

Is there any one place from which one can view the totality of all that makes up Virginia?

No, but if one were to make the attempt, he or she would do well to stand somewhere where the Blue Ridge Mountains are at their most majestic. This, the separation between the flat midlands of the state and the soaring mountains of its western part, is the area that speaks most to the wonders of Virginia, a place that has kept relevant, culturally speaking, through more decades and generations than any other. Massachusetts has its Pilgrims and its Puritans, but Virginia has Captain John Smith and Pocahontas.

What do they mean by the license plate "Virginia Is for Lovers"?

The state board of tourism has never made it explicit, and we can therefore surmise what is meant. Virginia is for lovers of culture, of horses, of Civil War reenactments, and so forth. Virginia is for lovers of Virginia Beach, the Shenandoah Valley, and the memories of Jamestown and Colonial Williamsburg. Does this mean the people of Virginia are more talkative and friendly than those of other, neighboring states? It sure seems like it!

Is Virginia one of the last holdouts of the old Anglo-Saxon culture that once seemed so dominant across the United States?

Not in real ethnic terms; the state has plenty of recent immigrants. But in its cultural heritage, Virginia seems like a place that has only known noble-born Englishmen and women who know how to ride horseback and hunt foxes. One certainly can dismiss this, saying it is all a cultural construct, but the constructs around which we build our thoughts and expressions tend to endure. The chances are that Virginia will continue to show off its long history, and that it will only enter the modern world on its own terms.

EARLY HISTORY

Who were the Native Americans of what we now call Virginia?

Humans may have lived in Virginia for thousands of years, but we can only speak to those who were there when the first white settlers arrived. In the spring of 1607, almost 200 colonists showed up on three ships. Coming into Chesapeake Bay, they arrived at a place where the water was so deep that they could tie their ships to trees. From that immediate need arose the village of Jamestown, the great-great-grandfather of Virginia, and of much of Southern culture in the entire United States.

Why are the Jamestown settlers so little celebrated when compared to the *Mayflower* Pilgrims, for example?

An excellent question. Most of the great nineteenth-century American historians lived either in New England or New York State, and they therefore extolled the virtues of their first settler groups, rather than those that came to the South. Then, too, the ugly memories of the Civil War led many Northerners to disparage the South and its people. Therefore, the *Mayflower* people, and the Puritans who settled Boston and Salem, are much better-known, even though the Jamestown colonists eventually claimed a larger land space.

How and when did tobacco become so important to Virginia's economy?

Captain John Smith and most of the other colonists did not intend to remain in Virginia. They came with the anticipation of finding gold and of returning to England as rich men. When this did not happen, they looked at other options. Jamestown colonist John

Pocahontas saves the life of John Smith in this 1870 lithograph.

Rolfe—who married Pocahontas in 1613—was the first to cultivate tobacco, having learned how to do so from the Indians. Rolfe shipped the first tobacco to England, where it soon became the rage.

Tobacco soon became the mainstay of the Virginia colony. English men and women harvested the plant and cured it; Dutch ships carried it to England and practically all other European nations; and soon a brand-new luxury good had been introduced to a wide market. King James I was so frustrated that he wrote *A Counterblaste to Tobacco*, urging his subjects to stay away from the noxious weed. They paid him little attention, however.

Is there anything to the much-loved story of Pocahontas saving Captain John Smith from certain death, at the hands of her father's executioner?

We can neither confirm nor deny. What we can say is that it is entirely possible. For many years, historians have debunked the episode, saying that Smith made it up many years after the event. While this cannot be ruled out, one cannot prove a negative. Until some certain evidence appears, it seems safer to give Smith and Pocahontas the benefit of the doubt.

451

Is it possible to separate slavery from tobacco? Or are they too intimately linked?

Tobacco came first, but it would not have been as successful without slave labor. Only the arrival of the first slaves from Africa—dated to the summer of 1619—made large-scale production of tobacco possible.

Does this mean that Virginians—and other whites—can let themselves off the hook? Of course not. Race slavery was one of the most pernicious and destructive of all economic systems ever created. And the means that the slaveholders employed—including the use of iron collars, coffles, and hunting dogs—are simply too horrible for many of us today to believe. If we are to look for any sort of justification, it lies in the idea that once an economic system is established, it becomes difficult to break. Virginia saw its first slaves in 1619; by 1700, the system had become so deeply embedded that very few white people even questioned it.

I've heard of Bacon's Rebellion but don't know much about it. Were slaves involved?

Some were, but Bacon's Rebellion (1675) was primarily a rising of the smaller planter class and the newly arrived indentured servants. Led by Nathaniel Bacon, sometimes described as America's first democrat and first political incendiary, the rebellion came very close to success. Virginia's colonial governor, Sir William Berkeley, had to agree to many of the rebels' demands, but when the tables were turned he went back on his word. Roughly twenty men were hanged (Bacon had died during the rebellion itself). The single most important result is that the white planters began to favor the importation of ever more black slaves, who, they judged, were more reliable and less likely to rebel.

When did Virginia become the land of slaveholders who argued for greater liberties for themselves?

This is one of the oddest, and most peculiar, of all juxtapositions. With the notable exception of Thomas Jefferson and a handful of others, most well-bred Virginia gentlemen never considered freeing their slaves, even as they argued and fought for American independence.

How important is *Roots* to our understanding of the experience of black Africans?

Alex Haley's book, made into a television miniseries in 1978, is one of the most influential stories ever told. Millions of people—black and white—watched on those cold winter nights in 1978, and for many of them, discussions of black and white, and what slavery really meant, have never since been the same. Through the life of Kunta Kinte, and his descendants, the viewer was able to witness the struggle of black people in North America and to marvel at how they have endured.

Farmers burned the city of Jamestown as part of Bacon's Rebellion in 1675.

By 1750, the image of the white Southern gentleman—who at that time was usually a Virginian—was complete. He was a fine horseman, a bit of a scholar, and he knew a great deal about the tobacco grown on his lands, even though he did little of the work himself. These Virginia gentlemen tended either to go to England for their education, or to be tutored at home, and in either case they grew up with strong ideas about the rights of men, which in this case was restricted to the rights of white men.

Was there ever a time when it seemed slavery might die of its own weight?

Quite a few prominent Virginians hoped that it would do so. Tobacco prices fell steadily during the eighteenth century, and it seemed that many plantations would be forced to free their slaves. But the growing controversy over taxes, and the impending conflict with Great Britain, kept these ideas to a minimum.

What famous speech took place in Richmond in 1775?

Founding father Patrick Henry gave a speech to the Virginia Convention in St. John's Church in Richmond in 1775, a year before he became the first governor of Virginia. His words "Give me liberty or give me death!" became legendary:

> Gentlemen may cry, peace, peace—but there is no peace. The war is actually begun. The next gale that sweeps from the north will bring to our ears the clash of resounding arms! Our brethren are already in the field! Why stand we here idle? What is it that gentlemen wish? What would they have? Is life so dear, or peace so sweet, as to be purchased at the price of chains and slavery? Forbid it,

453

Almighty God! I know not what course others may take; but as for me, give me liberty, or give me death!

How important was Virginia to the success of the American Revolution?

Removing Virginia from the scene, it is nearly impossible to construct a scenario under which the Revolutionary War would have been won. The Old Dominion supplied the single largest number of soldiers for the cause, but it also provided a majority of the most eloquent leaders in the Continental Congress. Thomas Jefferson and James Monroe may be the best-known, but Peyton Randolph, Patrick Henry, and others supplemented those actions. Then, too, the military efforts of the Thirteen Colonies—turned into the Thirteen States—came to fruition on Virginia soil, at the Siege of Yorktown.

Was there any possibility that the American revolutionaries would flub the opportunity presented to them at Yorktown?

This was one of the few times in the history of the Revolutionary War that things went "right," that the best efforts of most of the people involved bore fruit. Of course there was the possibility that the British, led by Lord Charles Cornwallis, would escape before the trap was sprung, but once George Washington and the Continental Army had them surrounded at Yorktown, with the French fleet under Admiral François-Joseph-Paul de Grasse containing them at sea, the chances were that American independence would finally be achieved.

VIRGINIA IN THE LIFE OF THE NATION

What was Virginia like in the two or three decades that followed the winning of American independence?

So long as one was white, middle class, and of a certain social standing, life in Virginia was by far the best it had ever been; it was during this period that many people, around the nation, expressed the opinion that to be a Virginian was the grandest thing imaginable. This was when George Washington established the presidency, when Chief Justice John Marshall established the power of the Supreme Court, when Thomas Jefferson was chosen for two consecutive terms, and when Lewis and Clark went west, in their epic crossing of the continent. Between about 1790 and 1820 was the high point for Virginia, as a state within the nation and as the state that led the nation.

When did Virginia start to "slide" down from its lofty pinnacle?

The forty years between 1820 and 1860 were not kind to the Old Dominion. Tobacco prices dropped consistently, and too much production of the leaf exhausted the Virginia soil. Slavery remained widespread; the number of black slaves increased; and no one could think up any reasonable path to the eradication of the institution. Virginia essentially drifted for many years. In the public sphere, it rested on its laurels, to the extent that the leaders of the period after 1860 were distinctly less notable than their predecessors.

Why did Virginia join the Confederacy in 1861?

It certainly was not because most of its people expected an easy or quick victory. Unlike the South Carolinians or Texans, for example, Virginians lived in close proximity to the North, and they knew its economic and military power. Virginians had few illusions about the war, but a slim majority of them believed it necessary to defend their rights; that those "rights" involved the right to hold others as slaves remains one of the great conundrums for any who studies the period. The personal dilemma of Robert E. Lee mirrored that of the state as a whole. Lee was a native Virginian who loved his state. He also was a sworn officer of the U.S. Army, and he had found great satisfaction in that role. He made his painful choice in April 1861, the same month that the Virginia special session voted to secede from the Union.

Was it inevitable that Virginia would bear the brunt of the fighting between North and South?

Yes. The only way to avoid this is if Virginia had won enough battles early in the war to force the center of action northward into

The South's greatest general was Robert E. Lee, who led the Army of Northern Virginia, the main force of the Confederate States of America.

455

Maryland and Pennsylvania. Lacking this, the Old Dominion was, quite naturally, the centerpiece of the long and dreadful Civil War. We can praise the heroism of the soldiers and generals, and we can admire the many sacrifices made (on both sides), but at the end of the day, most of us conclude that it was all too much. This is especially true for Virginia, which suffered the greatest number of battle casualties and saw its soil torn up, time and again, by the movement of armies. The 1970 song "The Night They Drove Old Dixie Down" expresses it well: "Virgil Caine is the name, and I served on the Danville train; 'til Stoneman's cavalry came, and he tore up the tracks again."

Has anyone ever been able to fully reconstruct the scene where Robert E. Lee met Ulysses S. Grant?

In sheer physical terms, it is easy to say that two men—one Northern and the other Southern—met in the parlor of the home of grocer Wilmer McLean, and that they arranged the surrender of the Army of Northern Virginia. This is but the bare bones, however; it does not indicate the enormous tension and drama that existed as Lee and Grant met in the village of Appomattox Court House. Two societies, which had lived for eighty years in peace, had now fought a dreadful and destructive war that lasted four years. Perhaps 750,000 people had died and a far larger number had been wounded. Four million black slaves had officially been emancipated, but there was no certain path to their true freedom or economic security. Lee and Grant both were smart enough to realize that what they accomplished on April 9, 1865, was but the beginning.

How did Virginia fare in the decades that followed the Civil War?

Poorly. The state remained in bad shape, economically and psychologically, well into the early part of the twentieth century. There was pride, to be sure, about Virginia's heroic role in the Civil War, but also great pain over the sacrifices that had been made. Then, too, there was no obvious path forward, no clear way to recoup the great losses, in men and materiel.

When did the turnaround begin?

By the time World War I began in 1914, Virginia was starting to come out from its long post-Civil War hangover. That there were so many military schools in the Old Dominion helped; then, too, a resurgence of pride came with Virginians playing an important role in the recovery of the South after the war.

How and when was Colonial Williamsburg established?

The Rockefeller family has often given generously to preserve aspects of American history, and in the 1920s, John D. Rockefeller Jr. gave the funds that allowed for the making of CW, as locals call it. The idea was to enshrine the virtues and values of Thomas Jefferson's generation, those remarkable Virginians who did so much to bring about the making of the United States. The raw materials were all there.

The charm of the restored streets and shops of Colonial Williamsburg has made it a popular attraction for casual tourists and those who enjoy history alike.

Buildings last longer in the South than elsewhere, and many of the original eighteenth-century buildings still remained. Major preservation work was done, and some replicas were used, but by and large the results were spectacular. The authenticity of Colonial Williamsburg was impressive. Critics, however, pointed out a weakness: the lack of an African American presence.

How could the designers of America's premier colonial village fail to put the black people in the scene?

It's a measure of how far the nation has come since the 1930s, when those decisions first were made. At that time, many readers of early American history took for granted that the black people were simply servants or slaves, who faded into the background when the guests arrived. By our current standards, this was simply scandalous, but it made sense to the Americans of the Great Depression era.

Things changed rather swiftly in the 1960s and 1970s. Visitors from many other states complained of the lack of a black presence, and Colonial Williamsburg adjusted. Even today, there are critics of the living history area, saying it does too much to praise the success of the white upper class, but nearly everyone agrees that CW has come a long way since its first conception.

How many U.S. presidents were born in Virginia?

Eight: George Washington, Thomas Jefferson, James Madison, James Monroe, William Henry Harrison, John Tyler, Zachary Taylor, and Woodrow Wilson.

When did Virginia Beach become so important, both to Virginia and to the national image of Virginia?

When we first think of Virginia, we tend to think of smoky blue mountains and endless valleys, but the state has a fine long section of beach just south of Cape Henry, which guards the entrance to Chesapeake Bay. Historically, this area played a small role in the development of the state, until about 1935. Ever since, it has been one of the most dynamic parts.

Virginia Beach is indeed a city—the second largest in the state—but it is also a state of mind: a place in which to escape from the demands of the modern world. Perhaps it is not by chance that the Tennessee-born psychic, Edgar Cayce, chose to locate here. This is where he performed his nearly 20,000 past-life readings. Though he was a dedicated mystic, and not a salesman, the image of Cayce has been used, or employed, by many moneymakers ever since.

How did Virginia do during World War II and the aftermath?

The Old Dominion began a slow rise to prominence in the decades that followed World War II. Sometimes the attention was notoriety, as when Prince Edward County declared "massive resistance" to the whole plan for desegregation of the schools. At the same time, however, one almost always found pockets of progressive thinking and cultural change. The very popular television program *The Waltons* had a lot to do with reintroducing Virginia to the rest of the nation.

How did the fascination with the Civil War help in bringing Virginia "back"?

Anyone who enters an American bookstore is struck by how many titles there are on the Civil War. This was the case as early as 1985, but the success of Ken Burns's *The Civil War* series on PBS, which aired in the autumn of 1990, marked the point of no return. Since then, thousands of titles have come off the shelves, and the book buyers keep coming.

How important was *The Waltons* in forming our modern-day conception of rural Virginia?

For nine seasons, *The Waltons* showed Americans what their rural roots are like; for 210 episodes, Americans heard the evening utterances, "Good night, John-Boy," "Good night, Mary Ellen," as the large Walton family wished each other sweet dreams. The television program was set in the Blue Ridge Mountains, just above Charlottesville, and the juxtaposition of old rural values and newfangled ideas—coming from the University of Virginia—could not have been more poignant. Some viewers simply adored John-Boy, while others lavished affection on Mama and Daddy. Nearly all viewers agreed that Grandma and Grandpa were the most authentic of the group.

Virginia benefited mightily. While the major Civil War sites had been kept in good condition, hundreds of smaller battles and skirmishes had been forgotten. They now came back to public attention, and it seemed as if every small Virginia town was determined to have its slice of the Civil War pie. If the Civil War represented the breakthrough on television's small screen, then *Gettysburg*, filmed in 1993, was the blockbuster at the movie theatres.

Will the Civil War craze ever fade, and if so, what might that do to Virginia's economy?

The chances are that the craze will continue, and perhaps even amplify. An entire generation of youngsters have been raised on Civil War stories; perhaps the challenge, for the storytellers, is to do so in more inclusive ways.

WASHINGTON

Nickname: "The Evergreen State"
Capital: Olympia
Statehood: November 11, 1889; 42nd state

AT A GLANCE

What are the most popular signs and symbols of the Evergreen State?

The willow goldfinch is the state bird, and the rhododendron is the state flower. The western hemlock is the official state tree. There is no official motto for Washington, but the unofficial one is "Alki," meaning "bye and bye" or "hope for the future."

Is there any one place from which one can survey the grandest parts of what is Washington State?

Some people might disagree, voting for another spot of their choice, but for the typical visitor or tourist the answer is surely from the top of the Space Needle, in downtown Seattle. Built in time for the 1962 World's Fair, the Space Needle highlighted Washington's dramatic progress during the twentieth century and pointed in the direction of where the United States intended to go next: outer space.

How big is Washington?

The eighteenth largest state has an area of 71,298 square miles (184,661 square kilometers) and an estimated 7,170,351 people (thirteenth in the nation).

Is it true that Washington, and most of the Pacific Northwest endures one rain shower after another?

It's not! While it rains frequently, and locals usually carry umbrellas, the area is not subject to the type of intense pounding known to Americans of the East Coast. Washington's rain tends to be a rather boring drizzle, which often yields, about twenty minutes later, to a rather gorgeous sky. And just about the time that the tourist is used to that beauty, the scene changes, the clouds return, and another light rain falls. None of these rains are of biblical proportion, however, and the typical Washington resident has long since learned to live with them.

Is it true that Washington has more outdoor enthusiasts, and recreational boaters, than almost any place in the Union?

The Space Needle in Seattle, Washington, is 605 feet (184 meters) tall. Built for the 1962 World's Fair, it remains today as a great place for a high vantage point of the surrounding landscape.

Almost any place except Oregon. Between them, the Evergreen State and the Beaver State have an endless supply of people who love the outdoors, eager to purchase their tents and equipment at Eddie Bauer, and so forth. If you had to trace it all the way back to an historical precedent, you might say that it commenced somewhere on the Oregon Trail, or, just as possible, that it's an outgrowth of the incredible enthusiasm Pacific Northwesterners had for gold fever in Alaska.

Do Washingtonians discuss the weather very much?

Not really. To them, as a people who love the outdoors, the weather is part of Mother Nature's plan. It's the outsider, the recent arrival, who talks about it constantly.

Can the Pacific Northwest person, or the Washingtonian more specifically, be recognized in a crowd?

No. The majority of Washington residents are third- or fourth-generation descendants of Midwesterners who came west, either by covered wagon or steamship. They therefore carry with them a mixture of New England and Midwestern characteristics, and many of them would be perfectly at home in Ohio or Indiana. The big difference comes when one examines the more recent arrivals. Washington is home to a large and growing Asian American population.

EARLY HISTORY

For how long have humans lived in what we call the state of Washington?

For somewhere between 10,000 and 12,000 years. We can't be more specific. These early comers were almost certainly descendants of the reindeer-hunting tribespeople who crossed the Bering Strait a few thousand years prior to that, but there are some intriguing finds in Washington, including some bone samples that look more Chinese than northwest Asian. Lacking anything conclusive, we can say with some confidence that Washington was primarily populated by some of the earliest Native Americans, and that a great many of their descendants were there to greet Captains Meriwether Lewis and William Clark in 1805.

I've heard that the Indian culture in Washington was quite different from what it was in, say, California. Is that accurate?

It is. The Indians of present-day Washington lived in a bountiful world, one where deer, elk, and bear (at least for the most daring hunters) were readily available, but the primary, overriding concern was for the fish. The many different fish of the Pacific Northwest, the salmon most especially, provided an excellent source of lean protein for the Native Americans, who seldom went hungry. Our evidence for this comes from the type of fish reported by Lewis and Clark and other explorers, and by the fact that of all the Native American tribes, only those of the Pacific Northwest practiced the so-called *potlatch*. This ceremony was a great giveaway, a day on which the wealthiest and most powerful man in the village voluntarily gave away all his possessions. At the end of that day, he was materially poor but spiritually and culturally enhanced. It was the man who could, and did, give away the most who was the most honored.

How long did these Indians go without their lifestyle being disturbed?

Hundreds, perhaps even thousands, of years. Pacific Northwest Indian culture was remarkably stable. It was not until the 1540s that a handful of Spaniards showed up, and it was not until two centuries later that a handful of British ships appeared along the coast. What the Native Americans thought of these early arrivals has not been determined, but the chances are they did not see them as a major threat (they were mistaken!).

What was the first that the outside world heard about Washington and the Pacific Northwest?

Captain James Cook came to Washington in 1778, and his journals, often reprinted, described the natural beauty of the area. Some of the land and waterscapes are named for Britons (such as Mount Hood), while others, like the Strait of Juan de Fuca, get their titles from Spaniards. Cook waxed about the beauty of the area, but it was his report on the availability of beaver fur that drew those who followed him. In the late eighteenth and early nineteenth centuries, the fur trade was at its height, fortunes were being made, and many people wanted to get in on the action.

How important were Lewis and Clark to our understanding of the Pacific Northwest?

We normally associate these two men, and the forty-odd men they led, with the Great Plains and the Rocky Mountains. This is not an error: the Lewis and Clark expedition did pioneer the way across the North American continent. But when they came down the west side of the Rocky Mountains and entered the Columbia River and its tributaries, Lewis and Clark recognized they were in an entirely new world. The Indian tribes along the Columbia appeared to have lived there a long time, and their cultures seemed in no way threatened or imperiled by the appearance of these white explorers. Explorers such as Lewis and Clark were accustomed to thinking of most Native Americans as materially poor; this was not the case in the Pacific Northwest. When Lewis and Clark's journals were published less than a decade later, they opened the eyes of thousands, perhaps hundreds of thousands, of white Americans about the possibilities that existed on the other side of the continent.

Who were the first permanent white settlers in Washington State?

We can't count the group that settled Astoria in 1812, because they were on the south side of the river. We therefore give the nod to John McLoughlin (1784–1857), a factor of the Hudson's Bay Company, who established a permanent settlement at Fort Washington in what is now Vancouver, Washington. For the next twenty years, McLoughlin played host to all manner of fur trappers and traders—British, Americans, and some others too. All this time, McLoughlin hoped that Great Britain would make a permanent claim to the region, but he would be disappointed.

WASHINGTON IN THE LIFE OF THE NATION

How did Washington come under the American flag?

It wasn't a preordained matter. The Spaniards had given up their claim, but the British were pushing theirs and even the Russians, whose base was in southern Alaska, were making noises of their own. Britain and America, wisely, decided to postpone the matter for some years, and during that interim the area was known as the Oregon Country, even though it was much bigger than the present-day state of Oregon.

In 1844, James K. Polk won the American presidency after a campaign in which he called for "Fifty-four Forty or Fight!"—a reference to the American boundary that went all the way to 54 degrees 40 minutes of north latitude. Had he gained all this, there would be no west coast of Canada today! But in 1846, British and American commissioners decided, instead, to draw the international boundary at 49 degrees north latitude. To ward off future conflicts, the commissioners also agreed that the ships of both nations would have access to the Strait of Juan de Fuca. Though no one planned it at the time, this meant that Seattle and Vancouver would, in time, grow up on opposite sides of the boundary, and that the Pacific Northwest would be home to British and American mercantile concerns.

Why did Washington take so much longer than Oregon to be settled?

About 90 percent of all the Americans who made their way to Oregon came by horse, covered wagon, or foot, and about 90 percent of all who came to Washington State did so by ship, whether by sailing or steam-powered vessel. Of these two alternatives, the landward journey was much more feasible in the 1840s and 1850s, as there weren't enough ships in the whole merchant marine to bring all those settlers by sea. So, even though Oregon and Washington share many things in the current day, their pattern of settlement was quite different.

When did the settlers finally begin to arrive?

Not until the 1870s and 1880s. Once they came, however, these new arrivals showed all the aggression and gumption that is usually identified with American arrivals. The Native American presence weakened considerably at the time of the Civil War; by the end of the nineteenth century, it was hard to find any Indians, at least in the coastal regions of Washington State.

Seattle, Tacoma, and Olympia were all natural places to settle. It should come as no surprise that the first settlers chose to locate in these places; Washington was essentially settled in a pattern that ran from west to east, defying much of the logic of what we associate with nineteenth-century patterns. From the beginning, the major towns were identified with merchant concerns. In the gold fever that followed, it was usually the men (and sometimes women) who sold tents, pickaxes, and shovels who became rich, rather than the miners themselves.

Was statehood difficult for Washington to achieve?

No. The fact that so many American settlers came by sea meant that numerous ship captains posted logs and journals of their trips to the Pacific Northwest, and it was clear   465 that this area would be a major benefit to the nation as a whole. Statehood was achieved in 1889.

What was life in Washington State like toward the end of the nineteenth century?

The fishing industry was in its early days, but it was apparent that this was one incredible gold mine, and very few of the early fishermen suspected it might ever be tapped. But the really big killing, the one that lived in the hopes and dreams of thousands of men, was the gold that was discovered in the Yukon Territory (which later became part of British Columbia). The gold was found in regions that belonged to Queen Victoria's Britain, but the Americans in the Pacific Northwest were eager to get their share. Seattle became the port of departure for many thousands of men headed to the gold fields, and, as usual, it was the merchants who came off the best.

How important is Seattle—and Puget Sound—to the shipping routes of the Pacific Northwest?

One can feel the answer simply by gazing from Pike's Market down to the harbor: Seattle's waterways are filled with shipping. The area is often referred to as the "Gateway to the Orient," and this began early. It was thanks to the vision of President James K. Polk that the vital waterways of the Pacific Northwest came into American hands; in the three generations that followed, many fortunes were made shipping goods to China and Japan.

How did Washington fare during World War I and World War II?

In both cases, war proved a powerful stimulus to the state economy. This does not mean that all Washingtonians supported World War I; many were dead-set opposed to it. The best-known of all the protesters was John "Jack" Reed, who later flew to Moscow and wrote his seminal *Ten Days That Shook the World*.

How did the aerospace industry become so large in Washington State?

The first making and flying of aircraft was primarily a Midwestern phenomenon, and the Pacific Northwest, with its frequently cloudy skies, did not seem like the ideal place for

Washington's Puget Sound has long been a center of trade and commerce, as well as of beauty (from a 1912 photo).

the industry to expand. Boeing opened its doors in 1936, however, and the company boomed as a result of demand in the Second World War. Boeing turned out the B-52 super fortresses that made American victory in the Pacific war a virtual certainty.

What was the single worst day of Washington state history?

Beyond doubt, this was May 18, 1980, when Mount St. Helens, or, rather, the volcano beneath, suddenly blew its top. Rumblings had been detected for weeks, but no one, including the best-informed scientists, had any anticipation that the mountain would blow, or that so much ash would come. An area thousands of acres wide was completely wrecked; trees fell down and vegetation and wildlife were completely altered. About eighty people died in the immediate aftermath of the explosion.

No further explosions have occurred since the Mount St. Helens incident, but it made people of the Pacific Northwest acutely aware that they live on one of the extensions of the so-called Pacific Rim, which includes hundreds of volcanoes, stretching from the South Pacific all the way to Chile. Surprisingly, Mount St. Helens was a boon for the environmental movement. Many more people began suggesting that it was best to leave nature alone.

When did Seattle become the center for Starbucks Coffee?

The first café opened in 1971. Within ten years, Starbucks was making record profits; a decade later, it had stores all over the United States and was moving abroad in search of new customers. Coffee has been part of the American experience for more than two centuries, but the new craze that commenced in Seattle brought a new twist to it: as a re-

Washington residents are known for their love of coffee, especially in Seattle.

sult of Starbucks, Americans expect fancy flavor in their coffee, as well as a stimulant to start their day.

How did the computer craze come to Seattle?

Bill Gates (1951–), now one of the richest men in the world, was a Washington State native, but he was living in New Mexico when he made one of his big breakthroughs, which led to the making of faster, more consumer-friendly computers. Gates started Microsoft as a revolutionary company and intended to steal profits from older, stodgier companies like IBM, but by the beginning of the twenty-first century, Microsoft seemed as "establishment" as any other large corporation. With its headquarters in Redmond, and Gates's amazing mansion just a few miles away, Microsoft was poised to influence computer trends for decades to come.

When did Amazon become one of the giants in retailing?

New Mexico native Jeff Bezos (1964–) was working at a rather cushy job in a hedge fund on Wall Street when he learned in 1994 that a new Supreme Court ruling would open the way for shipping and delivery, based on orders coming over the Internet. Bezos started amazon.com in his garage, but within a few years he had a large corporate headquarters in Seattle and several enormous warehouses close by. Bezos's strategy was simple but also revolutionary: eliminate the middleman by shipping direct, without having actual chain stores or a large workforce. Just as Chicago was the city most involved in creating the new American retailing c. 1910, so Seattle was the staging ground for the new Internet-based shopping experience. As of 2016, Amazon shows no sign of slowing down; instead, it seems primed to enter virtually every retail market, from books to clothing, and from shoes to cement.

What was life in Seattle like at the turn of the twenty-first century?

Admirers of the city and state claimed that they represented the future, that Seattle would one day displace Manhattan as the American city *par excellence*. Visitors who toured Pike's Market in the downtown tended to agree. Critics and detractors claimed that Seattle could never equal Manhattan, or other East Coast cities, because it was pointed in the wrong direction—east. That, the admirers claimed, was precisely the point.

Seattle and Washington still had their revolutionaries, the youngsters who did not admire or even respect all the emphasis on corporate solutions. The riots against the meeting of the WTO (World Trade Organization) in downtown Seattle in 1999 were the most severe of all those across the United States. Generally speaking, however, Washington State seemed one of the best places for the old and the new to meet.

What Washington county was renamed—without actually being renamed?

King County was created as a county in December 1852, a few months before Washington became a territory in 1853. The county was named after William Rufus King, who had just been elected vice president as Franklin Pierce's running mate. In February 1986, the King County Council voted to "rename" King County so that it was named after civil rights leader Martin Luther King Jr. The change occurred due to the discovery that the late vice president had been a slaveholder.

What will the Evergreen State look like a generation hence?

Given the incredible rate at which change has taken place since about 1960, it would be foolish to make too strong a stance on this question. But given Washington State history, it seems likely that while corporate strategies will remain important, the Evergreen State will continue to be influenced by its rural and environmental past. There are more backpackers, hikers, bicyclists, and recreational boaters in western Washington, pound for pound, than any other place in the nation.

Nickname: "The Mountain State"
Capital: Charleston
Statehood: June 20, 1863; 35th state

AT A GLANCE

What are the most popular signs and symbols of the Mountain State?

"Mountaineers Are Always Free" is the official state motto, coined in 1863. The cardinal is the official state bird, and the rhododendron is the state flower. The sugar maple is the state tree.

How large, or small, is West Virginia?

Comprising 24,231 square miles (62,758 square kilometers), West Virginia is forty-first among the fifty states in geographic size. The population of 1,854,304, as enumerated in 2010, shows that West Virginia is thirty-eighth among the states in population.

How did West Virginia become so utterly different from its neighbors?

Geography has a great deal to do with it. From its earliest beginnings, West Virginia was set apart both from the East Coast and the Midwest. The mountains for which West Virginia is so justly famous made it difficult for the area to be settled, and when the pioneers did arrive, they fashioned a way of life that had antecedents—to be sure—but which took on a flavor all its own. As a result, the people of the Mountain State are, indeed, among the most unusual to be found east of the Mississippi River. Sometimes it seems as if they belong in the Rockies rather than the Appalachians.

We know that West Virginia is the Mountain State. Can it equally be called the River State?

That expression has seldom been used but it would fit. West Virginia has many rivers, some of which end as tributaries to the Potomac, and others of which flow all the way to the Ohio. These rivers cut the state into many sharp corners and angles, which add great natural beauty but, along with the mountains, also make the state difficult to traverse. In recent times, the building of the New River Bridge was a signal accomplishment, knitting together parts of the state that had previously been separate. It would take the building of at least a dozen more such bridges to really make West Virginia cohesive, however.

Do West Virginians talk about the weather very much?

Only in order to sing its praises. West Virginia is, on average, about seven degrees cooler than Virginia, and even in the heat of high summer, one can find plenty of places in which to remain cool. West Virginia also does not suffer from the extreme cold that can sweep down from Canada into the lower Midwest. The state enjoys abundant rainfall. About the only negative that can be voiced is the amount of snow that falls; sections of the mountains receive as much as ten feet of snow per winter.

Can the West Virginian be told apart from his or her Virginia, Ohio, and Pennsylvania neighbors?

The West Virginian is the single most distinctive type found on or near the East Coast. Talkative, friendly, and expansive, the West Virginian has a hearty approach to life, which has been developed by a strong acquaintance with tragedy. It's a rare West Virginian who has not lost a friend or relative to the mining pits and tunnels. Until about the 1950s, the Georgia cracker was still a recognizable type, and he was equal to the West Virginian in cultural style. Since the 1960s, however, the West Virginian remains practically alone among Americans east of the Mississippi River.

Why do so many coal and natural gas companies demonstrate such interest in West Virginia?

The first companies to dig for coal only knew that they found the black stuff in prodigious amounts, but the companies that bid for contracts, and request permits today, realize that West Virginia is the richest part of a very rich mineral area known as the Marcellus Shale Formation. Stretching from the Catskills in New York to much of central Pennsylvania, and stretching south to encompass nearly all of West Virginia, the Marcellus is one of the great wealth producers on the East Coast, and if the natural gas companies have their way, it will continue to be so for a long time to come.

Hydraulic fracturing—better known simply as "fracking"—has plenty of critics. They claim that the process pollutes rivers and streams and that it frequently destroys

The natural beauty of the West Virginia mountain forests is undeniable.

the fresh water supplies in the very towns it is supposed to benefit. But given the enormous natural gas boom that began around 2005, it seems unlikely that fracking will go away anytime soon. The controversies that surround it, too, will continue.

EARLY HISTORY

For how long have humans lived in what we now call the Mountain State?

For at least 12,000 years. Very little is known about the earliest of these peoples, but some of their descendants belonged to the Mound Builder culture that erected earthen mounds in almost a dozen of the states. West Virginia has dozens, perhaps scores, of mounds, some of which are seven stories tall.

When the first white settlers arrived, they found Shawnee, Wyandot, and other Indian tribes in West Virginia. None of these tribes dominated the region, however. Like Kentucky, with which West Virginia shares some characteristics, the Mountain State was terrific for hunting and fishing, but was not populated to a great degree. Many of the Indians summered in West Virginia and then returned to Ohio.

473

When did the first white settlers arrive?

They started coming over the Blue Ridge Mountains early in the eighteenth century. Some came south from Pennsylvania, but the majority were Virginians, eager to find more elbow room, as they expressed it. One of the first known settlers was a Welshman named Morgan Morgan, who settled near Bunker Hill at a site that is a premier historical attraction today.

The early pioneers found out, almost immediately, that West Virginia was not Virginia. Tobacco grew here, but not nearly as well as along the coast, and most pioneer families grew a large variety of crops rather than concentrating on any one. Some slaves were brought into the area, but West Virginia never developed a strong "slave culture" as did Virginia. Many younger sons of prominent Virginia families moved to West Virginia because their elder brothers inherited all the family land.

What were relations with the Indians like?

The Native Americans were not friendly; on the other hand, they did not wish to start a shooting war with the white settlers. But in 1774 one conflict did take place, called Lord Dunmore's War, which centered on the wrongs done to Logan, a Mingo chief, whose family was massacred. The last royal governor of Virginia, John Murray, Lord Dunmore, gathered about 1,500 men and pursued the Indians through the part of Virginia that would eventually become West Virginia. The Battle of Point Pleasant (October 1774) was fought where the Scioto River flows into the Ohio, and a major granite monument stands on the site today. The Indians were defeated and were forced to make peace. Under the treaty that followed, most of West Virginia came into Anglo-American hands.

Did West Virginia play any role in the Revolutionary War?

Quite a few men from the area served; among them were the sharpshooters of Daniel Morgan's regiment. But because West Virginia was still part of the Old Dominion, Virginia gained the credit for almost everything the mountaineers accomplished. Soon after the war ended, the West Virginia area was chosen as the site for one of two federal arsenals: Harpers Ferry, which is where Virginia and Maryland come together. Thousands of muskets, rifles, and swords were manufactured there.

At the turn of the nineteenth century, West Virginia seemed likely to remain a province, or adjunct of the Old Dominion. A distinctive way of life had already developed, but West Virginia had neither the population nor material resources to justify any sort of break from Virginia. There were some interesting developments, however, in the discovery of coal and natural gas. West Virginia settlers established the first pumping station for natural gas in the entire nation.

How did John Brown—the legendary abolitionist—ever become so identified with West Virginia?

If one removes the humor that is so large a part of the West Virginia character, then
John Brown would be almost the archetypal West Virginian: physical, manly, and de-

termined to achieve his goal. In Brown's case, the goal was to set free the African American slaves, and he saw the mountains of West Virginia as tailor-made for this. Ten years before he made his famous raid on Harpers Ferry, Brown had a long conversation with abolitionist Frederick Douglass. Pulling out of a map of the mountains, Brown declared that these mountains were the home of free men, and that they would be the perfect refuge for the freed slaves. Give him just a few hundred men of daring and skill, Brown declared, and he could fend off the attacks by all the slaveholders in the entire South.

When did the raid on Harpers Ferry take place?

On October 16, 1859, Brown and about twenty accomplices attacked and captured the federal arsenal at Harpers Ferry without the loss of a man. Brown had about 1,500 wooden pikes that he intended to give to the slaves, and he planned to lead an army of them against the slave power, as he and others deemed it. But things began to go wrong almost immediately.

Brown captured the arsenal, but he and his friends were soon trapped inside its walls. The Virginia militia arrived, as did a group of U.S. Marines, led by Colonel Robert E. Lee. They stormed Harpers Ferry, and Brown was wounded and taken prisoner. By rights, that should have been the entire story, but Brown performed so brilliantly, and heroically, at his trial, that he won the sympathy of almost everyone present. He was hanged in December 1859, but his legend had just begun to grow. Throughout the Civil War, thousands of men marched while singing "John Brown's Body." Brown's action can be criticized on many levels, but in his heroism, his careless disregard for the odds, he acted very much like a West Virginia mountain man (even though he was born in Connecticut).

How did West Virginia finally become separate from Virginia?

When the Civil War began, West Virginia was split, with about two-thirds of its people strongly for the Union and the remaining third for the Confederacy. In October 1861, a

Is there anything to the story of John Henry?

Definitely. The trouble is separating fact from legend. In this way, the John Henry story is a good deal like that of Robin Hood, from English folklore.

The Chesapeake and Ohio Railway dug a tunnel under Big Bend Mountain in West Virginia and encountered plenty of difficulties along the way. The company brought in a steam-powered drill, and the story goes that Henry, an African American of great strength, declared he could dig faster and better than any machine. That heroic effort was required to get that tunnel dug, and built, is beyond dispute. Whether Henry did, in fact, accomplish his great work and then collapse, dead on the ground, remains a matter of dispute. The country singer Johnny Cash made the legend even stronger with his fine song "The Legend of John Henry's Hammer."

vote was taken, and the Union side won by almost ten-to-one. As a result, the counties of West Virginia organized themselves, and in June 1863, West Virginia entered the Union as the thirty-fifth state.

West Virginia is primarily known for its freedom fighters, the men who went with the Union, but one of its most heroic sons fought for the Confederacy. Thomas "Stonewall" Jackson, perhaps the most legendary of all Confederate commanders, was born and raised in West Virginia. When the Civil War commenced, he marched with his cadets to Richmond and offered his service to the Confederacy. Like John Brown, Jackson was a person utterly devoid of humor or carelessness; with him, everything was intentional. Though he marched and fought for the Confederacy, Jackson did so with the vim and vigor of a West Virginian.

What was life in West Virginia like in the decades that followed the Civil War?

West Virginia was now its own state, with its capital in Charleston, but it had a very difficult time in the early years. The state did not have the farming capacity of its neighbors, and it seemed doomed to forever be one of the poorest states of the Union. Discoveries of oil, coal, and natural gas followed, however, and West Virginians took heart. What they did not anticipate was the tyranny they would experience from the coal companies.

How bad were conditions in the coal tunnels and mines?

They could hardly have been worse. Today, when we see images of men filing into the mines, they at least wear brightly colored steel helmets; this was not the case in the

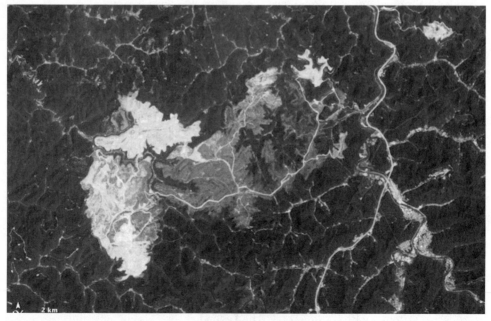

This NASA satellite photo of a region of West Virginia clearly shows the extensive damage to forests from a strip mining coal operation.

late nineteenth century. Eager to extract all that they could, the coal companies abused their workers to a degree seldom seen in American history. Mines were terrible places where the men worked eleven- to twelve-hour days, but the weariness they endured was nothing compared to the danger. The mine tunnels were in constant danger of caving in.

What was the single worst day in West Virginia history?

Beyond a doubt this was December 6, 1907. Early that morning, hundreds of workers filed into the Monongah mines in northeast West Virginia. Bells and alarms were heard around nine that morning, and the public learned that a major tunnel had collapsed. Tragically, 362 men died that day.

How did West Virginia fare during the First World War?

The demand for coal brought better economic times, but common miners found that their life was not much better than before. West Virginia miners participated in the great coal strike of 1919, led by the United Mine Workers.

How did the Mountain State fare during World War II?

The Second World War was a definite boon for many young men who escaped the mining towns and camps, but social and economic conditions in West Virginia did not improve. Neither the 1950s, which saw general prosperity throughout the nation, nor the 1960s, which witnessed the youth rebellion and impatience with established authority, did much to alleviate conditions in West Virginia. The only noticeable change was that the coal companies changed their way of extraction and went in heavily for strip mining.

Unlike tunnel mining, strip mining really strips the mountain or hill, reducing it sometimes to nothing. Whole sections of the West Virginia landscape changed during the 1970s and 1980s, as the coal companies did their best to extract all they could.

What is the Green Bank Telescope?

It's the largest fully steerable radio telescope in the world and the world's largest moveable land object. Dedicated in honor of Robert C. Byrd, West Virginia's longtime U.S. senator, the Green Bank Telescope is so important to astronomy, and to our hope of discovering life elsewhere in the universe, that radio silence is maintained in the area for thousands of acres. The first Green Bank Telescope was in place from 1962 until 1988, when it collapsed. The present one was built between 1991 and 2002.

Who was Cecil Underwood?

Underwood was both the youngest and oldest person to serve as governor of West Virginia. When he became governor in 1957, he was thirty-four years old and served just one term. At that time, the state constitution did not allow governors to serve consec-

The Green Bank Telescope in West Virginia is the largest fully steerable radio telescope on the planet.

utive terms. He ran for U.S. Senate instead, but he lost. He ran for governor again in 1964, 1968, and 1976, but lost each time. But in 1996, he ran again and won. On his second inauguration day—forty years apart—he became the oldest West Virginia governor at the age of seventy-four. He again served just one term.

When did West Virginia come under the gaze of the natural gas companies?

It began as early as the 1960s, when coal was suddenly less lucrative than previously. But the acceleration became a rush around 2005. "Peak oil"—when the maximum amount would be extracted from the ground—took place in 2004, and natural gas companies began a wholesale attempt at new discoveries. They knew they would find natural gas in West Virginia, but they didn't know how much.

Since 2005, fracking has been the rage in West Virginia. The difference between this and the great boom in coal production, a century earlier, is that the inhabitants know the value of what they possess.

What was life in West Virginia like at the beginning of the twenty-first century?

The same old pessimism prevailed among many residents, who complained that they were victims of the oil and natural gas companies, just as their grandparents were of coal. But there was also a new hopefulness, based on the knowledge that one of the world's great reservoirs of natural gas lies just beneath the West Virginia soil. Some state residents were 100 percent against fracking, while others cautiously explored the possibilities. The negative, to be sure, was that fracking had the capacity to wreck wells and even aquifers. But if a safe way could be found to extract the natural gas, quite a few West Virginians might be better off than their parents and grandparents.

ODDS AND ENDS

What is one of the most incongruous sights in West Virginia?

The Palace of Gold built by Hare Krishna devotees. Completed in 1979, the temple stands out on a local mountaintop in Marshall County and practically shouts to the world that West Virginia houses more than Bible-thumping coal miners.

Will West Virginia be able to maintain its down-home way of life in the decades to come?

Very likely it will. Nature made the Mountain State what it is. Even the most determined of human actions have not altered the basic character of the state and its people. The chances are that people will still sing "Take Me Home, Country Roads" and "The Legend of John Henry's Hammer."

WISCONSIN
1848

Nickname: "The Badger State"
Capital: Madison
Statehood: May 29, 1848; 30th state

AT A GLANCE

What are the most popular signs and symbols of the Badger State?

"Forward" is the official state motto. The robin is the official state bird, and the wood violet is the state flower. The sugar maple is the official state tree.

How large, or small, is the Badger State?

Comprising 56,153 square miles (145,436 square kilometers), Wisconsin is twenty-sixth among the fifty states in geographic size. The population of 5,742,713, as enumerated in 2010, means that Wisconsin is twentieth in terms of population.

Is Wisconsin more than the land of milk and cheese?

To be sure. What the state really lacks is a cultural spokesman; it has no equivalent to Garrison Keillor, the homespun radio performer who has made Minnesota so much more known to the rest of the nation. Wisconsin has much to be proud of, however, including a sturdy, self-reliant population and some of the best colleges and universities in the United States.

How did all those lakes (15,000-plus) ever come to be?

They are a product of the last Ice Age, which ended around 14,000 years ago. The glaciers came south, carving up the land and creating areas of variable height. The lower

481

level ones were filled with water at the end of the Ice Age, and the lakes we see today are the result.

Wisconsin has plenty of farmland, but it is the lakes that stick in the popular mind. Images of French fur trappers finding their way through endless ponds, lakes, and streams are not far-fetched. Today, however, Wisconsin has a nice blend of farm, factory, and places of higher learning.

Do the people of Wisconsin discuss the weather very much?

They do, to a greater degree than most of the people in other states. This is because Wisconsin fronts on the Great Lakes, and it has no shield against the Arctic cold that often comes south in January and February. Summers are generally more tolerable, but the heat that bakes the flat part of the state can be severe. Wisconsinites are well accustomed to the changeability of their weather, but they still make it part of their daily talk.

EARLY HISTORY

For how long have humans lived in what we call the state of Wisconsin?

For at least 10,000 years. We don't know the names or identities of the early peoples, but we believe that they found the area useful in terms of hunting and fishing. Discoveries of earthen mounds are made on occasion, but the lives of most of these Archaic peoples are largely unknown. Not so with the more recent Native Americans.

When the first European explorers and settlers arrived, they found several tribal groups in present-day Wisconsin. The Sauk, Fox, Miami, Winnebago, and Ojibway are the best-known. Virtually all of these peoples found the first Europeans—French mostly—to be a curiosity rather than a threat. Only when the fur trade began to boom, and more explorers arrived, did the Native Americans realize that these foreigners had the capacity to change the landscape.

Was there any chance that Wisconsin could have become the center of a French empire in America?

Not really. France did not send people in large enough numbers to make that happen. There *was* the chance, however, that Wisconsin could have been the center of the Midwest, thanks to the number of fur trappers and fur traders that came to the area. These were French, Irish, Scots-Irish, and others. For a time, there were as many Hudson's Bay merchants in Wisconsin as there were Anglo-Americans.

When did the United States first take notice of Wisconsin?

The area officially came to American control in 1783 with the Peace of Paris, but actual settlement did not come about till the end of the War of 1812. Even then, many Anglo-

American settlers were inclined to remain in more southerly areas, such as Indiana and Illinois. Wisconsin's development accelerated after the opening of the Erie Canal in 1825, however, because would-be settlers could come over the Great Lakes instead of by land.

Corn and wheat were major reasons why settlers came to Wisconsin; they saw the flat prairie land as ideal for the planting of cereal crops. More than a dozen towns were settled by 1830, the year the Black Hawk War caught the upper Midwest by surprise.

I've often heard of the Black Hawk War, but somehow it usually gets folded in with stories of Abraham Lincoln. Did it take place in Illinois?

No. Chief Black Hawk was a leader of the Sauk tribe, who watched with regret as his people sold the remainder of their lands in western Illinois to Anglo-American settlers. He moved across the Mississippi River to Iowa, but was persuaded in 1832 to go back to Illinois to fight for the land his people had lost.

Though Black Hawk lived in Iowa and the lands for which he fought were in Illinois, the crucial, climactic battle was in Wisconsin. The Battle of Bad Axe, in the southwestern part of the state, ended in complete victory for the Americans. Black Hawk was taken prisoner, but he soon became a much-admired cultural figure, with his portrait often painted. The people of Wisconsin, like their neighbors in Illinois and Iowa, correctly saw the Black Hawk War as the end of the Indian wars. From this point on, there were no martial impediments to the settlement of the Upper Midwest.

WISCONSIN IN THE LIFE OF THE NATION

How and when did Wisconsin achieve statehood?

Few states went through so long a process. Wisconsin was originally part of the Northwest Territory (1787–1800), then part of the Indiana Territory (1801–1809), then part of the Illinois Territory (1809–1818), and finally a part of the Michigan Territory (1818–1836). Throughout this time, there were not enough settlers, or a loud enough voice in Congress, to bring about a desired change. But success in the Black Hawk War played a crucial role. The number of emigrants from other states, as well as from abroad, increased greatly, and by 1850, there were more than 200,000 people in Wisconsin. This was more than sufficient for statehood, which was achieved

This circa 1890 painting by Samuel Marsden Brookes shows the grounds where the Battle of Wisconsin Heights occurred during the Black Hawk War.

on May 29, 1848. Madison was the state capital right from the start. By then, however, Wisconsinites had spread to most other parts of the state, and the area was well charted and mapped. By odd chance, Wisconsin had the opportunity to participate in the making of the Civil War, at least from a political standpoint.

How did the Republican Party get its start?

In the early 1850s, it was apparent that the Whig Party was no longer functional and that the Democratic Party was led by Southern politicians, or by Northern ones who favored the Southern cause. A new party was clearly needed, and it was in Ripon, Wisconsin, at a convention of anti-slavery groups, that the Republican Party was formed. Wisconsin is a long way from the seat(s) of the Civil War, but it played an important role in establishing the party that would fight the war to its conclusion.

How important was Wisconsin's role during the American Civil War?

The Union could have won the war without Wisconsin, but the same can be said for some of the other northernmost states. But on a moral level, Wisconsin was important because it was one of the few areas in the Midwest where white people seemed genuinely to care about blacks and the issue of slavery. Ohio and Indiana both furnished far more soldiers to the Union cause, but both states were filled with people who cared about blacks in the abstract, while not wishing to have them as neighbors.

Roughly 90,000 Wisconsinites fought in the Civil War. They performed well under fire and had numerous memorable moments. The single most startling was at the Battle of Lookout Mountain in Tennessee in 1863. Nineteen-year-old Arthur MacArthur (father of the better-known Douglas MacArthur) was ascending the ridge when he saw the color-bearer of the regiment fall. Seizing the colors, MacArthur shouted "On Wisconsin!" which remains the unofficial state motto.

What was the most important industry in the wake of the Civil War?

Lumber. Wisconsin had enormous sections of forest, some of it virgin, in 1865, and loggers from virtually all the neighboring states descended, hoping to take out the best and biggest logs. Some of the photographs are difficult to believe, so large are the logs. This foresting was done in an enthusiastic manner—Wisconsin is the land of Paul Bunyan!—but it was not performed wisely or with forethought; as a result, the state began to head toward deforestation in record time.

What was the single worst day in Wisconsin history?

On October 8, 1871, on precisely the same day as the famous Chicago Fire, an enormous forest fire struck the eastern part of the state. The flames rushed toward Peshtigo. Not only was the town destroyed, but more than 1,200 people lost their lives. The U.S. Forest Service was still a long way in the future, but this terrible event caused people to think about the need for forestry regulation.

Many theories and conspiracies have flourished as to how Chicago and Peshtigo were practically destroyed by fire on the same day. The most plausible theory points to a series of wind changes that caused fires of a normal size to become much larger.

I seem to see the name Oshkosh on all sorts of items. When did that town become so important?

Oshkosh started with the production of wooden doors and wagons and spread into other products. The people of Wisconsin delighted in turning towns into specialty areas; for example, Sheboygan was the chair capital of the Midwest and Fond du Lac produced the best wooden iceboxes.

Which industry became most important at the turn of the twentieth century?

The milk industry. Cattle had already thrived on the Wisconsin prairie for a half-century, but a commensurate demand for

A display of milk bottles dating back to the 1870s is proudly displayed at the Wisconsin Historical Museum in Madison.

milk nationwide led to a boom in the production and price at the turn of the century. Wisconsin workers flocked to the new moneymaker, and this eventually led to the state turning out 3 billion gallons of milk per year. It's no exaggeration to say that consumption of Wisconsin cattle products have led the people of the American Midwest to be, on average, taller, heavier, and stronger than their counterparts on the East or West Coast.

PROGRESSIVE POLITICS IN WISCONSIN

When did Progressive politics come to Wisconsin?

When we spell Progressive with the capital "P," we refer to the special brand of politics that emerged in the 1890s and lasted into the 1920s. Nationwide, politics entered a new era, with political leaders and their supporters vying to see who could create the cleanest image. They were more successful in Wisconsin than almost anywhere else. The person who did more than anyone else to establish a Wisconsin image in national politics was Robert "Fighting Bob" La Follette Sr.

485

How did one person manage to accomplish so much in one lifetime?

Fighting Bob La Follette was the son of a farmer, who died when he was only seven. He rose rapidly in Wisconsin politics and was elected governor in 1900. Twice reelected, he brought about more change than any governor of his time, and some argue more than any other American politician of the century.

Wisconsin was the first state to use a direct primary system for the nomination of state officials. It was the first to contemplate state ownership of factories (though this did not take place). After La Follette was out of the governor's mansion, the state went on to establish the nation's first teachers' pensions and, later, the first workers compensation law. Through all of this, La Follette was seen as the guiding spirit: he enlisted the help of academics at the University of Wisconsin to make his "Wisconsin Idea" more available to the general public.

How did Wisconsin fare during the two world wars?

Because Milwaukee had the highest percentage of German-born citizens of any city in the nation, and because so many Germans had immigrated to Wisconsin in the 1880s, it was dangerous for any Wisconsin politician to favor entry to World War I. Fighting Bob La Follette, now in the U.S. Senate, voted against entry to the war. Anger against his stance was generally directed toward La Follette himself, however; Wisconsin did not suffer a backlash during World War I.

On the other hand, the people of Wisconsin broadly welcomed World War II. They wished to banish the image of their state as recalcitrant, and Wisconsin sent about

200,000 men to fight in the war. The state's meat and dairy industries boomed throughout the war and established a prosperity that lasted well into the 1970s. Among other things, this enabled Wisconsin to fund one of the finest examples of public higher education.

When did the Wisconsin State Capitol acquire its magnificent look?

The Capitol in Madison was built of white granite, and the work was entirely accomplished in 1917. The contractors and builders had no way of knowing that their work would coincide with the beginning of the First World War. Wisconsin emerged from that war with an outstanding new capitol, one that has served as a model for several others.

"Fighting Bob" La Follette.

For how long has the University of Wisconsin been known as the Harvard of the Midwest?

Some Wisconsinites might disagree, preferring to be called the "Berkeley of the Midwest." But the reputation began in the 1950s and hit its peak during the late 1960s. Not only was the entire system of public higher education more affordable than most, but its professors were drawn from the very best schools. The late 1960s witnessed many student strikes and protests in favor of the Civil Rights movement and, generally, against the war in Vietnam. All the seventeen different campuses were fully merged by 1972.

Who was Joseph McCarthy and how bad a leader was he?

In terms of *effectiveness*, he was pretty darned good, meaning that he was able to persuade a lot of people to see things his way. The "bad" quality comes from the fact that he was mean-spirited to a degree seldom seen, even in American politics.

In January 1950, Senator McCarthy, who had served in the Navy during World War II, brought out a list of 123 persons, who he claimed were known Communists somehow serving in the State Department. Today the charge seems absurd on the face of it, but state and national listeners paid attention. For nearly three years, McCarthy became the third-most powerful person in the land, behind only the president and the Speaker of the House of Representatives. His excesses finally led to his fall, in the Army-McCarthy hearings of 1954. That he was a spectacular example of the worst type of American politician cannot be denied; that he hurt Wisconsin's image is almost equally certain.

What were the major controversies in Wisconsin toward the end of the twentieth century?

The Badger State was in good shape as the new century commenced. The state university system was still highly regarded, though it was not at the very top as it had been in, say, 1965. Both agriculture and industry were doing reasonably well, and many young people still migrated from other states either to go to school or to work in Wisconsin. But in the beginning of the second decade of the new century, Wisconsin became the center of a longstanding debate over how the pay and benefits of public educators should be funded.

How influential was McCarthy on American culture?

McCarthy's deeds led to the term "McCarthyism." Merriam-Webster's dictionary defines it as so: "A mid-20th century political attitude characterized chiefly by opposition to elements held to be subversive and by the use of tactics involving personal attacks on individuals by means of widely publicized indiscriminate allegations especially on the basis of unsubstantiated charges."

Wisconsin was one of the safeguards of the teachers' unions, and it was with great surprise that the rest of the nation watched while a new governor, and a majority in the legislature, attempted to rid the state of the principle of collective bargaining. But in 2013, the legislature voted to eliminate collective bargaining, meaning that all previous agreements reached with the various teachers' unions were in jeopardy. As of 2016, the ramifications are still unclear, but it remains a subject of great interest and concern in Wisconsin.

POPULAR RECREATION

What do Wisconsinites do for fun?

Paddling the many rivers and streams is a regular pleasure for many of the people of Wisconsin. Arts and crafts continue to play a major role. They also like to root for the Green Bay Packers of the National Football League. Few sports teams have built so iconic an image as the brawling Packers.

Where will the Badger State be a generation from now?

One hesitates to bet against Wisconsin, on the football field or off. The Badger State has consistently been a winner, whether in higher education, farming, or organized sports. Of course the state faces numerous challenges, not the least of which is the flight of many of its most prosperous citizens to warmer southern climates.

WYOMING

Nickname: "The Cowboy State"
Capital: Cheyenne
Statehood: July 10, 1890; 44th state

AT A GLANCE

What are some of the most popular signs and symbols of the Cowboy State?

"Equal Rights" was adopted as the official state motto in 1955, in recognition of the fact that this was the first state where women obtained the right to vote. The meadowlark is the state bird, and the Indian paintbrush is the state flower. The cottonwood is the official state tree.

How large, or small, is the Cowboy State?

Comprising 97,813 square miles (253,335 square kilometers), Wyoming is tenth in rank among the states in terms of physical size. Its population of 582,658, as enumerated in 2010, is dead last of the fifty states.

Is there any state that says "West" quite as loud and clear as Wyoming?

Not even close. Colorado's mountains are, on average, higher, and Montana has more wide open space, but Wyoming has been the destination of choice for those who crave a genuine, authentic experience of the American West ever since the first dude ranch was established in the late 1880s. Wyoming has a special combination of nineteenth-century grit, twentieth-century development, and twenty-first-century technology.

Had the federal government not stepped in and created the National Park system, Wyoming would be known only to those fortunate enough to possess camping gear and high-priced equipment; as a result of the park system, millions of Americans have toured Yellowstone and Grand Teton national parks.

What is the breakdown of Wyoming?

Specialists declare that there are three parts of Wyoming. The best-known is in the northwest section, home of Yellowstone National Park and Grand Teton National Park, a land of stunning mountains, river valleys carved by lava flow, and vast numbers of wild animals. One could easily spend a year in these parks and not see them all. But there are two other sections to the state.

Devils Tower inspired Indian legends, as well as being the setting for the conclusion of the 1977 classic science-fiction movie *Close Encounters of the Third Kind.*

Devils Tower, the first national monument of the United States, is the centerpiece of the northeastern part of Wyoming, a land known for its changeable weather and connection to Oregon Trail days. And southeastern Wyoming—home of Cheyenne (the capital) and Laramie (the University of Wyoming)—is the most civilized or sedentary part of the state. Of course this doesn't mean the people there are soft; it just means they are a little calmer than those of the truly wild West.

Are the people of Wyoming as rough and rugged as they appear?

They really are. Wyoming stands at the very center of where the Great Plains meet the Rockies, and for whatever reason, this is where the toughest of the tough folks moved to during the mid-nineteenth century. Their descendants are just as alert, observant, and ambitious.

One cannot find a better neighbor than Far Westerners. They are quick to help in an emergency. At the same time, they are clear that the people they help must learn to help themselves. Politically, they tend to be conservative, but it is a conservatism bred of individual choice, rather than knee-jerk response.

How many Native Americans live in Wyoming?

Indians form about 3 percent of the total population, but they are more visible than this percentage suggests. Wyoming Indians are proud of their heritage, which they display at pow-wows and fairs.

EARLY HISTORY

Who were the Native Americans in what we now call Wyoming?

So many tribes lived here that it is difficult to draw clear lines between their territories. Numerous Indian wars took place as the different tribes—Cheyenne, Sioux, Arapahoe, and others—jostled for position. All of their lives were dramatically altered when Spanish-bred horses from Mexico showed up sometime in the eighteenth century. The former walkers and hikers of the Great Plains became the roaming horsemen, and suddenly they were able to move into the lower Rocky Mountains.

The classic screen adaptation of Native American life is in the 1990 film *Dances with Wolves*. The film shows the Indians of the Great Plains in a much friendlier light than previous movies, and it shows that the rapid advance of the U.S. cavalry, as well as settlers, forced the Indians off the Plains and into the mountains. While the film certainly romanticizes aspects of Native American life, there is little doubt that boys of all ages have a permanent attraction to the Indian life. Just ask any of the tourists in Cody, Wyoming. Or ask their great-grandfathers, who sat breathless during Buffalo Bill Cody's Wild West Show.

Who were some of the first people of European descent to arrive in Wyoming?

The Lewis and Clark expedition missed the Equality State by about 200 miles. But on their return, Lewis and Clark gave permission to John Colter, like them a Virginian, to drop out of the Corps of Discovery in order to do some fur trapping on his own. Colter wandered for the better part of a year, and the stories sound very much as if he saw the Grand Canyon of the Yellowstone.

Colter died in Virginia just a few years later, but his stories were so memorable that they passed from one mouth to another, and when the first organized parties of explorers went into Wyoming, they discovered much of what he relayed was true. He can, therefore, be considered not only the first white person to see much of Wyoming, but also the great-grandfather, in a figurative sense, of Yellowstone National Park.

What was the Mountain Man era like?

During the 1820s, handfuls of ambitious—some might say reckless—fur trappers came to Wyoming. They spent months in the mountains, trapping the beaver, which provided a soft, warm fur for the making of hats, cloaks, and blankets. In 1825, the first Mountain Man rendezvous was held at the Green River in western Wyoming. For the next decade, this gathering saw the usually reserved Mountain Men blow off steam by firing their weapons, singing, and enjoying each other's company.

What brought the first white settlers to Wyoming?

It was the Oregon Trail that provided thousands of white Anglos with their first look at Wyoming, but they read about it in the journals of John Colter and a handful of explorers who came before.

The growing season in Wyoming is short, but there were benefits for those who came and settled early. The Homestead Act of 1862 brought thousands, and the first discoveries of oil helped bring even more. Wyoming grew up in a hurry, both during and after the Civil War. The state entered the Union in July 1869.

What role did Wyoming play in the U.S.-Indian Wars?

The Great Plains Wars are considered to have begun just a few miles west of Fort Laramie. The altercation between U.S. "bluecoats" and Sioux warriors with face paint was the start of a long series of conflicts. The United States nearly always won the wars, and it took the lion's share of the battles, but anyone who watches Western films from the 1950s and 1960s sympathizes with the outnumbered Indians. Theirs was a hopeless struggle, but they gave it all they had.

How important was the Civil War to the future of Wyoming?

The Civil War's conclusion in 1865 freed up tens of thousands of U.S. soldiers for service and many of them were dispatched to the Great Plains. The United States would surely have defeated the Indian tribes in the long run, but the end of the Civil War moved the process along.

What was the Johnson County War?

Most of us know—from Westerns and documentaries—that sheep and cattle raisers do not get along. This animosity increases when homesteaders are introduced to the mix. So it was in 1892, when the Johnson Cattle War was fought.

Cattle barons hired roughly fifty sharpshooters, with a daily pay rate, and a much-bigger bonus based on how many sheep farmers and rustlers they killed. The actual ca-

Because Yellowstone National Park is situated above a huge plume of hot and molten rock, there is a great deal of geyser activity and hot springs are everywhere. Tourists flock to see geysers like Old Faithful, but the same thing that caused the geysers to erupt may one day explode and destroy the valley and more.

sualties were rather low (less than a dozen on both sides combined) but the Johnson County War resulted in a standoff that was only settled when President Benjamin Harrison sent U.S. Army troops west.

When did national parks and national monuments become so important to the nation?

Hard as it is to believe there were no national parks till the 1870s, and the first national monument, Devils Tower, not until 1906. The idea of conservation or preservation hardly existed. But Wyoming had a lot to do with making the change.

Buffalo Bill Cody—the legendary Wild West man—is said to have killed over 4,000 buffalo in a six-month stretch in 1869. As the buffalo disappeared, people from all walks of life began to see that the resources of the Far West were not unlimited. Shortly thereafter, in 1872, Yellowstone was named the first national park.

When did the Indian reservation become established?

The Arapahoe and Eastern Shoshone are not friendly; in earlier days, they were deadly foes. But when the Arapahoe were established in the Wind River reservation in the 1880s, the Eastern Shoshone joined the Arapahoe for the space of one winter. The temporary

> ## Just how dangerous is the volcanic presence beneath Yellowstone National Park?
>
> If it ever blew off, the present and future of North America would be very much in doubt. Scientists believe that the last major eruption, about 400,000 years ago, was at least 1,000 times more explosive than the one at Mount St. Helens in 1980. The good news, however, is that any future eruption is probably a long way in the future. Even so, geologists monitor Yellowstone constantly.

arrangement became permanent only because the U.S. government refused to evict the newcomers.

Over time, the Arapahoe and Eastern Shoshone have learned to live and let live. They have separate tribal councils and regulations and do not mix very much socially.

What's so special about Devils Tower?

You really have to see it to believe it. One moment you're hiking along the broad fertile plain of eastern Wyoming, and suddenly you see a speck on the horizon, which, over the next two hours turns into a massive, almost rectangular object of stone and shale, pointed almost straight up. You can see, in a heartbeat, why the Native Americans consider this a sacred place, and why the first settlers, coming along the Oregon Trail, were filled with wonder.

Climbers have been keen to ascend Devils Tower ever since 1893, when a local man made the first successful attempt (one fellow later parachuted onto the top, but failed to have an exit plan!). These days, most hikers and climbers observe the voluntary ban on climbing during the month of June, when numerous Indian groups gather to perform rituals in and around the tower.

What national department store chain got its start in Wyoming?

James Cash Penney was working at a store called Golden Rule in the late 1890s when he was sent to Evanston, Wyoming, to help open a new store in 1899. He soon became part of the Golden Rule partnership. In 1902, Penney opened a new store in Kemmerer and eventually became full owner when the partnership dissolved. Penney soon opened stores in Utah and Idaho—and then nationwide. The original store in Kemmerer still operates as a JCPenney today.

Who was Nellie Tayloe Ross?

She was the nation's first woman governor. On October 2, 1924, Wyoming governor William B. Ross suddenly died. Secretary of State Frank Lucas was next in line of succession and took over as interim governor. A special election was held on November 4,

1924, in which the Democratic Party's nominated candidate, Ross's widow, Nellie Tayloe Ross, won. She was sworn in as governor on January 5, 1925, and filled out the remainder of her late husband's term. She ran for reelection in 1926 but lost. Seven years later, President Franklin D. Roosevelt named her the director of the U.S. mint, a position she held until her retirement in 1953.

How did World War I and World War II treat Wyoming?

The state provided its share and more of the young men who served, but the larger result was that the U.S. government became more aware of what it had in Wyoming. Large open spaces and a hardy population meant that new government installations could be built and staffed. The U.S. Air Force has its training academy in Colorado, but many Strategic Air Command sites are in Wyoming.

What was the high point for oil production in Wyoming?

The late 1960s saw more millions of barrels of oil than any previous time. The first energy crisis, in the early 1970s, should have seen Wyoming profit, but the state's leaders recognized the time had come to hold back. It is no coincidence that the nation's Strategic Petroleum Reserve is located in Wyoming. At the same time, however, coal and natural gas became the new, more sought-after sources of energy.

A 2007 photo of a wolf pack in Yellowstone. The National Park Services strives to maintain a healthy balance of wolves and their prey in the park.

When did wind power become so important to Wyoming?

The potential was there all along. According to the American Wind Energy Association, Wyoming is the seventh windiest state in the nation. But it took the creation of subsidies, many by the state government, to start the wind farms moving into production. Today, there are nearly 1,500 wind towers in Wyoming, and the projection is that there will someday be as many as 10,000.

When did wolves come back to Yellowstone National Park?

During the late nineteenth century, wolves were killed with great enthusiasm, and when the last in the park was killed in 1926, there was general jubilation. Roughly sixty years later, people became aware that the disappearance of the wolves was a negative for the natural habitat. If Yellowstone wished to declare that it was the only complete ecosystem in North America, meaning that all the original species could be found, it needed to bring back the wolves.

The National Park Service did the hard work in 1995–1996, bringing forty wolves to Yellowstone. At first there was real resistance and dislike, especially on the part of hunters, but a series of National Geographic films won the hearts of most viewers. The most stirring story was about wolf Number 42. Her sister, Number 40, was the alpha female of the pack, and she actually killed Number 42's offspring. But Number 42 turned the tables a few years later. With the help of her nieces, she killed her elder sister and soon became known as "Cinderella." Number 42 lived up to the name. Unlike her elder sister, she proved a good mother, aunt, and pack leader. When she died in 2006, there was great grief among the park staff.

What was life in Wyoming like at the beginning of the twenty-first century?

For the majority of Wyoming residents, life was just about as difficult and dangerous as it was for their grandparents. Of course, a number of modern inventions made some of the work quicker and easier, but many residents scorned these newfangled inventions, preferring to work on things in the old-fashioned ways. And for those who worked in the mining industry, in coal especially, the work seemed endless. None of this discouraged the typical Wyoming resident, however. An alternative state motto could be "Work Hard or Go Home."

How did Wyoming come to loom so large in national politics?

It's largely the result of a husband and wife: Richard and Lynne Cheney. High school sweethearts in their native Wyoming, Richard served in various roles (such as chief of staff for President Gerald Ford, U.S. House representative, and secretary of defense for President George H. W. Bush) before being elected vice president in 2000; Lynne served as chair of the National Endowment for the Humanities. Between them, the Cheneys brought a nononsense style to the George W. Bush administration, and a decidedly Wyoming, or Western, point of view. To them it was obvious that oil and natural gas were there for the taking and that the nation needed all it could obtain. Richard Cheney once was quoted as saying that the American way of life, complete with heating and air-conditioning, was "non-negotiable." While the Cheneys have had many critics, there is no doubt that they staked out their position and held it. The former vice president's longtime friend, retired Wyoming senator Alan Simpson, frequently compared him to Winston Churchill, saying he was a man ahead of his time and that he suffered much abuse as a consequence.

Is there any chance Wyoming will ever become "just another part of the country"?

Almost none. The landscape, the brilliant skies, and the endless rounds of difficult work mean that Wyoming is in a class of its own.

WASHINGTON, D.C., AND U.S. TERRITORIES

THE CAPITAL AND CAPITOL

What is the difference between a capital and a capitol?

The linguistics become a little involved because while a capital is usually a city, a capitol is usually one specific building. Washington, D.C., is the capital city of the United States, but the Capitol building—which houses the U.S. Congress—is the precise seat of government. To employ another analogy, London is the capital of the United Kingdom, but the Houses of Parliament, which sit right along the bank of the Thames River, are the precise capitol.

Was it inevitable that there would be a capital city, one like Washington?

No. The first seat of U.S. government was in New York, and the second in Philadelphia. During the 1790s, however, George Washington set into motion plans that resulted in the establishment of a true national capital, one based where no city had previously existed. Knowing his native Virginia very well, Washington was inclined to favor an area along the Potomac River. He did not have the entire say, however.

Congress was deeply divided over the question of geographic placement. Many senators and congressmen wished a capital city in the North, while many others favored a southern location. An historic compromise was brought about by Thomas Jefferson and Alexander Hamilton: the capital city would be on both sides of the Potomac River, built on lands ceded by Virginia and Maryland.

I notice that Washington, D.C., today is entirely on the north bank. How did that happen?

In 1846, the federal government returned the land on the south bank, which Virginia had previously ceded. This meant that Washington, D.C., would be completely on the north side of the Potomac, and, not so incidentally, on Northern soil.

The White House.

When was the White House built?

John Adams and First Lady Abigail Adams were the first presidential couple to reside in the White House, and they left decidedly mixed impressions, saying it was no better than what they had known in Philadelphia. But the White House took on a new, and second, life after the British burned sections of it in August 1814. Though it was not their intention, the British did a great favor to the young republic, boosting the patriotism of the people and increasing their enthusiasm for the national capital. Rebuilding of the White House began almost immediately, and by 1818 the modern structure—the one we know today—was essentially complete.

When was the U.S. Capitol complete?

There was an earlier structure that housed the Senate and House of Representatives, but it in no way compared to the one we know today. The grand design was drawn up in the 1840s, and when Abraham Lincoln delivered his first Inaugural Address in March 1861, the Capitol was substantially complete: only the dome was unfinished. The Civil War was a time of unparalleled growth for Washington, D.C., which saw its population double, and the establishment of numerous military camps in the suburbs. By Civil War's end, Washington, D.C., had expanded to about the physical size we know today. To be sure, it did not yet have the magnificent museums or memorials that millions of people visit each year.

Was there ever a "low" time for Washington, D.C.?

Not really. Once the grand buildings were erected—and the Washington Monument complete—the city took on a rather grand aspect that has never diminished. Foreigners were inevitably struck by the beauty and symmetry of Washington, D.C.: they attributed these to the fact that Washington was built as the federal city, rather than superimposed atop an earlier urban experiment.

When did the other beautiful buildings get built?

The various museums—most of them under the banner of the Smithsonian—were built early in the twentieth century but have been added on to ever since. The Pentagon came in the 1950s. Even in the rare times when something was not being built, Washington generally exuded positive energy. This was the center of U.S. national government, and, when the Cold War commenced, it was seen as the capital of the Free World.

Speaking of beauty, what is the story behind the cherry blossoms?

Several Americans travelling in Japan were taken by the beauty of the light pink and white Japanese cherry tree and urged Washington, D.C., officials to plant some in the city. It wasn't until the William Howard Taft administration that plans finally went into place. First lady Helen Herron Taft helped with the effort. An initial planting failed due to an insect infestation. A planting ceremony—led by Mrs. Taft and the wife of the Japanese ambassador—was held in 1912. Additional trees were planted through the years.

The first Cherry Blossom Festival was held in 1935 and now takes place every year—generally around the early part of April. Festival officials declare Peak Bloom Day as the day when 70 percent of the blossoms are open.

Was there a truly "high" point for Washington, D.C.?

There have been many, including a great number of huge parades, but in the sentiments of the nation, the greatest and grandest moment surely was in August 1963, when Reverend Martin Luther King Jr. delivered his "I Have a Dream" speech. Standing at the Lincoln Memorial, close to the Potomac, King sent forth a rhetorical blaze that has never been equaled in American national history. Many white Americans who had previously defended the practice of segregation were shamed by the eloquence of King's speech. Many other people—white and black—found that their support of racial integration received new strength from the speech.

Along with all this grandeur and success, are there any failures to report?

Quite a few. In the years just prior to the Civil War, human beings were still sold on the open market, sometimes within a few blocks of the White House. Washington, D.C., also has its share of problems associated with urban America in the early twentieth century. The capital city has many poor people—many of them African American—and there have been some truly depressing moments, such as when the city's mayor, Marion Berry, was charged with possession of drugs in 1990.

What is the future of Washington, D.C.?

Almost no one can imagine a scenario under which Washington ceases to be the capital of the nation. The place is imbued in tradition. Whether the District of Columbia should be governed differently, with greater freedom from the decisions of the U.S. Congress, is difficult to say. The chances are that Washington will remain a place of great, even compelling, contradictions, with a clear gap between rich and poor, insiders and outsiders. It will also continue to attract tourists from all over the world.

THE TERRITORIES

What are the most significant U.S. territories?

The islands of Guam (201 square miles, 544 square kilometers), Puerto Rico (3,425 square miles, 8,870 square kilometers), and the Virgin Islands (134 square miles, 347 square kilometers). There was a time, in the early twentieth century, when the Philippines (115,831 square miles, 300,000 square kilometers) were also a U.S. territory.

What are some of the most important signs and symbols of the various territories?

The seal of the Virgin Islands shows a yellow breast (the official bird) perched atop a yellow cedar (the official tree). The commonwealth flag of Puerto Rico has five horizontal stripes (all of them equal), three red and two white.

How does one define a U.S. territory?

These is no specific definition, but the process usually follows this cycle: absorption by the U.S. military, confirmation by the U.S. Congress, and then an arrangement for territorial delegates to the Congress. During the early nineteenth century, there were a number of territories (many of them carved out of the Louisiana Purchase), but it was understood that these eventually would become states. This was not the case with overseas territories that the United States acquired during the Spanish-American War.

In how many ways was 1898 the year of destiny?

For millions of Americans (those who backed the Spanish-American War), it was obvious that it was America's destiny to acquire many islands around the globe. To millions of others (those who opposed the war), 1898 was a sad year, the one in which the United States embarked on a truly imperial future.

The Spanish-American War commenced in May, and the fighting was all over by October, with the Americans winning nearly every contest. The most memorable event was the charge up San Juan Hill, performed by Colonel Theodore Roosevelt and his "Rough Riders," the regiment he had personally recruited. In December of that year, the set of treaties known as the Peace of Paris was signed, under which Spain gave up all claim to Cuba, Puerto Rico, Guam, and the Philippines. To put that in perspective, Spain had governed these areas for about three centuries. The United States did not gain sovereignty over Cuba, but the island was placed under an unofficial protectorate, which allowed the Americans to intervene in Cuban affairs at almost any time.

What was the big failure, so far as American imperialism was concerned?

From the point of view of the big corporations—those that had helped bring on the war in the first place—there was no failure; virtually all of the conquests of 1898 turned profits for American companies. But from a military point of view, the conquest of the Philippines turned out to be little short of a disaster. The Filipinos revolted against American rule within a year, and the long insurrection claimed many American and Filipino lives. The U.S. military was powerful enough to impose its will on the Philippines, but it did so at great cost to America's worldwide image; almost for the first time, the United States was seen as a brutal conqueror.

The United States held on to the Philippines until 1942, when the Japanese ejected the Americans. U.S. general Douglas MacArthur made good on his pledge that "I shall return," and the Philippines were once again under American rule by the end of 1944. This time, however, American rule was useful to neither the Filipinos nor the American self-concept, and the Philippines became fully independent in 1946.

How did the United States come to possess the Virgin Islands?

Located less than one hundred miles east of Puerto Rico, the Virgin Islands are a large group that over time have been owned by Great Britain, Denmark, and the United States (today there are only the British Virgin Islands and the American Virgin Islands). As it became increasingly apparent that the United States would enter World War I, negotiations began between America and Denmark, and on March 31, 1917, just days prior to the declaration of war, four of the Virgin Islands became officially American (the residents did not become U.S. citizens till 1927).

What was the American Anti-Imperialist League?

Most organizations do not define themselves with a negative such as "anti" and this may have contributed to the relative weakness of the anti-imperialist league. At its height, in the early twentieth century, however, the league had many prominent persons among its members, including Andrew Carnegie and Mark Twain. They concurred that imperialism was a distinctly European theme and that it had no place in the United States.

The streets of old San Juan have a charming international feel; and many Americans mistakenly believe that Puerto Rico is a foreign country, but it is part of the United States.

People primarily of African descent populate the Virgin Islands. They do not have voting rights in U.S. national elections, but they send a territorial delegate to the U.S. Congress. This person can participate in discussions on the floor of the House of Representatives but cannot vote.

What is so special about the case of Puerto Rico?

Puerto Rico means "rich port" in Spanish, and this term was applied to the port of San Juan, on the western side of the island. Puerto Rico was part of the Spanish Empire for more than 300 years, but it never generated much wealth for the Spanish motherland; rather, it was a significant strategic location, especially for the treasure fleets that sailed from Spanish Mexico. In 1898, Puerto Rico fell to American arms, and by the end of the year the island was a U.S. military possession. It became the Commonwealth of Puerto Rico in 1950.

What's significantly different about Puerto Rico is the size of its population (estimated at 3.7 million in 2014) and the number of people who come to the mainland United States. Puerto Ricans are U.S. citizens and do not need passports to come to the mainland; over time, New York, Boston, Philadelphia, and Miami have received the largest number of Puerto Rican arrivals. From the 1950s onward, Puerto Ricans have moved to the mainland, where they experience significant economic opportunity, along with subtle ethnic discrimination. During the 1970s, discrimination against Puerto Ricans reached its height, but the negative sentiment has backed off since that time.

How did Guam fall into American hands, and why has it remained that way?

Guam was another part of the Spanish Empire, dating from the time of Ferdinand Magellan. It came under U.S. jurisdiction in 1898 and later became an official territory. Guam is quite small (about 240 square miles) but it plays an important role in the U.S. military plans for the East Pacific. Guam has a brisk tourist trade, with most of its tourists coming from Japan. American military spending on aircraft and installations has made the island economically viable.

What is the future of the various U.S. territories? Will any of them become states?

Puerto Ricans have decided, over time, that being a commonwealth of their own and part of the United States is more advantageous than becoming an official state, though those opinions have wavered through the years. Countless politicians have supported either statehood or the right for Puerto Rico's citizens to determine its status. But bills have always failed in Congress. Many believe it has to do with partisan politics. The Democratic-heavy territory would add two senators and one representative—very likely Democratic—to Congress.

Other U.S. territories have not benefited as clearly from American governance, but it is unlikely that independence movements will begin. The only major success story, of a people going from territorial status to complete independence, is that of the Filipinos.

Would the United States be any better—or worse—off if it did not hold these various territories?

Mainland Americans generally do not recognize the advantages that accrue to them from possession of so many islands. When asked, they often reply that it doesn't make a bit of difference to them if the territories are independent or not. Only old-timers, particularly from the U.S. military, realize that the territories confer advantages—economic and military—on the mainland.

Timeline

1492	Columbus arrives in the Bahamas, inaugurating the Age of Discovery
1539	De Soto lands in Florida, commencing a three-year journey through the South
1540	Coronado sets out from Mexico, seeking the Cities of Gold
1562	French Huguenots arrive in South Carolina, but soon head for home
1564	French Huguenots establish Fort Caroline in Florida
1565	After eradicating Fort Caroline, Spaniards establish Fort St. Augustine, the longest continuously occupied place in the United States today (occupied by people of European descent)
1585	Sir Walter Raleigh sends colonists to the Outer Banks of North Carolina
1586	North Carolina colonists evacuated by Sir Francis Drake
1587	Second group of colonists settle on Roanoke Island; Virginia Dare is born
1590	Roanoke colonists are found to have disappeared completely
1598	Juan de Onate commences exploration and settlement in New Mexico
1603	Queen Elizabeth I dies; is succeeded by King James I
1607	English colonists establish Jamestown in present-day Virginia
1609	Santa Fe, New Mexico, is established
1620	The Pilgrims sail on the *Mayflower* and arrive in present-day Plymouth, Massachusetts
1626	The Dutch purchase Manhattan Island for a trifling sum
1630	The Puritans sail aboard the Winthrop Fleet and settle Boston and its vicinity
1633	The first Roman Catholic settlers from England arrive in present-day Maryland
1634	The Great and General Court of Massachusetts Bay is established
1636–1637	The Pequot War in southern Connecticut ends in complete victory for the English settlers
1644	Rhode Island & Providence Plantations receive a charter from England
1649	The English Civil War ends with execution of King Charles I

1650s	During the decade that follows King Charles' death, Virginia proves loyal to the Stuart dynasty, thereby earning the nickname "Old Dominion"
1651	The Navigation Ordinance is passed
1660	King Charles II ascends the throne
1664	English ships, sent by James the Duke of York, capture Manhattan Island from the Dutch
1669	King Charles II grants a sweeping charter for the colony of Carolina (not yet divided into North and South)
1675	King Philip's War rages in New England
1676	King Philip's War ends with Metacom's death
	Bacon's Rebellion nearly overturns royal government in Virginia
1682	William Penn obtains a charter for the land to be known as Pennsylvania, meaning "Penn's Woods"
1685	King Charles II dies and is succeeded by King James II, his younger brother
1686	The Massachusetts charter of 1629 is revoked
1688	The Glorious Revolution overturns King James II in favor of his daughter and son-in-law, William and Mary (for whom the Virginia college is later named)
1689	Boston overthrows its royal governor in a bloodless, one-day coup
	Manhattan does the same to its lieutenant governor
	King William's War—known in Europe as the War of the League of Augsburg—begins
1690	Bostonians capture Port Royal, Nova Scotia, but fail in their attempt to conquer Québec
1697	King William's War ends with the Peace of Ryswick
1700	Overall population of the colonies is roughly 250,000
1702	King William dies and is succeeded by his sister-in-law, Queen Anne
1704	Deerfield, Massachusetts, is destroyed by an attack from French and Indian forces
1710	Four Iroquois chiefs—known as the Four American Kings—arrive in London
1711	Britain sends a fleet and army in an attempt to conquer Quebec; the effort fails
1712	Queen Anne's War ends with the Peace of Utrecht
	Carolina is separated into North and South
1714	Queen Anne dies and is succeeded by King George I
1727	King George I dies and is succeeded by his son, King George II
1732	James Oglethorpe obtains a charter for what becomes Georgia
1739	The War of Jenkins Ear breaks out between Britain and Spain
1740	Reverend George Whitefield comes to the colonies for the first of seven trips
	The First Great Awakening begins
1744	King George's War—known in Europe as the War of the Austrian Succession—begins
1745	Farmers and fishermen from New England capture France's Fort Louisburg
1747	Knowles Riots in Boston

1748	King George's War ends with the Treaty of Aix-la-Chapelle
1750	Dr. Thomas Walker becomes first white person to pass through Cumberland Gap
1752	The American calendar is changed from the Julian to the Gregorian
1754	The French and Indian War begins with a skirmish fought in western Pennsylvania; the twenty-two-year-old George Washington plays a leading ole
1755	Boston is rocked by a powerful earthquake
1759	Québec City falls to the British
1760	Montréal falls to the British
	King George II dies and is succeeded by his grandson, King George III
1763	The French and Indian War ends with the Peace of Paris. Under its provisions, the British flag now waves over virtually all the land between the Atlantic and the Mississippi River
1765	King George III tries to force Americans to accept the Stamp Act
1766	The Stamp Act is repealed
1767	The Townshend Revenue Acts place new taxes, including one on tea, on the colonists
1770	The Boston Massacre takes place on March 5
1772	The *Gaspee* Affair proves that the people of Rhode Island are keen for liberty
1773	The Boston Tea Party takes place on December 16
1774	King George and Parliament announce the Coercive Acts to punish Massachusetts for the Tea Party
1775	The American Revolution begins with the Battles of Lexington and Concord
	The Battle of Bunker Hill is fought
	Daniel Boone establishes Boonesborough, Kentucky
	Americans make a valiant but doomed attempt to conquer Canada to turn it into the fourteenth colony
1776	The Second Continental Congress approves the Declaration of Independence, which clearly states that the former colonies now are "free and independent states"
1781	The Continental Congress approves the Articles of Confederation
1783	The Revolutionary War ends with the Treaty of Paris. Under its provisions, the United States gains title—on paper, at least—to most of the lands east of the Mississippi River
1785	Congress approves the Northwest Ordinance. Under its provisions, most of the lands of the Midwest will be settled in a rational, even scientific manner, in lots of 36 square miles apiece
1786	Shays's Rebellion in central and western Massachusetts persuades many leading Americans that a stronger form of government is necessary
1787	After four months, the Constitutional Convention approves the brand-new Constitution. Under its provisions, a path toward statehood is established, and it is agreed that all new states will be equal to the original thirteen.

	Delaware becomes the first state of the Union on December 7
	Pennsylvania becomes the second state of the Union on December 12
	New Jersey becomes the third state of the Union on December 18
1788	Georgia becomes the fourth state of the Union on January 2
	Connecticut becomes the fifth state of the Union on January 9
	Massachusetts becomes the sixth state of the Union on February 6
	Maryland becomes the seventh state of the Union on April 28
	South Carolina becomes the eighth state of the Union on May 23
	New Hampshire becomes the ninth state of the Union on June 21
	Virginia becomes the tenth state of the Union on June 25
	New York becomes the eleventh state of the Union on July 26
1789	George Washington is sworn in as the first president of the United States on April 30
	North Carolina becomes the twelfth state of the Union on November 21
1790	Rhode Island becomes the thirteenth state of the Union on May 29
1791	Vermont becomes the fourteenth state of the Union on March 4
1792	Kentucky becomes the fifteenth state of the Union on June 1
1796	Tennessee becomes the sixteenth state of the Union on June 1
1800	Population of the sixteen states reaches 5.3 million
1803	Ohio becomes the seventeenth state of the Union on March 1
1810	Population of the seventeen states reaches 7.2 million
1812	Louisiana becomes the eighteenth state of the Union on April 30
	War breaks out between America and Great Britain
1814	"The Star-Spangled Banner" is penned after the Battle of Baltimore
	Peace is signed between Britain and America on Christmas Eve
1815	Andrew Jackson wins the Battle of New Orleans (January 8) and becomes a legendary hero to thousands of Western frontiersmen
1816	Indiana becomes the nineteenth state of the Union on December 11
1817	Mississippi becomes the twentieth state of the Union on December 10
1818	Illinois becomes the twenty-first sate of the Union on December 3
1819	Alabama becomes the twenty-second state of the Union on December 14
1820	Population of the twenty-two states reached 9.6 million
1820	Maine becomes the twenty-third state of the Union on March 15
1821	Missouri becomes the twenty-fourth state of the Union on August 10
1830	Population of the twenty-four states reaches 12.8 million
1836	Arkansas becomes the twenty-fifth state of the Union on June 15
	Texas rises in revolution against Mexico. Though she wins independence, Texas is not allowed in to the Union, and she exists as a separate nation for nine years as the Lone Star Republic
1837	Michigan becomes the twenty-sixth state of the Union on January 26

1840	Population of the twenty-six states reaches 17 million
1845	Florida becomes the twenty-seventh state of the Union on March 3
1845	Texas becomes the twenty-eighth state of the Union on December 29
1846	War with Mexico begins
	Iowa becomes the twenty-ninth state of the Union on December 28
1847	The first Mormons arrive at Great Salt Lake
1848	Gold is discovered near Sacramento
	Peace between America and Mexico is signed
	Wisconsin becomes the thirtieth sate of the Union on May 29
1850	Population of the thirty states reaches 23.1 million
	California becomes the thirty-first state of the Union on September 9
1858	Minnesota becomes the thirty-second state of the Union on May 11
1859	Oregon becomes the thirty-third state of the Union on February 14
1860	Abraham Lincoln wins election as the sixteenth president of the United States
	South Carolina secedes from the Union on December 20
	Population of the thirty-three states reaches 31.4 million
1861	Kansas becomes the thirty-fourth state of the Union on January 29
	The Confederate States of America is formed in Montgomery, Alabama
1863	West Virginia, carved out of the Old Dominion, becomes the thirty-fifth state of the Union on June 20
1864	Nevada becomes the thirty-sixth state of the Union on October 31
1865	Lee and the Army of Northern Virginia surrender to Grant at Appomattox Court House
	President Lincoln is assassinated on April 14
1867	Alaska is purchased from Russia
	Nebraska becomes the thirty-seventh state of the Union on March 1
1869	The Transcontinental Railroad is completed with the link-up at Promontory Point in Utah
1870	Population of the thirty-seven states reaches 39.8 million
1876	Colonel George Custer and his men are wiped out at the Battle of Little Bighorn by combined forces of Lakota, Arapaho, and Northern Cheyenne Indians
	The United States celebrates its Centennial in Philadelphia
	Colorado becomes the thirty-eighth state of the Union on August 1
1880	Population of the thirty-eight states reaches 50.1 million
1889	North Dakota becomes the thirty-ninth sate of the Union on November 2
	South Dakota becomes the fortieth state of the Union on November 2
	Montana becomes the forty-first state of the Union on November 8
	Washington becomes the forty-second state of the Union on November 11
1890	Population of the forty-two states reaches 62.9 million
	Idaho becomes the forty-third state of the Union on July 3

	Wyoming becomes the forty-fourth state of the Union on July 10
1896	Utah becomes the forty-fifth state of the Union on January 4
1900	Population of the forty-five states reaches 75.9 million
1907	Oklahoma becomes the forty-sixth state of the Union on November 16
1910	Population of the forty-six states reaches 91.9 million
1912	New Mexico becomes the forty-seventh state of the Union on January 6
	Arizona becomes the forty-eighth state of the Union on February 14
1917	The United States enters World War I
1918	World War I ends on November 11
1920	Population of the forty-eight states reaches 105.7 million
1930	Population of the forty-eight states reaches 122.7 million
1940	Population of the forty-eight states reaches 131.6 million
1941	United States declares War on Japan on December 8 and three days later declares war on Germany
1945	Word War II ends on September 2
1950	Population of the forty-eight states reached 150.6 million
1959	Alaska becomes the forty-ninth state of the Union on January 3
	Hawaii becomes the fiftieth state of the Union, on August 2
1960	Population of the fifty states reaches 179.3 million
1970	Population of the fifty states reaches 203.3 million
1976	The United States celebrates its bicentennial with events all-round the nation
1980	Population of the fifty states reaches 226.5 million
1990	Population of the fifty states reaches 248.7 million
2000	Population of the fifty states reaches 281.4 million

Further Reading

Abbott, Carl, and others, eds. *Colorado: A History of the Centennial State*. Boulder, CO: Colorado Associated University Press, 1982.

Adams, Ansel, and Nancy Newhall. *The Tetons and the Yellowstone*. Redwood City, CA: 5 Associates, 1970.

Alaska and the Yukon. New York: Facts on File, 1983.

Allis, Marguerite. *Connecticut River*. New York: Putnam, 1939.

Annerino, John. *Canyons of the Southwest*. San Francisco: Sierra Club Books, 1993.

Bald, F. Clever. *Michigan in Four Centuries*. New York: Harper & Brothers, 1954.

Banta, R.E. *The Ohio*. New York: Rinehart & Company, 1949.

Barker, Elna, and Richard G. Lillard. *The Great Southwest: The Story of a Land and Its People*. Palo Alto, CA: American West Publishing Company, 1972.

Bartlett, Richard A. *Yellowstone: A Wilderness Besieged*. Tucson: University of Arizona Press, 1985.

Bean, Walton. *California: An Interpretive History*. New York: McGraw-Hill, 1968.

Beck, Warren A. *New Mexico: A History of Four Centuries*. Norman: University of Oklahoma Press, 1962.

Blegen, Theodore C., and Theodore L. Nydahl. *Minnesota History: A Guide to Reading and Study*. Minneapolis: University of Minnesota Press, 1960.

The Book of the States, Vol. 38. Lexington, KY: Council of State Governments, 2006.

Bowman, John S. ed. *The World Almanac of the American West*. New York: Pharos Books, 1986.

Boye, Alan. *Holding Stone Hands: On the Trail of the Cheyenne Exodus*. Norman: University of Nebraska Press, 1999.

Boyer, Crispin. *National Geographic Kids Ultimate U.S. Road Trip Atlas*. Washington, DC: National Geographic Society, 2012.

Bridger, Bobby. *Buffalo Bill and Sitting Bull: Inventing the Wild West*. Austin: University of Texas Press, 2002.

Brinkley, Douglas. *The Great Deluge: Hurricane Katrina, New Orleans, and the Mississippi Gulf Coast*. New York: Harper, 2006.

Brown, Daniel James. *The Indifferent Stars Above: The Harrowing Saga of a Donner Party Bride*. New York: William Morrow, 2009.

Burrows, Edwin G, and Mike Wallace. *Gotham: A History of New York City to 1898*. New York: Oxford University Press, 1999.

Burton, Sir Richard Francis. *The City of the Saints and Across the Rocky Mountains to California*. Boulder: University Press of Colorado, 1990.

Bushman, Richard L. *From Puritan to Yankee: Character and the Social Order in Connecticut, 1690–1765*. Boston: Harvard University Press, 1967.

Cappelli. Louis W. *Rhode Island: A Guide to the Smallest State*. Boston: Houghton Mifflin, 1937.

Caruso, John A. *The Appalachian Frontier: America's First Surge Westward*. Indianapolis: Bobs-Merrill Company, 1959.

Carter, Dan T. *The Politics of Rage: George Wallace, the Origin of the New Conservatism, and the Transformation of American Politics*. New York: Simon & Schuster, 1995.

Carter, Hodding. *Doomed Road of Empire: The Spanish Trail of Conquest*. New York: McGraw-Hill, 1963.

Cheney, Lynne. *Our 50 States: A Family Adventure across America*. New York: Simon & Schuster, 2006.

Clark, Erskine. *Dwelling Place: A Plantation Epic*. Yale University Press, 2005.

Crichton, Judy. *America 1900: The Turning Point*. New York: Henry Holt, 1998.

Cronon, William, et al, eds. *Under an Open Sky: Rethinking America's Western Past*. New York: W.W. Norton, 1992.

Cromie, Robert. *The Great Chicago Fire*. New York: McGraw-Hill, 1958.

Crompton, Samuel Willard. *The Cheyenne*. New York: Chelsea House, 2011.

———. *The Mohawk*. New York: Chelsea House, 2010.

Current, Richard Nelson. *Wisconsin: A History*. Urbana: University of Illinois Press, 2001.

Dary, David. *The Santa Fe Trail: Its History, Legends, and Lore*. New York: Knopf, 2000.

Davis, Edwin Adams. *Louisiana: The Pelican State*. Baton Rouge: Louisiana State University Press, 1959.

Davis, Julia. *The Shenandoah*. New York: Farrar and Rinehart, 1945.

Denton, Sally, and Roger Morris. *The Money and the Power: The Making of Las Vegas and Its Hold on America, 1947–2000*. New York: Knopf, 2001.

Didion, Joan. *Miami*. New York: Simon & Schuster, 1987.

Diefendorf, Mary Riggs. *The Historic Mohawk*. New York: Putnam, 1910.

Eckert. Allan W. *That Dark and Bloody River: Chronicles of the Ohio River Valley*. New York: Bantam Books, 1995.

Editors of Time-Life Books. *The Old West: The Townsmen*. Alexandria, VA: Time-Life Books, 1975.

———. *The Old West: The Pioneers*. Alexandria, VA: Time-Life Books, 1974.

Endoes, Richard. *Saloons of the Old West*. New York: Knopf, 1997.

Farris, John T. *The Romance of Old Philadelphia*. Philadelphia: Lippincott, 1918.

Federal Writers Project of the Works Progress Administration. *New Jersey: A Guide to Its Present and Past*. New York: Hastings House, 1939.

———. *Connecticut: A Guide to Its Roads, Lore, and People*. Boston: Houghton Mifflin, 1938.

———. *North Dakota*. New York: Oxford University Press, 1950.

Feintuch, Burt, and David H. waters, eds. *The Encyclopedia of New England: The Culture and History of an American Region*. New Haven: Yale University Press, 2005.

Finger, John R. *Tennessee Frontiers: Three Regions in Transition*. Bloomington: Indiana University Press, 2001.

Fishwick, Marshall S. *Virginia: A New Look at the Old Dominion*. New York: Harper & Brothers, 1959.

Flynt, Wayne. *Alabama in the Twentieth Century*. Tuscaloosa: University of Alabama Press, 2004.

Fradin, Dennis Brindell. *North Carolina*. Chicago: Children's Press, 1992.

Frankaviglia, Richard V. *Believing in Place: A Spiritual Biography of the Great Basin*. Reno: University of Nevada, 2003.

Hopkins, Virginia. *The Colorado River*. Secaucus, NJ: Chartwell Books, 1985.

Hulse, James W. *The Nevada Adventure: A History.* Reno: University of Nevada Press, 1978.

Hume, Ivor Noel. *Martin's Hundred*. New York: Knopf , 1982.

Galay, Alan, ed. *The Colonial Wars—An Encyclopedia*. Garland Press, 1997.

Goodheart, Adam. *1861: The Civil War Awakening*. New York: Knopf, 2011.

Grossman, James R., and others, eds. *The Encyclopedia of Chicago*. Champaign: University of Illinois Press, 2004.

Gutheim, Frederick. *The Potomac*. New York: Rinehart & Company, 1949.

Hoxie, Frederick C. ed. *Encyclopedia of North American Indians*. Boston: Houghton Mifflin, 1996.

Irving, Washington. *A Tour on the Prairies*, edited by John Francis McDermott. Norman: University of Oklahoma Press, 1956.

Jones, Jacqueline. *Creek Walking: Growing Up in Delaware in the 1950s*. Newark: University of Delaware Press, 2001.

Kaplan, Robert D. *An Empire of Wilderness: Travels into America's Future*. New York: Random House, 1998.

Karr, Paul. *New York City: An Explorer's Guide*. Woodstock, VT: The Countryman's Press, 2003.

King, Dean. *The Feud: The Hatfields and McCoys, the True Story*. Boston: Little, Brown, 2013.

Kizzia, Tom. *Pilgrim's Wilderness: A True Story of Faith and Madness on the Alaska Frontier*. New York: Crown, 2013.

Klein, Maury. *Union Pacific: The Birth of a Railroad, 1862–1893*. Garden City, NY: Doubleday, 1987.

Koeppel, Gerard. *Bond of Union: Building the Erie Canal and the American Empire*. Boston: Da Capo Press, 2009.

Laine, Don and Barbara. *The New Mexico Guide: The Definitive Guide to the Land of Enchantment*. Golden, CO: Fulcrum Publishing, 2005.

Lane, Mills, ed., *Georgia: History Written by Those Who Lived It*. Savannah, GA: Beehive Press, 1995.

Langlieb, David. *Philadelphia, Brandywine Valley, and Bucks County*. Woodstock, VT: The Countryman's Press, 2009.

Larson, T.A. *History of Wyoming*. University of Nebraska Press, 1965.

Least Heat-Moon, William. *PrairyErth (a Deep Map)*. Boston: Houghton Mifflin, 1991.

Lefler, Hugh T., and William S. Powell. *Colonial North Carolina: A History*. New York: Charles Scribner's Sons, 1973.

Linenthal, Edward T. *The Unfinished Bombing: Oklahoma City in American Memory*. New York: Oxford University Press, 2001.

Lockwood, C.C. *Discovering Louisiana*. Baton Rouge: Louisiana State University Press, 1986.

Lurie, Maxine N., and Marc Mappan, eds. *Encyclopedia of New Jersey*. Rutgers University Press, 2004.

Madison, James H. *The Indiana Way: A State History*. Bloomington: Indiana University Press, 1986.

McCafferty, Michael. *Native American Place-Names in Indiana*. Urbana: University of Illinois Press, 2008.

McGinty, Brian. *John Brown's Trial*. Harvard University Press, 2009.

McGrath, Roger D. *Gunfighters Highwaymen and Vigilantes: Violence on the Frontier*. Berkeley: University of California Press, 1984.

McLynn, Frank. *Wagons West: The Epic Story of America's Overland Trails*. New York: Grove Press, 2002.

McReynolds, Edwin C. *Missouri: A History of the Crossroads State*. Norman: University of Oklahoma Press, 1962.

———. *Oklahoma: A History of the Sooner State*. Norman: University of Oklahoma Press, 1954.

Meras, Phyllis, and Kathleen Imbric. *Rhode Island: An Explorer's Guide*. Woodstock, VT: The Countryman's Press, 2004.

Miller, Lee. *Roanoke: Solving the History of the Lost Colony*. New York: Arcade, 2000.

Milner, Clyde A, and others, eds. *Oxford Encyclopedia of the American West*. New York: Oxford University Press, 1994.

Miner, Craig. *Kansas: The History of the Sunflower State, 1854–2000*. Lexington: University Press of Kentucky, 2002.

Misuraca, Karen. *The California Coast: The Most Spectacular Sights and Destinations*. London, England: Voyageur Press, 2001.

Morgan, H. Wayne, and Anne Hodges Morgan. *Oklahoma: A Bicentennial History*. New York: W.W. Norton, 1977.

Morgan, Robert. *Boone: A Biography*. Chapel Hill, NC: Algonquin Books, 2007.

Morris, Willie. *My Mississippi*. Jackson: University Press of Mississippi. 2000.

Munroe, John A. *History of Delaware*. Newark: University of Delaware Press, 1979.

Nadeau, Remi. *Fort Laramie and the Sioux Indians*. Englewood Cliffs, NJ: Prentice-Hall, 1967.

Nash, Gary B. *First City: Philadelphia and the Forging of Historic Memory*. Philadelphia: University of Pennsylvania Press, 2002.

Norris, Kathleen. *Dakota: A Spiritual Geography*. New York: Ticknor & Fields, 1993.

O'Connor, Thomas H. *The Hub: Boston Past and Present*. Boston: Northeastern University Press, 2001.

Pagnamenta, Peter. *Prairie Fever: British Aristocrats in the American West, 1830–1890*. New York: W.W. Norton, 2012.

Parker, Watson. *Deadwood: The Golden Years*. Lincoln: University of Nebraska Press, 1981.

Pauketat, Timothy R. *Cahokia: Ancient America's Great City on the Mississippi*. New York: Viking, 2009.

Philbrick, Nathaniel. *Mayflower: A Story of Courage, Community, and War*. New York: Viking, 2006.

Powell, Lawrence Clark. *Arizona: A Bicentennial History*. New York: W.W. Norton, 1976.

Powell, Lawrence P. *Historic Towns of the Southern States*. New York: G.P. Putnam's Sons, 1900.

Powell, William S., and Jay Mazzocchi, eds. *Encyclopedia of North Carolina*. Chapel Hill: University of North Carolina Press, 2006.

Preston, Douglas. *Cities of Gold: A Journey across the American Southwest in Pursuit of Coronado*. New York: Simon & Schuster, 1992.

Raban, Jonathan. *Bad Land: An American Romance*. New York: Pantheon Books, 1996.

Ramage, James A., and Andrew S. Watkins. *Kentucky Rising: Democracy, Slavery, and Culture from the Early Republic to the Civil War*. Lexington: University Press of Kentucky, 2011.

Robinson, Elwyn B. *History of North Dakota*. Lincoln: University of Nebraska Press, 1966.

Ronda, James P. *Astoria and Empire*. Lincoln: University of Nebraska Press, 1990.

Roske, Ralph J. *Everyman's Eden: A History of California*. New York: Macmillan, 1968.

Rountree, Helen C. *Pocahontas's People: The Powhatan Indians of Virginia through Four Centuries*. Norman: University of Oklahoma Press, 1990.

Rushton, William Faulkner. *The Cajun: From Acadia to Louisiana*. New York: Farrar, Strauss & Giroux, 1979.

Samson, Karl. *Frommer's Oregon*, 8th ed. Hoboken, NJ: John Wiley & Sons, 2012.

Sandlin, Lee. *Wicked River: The Mississippi: When It Last Ran Wild*. New York: Pantheon Books, 2010.

Schneider, Paul. *Old Man River: The Mississippi River in North American History*. New York: Henry Holt, 2013.

Shirley, Glenn. *Six-gun and Silver Star*. Albuquerque: University of New Mexico Press, 1955.

Sisson, Richard, and others, eds. *The American Midwest: An Interpretive Encyclopedia*. Bloomington: Indiana University Press, 2007.

Shoumatoff, Alex. *Legends of the American Desert: Sojourns in the Greater Southwest*. New York: Knopf, 1997.

Silverberg, Robert. *Ghost Towns of the American West*. New York: Thomas Y. Crowell, 1968.

Snow, Peter. *When the British Burned the White House: The 1814 Invasion of Washington*. New York: St. Martin's Press, 2013.

Sprague, Marshall. *So Vast So Beautiful a Land: Louisiana and the Purchase*. Boston: Little, Brown, 1974.

Stadius, Martin. *Dreamers: On the Trail of the Nez Perce*. Caldwell, ID: Caxton Press, 1999.

Steen, Ralph W. *The Texas Story* Austin, TX: The Steck Company, 1948.

Story, John W., and Mary L. Kelley, eds. *Twentieth-Century Texas: A Social and Cultural History*. Denton: University of North Texas Press, 2008.

Straud, Patrick. *Montana: An Explorer's Guide*. Woodstock, VT: The Countryman's Press, 2008.

Taylor, Alan. *American Colonies: The Settling of North America*. New York: Penguin Books, 2001.

Tebeau, Charlton W. *A History of Florida*. Oxford, OH: University of Miami Press, 1967.

Tree, Christina, and Diane E. Foulds. *Vermont: An Explorer's Guide*. Woodstock, VT: The Countryman's Press, 2006.

Tubbs, Stephanie Ambrose, and Clay Straus Jenkinson. *The Lewis and Clark Companion: An Encyclopedic Guide to the Voyage of Discovery*. New York: Henry Holt, 2003.

Ulrich, Laurel Thatcher. *A Midwife's Tale: The Life of Martha Ballard Based on Her Diary, 1785–1812*. New York: Knopf, 1990.

Utley, Robert M. *The Lance and the Shield: The Life and Times of Sitting Bull*. New York: Henry Holt, 1993.

Vance, Randolph. *Ozark Superstitions*. New York: Columbia University Press, 1947.

Vermont: Extraordinary Wilderness Areas of the Green Mountain State, commentary by Tom Wessels. North Pomfret, VT: Thistle Hill Publications, 2003.

Vestal, Stanley. *Jim Bridger, Mountain Man*. New York: William Morrow, 1946.

Viola, Herman J. *Exploring the West*. Washington, DC: Smithsonian Books, 1987.

Wallace, Andrew. *The Image of Arizona: Pictures from the Past*. Albuquerque: University of New Mexico Press, 1971.

Wallace, Paul W. *Pennsylvania: Seed of a Nation*. New York: Harper & Row, 1962.

Waller, Ronald W., and others. *Massacre at Mountain Meadows: An American Tragedy*. New York: Oxford University Press, 2008.

Wallis, Michael. *The Real Wild West: The 101 Ranch and the Creation of the American West*. New York: St. Martin's, 1999.

Warden, G.B. *Boston: 1689–1776*. Boston: Little, Brown, 1970.

Watkins, T.H., and others. *The Grand Colorado: The Story of a River and Its Canyons*. Sanger, CA: American West Publishing Company, 1969.

Whayne, Jeannie. *Delta Empire: Lee Wilson and the Transformation of Agriculture in the New South*. Baton Rouge: Louisiana State University Press, 2011.

Williams, John Hoyt. *A Great and Shining Road: The Epic Story of the Transcontinental Railroad*. New York: Times Books, 1995.

———. *Sam Houston: A Biography of the Father of Texas*. New York: Simon & Schuster, 1993.

Wingered, Mary Lethert. *North Country: The Making of Minnesota*. Minneapolis: University of Minnesota Press, 2010.

Wishart, David J., ed. *Encyclopedia of the Great Plains*. Lincoln: University of Nebraska Press, 2004.

Wolfe, Muriel Sibell. *Montana Pay Dirt: A Guide to the Mining Camps of the Treasure State*. Athens, OH: Swallow Press, 1963.

Wolmar. Christian. *The Great Railroad Revolution: The History of Trains in America*. New York: Public Affairs, 2012.

Woolley, Benjamin. *Savage Kingdom: The True Story of Jamestown, 1607, and the Settling of America*. New York: Harper Collins, 2007.

Works Progress Administration in the State of Ohio. *The Ohio Guide*. New York: Oxford University Press, 1940.

The World Almanac and Book of Facts: 2015. New York: World Almanac Books, 2015.

Worster, David. *Dust Bowl: The Southern Plains in the 1930s*. New York: Oxford University Press, 1979.

Wright, Louis B. *South Carolina: A Bicentennial History*. New York: W.W. Norton, 1976.

Wright, Richardson. *Hawkers and Walkers in Early America*. Philadelphia: J.B. Lippincott, 1927.

Index

Note: (ill.) indicates photos and illustrations.

521

Dewey, John, 443
Dickinson, Emily, 209
Dickinson, John, 80
Dinkins, David, 319
Disaster City, Texas, 427
disasters, natural. See weather, state
Discovery, 348
Disney, Walt, 93
Disney World, 93
Disneyland, 93
District Court, U.S., 39
District of Columbia. See Washington, D.C.
Dix, Dorothea, 210
Dixon, Illinois, 135
Dixon, Jeremiah, 80
Dodge City, Kansas, 163
Dole, Edmund Pearson, 111
Dole, James, 111
Dole, Sanford, 111
Dole Food Company, 111
Dome Car, 254, 254 (ill.)
Dorchester Heights, Massachusetts, 211
Dorr Rebellion, 383
Douglas, Stephen A., 132
Douglass, Frederick, 475
Dove, 199, 199 (ill.)
Dover, Delaware, 77
Dover Air Force Base, 84
Doyle, Arthur Conan, 434
Dravo Corporation, 84
Dred Scott case, 200
Du Luth, Daniel Greysolon, Sieur, 227
du Pont, Éleuthère Irénée, 81
du Pont IV, Pierre "Pete," 82
du Pont, Pierre, 82
Dubuque, Iowa, 152
Dubuque, Julien, 150
Dukakis, Michael, 213–14
Duke, James Buchanan, 328
Duke University, 330–31
The Dukes of Hazzard, 174–75
Duluth, Minnesota, 227–31
Dummerston, Vermont, 441
Dunkin' Donuts, 154
Dunmore, Lord (John Murray), 474
DuPont Company, 78, 81
Durham, North Carolina, 328–29, 331
Dust Bowl, 164 (ill.), 164–65, 269, 339, 358
Duston, Hannah, 283–84

E

Earp, Morgan, 28
Earp, Virgil, 28
Earp, Wyatt, 28, 162
earthquakes. See weather, state
East Jersey, 293

East Pacific, 505
East Peru, Iowa, 152
East St. Louis, Illinois, 128, 130
Eastern Shoshone Indians, 493–94
Eastport, Maine, 195
Eastwood, Clint, 154
Ebenezer Baptist Church, 417
economies, state
    Alabama, 2, 7–8
    Alaska, 19
    Arizona, 29, 33
    Arkansas, 39, 41
    Colorado, 60, 63
    Connecticut, 72, 74–75
    Delaware, 78, 80, 83
    Florida, 88, 92, 95
    Georgia, 101, 103–4
    Hawaii, 113, 115
    Idaho, 123
    Indiana, 143, 145
    Iowa, 153
    Kansas, 164
    Kentucky, 172
    Louisiana, 184
    Maine, 192, 194
    Maryland, 199, 202, 204
    Massachusetts, 210, 214
    Michigan, 217–18, 220–22, 224
    Minnesota, 230
    Mississippi, 240, 242
    Missouri, 250–51
    Montana, 258–61
    Nebraska, 268–70
    Nevada, 279
    New Hampshire, 287
    New Jersey, 293, 295, 297–98
    New Mexico, 306
    New York, 312, 315, 321
    North Carolina, 328, 330
    North Dakota, 339–40
    Ohio, 346, 348
    Oklahoma, 357–58, 360
    Oregon, 366–68
    Pennsylvania, 373–77
    Rhode Island, 380, 386
    South Carolina, 392, 394–97
    South Dakota, 403
    Tennessee, 413–14
    Texas, 424–25, 428
    U.S. territories, 504–5
    Utah, 435–36
    Vermont, 439, 444
    Virginia, 450, 452, 455–56, 459
    Washington, 466
    West Virginia, 477
Eddie Bauer, 369, 462
Edison, Thomas, 295–96, 346
Eisenhower, Dwight, 19, 41, 114, 153, 158, 164, 288
Eisenhower, Mamie Doud, 153
Elizabeth, Queen, 325

Elliott Bay, 461
Ellis Island, 316 (ill.), 317
Elway, John, 58, 58 (ill.)
Ely, Nevada, 277
Empire Builder, 254 (ill.)
Empire State Building, 311, 318
Empty Quarter, 432
England. See also Britain, Great
    Arizona, 31–32
    Connecticut, 67, 71, 73
    Delaware, 80
    Georgia, 100–101
    Illinois, 131
    Indiana, 140
    Kentucky, 171, 173
    Louisiana, 179
    Maryland, 199
    Massachusetts, 210
    Nevada, 278
    New Hampshire, 283
    New Mexico, 306
    New York, 317
    North Carolina, 326
    Ohio, 343
    Pennsylvania, 373
    Rhode Island, 379, 381
    South Carolina, 391–92
    Tennessee, 411
    Utah, 434
    Vermont, 442
    Virginia, 450–51, 453
    Washington, D.C., 499
Englewood, Colorado, 60
Environmental Protection Agency, 348
Erie, Pennsylvania, 343
Erie Canal, 74, 220, 228, 315, 483
Escalante, Brother, 26
Espinoza, Victor, 172
Eugene, Oregon, 369
Eureka, Nevada, 277
Europe
    California, 51
    Connecticut, 71
    Kansas, 164
    Missouri, 245, 251
    Nebraska, 267
    New York, 316
    North Dakota, 337
    South Dakota, 402
Evacuation Day, 211–12
Evanston, Illinois, 128
Evanston, Wyoming, 494
Evers, Medgar, 241
expressions, state
    Alabama, 6
    Alaska, 13
    Arizona, 30
    California, 55
    Connecticut, 67
    Florida, 94–95